ELIZABETH & GEORGIANA

*The Duke of Devonshire
and his two Duchesses*

written by

CAROLINE CHAPMAN

in collaboration with
JANE DORMER

JOHN MURRAY
Albemarle Street, London

A catalogue record for this book is available from the British Library

ISBN 0-7195-6044 6

Typeset in 12.25/13pt Garamond MT by Servis Filmsetting Ltd, Manchester

Printed and bound in Great Britain by Creative Print and Design (Wales),
Ebbw Vale, Gwent

Contents

Illustrations

The author and publishers would like to thank the following for their kind permission to reproduce illustrations: Plates 1, 6, 12, 14 and 23, from the Devonshire Collection, Chatsworth, by permission of the Duke of Devonshire and the Chatsworth Settlement Trustees; 2, National Trust Photographic Library; 3, Sotheby's Picture Library; 4, National Trust Photographic Library/Angelo Hornak; 5, National Trust; 7, 13, 15, 17, 18, 20, 21, 22, 24 and 26, Dormer Archives; 8 and 16, Private Collection; 11 and 19, Mary Evans Picture Library; 27, Christie's Images.

Introduction

For almost twenty-five years of her life Elizabeth Foster lived in the shadow of Georgiana, Duchess of Devonshire, one of the most enchanting women of the late eighteenth century. While this was in many ways an enormous advantage, Bess's character and reputation have suffered grievously from continual comparison with the Duchess, both by her contemporaries and by posterity. She has been variously accused of insincerity, opportunism, superficiality, promiscuity, greed, and relentless social ambition. She has even been described recently as 'a wild slut'. Her love of art has been dismissed as merely a striving to emulate Georgiana, when in reality the seed was planted by her father long before she met the Devonshires. That personalities of the stature and intellect of Madame de Staël, Cardinal Consalvi and Edward Gibbon counted her as an intimate friend has also been largely ignored. Nor has she been given full credit for her devotion to her children, or for her deep affection for her stepson, Lord Hartington, an affection he reciprocated in her last years. Above all, she has been charged with being a faithless friend to Georgiana, and for using her relationship with the Devonshires to regain the position in society she had lost by making a foolish marriage.

The evidence to counteract these accusations is found not only in hundreds of previously unpublished letters from the Dormer Archives and elsewhere, but in her journals. Excerpts from the latter have been quoted by previous authors, but with few exceptions have been taken from Dorothy Margaret Stuart's *Dearest Bess*, until now the only full-length biography of Elizabeth Foster (apart from one other fictionalized account). Miss Stuart's excerpts often tell only part of the

ix

story, however; the omission of a single sentence from an original entry can affect a reader's perception of Bess. The resulting distortions are an inevitable pitfall of secondary sources, but I have enjoyed the luxury of having all 128 journals (transcribed and typed, they cover some 9,000 pages) on the desk before me throughout my years of research.

Should I have placed such faith in the journals? Cynics will claim that journals are ideal vehicles for self-justification and self-obfuscation, and certainly Bess wrote a large proportion in the full expectation that they would be read by others. But it is impossible to listen to a voice over a long period without developing an ear for what is true and what is false. There are many instances when Bess, forgetting her invisible audience, wrote with passion and sincerity. The sentiments expressed in the journals are often reflected in her letters, particularly those to her diplomat son Augustus Foster. They were separated for years at a time, and she wrote to him with directness and candour.

In my quest to paint a more balanced picture of Bess's character, I have neglected certain aspects of her life. As a resident of Devonshire House – a centre of political life in London for some twenty years – she could not fail to become involved in the politics of the day. But where Georgiana was active in the Whig cause – as vividly described by Amanda Foreman in her recent biography of the Duchess – Bess's role was more passive, as observer and meticulous chronicler of events. Nor have I dwelt at any length on the brilliant personalities who made up the so-called Devonshire House Circle, since they too have been admirably described by previous biographers and other writers. Instead I have concentrated on those areas of Bess's life which have been largely overlooked: her childhood and first marriage, her obsessive travelling, and her last years in Rome, where she became one of the city's best-loved and most well-known residents, renowned for her patronage of the arts, 'inexhaustible benevolence' and unfailing *douceur*.

Indignation is an excellent spur to a biographer, and I feel indignant that Bess has been so often unfairly portrayed in the past. Of her love for the Duke and Duchess, and of her fidelity to them in thought, word and deed, I am entirely convinced.

Acknowledgements

First and foremost I would like to thank Jane Dormer for her years of painstaking research and for her skilful transcription of Elizabeth Foster's journals. Without her permission to use her family's archives, this book would not have been possible.

I am also grateful to the Duke and Duchess of Devonshire for allowing me access to the Chatsworth archives, and for the unfailing courtesy and kindness of Peter Day, Keeper of Collections at Chatsworth, Charles Noble, Deputy Keeper of Collections, and their assistant Diane Naylor. I have been helped by many others during the course of my research, but I would like to express my particular gratitude to the following: The Hon. Simon Howard for permission to use the Castle Howard archives, and Dr Christopher Ridgway, Curator of Castle Howard, and his assistant, Alison Brisby; Stephen Parkin of the British Library's Rare Books; Ellen Phillips for her early encouragement and advice, and Liz Wyse for her years of gentle tuition. I would also like to thank Dorothy Abel-Smith, Ewan Cameron, Elaine Chalus, Lord Erne, Kathryn Bellamy and Rosemary Baird at Goodwood House, Terence Suthers at Harewood House, the staff of the London Library, Ian Pitt, Bianca Riccio, and John Shutter.

The agents for the book, first Serafina Clarke and then Mandy Little, have been endlessly encouraging and supportive. Caroline Knox at John Murray has guided the book through with tact, sensitivity and humour, and Liz Robinson's editing has been – quite simply – brilliant. But I could not have survived the last three years had it not been for the loving support of Catherine and Jess, or without Roger's seemingly endless patience and forbearance.

Caroline Chapman

I would like to take this opportunity to thank Caroline Chapman, the author of this book, for her Herculean efforts in producing such a coherent narrative. I would also like to thank my family for their help and patience: my husband Robert and his nephew Ian Glennie, my son James Sandbach and daughter and son-in-law, Emma and Graham Defries; also my stepbrother and late stepfather, Julian and Peregrine Fellowes.

I must mention especially Justin Archdale, for helping me with the research, transcribing many indecipherable letters and the like; Juliet Townsend, for transcribing some of the original journals and letters; and Martin Smyth and Emer Wilson of the Public Record Office of Northern Ireland (PRONI), and its former Head Dr Anthony Malcolmson, for all their assistance.

I would also like to thank the following for many invaluable contributions and advice: Lord and Lady Bellew, Patrick Clyne, Flora Fraser, James Irvine, John Kenworthy-Browne, the late James Lees-Milne, the Countess of Longford, Brian Masters, Teresa Miszewska, Alice Phipps, Stephen Pratt, the Reverend Brian Raistrich, Peter Rankin, Hilda Rawlings, John Martin Robinson, Francis Russell, Dr Bertrand Sauzier, Jim Smith, Nino Strachey, and Margaret Tiernan. I have insufficient room to mention so many others.

Jane Dormer

NOTE

No alterations have been made to contemporary quotes apart from an occasional change in punctuation to make them more intelligible, the writing out in full of some of the more confusing abbreviations, and a few spelling corrections or modernisations to avoid the appearance of typographical errors.

Dramatis Personae

THE HERVEYS

Frederick Hervey (1730–1803), Bishop of Derry and 4th Earl of Bristol – known after 1779 as the 'Earl-Bishop' – m. 1752 Elizabeth Davers (1730–1800). Of their six children, one (George) died aged 9; of the others,

Mary (1753–1842), m. 1776 as his second wife John Creichton, 1st Viscount (later 1st Earl) Erne; their only child, Caroline, m. 1799 James Stuart-Wortley, later 1st Baron Wharncliffe (she is Bess's niece 'Caroline Wortley');

John Augustus (1757–96), after 1779 Lord Hervey; known as 'Jack'; m. 1779 Elizabeth Drummond; their only child, Eliza (Bess's 'beloved niece') m. 1798 Charles Rose Ellis (later Baron Seaford); she d. 1803 (and her elder son eventually succeeded to the ancient Hervey barony of Howard de Walden);

Elizabeth Christiana (1758–1824), 'Bess'; m. 1776 John Thomas Foster; of their three children, Frederick (1777–1853), known as 'Fred', died unmarried; Eliza died soon after birth; and Augustus (1780–1848), diplomat and later 1st Baronet, m. 1815 Albinia Hobart;

Louisa (1767–1821), m. 1795 Robert Banks Jenkinson, later (1803) Lord Hawkesbury and (1808) 2nd Earl of Liverpool;

Frederick (1769–1859), m. 1798 Elizabeth Upton; later (1803) 5th Earl and (1826) 1st Marquess of Bristol.

As Lady Elizabeth Foster, Bess had two illegitimate children by the 5th Duke of Devonshire;

> Caroline (1785–1862), surnamed St Jules, known as 'Caro'; m. 1809 George Lamb, youngest son of Lady Melbourne (but possibly not of Lord Melbourne);

> Augustus (1788–1877), surnamed and always known as 'Clifford'; m. 1813 Elizabeth Townshend, known as 'Lizzy'; he rose to the rank of admiral and was cr. a baronet in 1838; in 1832 his half-brother Hart, 6th Duke of Devonshire, as Lord Chamberlain, appointed him a Gentleman Usher of the Black Rod.

THE CAVENDISHES

William Cavendish (1748–1811), 5th Duke of Devonshire, m. 1774 Georgiana, daughter of 1st Earl Spencer; of their three children,

> Georgiana (1783–1858), known as 'Little G.', m. 1801 George Howard, Viscount Howard of Morpeth, later (1825) 6th Earl of Carlisle;

> Harriet (1785–1862), known as 'Haryo', m. 1809 Lord Granville Leveson-Gower, later (1815) 1st Viscount and (1833) Earl Granville;

> William (1790–1858), Lord Hartington, known as 'Hart', later (1811) 6th Duke of Devonshire, did not marry.

The 5th Duke of Devonshire married Bess in 1809, less than two years before his death.

Georgiana Spencer's sister Henrietta-Frances (1761–1821), known as 'Harriet', m. 1780 Frederick Ponsonby (1758–1844), Viscount Duncannon and later (1793) 3rd Earl of Bessborough (whose mother was a sister of the 4th Duke of Devonshire); their daughter Caroline (1785–1828) m. 1805 William Lamb, later 2nd Viscount Melbourne, and had a notorious affair with Lord Byron, who later (1815) m. Lady Melbourne's niece and William's cousin, Annabella Milbanke; Harriet had a lengthy liaison with Lord Granville Leveson Gower (who later m. her niece Haryo Cavendish); the two children of the liaison, Harriette and George Stewart, were adopted by Haryo and Granville, in 1812 and 1813 respectively.

'This world is a comedy to those that think, a tragedy to those that feel'

Horace Walpole to the Countess of Upper Ossory, 16 August 1776

'Oh sentiment, sentiment! Sweet food of the soul! Where is the iron heart which you have never affected?'

From Jean-Jacques Rousseau, *Julie, ou la Nouvelle Héloïse*

Prologue

BESS FOSTER HAD the good fortune to be born into the Whig aristocracy during the latter part of the eighteenth century, an age of grace and elegance, squalor and refinement, of passion and profligacy, sentiment and sensibility, when the heart ruled the head and to hell with the consequences.

Portraits of the period depict a life of cultivated ease: a silk-clad couple strolls arm in arm through a sylvan landscape; pensive beauties drape themselves against Ionic pillars, a distant view of Rome or Naples shimmering in the background. A handsome duchess, apparently incapable of an act so primitive as childbirth, gazes fondly at her romping, rosy-cheeked children. Men in glowing scarlet uniforms strike martial poses, an arm outstretched in imitation of a Roman emperor; a wealthy earl leans against a tree stump cradling a shotgun, at once part of the landscape and its master. These are men to whom the habit of command comes naturally. That they are powerful, privileged and wealthy is no surprise: it is their birthright.

The Grand Whiggery were members of a tiny élite consisting of no more than three hundred families – 'all cousins', as Lord Melbourne once described them. This exclusivity had its drawbacks: only within its narrow compass could 'a good marriage' be contracted. To a twenty-first-century observer, the interweaving by marriage of the great Whig families is virtually impenetrable, the confusion intensified by the repetition of Christian names from generation to generation. Bess's family, the Herveys, favoured John, Frederick and Augustus; every Cavendish heir since the sixteenth century had been called William. Everyone else appears to have been called Robert, George or

Charles, Harriet or Caroline (except, unaccountably, George Gordon Byron, sixth Baron Byron of Rochdale, who was seldom referred to other than as Byron). But these were the chosen few. Beyond the high defensive walls of their West End properties seethed London's great metropolis, where life for the majority was a more brutal affair. People worked hard for their daily bread, robbed for it, occasionally rioted for it. Life on the London streets was dangerous, smelly and uncertain. But even their high walls could not protect the aristocrats from illness and disease, spare their wives the perils of childbirth or their children from dying in infancy.

Unlike the French aristocracy – who were afraid to leave Court for fear of missing a morsel of gossip – the Whig nobles retired to their country seats when Parliament was in recess. From splendid mansions which combined formal grandeur with informal comfort they gazed upon limitless vistas unsullied by signs of rival human habitation. The wholesale removal of villages which impeded the view was not uncommon. (Thomas Coke, however, having resited a hamlet, remarked a little sadly: 'I look around, not a house to be seen but for my own. I am Giant, of Giant's Castle, and have ate up all my neighbours.') They strolled in the park, rode to hounds, played cricket with their tenants, entertained the local squirearchy, and rearranged the landscape in the style of Capability Brown.

Secure in their supremacy, they pursued their own course through life, oblivious to public opinion or censure. The men spent half the night in their clubs and half the day in their beds, rising in time to attend Parliament by late afternoon. Politics was their life blood; in an age which saw the loss of the American colonies, the madness of George III, the fall of the French monarchy and the wars against France, there was much to be political about. They drank awesome amounts of alcohol and consumed gargantuan meals. Pitt the Younger thought nothing of dispatching two or more bottles of wine with his dinner; Lord Melbourne ate three chops and a grouse for breakfast. Staggering sums of money were lost at the gaming tables: Charles James Fox 'played deep' and lost £140,000 in three years.

Everyone (except, it seems, the Duke of Devonshire) spent several hours a day reading and writing letters: Bess's father once arrived in Rome to find ninety awaiting him. During lulls between social engagements, they read the Classics, poetry, philosophy, history, and Shakespeare. Women devoured romantic novels. 'There is scarce a young lady in the kingdom', grumbled *The Lady's Magazine* in 1773, 'who has not read with avidity a great number of romances and novels, which tend to vitiate the taste.' Vitiating or not, novels proliferated, quickening the blood and liberating the libido. Sensuality and sexuality were given free expression; sensibility was given free rein. Women formed passionate friendships with members of their own sex, expressing their feelings for each other in terms of emotional intensity. Men, too, were allowed to 'feel'. 'There's nothing in the world so noble', exclaims Charles Surface in *The School for Scandal,* 'as a man of sentiment!' To be individualistic, to pursue bizarre hobbies, to express yourself in any way you damn-well pleased was not merely acceptable, it was expected. Altogether, it was an age in which the eccentricities of the Hervey family could flourish.

I

The early years
1758–1776

'When God created the human race, he created men,
women, and Herveys.'

Variously attributed to Lord Chesterfield, Lady Mary
Wortley Montagu, Lady Townshend, and Voltaire

———————◆———————

Bess was born a Hervey (pronounced Harvey), one of the foremost families of England. As staunch royalists, Herveys had served the Crown since the reign of Henry VIII, and their estates at Ickworth near Bury St Edmunds had survived, even expanded, despite the vicissitudes of history. The first Hervey to be ennobled was Bess's great-great-grandfather, created Earl of Bristol in 1714 for supporting the Hanoverian succession. After the death of his much-loved first wife, the Earl married the heiress Elizabeth Felton. Noted by her contemporaries for her 'vivacity, eccentricity, and love of pleasure', it was reputedly she who introduced the wayward element into the Hervey genes. The activities of at least four of her seventeen children lend colour to this allegation: Henry was an incurable spendthrift; William was cashiered from the navy for brutality to his men; Thomas wrote eccentric pamphlets, fought numerous duels, and eloped with his godfather's wife. The eldest son of this unsatisfactory brood, while also distinctly unusual, was the most intriguing.

John, Lord Hervey was handsome, witty, a Classical scholar and a connoisseur of the arts. In 1730 he was appointed Lord Privy Seal and

Vice-Chamberlain of the Royal Household under George II and Queen Caroline. During his years at Court Lord Hervey kept frank and illuminating memoirs of the king and his family, and was famously satirized by Alexander Pope as Sporus (one of Emperor Nero's nancy boys), excoriated in such lines as:

> Amphibious thing! that acting either part,
> The trifling head, or the corrupted heart!
> Fop at the toilet, flatterer at the board,
> Now trips a lady, and now struts a lord.

This imputation of sexual ambiguity is not wholly unjust, since although John Hervey married for love the beautiful Molly Lepell, fathered eight children, fought a duel and seduced the Prince of Wales's mistress, the great love of his life was Stephen Fox, first Earl of Ilchester and uncle of Charles James.

Lady Hervey was widely praised for her beauty, intelligence and engaging manners – all attributes Bess possessed in abundance – but there was another and more durable gift which may have passed from grandmother to granddaughter: Lady Hervey, declared Lord Chesterfield, 'has all the reading that a woman should have, and more than a woman need have . . .' This gift, fostered by her father, sustained Bess through life. 'I believe nothing is more necessary than constantly supplying the mind with information,' she later told a daughter-in-law, '& above all to avoid trash, it cramps the mind & intellect . . .'

Of the children born to Lord and Lady Hervey, the eldest son, George, is best remembered for having challenged Lord Cobham to a duel for spitting into his hat; the second, Augustus, rose to the rank of admiral, enjoyed numerous amorous adventures and secretly married the notorious Elizabeth Chudleigh, a lady celebrated for her appearance at a ball wearing only a wisp of gauze and a seductive smile who subsequently committed bigamy by marrying the Duke of Kingston; a daughter, Mary, married an Irish rake and bore a son who was later hanged for murder. The third son, Frederick, was Bess's father.

In his youth Frederick showed no sign of the erratic behaviour of his father's generation. According to the antiquary William Cole, who knew him at Cambridge, 'His good sense, great good-nature and affability gained him the love and esteem of all who knew him; and his sprightliness, wit, vivacity, ingenuity and learning proved him to be a genuine Hervey . . .' Though initially destined for the law, Frederick abandoned his studies to take holy orders; a year later he obtained the post of Clerk of the Privy Seal, becoming Principal Clerk five years later. In 1752 he married Elizabeth, daughter of the prosperous land-owner Sir Jermyn Davers, of Rushbrook Hall in Suffolk.

Though outwardly pillars of Suffolk society, Elizabeth Davers's parents had lived together for ten years before marrying, and their first two sons were born out of wedlock. The third son, Robert, inherited the title on the death of his father but in 1761 left England 'in a pique' for America, where he 'sought the most savage and uncultivated spots' and was attacked and murdered by Indians. His two younger brothers both committed suicide: one shot himself on board ship, the other in his mother's greenhouse. In the space of seven years Bess's mother lost three of her brothers; what lay behind these tragic deaths is unknown, although it was said of the formidable Lady Davers that she was 'ever unparental' to her sons.

While no beauty, Elizabeth Hervey was a woman of charm, piety and enormous good sense. She was to prove a tender mother and, despite years of provocation, a loyal and dependable wife. Since the marriage was strongly opposed by both families – the Herveys were Whigs, the Daverses were Tories – and Elizabeth's dowry was small, it would seem that the couple married for love. This is borne out by Frederick's fond references to his wife as his 'true counterpart' and his 'Excellent', though these affectionate sobriquets were later amended to 'the majestic ruin'.

Some time in 1755 Frederick and Elizabeth Hervey settled in a small house at Horringer, near Ickworth, where their fourth child, Elizabeth Christiana (generally known as Bess), was born and baptized in the local church on 13 May 1758. The family already consisted of Mary, the eldest, and two boys, George and John Augustus (known as Jack). In appearance, Bess was undoubtedly a Hervey: small, fragile and fine-boned. With her large hazel eyes, curling brown hair and delicate fea-tures, she was an engaging child. Inheriting also the frail constitution of the Herveys, she was plagued throughout her life by sudden violent fevers and 'oppressions on the chest'.

In 1761, following the birth and immediate death of a third son, the Herveys left Horringer for London. Where they lived is unknown, but they may have stayed for a while in Lord Bristol's imposing house in St James's Square. With four children to feed, Frederick had been des-perately trying to obtain ecclesiastical preferment, but by 1763 had achieved no more than the poorly-paid post of Chaplain to King

George III. Two years later, he suddenly uprooted his family and went abroad. His reasons for doing so are unknown, but the comparatively low cost of living on the Continent may have influenced his decision. It was Frederick's first trip abroad, and it marked the beginning of his obsession with travel. This powerful urge to keep moving, to turn another corner to see what lay beyond, was fuelled by a spirit of ceaseless enquiry, and these were two more facets of his character which he passed on to his daughter Bess.

The Herveys took with them three of their children, Mary, George and Bess, aged twelve, nine and seven respectively. The second son, Jack, was left at Bury with his maternal grandmother. Accompanied by nurses, tutors and numerous servants, the party set sail for Ostend. Despite its size, it would have aroused little comment; since the end of the Seven Years' War in 1763, the English had taken in droves to going to the Continent. Principally they were wealthy young men of noble birth, despatched abroad on a Grand Tour to bridge the awkward gap between university and manhood. It was piously hoped the young milords, chaperoned by their tutors (known as bear-leaders), would steep themselves in the art and culture of Europe, broaden their minds and return as grown men without, God willing, having contracted 'the perils of Venus' in the back streets of Naples.

The Herveys' first destination was Spa, near Brussels, a small town lying in a sheltered valley in the Ardennes. In the latter part of the eighteenth century it was one of the most fashionable of the European watering-places. During their stay, George died of an unspecified illness. For Bess, plucked out of the nursery and living in a strange town, this was profoundly disturbing; for her parents, it was a body blow. At that stage the family was close-knit and harmonious, and the children were brought up in the relaxed, affectionate manner inspired by such writers as John Locke and Jean-Jacques Rousseau, both considered 'admirable models' by Frederick. Children were no longer to be required to address their parents as 'sir' and 'madam', nor to be dressed as diminutive adults; instead, they were treated as individuals, doted on and indulged.

Yet when the grieving family left Spa it was to lodge Mary and Bess with a Mademoiselle Chaumelle in Geneva, to be taught French and Italian, the two foreign languages considered essential for aristocratic young ladies. Frederick and his 'Excellent' then departed for Italy and did not return for more than a year. Though it would be wrong to judge this abandonment by today's standards, it must surely have affected the children. Mary was a calm, sensible child, but Bess was emotional, highly-strung, and already prey to her 'too feeling heart'. It is little wonder that Mrs Hervey often referred to her as 'poor dear little Bess'. 'I fear,' she later wrote to her daughter, '. . . that you have inherited your mother's anxious temper about those you love, but conjure you, by the well-known suffering of it, to struggle hard against it while you have youth and spirits to do so, and to incline as much as you are able to the best side of every object.' Mrs Hervey spent much of her married life trying to see the 'best side of every object', but her letters reveal a longing to be with her children rather than rattling about Europe with her husband.

The girls' only contact with their parents was by letter, and the post took three to four weeks, ceasing altogether when snow blocked the Alpine passes. Some of the parental letters show a remarkable lack of imagination: it can have brought little comfort to Mary and Bess to hear how their mother had been obliged to spend the night alone in her carriage when it became stuck fast on a precipitous mountain track, or that their father, while climbing Vesuvius with his friend Sir William Hamilton, had been badly injured during a minor eruption. Frederick's description of his accident spares his daughters none of the gory details: struck on the arm by a red-hot stone, he was confined to bed for several weeks.

Frederick and Sir William had been at Westminster School together. They were exactly the same age, and shared a passion for art and antiquity. Since his appointment in 1764 as British Minister to the Court of Naples, Hamilton had become fascinated by Vesuvius; within four years of his arrival he had climbed the volcano no fewer than twenty-two times. Frederick was infected by his friend's enthusiasm for the study of geology and vulcanology, interests which persisted until they were usurped by his mania for collecting works of art.

Frederick and his 'Excellent' were still in Naples when news reached them that Frederick's eldest brother, Lord Bristol, appointed Lord Lieutenant of Ireland, had promptly named Frederick his First Chaplain. They returned to England, retrieving their daughters *en route*. Thanks to Lord Bristol's continued nepotism, Frederick soon became a bishop, of Cloyne in 1767, and a year later of Derry, the wealthiest bishopric in Ireland. Mrs Hervey and the children duly left Bury St Edmunds to join the new bishop in his palace in the walled town of Londonderry on the banks of the River Foyle.

From the first Frederick had an impact upon the church, people and politics of Derry. Besides renovating his cathedral and palace, he built bridges, improved roads, drained marshes, and visited every parish in his diocese. What particularly endeared him to his parishioners was his resolve never to appoint an Englishman to an Irish benefice. Although he abandoned his diocese for years at a time, and despite his often unruly and controversial behaviour, Frederick's insistence on religious and political tolerance and his efforts to ease Catholic oppression show him to have been years ahead of his time. Such independence of thought might be admirable, but there was something reckless and ungovernable about Frederick, a carelessness about the feelings of others which at times was almost cruel. He once obliged some of his clergy to compete for a rich living by taking part in a race across country. Too fat and unfit for such physical exertion, not a single cleric reached the finishing line. Highly amused by this game, Frederick presented the living elsewhere.

The Bishop's Palace in Londonderry was described in the mid nineteenth century as a 'substantial and commodious building'. Behind it lay an extensive garden bounded on two sides by the town walls – a paradise for young children. The bishopric owned another large garden outside the town walls where Frederick erected a summerhouse, fifty feet long with a fine Classical portico, which he called his Casino.

In 1767 Mrs Hervey had given birth to another daughter, Louisa; in 1769 Frederick was born. Barely eighteen months later, the family was again uprooted. The Bishop's pastoral exertions had brought on an attack of gout, which he proposed to cure by pursuing his geological studies abroad, taking with him his thirteen-year-old son Jack, by then a midshipman in the Royal Navy. Instead of installing his wife and the rest of his family in a rented house in Bury St Edmunds – which he could well have afforded – he distributed them piecemeal around the town; Bess and the infant Frederick found themselves lodged with a mysterious Dr Mandeville in Bury market place. In the twelve years of her existence, Bess had thus only twice spent three consecutive years in one place, and had endured one year of total separation from her parents; now she was to live apart from the rest of her family again. Today her childhood would be described, if not as deprived, then certainly as unsettled.

After two years abroad the Bishop and Jack returned, and the family left again for Londonderry. The town, though picturesque, was a long way from the bright lights of Dublin; for Mary and Bess, already dreaming of fashion and romance, it must have seemed distressingly remote from either. As the Bishop believed in regular hours and a strict diet, life at the palace was simple, frugal, and dull. While their father darted from one fantastic project to another, such as the adornment of his cathedral and of many of his churches with elaborate spires, the two older girls spent long hours in the schoolroom. The education of well-born girls in the eighteenth century was traditionally limited to social accomplishments such as music, sketching, dancing and deportment; Bess's remarkable grasp of ancient history and her familiarity with the Classics suggest that she was taught them from an early age, and was an extremely able and receptive pupil. To a love of learning she added a bright enquiring mind, quick perception, and a face of fragile beauty. At the age of fourteen she already showed signs of becoming the 'bewitching animal' who so fascinated Edward Gibbon, the great historian, when he met her some years later.

In March 1775 Lord Bristol died, to be succeeded by the nautical, bigamous and childless Augustus. Frederick not only inherited ten thousand pounds but became heir presumptive to the Bristol title and thirty thousand acres of family estates in Suffolk and Lincolnshire. Perhaps enticed by this sudden improvement in the eligibility of the Bishop's elder daughters, two suitors promptly appeared on the scene. The first, a widower with antiquarian tastes, a Mr Trant, proposed to Mary; when she refused him, he proposed to Bess, only to receive the same reply. In a letter to his agent in Italy the Bishop blithely recounted these events, concluding: 'Mary is now likely to be married to Lord Erne of this kingdom, he is a most unexceptionable Man . . . & is in love with her to the eyes.' Almost as an aside, he added, 'Unfortunately, he is a widower & has children: this staggers her . . .' No wonder: Mary was twenty-one, while Erne was twice her age, with four children. The Bishop, however, saw these as minor drawbacks, since his future son-in-law's annual income was nine thousand pounds and he possessed 'a very beautiful seat' in Ireland. Besides, Frederick had other things on his mind.

In the far north of Derry, on a treeless headland lashed by the Atlantic gales, the Bishop had decided to build a house; and not any old house. It was to have modern conveniences (possibly the first to be installed in Ireland) and – when two long wings were added to the original villa – galleries in which to display the Bishop's ever-growing collection of paintings and sculpture. When the house was completed, it was said to boast 'as many windows as there are days in the year'. Subsequently named Downhill, and the first of three palatial edifices he was to erect in his lifetime, it was the only one he ever properly occupied. By the summer of 1776 the shell of the house was standing. If the Bishop had not been so immersed in his grandiose construction, he might have taken a more intelligent interest in the suitability of John Thomas Foster, the young man who was now courting his daughter Bess.

2

A marriage and a meeting
1776–1782

'I can never consent to her being put again into the
power of a Person who has already so much abus'd it, &
who appears to me to have but *one selfish brutal passion
which actuates him even at this moment . . .'*

Lady Bristol to her husband, August 1780

———————◆———————

JOHN THOMAS FOSTER was the son of the Reverend Dr Thomas
Foster, rector of Dunleer, a small town in County Louth. His
mother had died in 1774, and a younger brother in infancy. Dr Foster
had lavished money and affection on his only child, sending him first
to Trinity College, Dublin and then to Christ Church, Oxford. This,
an unusually extensive education for an Irish gentleman of the period,
was followed by a Grand Tour which inspired in the young man a taste
for travel. Writing to his old friend, the statesman John Baker Holroyd
(later Lord Sheffield) in 1775, Dr Foster bewailed his son's 'fondness
for rambling' and his pursuit of the pleasures of Dublin. A year later
he told his friend: 'Jack does not seem to me to have any tendency to
marriage & I don't like him the better on that account . . . Thus far I
have done all in my power for his Happiness, the rest he must contrive
& manage for himself.' As to the kind of girl his son should marry, the
rector was philosophical: 'He must please himself, but I hope it will be
in one who will not disdain to live in Ireland.'

Since their arrival at the time of the Cromwellian Settlements the

Fosters had become one of the most able and liberal-minded families in Ireland, with large estates in County Louth and close connections to Irish politics. John Foster's uncle Anthony was Chief Baron of the Exchequer in Ireland and his cousin, another John Foster, was later Chancellor of the Exchequer in Ireland and then last Speaker of the Irish House of Commons. In 1776, at the age of twenty-nine, John Foster himself entered parliament as member for Dunleer. For the Bishop, anxious for the support of liberal parliamentarians in his crusade for Catholic relief, his prospective son-in-law's political connections may have blinded him to the fact that Bess possessed the intelligence, charm and beauty to make a far more brilliant match. Bess herself later maintained she had married Foster 'on the advice' of her father, and told her friend the Duchess of Devonshire that when her father asked if she loved the young man, she had confessed 'that his behaviour had not won my affection, but I assured him [her father] that my behaviour towards him [Foster] would give him satisfaction, and that he [Foster] should never know whether it was from love or duty.' Even if subsequent events had coloured what Bess told the Duchess, she clearly had not married Foster for love. Her meek acceptance of the match implies either a lack of self-knowledge, or fear of her father – or a combination of the two.

Whatever may have been Mrs Hervey's private assessment of Foster, she would have been obliged to defer to her husband's view. But she was a perceptive woman, and must have seen the dangers inherent in the match. Bess was only eighteen years old, and apart from the widower Trant, no serious contender, it appears that she married, or was persuaded to marry, the first man who came her way. This was surely unnecessary in those enlightened times, when the average age for girls to marry was twenty-four, and marriage for love, even among the aristocracy, was becoming increasingly common.

Years later, when the marriage was disintegrating, Mrs Hervey reminded the Bishop of 'the alarm' Bess had taken *just before* they married, at a harsh and tyrannical sentiment which he [Foster] had express'd'. So Mrs Hervey had been wary of him from the start. But she became fond of him in time. 'Assure Mr Foster of my sincere affection,' she wrote to Bess six months into the marriage. 'He loves you too well for me not to feel a true regard for him, and I flatter myself that a well-founded esteem and perfect harmony will subsist amongst us all as long as we live.' Yet there are some puzzling aspects to the match: why did Mrs Hervey never meet Dr Foster or visit the rectory at Dunleer, and why did Dr Foster not meet Bess until she had been married to his son for several months?

After four active years in his diocese, the Bishop felt it was high time for another sortie abroad. The party that set off for Brussels in the autumn of 1776 consisted of the Bishop, Mrs Hervey and their youngest daughter Louisa; Mary, who had married Lord Erne earlier in the year; Lord Erne's two daughters; Bess; and John Foster. On 16 December Bess and John were married in Brussels, and for the next six months remained with Bess's family. This time spent on the Continent, which may have included a visit to Paris, proved a revelation to Bess. Brussels, with its delightful gardens and squares, its inns and ordinaries (precursors of the restaurant) the equal of any in France, and its fine opera house, gave her a taste for the Continental way of life. With her father as guide and mentor, she also developed a passion for art and architecture so genuine as to become a mainstay of her life. So completely did she absorb her father's views that it took some years for her to develop her own.

In early April 1777 Dr Foster wrote ecstatically to Holroyd: 'Elizabeth is certainly with Child.' After a visit to Bess's relations at Ickworth and Bury, the couple joined Dr Foster in London before all three visited Holroyd and his wife at Sheffield Place in Sussex. Writing to Holroyd to confirm their imminent arrival, the rector gave an oblique clue to his first impressions of his new daughter-in-law: 'Shall I tell you how I like her? No, I will not raise prejudice – but surely it will be *J.F's* fault when he is not happy.'

Holroyd was a close friend of the great historian Edward Gibbon, and later became custodian of his papers, editing and publishing his *Miscellaneous Works*. The two men had met in Lausanne just before Gibbon set out on his Grand Tour, during which he conceived the idea of writing his famous history. Though twice her age, Holroyd was enchanted by Bess and this first meeting marked the beginning of a close association. Soon after the birth of her first child she began to write him long, affectionate letters which reveal details of her life not found elsewhere, the earliest of her letters to survive. It was also Holroyd who later introduced Bess to Gibbon. Gibbon proved himself equally smitten, describing her to his old friend Georges Deyverdun as 'a delightful little creature, but ever so slightly naughty'.

Though Mrs Hervey was confident that Foster had 'a steady well-founded Affection' for her daughter, Bess was not looking forward to bearing his child. 'I shall chide you', her mother responded, 'if you become a mother so *tristement.* I had reckoned about your feeling the full value of it, and I still think that when your fears are over you will think you are well paid for your *pains.*' Nor did Bess want to breastfeed the baby, a practice eulogized in the novels of Samuel Richardson and subsequently by Rousseau, whose book *Émile* condemned the traditional use of wet-nurses. Her mother advised 'the hartshorn and oil with hare-skins, used as I did, to backen your milk . . .' (presumably a contemporary method of encouraging the cessation of lactation). Another letter counselled her daughter against late nights and too much exercise, and to leave off her corsets until the baby was born.

Some time in July, Bess and John Foster left for Ireland. On their way to Dublin they visited the rectory at Dunleer, which for part of the year they were to share with Dr Foster. With its austere Irish-Georgian exterior, it was a shock to Bess, who was hoping for something grander. The church, which lay half a mile from the rectory, was not just plain but stark, both inside and out. Bess's letter to her mother describing her new home has been lost, but Mrs Hervey's response leaves little doubt as to its contents: 'I am shocked dear Bess at your account of *your Dungeon* which I had conceived a Place of comfort & which I almost suspect is seen in its worst light by *People who only want a pretext to ramble.*' With her usual good sense, Mrs Hervey recommended that the bed chambers should be hung with 'light chearful papers', and that 'music, drawings, Books, & the little Boy, will give ye old House another face . . .' Dr Foster, she added, 'whom I presume has more goodness than delicacy, has not thought of polishing his House, tho' he has paid so liberally for polishing his Son.' In other words, Bess should make the best of the situation. But it was perhaps this first sight of the 'dungeon' at Dunleer, and the thought of spending hours in that grim little church, that confirmed Bess's misgivings about her marriage.

From Dunleer they travelled the thirty-six miles to Dublin to stay in Dr Foster's town house in Dawson Street until the baby was born. Dawson Street presented a far more cheerful prospect than Dunleer: lined with fine Georgian houses with pillared porticoes and cast-iron railings, it runs between the handsome square of St Stephen's Green and Trinity College, the heart of eighteenth-century Protestant Dublin.

On 3 October 1777 Bess gave birth to a son. Mrs Hervey told Mary that the baby was 'certainly *hurried* into *the world* before *his time*', which indicates he was premature; he was christened Frederick Thomas. Mrs

Hervey's response to her daughter's letter describing the birth (since lost) suggests that Bess was prone to self-dramatization: 'The *Horror* of it, I flatter myself you had magnified, and that you find the pleasure of being a Mother beyond that you had conceived it to be . . .'

Once Bess had surfaced from her month-long lying-in, her correspondence with Holroyd began. In view of his friendship with the Foster family, it is surprising that she felt able to express her views to him so candidly. In December she confessed that she found all babies 'much alike', but added that she looked upon her son 'as a Creature dependant upon me, and irresistibly engaging the affections'. But 'As to Dublin as a metropolis, 'tis poor as a City, dirty, and as a place of amusement dull. The civilities the Castle [the Lord-Lieutenant] has shown me, & the partiality of some individuals, makes me pass some of my time pleasantly, but *pour le reste, je m'ennuie à la mort*.' Three months later there was little sign of improvement: 'Upon the whole, notwithstanding their Routs, Balls and Assemblys, there is but a few people, the Opera and still more the miserable situation of Dunleer, that would make me regret Dublin. There is much dissipation with little amusement or vivacity to justify it.' This is scathing stuff, and odd too, for it was a time when Dublin was considered by many English residents and visitors to be as sophisticated as Paris or London. Bess admits to being the object of flattery, but maintains that the 'admiration of a buzzing crowd' neither pleased nor satisfied her. In general, the women were poorly dressed, 'ill educated & indelicate'; as for the men, they were 'too much engrossed by Politicks to engage much in society . . .' This lack of male society was a real privation for Bess, who much later told a daughter-in-law: 'Some Man one can always find to talk to, because books or politicks will bring people out according to their capacity & situation, but nothing is so tiresome as making conversation with a Woman who only talks of dress or domestic affairs.' With a few notable exceptions, this stated preference for the company of men was to hold true throughout Bess's life.

Bess's distaste for Dublin and its society was exacerbated by letters from her mother, now in Rome, who tantalized her with accounts of the glories of the 'Eternal City' and of her father being 'everlastingly employ'd in buying ornaments for the Downhill'. But Bess's suggestion that she and John Foster should join them there was seen by her mother as an excuse for more 'rambling' and firmly discouraged. On Bess's first wedding anniversary Mrs Hervey wrote her a bracing letter reminding her of her duties as a wife, observing that 'You have both too much good sense to believe each other, or yourselves, faultless', and adding, optimistically, 'I expect that you will enliven the *too serious* character of your Husband, & that his gravity will *gently* temper your fire & vivacity.' There is an implication that Bess had expressed misgivings about her marriage, and that the once pleasure-seeking Foster had settled in earnest to his duties as a member of parliament. The Bishop, whose interest in his children was sincere but fleeting, blithely ignored any signs of discontent and increasingly used Bess as a means of communicating his political views to John Foster – or 'the Senator', as he now called him.

Some note of desperation in Bess's letters did however move her mother to suggest that when she and the Bishop returned to Ireland, the Fosters should live near them at Downhill. 'And if we could get Ld Erne to take Walworth [a neighbouring property] . . . I think we might altogether make a society amongst ourselves . . . We would have music & drawing, & reading & keep good Horses & Cabriolets & Boats etc. etc. & above the rest all love one another, & let me assure you dear Bess there are few plans that offer more happiness than this.'

Mrs Hervey's inclusion of the Ernes in this merry plan was probably because Mary's marriage was also causing her parents concern. 'He tires her to atoms', the Bishop complained to Bess, 'by his silly difficulties, and his endless irresolution. Great God, how ill she is matched!' But he changed his tune when Mary became pregnant. 'Have you seen Lord Erne? Is he on tip-toes? Isn't *Mary* a sweet creature to be at last multiplying herself, and providing comforts for *her* old age and mine. I am in raptures with the thought of seeing you all at the Downhill, and have some thoughts of building barracks for children. Go on, my dear Eliza, and never fear hurting your consititution by honest child-bearing, since for one Mother that grows thin with this work, there are five hundred old maids that grow more thin for want of it.' The Bishop's letter was written two days after Bess herself had lost her second baby, a girl who lived only eight days.

To judge from her parents' letters, Bess had not been well for some time before the baby's birth. Her mother, who always maintained that her daughter's frail constitution had been 'overturned' by a childhood illness, had urged her to take the medicine she had sent, 'for if I find you *thin* and coughing I shall chide you as usual . . .' Her father had recommended she should take the waters at Bath, even offering to pay her expenses – a sure sign of his concern. In November he had been uneasy that Bess intended lying-in at Dublin, where the air was bad:

'Air, my dear Elizabeth, is nothing more than a Fluid whose purity and Impurity depend almost entirely upon the greater or less degree of its elasticity: in great cities and Marshes, there can be little elastick air . . . Dublin is both a great city and a Great Marsh; judge therefore, what a stagnant air it must always contain. Fear it, my dear Ophelia; fear it.' To this concern for their daughter's health, Mrs Hervey had added a further worry: that Bess seemed to dread having another baby. 'It is amazingly unnatural', she wrote to Mary, '& I don't understand it . . . but . . . one cannot enter into [the heart's] recesses, or account for its cravings and disgusts.'

There is no mention of the baby's death in any of the surviving correspondence. The only record of her brief existence is found on the flyleaf of Dr Foster's red leather prayer book: 'Jack's & Elsie's Daughter born Nov. 17, 1778 in ye eighth month, lived 8 days. I baptis'd it Elizth.' So the baby had been premature; even if Bess, who had carried her through a difficult summer, was reluctantly pregnant, her sense of loss must have been terrible. (Despite a marked improvement in a child's life expectancy by mid century, the death rate was still depressingly high. Gibbon, for example, was the sole survivor of a family of seven; the poet Thomas Gray, the sole survivor of twelve.) Apart from her husband, she had no member of her family to console her, and because of the time it took letters from Italy to reach her, the first she received from her mother – counselling her about breastfeeding – arrived a month after the baby had died.

Bad air was much on the Bishop's mind as he, Mrs Hervey and Louisa had all been very ill with 'influenza' (almost certainly malaria), Louisa dangerously so. Their convalescence again postponed their return to Ireland, a return which Mrs Hervey eagerly anticipated in almost every letter to her daughters. 'Why', she exclaimed to Bess, 'are we to be hundreds of miles asunder?' And to Mary: 'How lonely I am become . . . I never could bear travelling, but nobody credits it!' (For 'nobody', read the Bishop.)

When the Irish House of Commons was in recess the Fosters returned to Dunleer, where the 'dungeon' may well have been improved by 'chearful papers' but the continual presence of her aged father-in-law creeping about the house in his clerical black, and the austere way of life of a parochial rectory, was to Bess like being buried alive. With her beauty, breeding and thirst for culture, surely she had been destined for a more brilliant world than that of Dublin, Derry and Dunleer; but she was trapped. By late 1778 Mrs Hervey was confiding to her oldest daughter Mary that Bess was bored with Ireland in general and with Dunleer in particular. 'Poor dear Bess', she continued, 'I am afraid feels solitary.'

When the Bishop and his wife finally returned to England in the summer of 1779, Mrs Hervey was prevented from continuing to Ireland by Louisa's persistent ill health; yet another year was to pass before she was reunited with Bess. The Bishop went alone to Londonderry, and failed to make any effort to see his daughters; the arrival from Italy of crates of works of art for Downhill, his diocesan affairs and a fresh onset of gout combined to keep him in the north. Instead, he wrote Bess long letters justifying his absence abroad and deploring the decline of Ireland: 'Can any country flourish where two-thirds of its inhabitants [the Roman Catholics] are still crouching under the lash of the most severe illiberal penalties that one set of citizens ever laid upon the other?'

In December 1779 the Bishop's brother Augustus died, and he became fourth Earl of Bristol, inheriting the extensive Ickworth estates and an annual income of some twenty thousand pounds. Despite this radical change in his fortunes, the Earl-Bishop – to use Horace Walpole's rather spiteful designation – remained in Ireland for another year, leaving his wife, now Countess of Bristol, to wrestle with his tangled affairs at Ickworth. Lady Bristol began by moving from her mother's house in Bury (Lady Davers died in February 1780) into Ickworth Lodge, a converted farmhouse set in the park at Ickworth, where she was to live for the rest of her life. It was cramped and inconvenient, but had a large garden which boasted melon beds, damson trees and filbert hedges. Although still standing today, the house has been altered beyond recognition.

In the early months of 1780, Bess moved restlessly between Dunleer and Dublin. While on naval service in Canada her brother Jack (now Lord Hervey) had married a gentle, modest girl named Elizabeth Drummond; Bess was at Dunleer when he stopped briefly at Dublin on his way home to England. Although she had not seen her brother for more than three years, Foster tried to prevent Bess going to Dublin by pretending that none of his horses were available. Somehow, she contrived to get there. Jack, quick-tempered, passionate and headstrong, with a deep affection for his sister, would have been unequivocal in his sympathy and support. It was perhaps this meeting that gave Bess the courage to leave John Foster. Three months pregnant again, she travelled north with her son to Downhill to see her father. The Earl-Bishop, however, received her with little enthusiasm; a distraught daughter running away from her politically useful husband was an inconvenience, and he advised her to either return to the husband she should never have left, or go to her mother at Ickworth. Bess chose Ickworth, but failed to inform Foster of her decision.

Enter Mr Churchill. Oddly enough, what is known of Mr Churchill comes from the pen of the Earl-Bishop. Writing in April to Bess, defending himself against an accusation by the Lord-Lieutenant that he had encouraged unrest in Ireland, he added that she was 'at liberty to show this letter to our excellent friend Mr Churchill whose clear head and warm, virtuous heart will easily distinguish & cannot fail to approve the propriety of my conduct.' Either in the role of 'excellent friend' or as potential lover, Mr Churchill met Bess as she embarked at Donaghadee for Port Patrick in Scotland. When news of this reached Foster, he set off at once, catching up with the couple at York. Mr Churchill was sent on his way, while Bess and Foster continued their journey to Ickworth, arriving sometime in August on Lady Bristol's doorstep.

Lady Bristol was shocked to find that the daughter she had not seen for more than three years had lost her youthful sparkle and was now 'the picture of woe, & despair, her health ruin'd, & all her prospects blasted . . .' Writing to the Earl-Bishop after a long interview with Foster, though conceding that Bess deserved censure for her conduct with regard to Mr Churchill, Lady Bristol gave John Foster no quarter. She wrote of '*meannesses*' which 'stamp his character for one of the *basest* and most incorrigible that can be conceiv'd'; described how on her return to England she had been told that the late Lord Bristol and 'all our relations and Friends' – who had seen the couple when they visited Ickworth and Bury *en route* to Ireland – had spoken of 'the great harshness' with which he treated Bess and recognized it as 'an incorrigible defect in his character', since he treated his father in the same way. 'The more I talk to him,' Lady Bristol concluded, 'the more I perceive his duplicity, want of feeling & selfishness, and I can never consent to her being put again into the power of a Person who has already so much abus'd it, & who appears to me to have but *one selfish brutal passion which actuates him even at this moment . . .*'

Despite this condemnation of her son-in-law, Lady Bristol made genuine efforts to save the marriage, principally, it seems, because the Earl-Bishop insisted that she do so. To Mary, however, she confided that in her view hope of a reconciliation was useless. 'It was totally against my opinion as to *happiness*, but your Father's orders, & her *situation* call'd for it . . . dejection and despair are wrote on her countenance, & tho' I have no doubt that time might wear out her *attachment*, I believe nothing *can remove her* disgust . . .' What Lady Bristol meant by 'her *situation*' is unclear: she may have been acknowledging that Bess had no legal grounds of complaint against her husband, that she had been compromised in the eyes of the world by her association with Mr Churchill, or simply that she was pregnant.

In December 1780 Bess gave birth to another son, Augustus – the second baby at Ickworth Lodge, Jack's wife having given birth to a daughter, Eliza, in August. The house must have been bursting at the seams, since the company also included the Earl-Bishop's younger brother General William Hervey, just returned from ten years' service in Canada; the Ernes and their daughter Caroline; and the two youngest Herveys, Louisa and Frederick. In late December, the Earl-Bishop himself arrived; it was the last time the entire family was together under the same roof. The only person absent was John Foster, who had sought refuge in London.

In early 1781 reports reached Bess from Ireland of an 'intrigue' between Foster and her maid, Madame Wagnière. These were seized upon by the Ickworth camp; if they were true, Bess at last had grounds – other than her 'disgust and contempt' – on which to separate from her husband. Lady Bristol told Mary that the intrigue had been going on for eight months, and that Madame Wagnière had complained of '*forcible attempts*' by Foster, while he maintained it was she who was the seducer. As far as Lady Bristol was concerned, Foster was 'in *all things* "mud of ye streets"'.

For Bess and her mother – though not for the Earl-Bishop – it was the last straw. In an undated draft of a letter, written in Lady Bristol's hand, Bess informs her husband that 'it is my fixt wish & determination not to return to you'. She maintains that her 'intentions leaving Ireland were proper', though 'the consequences [Mr Churchill] that attended it [were] improper, but accidentally so', and condemns his conduct towards her as 'the mean *concessions* of a sensual passion that feared to lose its object'. She concludes: 'I must assume a steady determination, & rather than prostitute myself to such a person as I can neither Love nor Esteem, will submit to give up those Children I had hoped to have placed my Joy and Pride in . . .'

At that date, divorce was impossible except for the very rich, and then only by a private Act of Parliament. A 'private' separation, as it was known, was the only option, but neither party could remarry, and the husband had the legal right to claim custody of the children. Though formal separations became increasingly common as the century progressed, by insisting on a separation from John Foster Bess was none the less consigning herself to limbo; that she preferred limbo is clear evidence of her aversion to her husband. The frequent references to her 'disgust', and to John Foster's 'sensual passion', imply that he had forced his attentions on her. At no time does she admit to what may have been another powerful motive for wanting to be free of John Foster: a conviction that she had married beneath her. She had, after all, been born into one of the foremost families of England; even as the daughter of a bishop, she might have expected to do better than an obscure Irish MP; as the beautiful daughter of a wealthy earl she could have aimed for the upper reaches of the aristocracy – but her father had succeeded too late to save her from Dunleer. After five years, the marriage was over; once John Foster had left Ickworth in the spring of 1781, Bess never saw him again.

In June Bess received a heartbroken letter from Dr Foster, in which he insisted that his son's only fault as a husband was that he *'loved too well'*, and reproached her for leaving him. Two further reproaches ring true – his wish that she had been 'more sparing' in expressing her dislike of Ireland, and his recognition that his hope motherhood would satisfy her 'must now give way to the charm of high Life & the pursuit of Pleasures which are not be be found *here*'. He refused to accept that his son had seduced the maid: 'Did you not live altogether above three years before, & did she ever complain of such rudeness from her Master?' As for Mr Churchill, he was a man of small understanding who had poisoned Bess against her husband: 'You will not deny your sincere affection for him before you knew Mr Churchill.' Moreover, Dr Foster disclosed, Mr Churchill had a wife and family in Scotland. (Years later, Bess assured her son Augustus that she had never been unfaithful to his father.)

In the autumn the Foster family, though they had consented to the terms proposed by the Earl-Bishop, tried to make Bess change her mind. But, as she told Holroyd (now Lord Sheffield), 'as feelings guide me & not either prudence or interest I have continued firm, & will submit to any state of penury rather than proffer myself again to a Man I cannot esteem, & must dislike.' The Fosters gave in. In November Bess summed up her situation to Lord Sheffield: 'The dreary prospect I have before me gives me a horror of pursuing the journey which my Youth makes it too probable should be a long one. I feel lost to myself . . . & the world, every power of affection, every feeling of tenderness my nature is fraught with, turns but to increase my misery . . . I look on [my children] & know they are to be torn from me & taught to forget me.' Her brother Jack put it more succinctly: 'A Gloomy Dismal Fate, I am afraid is her lot,' he told Mary.

While Bess was still at Ickworth she was seen by Mrs Dillon, one of the Bishop's nieces. In a letter to her husband Mrs Dillon painted a sad little picture of Bess, and a damning one of the Earl-Bishop:

Never was a story more proper for a novel than poor Lady Elizabeth Foster's. She is parted from her husband, but would you conceive that any father with the income he has should talk of her living alone on such a scanty pittance as £300 a year! And this is the man who is ever talking of his love of hospitality & his desire to have his children about him . . . It is incredible the cruelties that monster Foster made her undergo with him; her father knows it, owned him a villain, & yet, for fear she should fall on his hands again, tried at first to persuade her to return to him.

In January 1782 the family decided that Bess and Mary should move with their three children to lodgings in Bath. Mary was now living separately from Lord Erne, but had been allowed to keep her daughter Caroline. The sisters were obliged to live on the meagre allowances agreed with their husbands and supplemented by their father's annual £300 each: Bath was cheaper than London and was, besides, a delightful place.

Bath had been a fashionable spa since the early seventeen-hundreds. A guide book of 1800 cites it as 'one of the *most agreeable* as well as *most polite* places in the Kingdom . . .' During the 'season', which began in April, it not only attracted the gouty, the sick and the infertile, but over the years had become something of a marriage market. Balls, concerts and the theatre helped to relieve genteel boredom, but the real business of the day was quaffing glasses of warm mineral water in the Pump Room or bathing in the sulphurous waters of the King's Bath. Though the rules of society did not allow women in Bess and Mary's position to be seen in places of public entertainment, a walk along the vibrant streets any day during the season would bring them into contact with the cream of English society.

In May an event occurred which changed Bess's life for ever: she and Mary received a visit from the Duke and Duchess of Devonshire.

To find this illustrious couple on their doorstep must have thrown the sisters into some confusion. Georgiana was one of the most glamorous figures of her day, while the Duke exuded the unmistakable aura of one born to a life of wealth and privilege. That this casual visit, prompted by kindness, should have had the remarkable sequel it did almost suggests the hand of Fate. To the two sisters, the interest shown in them by their visitors must have seemed incomprehensible. They could not have known that the Duke and his Duchess were desperately bored. Their marriage in 1774, begun with such bright promise, had grown stale. They were both seeking diversion, and it fell to Bess to supply it.

Eight years before, when the Duke married Georgiana Spencer and installed her at Devonshire House in London, her impact on society had been dramatic: within months she had transformed the great sombre building on Piccadilly into the most sought after venue for the Whig élite. Society, jaded by a constant round of pleasure, was enchanted with her glowing personality and the atmosphere of reckless gaiety she created – a spectacular achievement for a girl just turned eighteen. Had this extraordinary success been based solely on her beauty and position it might have burnt itself out in a year, but it was built on more durable foundations. While she was not as clever as Lady Melbourne, and had neither the physical perfection of Mrs Crewe nor the allure of Lady Jersey (all leading figures in society), Georgiana possessed compassion, kindness, generosity of spirit, and a singular gift for inspiring love in all who knew her. Even the principal commentators of the time – who were not easily moved – saluted her as a phenomenon. Horace Walpole praised her 'flowing good nature, sense, and lively modesty'; Mrs Delany, then in her eighties, admitted to being '*quite* in love with her'; for Nathaniel Wraxall her appeal lay not so much in her face and figure as in the 'amenity and graces of her deportment, in her irresistible manners and the seduction of her society'. He added shrewdly: 'Her heart may be considered as the seat of those emotions which sweeten human life, adorn our nature, and diffuse a nameless charm over existence.' It was Georgiana's heart that was her problem.

In a letter to Gibbon Bess later declared Georgiana to be as 'handsome as an archangel'. The historian agreed, adding: 'To express that infallible mixture of grace, sweetness, and dignity, a new race of being must be invented, and I am a mere prose narrator of matter of fact.' If a man of Gibbon's felicity with words felt himself unable to do justice to Georgiana, he was not alone: though she was painted by the greatest artists of her day, none seemed able to capture her extraordinary appeal. As Fanny Burney perceived, 'Vivacity is so much her characteristic, that her style of beauty requires it indispensably; the beauty, indeed, dies away without it.'

The Duke, by contrast, was seldom painted. The few portraits show a grave-faced man who regards the viewer with a certain wariness, his youthful shyness masked in maturity by an air of apparent indifference. Wraxall pronounced him 'tall and manly, though not animated or graceful, his manners always calm and unruffled. He seemed to be incapable of any strong emotion, and destitute of all energy or activity of mind . . . Yet beneath so quiet an exterior he possessed a highly improved understanding . . .' Others were less complimentary. During one of his 'Tours' John Byng, a contemporary of the Duke, avoided an inn at Skipton in Yorkshire on the grounds that it was 'a gawky, dismal, ill-contrived thing built by and resembling the Duke of Devonshire'.

At the age of sixteen William Cavendish had become fifth Duke of Devonshire and the possessor of an immense fortune. Apart from his two main residences, Devonshire House in London and Chatsworth in Derbyshire, he also owned four other properties in England and one in Ireland. For generations the Cavendish family had lived up to their motto *Cavendo Tutus* ('Safe by being Cautious') and acquired a reputation for integrity and a sense of duty that commanded universal respect. One did not trifle with a Cavendish.

By the time she met the two Hervey sisters Georgiana, though still as popular as ever, was disillusioned with her life and her marriage. To the disgust of the Duke's family, she had suffered numerous miscarriages. Not only had she failed in her principal duty – to produce children, particularly a son and heir – but she had also failed to win the affection of her husband, who patently preferred his club, the company of his friends, and the bed of his mistress, a dressmaker named Charlotte Spencer (no relation of Georgiana). And she had become a compulsive gambler. She gambled all night, and slept all day. Within a year of her marriage she was in debt. Too afraid to confess her losses to the Duke, she confessed them to her mother.

Should Georgiana have ceased at any time to be conscious of her shortcomings, she had her mother to remind her. Lady Spencer was one of those inestimable women for whom the world had nothing but praise: she was intelligent, well-educated, cultured, an admirable wife and a loving mother. Even the Earl-Bishop spoke of her as his 'model of a woman'. Georgiana was born in 1757 (a year before Bess), her brother George a year later, and her sister Harriet in 1761. The loss of two further daughters in infancy had turned Lady Spencer to religion. It had also turned her to gambling. Though aware of her inconsistency, Lady Spencer never ceased to chastise her daughter for sharing this addiction. Her love for Georgiana was obsessive, her involvement in every aspect of her daughter's life invasive and ultimately destructive. Georgiana adored her mother with equal intensity: '. . . you are my best and dearest friend,' she told her. 'You have my heart and may do what you will with it.'

Even before Georgiana's marriage, Lady Spencer was counselling her against falling into 'dissipation, vice and folly'. As she watched her precious daughter fall with considerable abandon into all three, the daily letters became relentless in their criticism: Georgiana's way of life was condemned, her friends scorned as 'vicious and profligate', her duties as a wife enumerated. Twenty years later Lady Spencer was still writing similar letters, ending one in 1795, 'but I expect much more from you'. However hard Georgiana tried to live up to her mother's expectations, it seemed impossible to satisfy her.

One of Lady Spencer's letters reminded her daughter that her 'exalted station' obliged her 'to many duties, an universal charity, an active humanity', and it may well have been she who suggested Georgiana should call out of kindness on the Hervey sisters, daughters of her old acquaintances the Earl-Bishop and his wife.

The Devonshires were in Bath to take the waters, Georgiana because they were considered an aid to fertility and the Duke on account of his gout. Initially, Mary and Bess were little more than a welcome distraction. 'You cannot conceive how agreeable and amiable they are,' Georgiana told her mother, 'and I never knew people who have more wit and good nature.' Later, a proprietary note creeps in: 'If you see Lady Bristol, I wish you would say as from yourself that the D. and I are very happy in seeing a great deal of Lady Erne and Lady Eliz., for that strange man Lord Bristol is, I have a notion, acting the strangest of parts by Lady Eliz. and we thought perhaps if it was known we saw something of them it might make him ashamed of not doing something for her.' It was typical of Georgiana to use her rank and connections to help someone in trouble.

From that point, there was no further mention of Mary. All Georgiana's attention was focused on Bess, who having weaned the baby, Augustus, lived in daily dread of the arrival of Mr and Mrs

Marshall, the couple deputed by Foster to take the boys back to Ireland. Bess had endorsed her husband's choice of the Marshalls; she had known them in Dunleer, and had 'total reliance on their affection'. Even at the moment of parting with her sons, Bess did not waver in her resolve to separate from her husband. On 19 June she wrote to him from Bath: 'I have attended the children as far as their first day's journey, & I shall suffer tomorrow more than I can express to you. I had hoped to have trained them up to be our mutual pride & pleasure, but must now be satisfied only to hear that you love & cherish them, but do this & be kind to them & they have a disposition amply to reward you.' In the circumstances, it was a restrained and dignified letter, and the first indication of her love for her children. Her apparent lack of maternal instinct, especially when they were babies, may be attributable to her increasing 'distaste' for their father, since she later proved herself the most loving mother imaginable.

Foster wrote to Bess when the boys arrived. She replied: 'I am extremely gratified by the affection & Approbation you have shown & expressed for the dear children . . . Do not, I conjure you, teach them to forget me, be kind to them both, & may they afford you all the happiness that is denied to me.' Although Bess had damned John Foster as a husband, there is nothing to suggest that he was not a good father, with one grave exception: he steadfastly refused to allow the boys to see Bess. Despite repeated efforts on her part, she did not see them again for fourteen years.

Years later Bess described her plight to Augustus: at the age of twenty-four she was '. . . a wife and no husband, a mother and no children . . . [left] by myself alone to steer through every peril that surrounds a young woman so situated'. She was the classic damsel in distress, the embodiment of the current sentimental fashion for tragic, forsaken heroines. And the Duke, though an unlikely St George, appeared to be only too willing to play the knight in shining armour. Besides, what full-blooded male would not enjoy being seen about Bath in the company of not just one beautiful woman, but two? As Wraxall noted of the Duke, 'the somnolent tranquillity of his temper [did not] by any means render him insensible to the seduction of female charms.'

It may have been Bess's misery over the loss of her children that prompted the Devonshires to invite her to accompany them to Plympton, where the Duke, as an officer in the Derbyshire Militia, was required to attend the military camp. 'The Duchess of Devonshire's behaviour on this occasion is *heavenly*,' Lady Bristol wrote to Bess, '& your distress will have been . . . relieved by your father's £100 . . . We look upon your *Journey* & your *summer* as most happily allotted . . .' (Both Foster and her father had failed to pay her allowance, and Bess was already in debt. The hundred pounds were to repay Georgiana.) In August Bess wrote to Lord Sheffield from Plympton to say that she had let herself 'be carried to Town by the D. & Dss of Devonshire, then brought here, where in the midst of "War alarms" we enjoy real peace, & much pleasure. The fact is they both spoil me as much as you & dear Lady S[heffield] used to do.'

Bess and the Devonshires had become inseparable. They went riding or drove out together, played backgammon and read Shakespeare. Often they just 'dawdled and drew'. 'How comfortable this is,' Georgiana told her mother, '& how much more one enjoys oneself than in the hurry of a town.' This remark perhaps contains the key to the rapidity of Bess's intimacy with both the Devonshires; had they met in the 'hurry' of London, where Georgiana and the Duke lived virtually separate lives, such closeness between all three would have been impossible.

Bess has been criticized for allowing herself to be 'carried' off by the Devonshires, and for thereafter insinuating herself into their society as a way of escaping poverty and a bleak future. But at that stage, low in both health and morale, she surely lacked the confidence for such calculating behaviour. She was younger than the Duke by ten years, and possibly even a little in awe of him. Georgiana's glamour and sophistication must have been daunting to a girl who knew nothing of the fashionable world, and apparently had no friends and no money; the glittering world of the Devonshires was a far cry from the rectory at Dunleer. Suddenly, she found herself the focus of two unhappy people. Though at first surprised and flattered by their attentions, perhaps she began to see that her effect on their marriage was beneficial. When Georgiana told her mother 'We all go on deliciously here, and are so comfortable that we look upon it as a misfortune when we are obliged to go out', it was the first time for years that she had expressed such quiet contentment. How – and, indeed, why – should Bess have resisted being carried off and spoilt by them? For her to be taken up by the Devonshires at such a moment in her life was little short of a miracle. She cannot have foreseen that a summer spent in their company would lead to a friendship lasting until Georgiana's death, or that she would fall in love with the Duke.

Lady Spencer, who should have been relieved that her daughter had exchanged a life of 'vice and folly' for the joys of reading Shakespeare, was quick to detect a change in Georgiana. 'Those were happy days, my dearest child, when every thought of your innocent heart came rushing out without a wish to disguise it . . . I see you on the edge of a thousand precipices, in danger of losing the confidence of those who are dearest to you . . .' In August Georgiana's sister Harriet and her husband Lord Duncannon joined the Devonshires at Plympton. Instead of spurning the interloper, Harriet was as charmed by Bess as her sister. Four years younger than Georgiana, Harriet was an intelligent woman, with a strong, clever face and dark eyes. She was passionately fond of Georgiana, yet generous enough never to resent Bess's hold on her sister's affections.

By September, Georgiana and Bess were writing poems to one another. Georgiana's describes her state of mind before they met: 'Ere sorrows had obscur'd my day/your sweetness charm'd my better day/And doubly blest the pleasures few/That were increas'd & shar'd by you.' This is followed by generous praise of Bess, and a touching plea for her affection: 'Combining with an *upright mind*/a heart affectionate & kind/for all in you united trace/Perception, honor, sense & grace/Oh can you Bess your task fulfill/And daily faulty love me still?' In her reply – entitled 'Little Bess's answer' – Bess expresses her gratitude for Georgiana's praise and friendship and extols her in return, but her words show signs of self-regard and affectation which are absent from Georgiana's. The poem contains two revealing lines: 'How the faults which you blame she'd learn to correct/And coquetry no more her manners direct.' Whether the 'coquetry' had been aimed at the Duke or at others of the fashionable crowd gathered at Plympton is impossible to tell, but the word – or variations of it – cropped up again in letters to Bess from both her mother and Georgiana. Certainly Bess 'flirted' with the Duke; her whole manner, whether consciously or not, was flirtatious: she had only to give one of her demure sidelong glances for the damage to be done. 'No man could withstand her,' wrote Edward Gibbon. 'If she chose to beckon the Lord Chancellor from his Woolsack in full sight of the world, he could not resist obedience.'

In November the Devonshires were to join Georgiana's parents at Hotwells, a spa near Bristol. When she heard that Bess would accompany them, Lady Spencer pleaded that her husband was too ill to see strangers. 'Ly Eliz: comes with us, my Dst Mama,' Georgiana firmly replied, 'but . . . she is the quietest little thing in the world, and will sit and draw in a corner . . . or be sent out of the room, or do whatever you please . . . I hope to see her set out for Nice within the month.' This letter is interesting on three counts: it paints a picture of Bess as a biddable mouse; it shows that Georgiana, who seldom defied her mother, was prepared to do so where Bess was concerned; and it reveals that the possiblity of Bess wintering abroad had already been discussed.

Bess had been unwell for some time. Prone since childhood to bronchial troubles, in September she was diagnosed as showing early symptoms of consumption. The eighteenth-century remedy for tuberculosis was to go abroad, preferably to the Mediterranean, but given her penurious state, this solution was clearly beyond her resources. In their anxiety to help her, the Devonshires devised a plan. The Duke had an illegitimate daughter by his mistress Charlotte Spencer, born within a few months of his marriage to Georgiana. Had he himself not told his wife about the liaison, she would have learned of it from the newspapers, which scrupled no more then than now to expose private matters to the public gaze. But for a man to have a mistress was considered by society as entirely *comme il faut*, and any offspring were often raised by his family; when Charlotte Spencer died, her child, Charlotte Williams, was 'adopted' by the Devonshires and lodged with a Mrs Garner at their expense. For Bess to go abroad for her health, taking Charlotte with her to further the child's education, seemed an ideal solution. The Devonshires would not have put it so crudely, but that did not prevent others from describing Bess as acting the part of paid governess (she was to receive £300 a year).

There may have been other reasons for despatching Bess to foreign parts. A letter from Georgiana to her mother in October contains a passage which could imply a suspicion that Bess's relationship with the Duke was not simply one of friendship: '. . . so weak am I that I yield to things that hurt me, with my eyes open.' This was written before the Devonshires took Bess to stay with the Spencers at Bristol, when Lady Spencer had ample opportunity to observe the three together. They now used nicknames for each other: the Duke was 'Canis', presumably because of his love of dogs (ardently shared by Bess); Bess was 'the Racoon' or 'Racky', probably because of her wistful expression and large eyes; Georgiana, for reasons which remain obscure, was 'Mrs Rat'. Lady Spencer must have been both surprised and disturbed by the level of intimacy they had achieved in so short a time, and can hardly be blamed for wishing Bess elsewhere. Aware of her hostility, Bess strove to overcome it; but the means she employed, which included writing obsequious postscripts to Georgiana's letters, only alienated Lady Spencer further.

In late October, Georgiana suspected she was pregnant. Until the three-month danger period was over, Bess and the Duke devoted themselves to her care. Georgiana later recalled a journey they made to Bath during this time: '. . . what could be more interesting than our journey last year – a Man and a woman endowed with every amiable quality and loving one another as Brother & Sister, Nursing & taking care of a Woman who was doatingly fond of them & who bore within her the child that was to fulfill the vows and wishes of all three.' Georgiana's unborn baby had become a tangible symbol of their friendship.

A month before her departure abroad, Bess received the shocking news that after thirty years of marriage her parents had separated. It seems they had gone for a drive together in apparent harmony but returned not speaking to one another (and they never did so again). Only the coachman knew what had occurred and he, with commendable discretion, refused to reveal it. Lord Bristol had packed his bags and left for Ireland. His parting gesture was to let Bristol House in London for three years, thus condemning his wife and the two youngest children to a life of rural obscurity at Ickworth Lodge. Bess's anxiety about her mother is evident from a letter from Lady Bristol written in February 1783 and addressed to her daughter at Nice:

> I am sorry that my situation has sat so heavy on [your mind] for I can give you no comfort on that subject except by assuring you that my mind is quite above and out of the reach of the oppression I receive, and the insults which accompany it . . . & even my resentment is softened down into compassion for the frailties of human nature, and for the wreck which warring passions bring upon it: my own happiness has long been an empty sound . . .

3

Grand Tour
1782–1784

'My dearest, dearest, dearest Bess, my lovely friend,
nothing would give me so much pleasure as an
unexpected letter from you . . .'

Georgiana to Bess, 25 January 1783

———————————◆———————————

FOR A WOMAN, especially a girl of twenty-four, to travel abroad
without a male escort was both highly unusual, and a major under-
taking. By virtue of her rank, and her position as the Duke's represen
tative, Bess was in charge of the small party which left England at the
end of December 1782. It consisted of the eight-year-old Charlotte
(nicknamed Louchee because of her squint), Mrs Garner (who had
been looking after the child), a maid, Mrs Ashburner, and a Mr Hunter,
who was to be responsible for their travel arrangements. All of them
caused problems: Mrs Garner proved to be 'diabolical', Charlotte a
reluctant student, Mr Hunter extravagant, and the maid tiresome
enough for Bess to shed her the second time they passed through Lyons.

The eighteenth-century traveller had a wide range of guides from
which to choose. Some, like Thomas Nugent's *Grand Tour*, were
written specifically as guidebooks; others, such as Mariana Starke's
Letters from Italy, were not, but nevertheless contained much inciden-
tal practical advice. Bess had certainly read Laurence Sterne's *A
Sentimental Journey through France and Italy*, and possibly Tobias Smollett's
cantankerous *Travels in France and Italy*. While Sterne was full of the

romance of travel, Smollett would have prepared her for the innumerable hazards in store.

Not least of these was money. It was not necessary to travel with heavy bags of coins, for a system of letters of credit drawn on designated banks along the route could be established. However, as this relied on the erratic postal services, a traveller could find himself arriving ahead of his authority to draw funds. By the 1770s a form of credit known as circular notes had evolved – today's travellers' cheques in all but name – and these would have been far more efficient for Bess (since her itinerary kept changing), but the Devonshires continued to use the traditional letters of credit.

Then there was the problem of what to pack: Mariana Starke advised a host of necessities, not least of which was a travelling *chaise percée* (close-stool) which fitted into the well of the carriage. Other items included sheets, pillows, blankets, towels, pistols, a pocket-knife (to eat with), tea, mosquito-nets, a padlock (few rooms boasted locks), essential oil of lavender (a few drops scattered over the bed repelled bugs and fleas), numerous spices and condiments, and a well-stocked medicine chest – a list which speaks eloquently of damp beds, tasteless food and a dearth of doctors. As Bess could hardly have flourished a pair of pistols, it was presumably Mr Hunter who was in charge of firearms, a prudent defence against highwaymen and wolves.

Another indispensable item was a leather *portefeuille* in which to carry the multifarious documents required. These included copies of the precious letters of credit, letters of introduction, letters of recommendation to all British embassies, health certificates (to prove the traveller had not come from a town in quarantine), and passports. As English passports were not recognized on the Continent until the nineteenth century, the traveller had to obtain a new one for every territory he entered. One traveller planning a journey from Rome, in the Papal States, to Naples, in the Kingdom of Naples, complained that he had to go to the police in Rome to get his 'passport passed, then to the Governor to get it signed for Naples, and afterwards to the Consul of Naples to get it countersigned' – all this to travel a hundred and fifty miles.

An important item in Bess's luggage was a small notebook. Together with countless other young ladies of her ilk, she had decided to keep a journal, a practice gently satirized by Henry Tilney in Jane Austen's *Northanger Abbey*: 'Not keep a journal!' Tilney exclaims to Catherine Morland. 'How are your absent cousins to understand the tenour of your life in Bath without one? . . . How are your various dresses to be remembered, and the particular state of your complexion, and curl of your hair to be described in all their diversities, without having constant recourse to a journal?' The notebook was the first of some 128 which Bess filled over the next forty-two years, their contents much less frivolous than Tilney suggests. Her Grand Tour journals read like a cross between a history lesson and a lecture on art appreciation, and are peppered with quotes from Shakespeare and the Classics. She becomes mired in endless detail; there are too many olive groves, rushing torrents and jutting rocks, proof of the influence of Ossian and Rousseau, who preached a new reverence for nature untamed, the picturesque and the romantic. They were undoubtedly written for others to read, but they also proved an invaluable *aide-mémoire* for her future travels. Bess's greatest gift as a journalist – the ability to remember conversations seemingly verbatim, a talent inherited from her grandfather Lord Hervey – developed later.

Bess began her journal on 29 December 1782 with a brief description of the embarkation at Dover. She makes no mention of her emotions on leaving England, nor does she comment on her companions. At Calais they stayed at Dessein's, the best-known hotel. The following day they departed for Paris in a *carosse,* a vehicle like an English stage-coach with room for six passengers and drawn by four horses. Bess comments on the postilions 'who wear their nightcaps under their hats and the most enormous boots [and] always look as if they would overpower the poor miserable horse they ride . . .' English tourists invariably derided the quality of French horses, and considered postilions to be spectacularly vile. Smollet had condemned them as 'lazy, lounging, greedy and impertinent'.

After a succession of 'execrable' roads and numerous 'indiffirrent' inns – though there is no mention of the athletic fleas she must have encountered they reached the French capital. Paris she considered inferior to London, the streets narrow, unpaved and dangerous. The shops, however, 'afforded great variety, & great perfection & taste . . .' She attended the opera but, while 'struck with the magnificence of the spectacle', disliked the singing. Marie-Antoinette was in the audience, and Bess 'was pleas'd with her sending to inquire who I was' (that her presence should be noticed illustrates just how small society was in those days). She was also conducted around the palace of Versailles by Comte d'Adhémar, who had been French minister at Brussels at the time of her marriage. Parts of the palace she considered 'shabby and old', the rooms 'dark and bad', but the Hall of Mirrors was 'superb'.

Georgiana, who had known the French Queen and her intimate companion the Duchesse de Polignac for some years, had arranged for Bess to meet the latter. Introduced by Georgiana as her 'most loved friend', Bess was received by the Duchess 'as if we had long been friends'. As governess to the royal children, the Duchess – or Little Po, as she was called – took Bess to see the two-year-old Dauphin.

From Paris, Bess and her entourage took the customary Grand Tour route south via Lyons to the Rhône, then on by barge to Avignon. From there they travelled overland through Aix towards Nice, spending one night in an inn where they had no blankets – in February. The coastal road was full of surprises: one inn was overrun with cats 'almost wild that jumped to the ceiling, & top of the Bed'; another was 'very dangerous to sleep at from the number of robbers'; the following morning they were startled by a wolf bounding across the highway. At Nice she came to rest at the house of an old friend of her parents, Lady Rivers.

Throughout her four weeks on the road, Bess had written numerous letters home. At least six of them were to Lady Bristol – a measure of her concern for her mother's situation. The first surviving letter received from Georgiana, written on 25 January, begins: 'My dearest, dearest, dearest Bess, my lovely friend, nothing would give me so much pleasure as an unexpected letter from you . . .' It was enclosed in a box of chintz and muslin, 'some chip [straw] hats and some tea, in case you should not get good at Nice . . .' One passage, written partly in French, shows Georgiana to be still unsure of the strength of Bess's affection for her: 'If I am mistaken and that you are grown "*Ah te voilà ma petite*" to your G. throw this into the sea. But that is not possible, forgive me, my angel, I believe I sometimes say these awful things to you just to have the pleasure of hearing them contradicted.' None of Bess's early letters to Georgiana and the Duke have survived, but notes in her journal indicate that she had sent the Duke some of the famous Côte Rôtie wine from Condrieu, and Hermitage from Tournon. A letter to the Sheffields in early February shows that she was homesick, mourning the loss of her children, fearful for her future, and suffering from fevers and from pains in her chest. She had found a little house close to the sea where she meant to 'live quiet & retir'd' and do nothing but 'ride, draw, & practise musick' – and presumably instruct Charlotte: despite her role as governess, Bess seldom mentions the child. When Georgiana first met Charlotte in 1780 she described her to her mother as 'amazingly like the Duke' and 'vastly active and vastly lively'; Bess found her quick to learn, but reluctant to apply herself without strict handling.

Bess's rides in the hills above Nice attracted the attention of the local peasantry, who were astonished to see a young Englishwoman dressed in a white riding habit and a befeathered hat mounted on a fine English horse. 'Would you believe it,' she told Lord Sheffield, 'they have dedicated a beautifull fountain here to me . . .'

Bess's desire to live a secluded life may have stemmed from other motives than a wish to regain her health. Lady Bristol's letters in the early months of 1783 allude to several mysterious gentlemen – all, maddeningly, referred to by their initials only – who had clearly played some part in Bess's life before she left England. Mr F. (John Foster) is mentioned briefly, he having had the impertinence (in Lady Bristol's view) to ask Bess whether she had received any money from her parents. Lady Bristol advised Bess to ask him how he 'thought you had been maintained for the eight months he had left you without a shilling'. But who was L.A.P., and why was Lady Bristol so relieved that Bess had refused 'what he had solicited'? She felt confident, however, that Bess was 'getting into port again, though the current may be a little against you, and oblige you to work for some time at the oar . . .' She believed, too, that Bess now had 'good sense and steadiness enough to lay down the coquette without adopting the prude . . .' Another letter declares a wish that Bess 'was not so punctual' about writing letters to H., 'for by that means you make absence no advantage, and you are still the dupe of his expressions'. But it is not only the owners of the initials that intrigue; in February Lady Bristol entreated Bess to cease feeling guilty for causing her so much 'uneasiness . . . for thou art the sheep that was lost and is found again . . .' Though she approved of Bess's retired way of life at Nice, she adds sternly: 'Something decisive in your conduct was necessary to make an impression and to put you upon a new footing.'

Lady Bristol's enigmatic comments a month later are still more tantalizing. Concerned that Bess's health has not improved, she wonders if the climate is unsuitable – or is it 'still the effects of your long journey, and the scene you went through; or a wound that is still festering, though you think it healed; or the absence from your friends [the Devonshires]; or the severe judgement you are passing on yourself?' What 'scene' had Bess gone through, and when, and with whom? The only possible clue, although it thickens the plot rather than unravelling it, is a remark in Lady Bristol's first letter after Bess left England: 'I pity you for the meeting at Dover, and long to know the result.'

It would seem from all these innuendoes that Bess had emerged from five years of marriage – the majority of which she had spent pregnant and immured at Dunleer – with something of a bang. Like all beautiful women, she was beset by temptations; to resist them required a strength of character and clarity of purpose which she had yet to develop. Meanwhile her susceptibility to flattery, which she had earlier condemned to Lord Sheffield as incapable of 'satisfying the heart', might lead her into ever deeper waters: as she was still a married woman, no liaison could lead to an honourable conclusion.

While she was at Nice, Bess heard constantly from her 'lov'd friend'. Georgiana's letters now began to contain political news, an indication of her increasingly close involvement. In January Bess noted in her journal Georgiana's information that the peace marking the end of the American War of Independence was '"thought a very bad one, & Ld Shelburne's mismanagement is said to be wonderfull"'. In February Shelburne resigned as leader of the government. In April George III, despite his loathing of the Whigs in general and of Charles James Fox in particular, was forced to accept a government formed under Lord North, with Fox as Foreign Secretary.

Georgiana had become so involved in Bess's life that she was even corresponding with John Foster about the two boys. In April she told Bess he seemed so amenable that she had conceived a plan for Augustus to be sent to school in England, the cost to be borne by the Devonshires. Georgiana's generosity did not end there: she implored Bess 'to attend strictly to your dear health, but likewise to every amusement for your mind that would not be hurtful to it or imprudent . . . For this purpose Dearest Bess if you refuse to receive from your sister . . . what is really your own [she means money], you overwhelm her heart with sorrow. Let therefore your Canis and G. give you what is necessary for making your stay agreeable or by heavens you break my heart.'

Georgiana had the rare gift of persuading people to believe that by accepting something from her they were doing her a favour. Bess was certainly not proof against such strategy, any more than she was against Georgiana's openly declared need for her. Georgiana urged

Bess not to return to England until after her baby was born, 'for fear of the agitation it would cause us both'; when she did return, it must be to Devonshire House, for a month at least.

> And as *your little pride,* and perhaps circumstances, may make it as well that you should not absolutely live in the house always with your brother & sister, I will look out immediately for a house for you near us on condition that you are less in it than here . . . You should have your children with you . . . You shall be on the best & most friendly terms with all your family . . . but independent of them, and your Brother and Sister – your Canis and G. – shall be the only ones whom you shall allow to share with you . . . Am I too presuming in making myself & Canis the principal movers in the scheme of your future life?

It would have been remarkable – and positively perverse – if Bess had declined to adopt Georgiana's rosy 'scheme' for her 'future life'.

By May, Nice was too hot: Bess and her entourage boarded a ship for Toulon. From there they travelled inland to Avignon, then by barge up the Rhône to Lyons, the river so swollen by meltwater from the Alps that teams of oxen were required to haul the barge against the current. After a month at Lyons the little party, now reduced to four by the abandonment of Mrs Ashburner in a convent, travelled east to Geneva.

Bess's concern for Georgiana, with her history of miscarriages, and whose pregnancy had been difficult, is evident from a letter written during the journey north. 'Dearest ever ever dearest Love, why have I no letters from you? I cannot express nor describe the anxiety I feel from it, nor how my peace depends on every thing that concerns you . . .' This was followed by a request for money (which she insisted should be merely a loan), tempered by promises that at Lyons she would 'begin a plan of reform' of her expenditure.

At Geneva Bess received the long-awaited news: Georgiana had given birth to a daughter on 12 July. 'She really is uncommonly hand-some,' wrote the ecstatic mother. 'Her eyes are Beautiful. How gulchy you would have been at her birth . . .' The child was christened Georgiana, but usually referred to as 'Little G.' Bess's response was written on 20 July: 'My wish, my fondest wish, is thus accomplished, You are a Mother! . . . 'Tis still almost as a dream to me & so difficult is it for a heart oppressed & long accustomed to sorrow to bear up under Joy that I quite sank away at the news I have been pining for . . . Oh my best Love, my heart since I have known you has formed no wish but for your happiness, no prayer but for blessings on you & to deserve your Love . . .' The letter continues in this vein for several pages. She then describes her consternation when she found Georgiana's courier at her door. Immediately fearing bad news, her 'tearless brain grew hot; & I really thought for some time that I should have gone mad . . . I bid him speak on & at last tears came to my relief; I blest God that you was well & today I feel the full extent of *our* happiness. Kiss *our* Child for me: how happy are those who have a right to be its god-mother, but I am to be its little mama; Canis said so.'

While this letter may seem excessively emotional, almost hysterical, it takes its tone directly from Jean-Jacques Rousseau's *La Nouvelle Héloïse* of 1761, one of the most popular and influential novels of the eighteenth century. In a series of letters, *Héloïse* tells the story of the passionate if wildly idealized relationship between a young tutor, Saint-Preux, his pupil Julie and her friend Claire. Young women like Bess and Georgiana were stirred by its outpourings of emotion and the intensity of feeling, as much between Julie and Claire as between Julie and Saint-Preux. The letters of Bess and Georgiana express sentiments no less passionate than those of the two fictional women. Bess, in describing her physical prostration on receiving the news, is trying to convey the depth of her joy and relief that Georgiana had, at last, been safely delivered of a child. It is pure *Héloïse*. And her reference to '*our* child' is not presumption, but an echo of the term initiated by Georgiana herself.

'What oh what are you doing now my best & beloved love,' Bess wrote three days later. 'When you can write send me a little detail of how you pass your time, when you suckle the little treasure . . . in short every thing about you.' Though the Duke seldom put pen to paper, on 29 July he told Bess 'the Duchess thinks the child is much such a little thing as you, and I think so too, only she is not so naughty and so apt to be *vexed*.'

Even the pure Swiss air had not cured Bess of the pain in her side, and she decided to go to Lausanne to consult the famous Swiss physician Simon Tissot (also known for his treatise on masturbation, which he attributed to idleness and the reading of meretricious novels). Gibbon, a resident of Lausanne, must have seen her – though she makes no mention of it in her journal – as he told Lord Sheffield: 'Your later flame and our common Goddess, the Eliza, passed a month at the Inn the greatest part of the time either in fits or taking the air on horseback.' From Lausanne she journeyed by boat up Lac Léman to Vevey, accompanied not only by Charlotte but also by two mysterious gentlemen, Monsieur Gambier and the Chevalier Ternu. This interesting fact is recorded in her journal, sandwiched between descriptions of '*jolies villages*' and '*superbes rochers*' (this section is written in French). The excursion lasted several days and included a side trip to Meillerie (sacred to Bess as the place where Saint-Preux, hero of *La Nouvelle Héloïse*, contemplated suicide out of love for his Julie), and one night spent in a cottage sheltering from a storm. Bess records that Charlotte occupied the bed, while she slept on the floor and '*mes amis*' on chairs. Bess's account of this adventure provoked a horrified response from Georgiana on 19 August:

> I think that the innocence of your conduct and intentions does not make you aware enough of the danger of your situation. You see after all the resolutions you made about not receiving men, you have been living alone with 2 . . . Suppose you had at any place seen a beautiful young woman arrive, travelling by herself, who, tho' there was nothing against her, had had imprudencies laid to her charge, and that you saw this young woman giving parties and living with two men, both suppos'd to be in love with her – with all your candour you would think her imprudent. I declare to God, my sweetest Bess, I do not fear the *essential* with you one moment, but to you the opinion of the world is of so much importance for every future scheme, and so many of our women lately have gone into Switzerland and Italy when in scrapes, that you should be doubly cautious to shew you are not that kind of person.

Georgiana then implored Bess not to meet a certain chevalier in Turin (it seems he was not the same chevalier as the one at Vevey), but to find some women to live with while in Italy, 'let them be ever so disagreeable'. 'My angel love,' she concludes, 'the world is so alive about you that I have even heard that ridiculous storys have been made of your being crown'd at the fountain at Nice.'

Bess's reply, which took her five days to write and covered nine pages, was dated from Turin on 8 September, soon after she had crossed the Mont Cenis pass into Italy. The letter is a disturbing mixture of extravagant excuses for her conduct, genuine contrition at having caused Georgiana such distress, and frequent references to her social success. 'Never was your little Bess so surrounded as last night', she gushes, and at least four more ardent admirers had appeared on the scene. Lurching wildly from one subject to another, the letter gives the impression that Bess has completely lost her bearings, if not her head. She even suggests that her father has sent men to spy on her.

Towards the end of it she admits that the trip to Vevey with the two men was ill-judged, and concludes with her sanest comment through-out: 'There are situations & circumstances when even the partiality one may meet with is distressing. Rome's antiquities will suit me better than the Court of Turin.' Two weeks later, in a letter which if read in its entirety strikes a note of desperation rather than self-pity, Bess tells Georgiana that she feels abandoned by her family; that her heart 'like a bruised Plant' cannot 'regain its vigor'; and that her soul is 'laden with all that is most bitter, and is burning itself up with feelings of dis-tress that are all but terrifying'.

Georgiana's concern that her dearest Bess was skating on ever-thinning ice demonstrates her awareness, gained from personal expe-rience, of the necessity for a woman to protect her good name. Bess's blithe assumption that she could behave as she pleased was born of youthful arrogance, rather than lack of virtue – although Georgiana's reference to Bess having had 'imprudencies laid to her charge' recalls Lady Bristol's concern over her daughter's morality. Bess had yet to learn that discretion was the key to survival in society. In Lady Melbourne's view, 'Anyone who braves the opinion of the world sooner or later feels the consequences of it.' Bess, after all, was a Hervey, and Herveys were watched by the world with particular atten-tion: sooner or later they could be guaranteed to behave badly.

Indeed, Bess's father was already behaving outrageously badly. Having abandoned his wife at Ickworth, he went straight to the house of a Mrs Mussenden in Ireland. Mrs Mussenden, though undeniably a close relative by marriage, also happened to be very young and very beautiful. To Mary her father merrily recounted the 'innocent spirits, gay society and indefatigable attentions' of 'this *chère cousine*'. Mrs Mussenden was to prove only the first of several *amitiés amoureuses* enjoyed by the Earl-Bishop in his latter years, all now judged to have been no more than flirtatious friendships. But at the time it naturally caused a scandal, aggravated in November by the publication in *Freeman's Journal* of an anonymous letter in which Lord Bristol, though not specifically named, was accused by implication of having seduced Mrs Mussenden.

All this was very painful to the family, particularly to Lady Bristol. To receive Bess's account of her trip to Vevey only added to the poor woman's distress. In a December letter she warned Bess that when she saw her 'borne away by the defects in your character, or blinded by your own approbation acting so as I think will provoke the censure of the world, I must tell you of it. I hope it is not with *aigreur* [sharpness], but I own it is with strong feelings, because I see you in a situation in which you have everything against you. I am grieved to say that your father's very extraordinary conduct has given rise to many ill-natured reflections on the whole family.'

But the Earl-Bishop's association with his young cousin was not the sole reason he was attracting attention. His brief colonelcy of the Irish Volunteers (an armed body of Protestant patriots) during the Dublin Volunteer Convention in November 1783 – at which he created a sensation by parading through Dublin clad in episcopal purple, his knee and shoe buckles blazing with diamonds – and his conduct during the sittings of the Convention had aroused the suspicion, even alarm, of the British government.

In Turin Bess was having a panic over money. Either she had been extravagant, or the system of letters of credit had broken down. Georgiana, typically, blamed herself: 'I find you are kept in Turin for want of money. Good God – Good God – and all my fault.' Oddly enough, in a letter thought to belong to the same period, Bess refers to some money she had *returned* to the Duke, given her by her father (curiously, he is referred to here and elsewhere as 'Pansey'): 'I never know how to keep money & a day later it might have been gone heaven knows where.' Bess adds a touching declaration of her gratitude to Georgiana: 'The more I think, the less I can guess what you can mean in your letter by your obligation to me. I only know you can have none to such a bankrupt as me. I owe you every thing, & can repay you nothing.'

Although Georgiana's letters were full of delight in her little girl, her state of mind was precarious. Her gambling debts were mounting, the Duke's agent Mr Heaton had made a baseless assertion that she was having an affair with the Prince of Wales, and at the end of October her father died. When Bess heard of Lord Spencer's death, she went into mourning. 'I thank you my *kindest love for wearing mourning*,' Georgiana wrote to her from Bath. 'Where could I find another heart like yours . . .'

In December the Duke too wrote to Bess from Bath. It is an affectionate and endearing letter, and gives a rare glimpse of a man whose personality remains largely elusive.

This place has been very unpleasant for me compared to what it was a year and a half ago, for then I had the Rat [Georgiana] and Bess and good health and fine weather . . . There are many places in Bath that put me so much in mind of you that when I walk about the town I cannot help expecting upon turning the corner of a street, to see you walking along it, holding your cane at each end, and bending it over your knee. But I have never met you yet, and what surprises me likewise very much is, that somebody or other has the impudence to live in your house in Bennett Street.

By the time she received this letter Bess was in Rome, having spent two weeks immersing herself in the glories of Florence on her way south. She had apparently survived the problems of travelling in Italy – the heat, the appalling roads, the grasping innkeepers and importunate beggars, dastardly coachmen and ruffianly postilions – and at Bologna seems to have avoided contracting a complaint known as the Itch, said to be caused by the local wine. There were other privations especially trying to women: 'There are', wrote Samuel Sharp, 'no such things as curtains, and hardly, from Venice to Rome, that cleanly and most useful invention, a privy; so that what should be collected and burried in oblivion, is forever under your nose and eyes.' 'Italy' at this time was divided into several states, thus the currency was a nightmare: the traveller required three different kinds of lira – the Milanese, the Austrian and the so-called 'Italian' – and must learn to differentiate between almost fifty sorts of coins. Tuscany alone used the sequin, the scudo, the livre and the paul. With the help of the 'extravagant' Mr Hunter Bess had obtained the obligatory health certificates from the town authorities, and had learnt the exact amount required to bribe the customs officials to prevent them ransacking the luggage. Yet in spite of all these trials, her journals lack the endless grumbles of Smollett and others. With her love of continual novelty and of the arts and ancient history, and her ardent appreciation of the beauties of nature she made an ideal tourist.

'If Mr Gibbon is within hearing,' Bess had written to Lord Sheffield in 1781, 'send my admiration of his works . . . & tell him I mean to make them a particular study as long nights & early candles are established.' The second and third volumes of Gibbon's *Decline and Fall of the Roman Empire* were published this year, and her study of this masterpiece – later compared by Thomas Carlyle to 'a kind of bridge that connects the ancient with the modern ages. And how gorgeously does it swing across the gloomy and tumultuous chasm of these barbarous centuries' – had instilled in her a passion to see for herself the wonders of ancient Rome. But by the late eighteenth century the city's decay was already far advanced, its ancient monuments buried, looted, or obscured by recent building. Mariana Starke complained of the pestilential air emanating from the choked-up sewers, James Boswell was shocked to find parts of the Colosseum 'full of dung', and a weekly livestock market took place in the Forum (hence its name, Campo Vaccino, the cattle pasture). But Nugent insisted that 'one cannot walk fifty paces without observing some remains of [Rome's] ancient grandeur', and Bess shared Nugent's view. With the guidance of Thomas Jenkins, one of the best of Rome's *ciceroni*, she carried out an exhaustive study of the city. Her description of part of the Forum demonstrates how powerfully it affected her:

> The three Columns of Jupiter Stator are noble . . . & stand free & apart. One other column also nearer the Capitol very fine: on the pedestal an inscription to Phocas. The Arch of Severus much sunk, but all are so hid by modern buildings, & the whole appearance so inferior . . . that it creates a constant regret in seeing them . . . Still I must consider this as almost sacred ground, & revere the great, generous & Imperial Heroes that formerly governed & honor'd it.

On Christmas Day Bess attended High Mass celebrated by Pope Pius VI in St Peter's. Also present were Joseph II, Emperor of Austria, and Gustavus III, King of Sweden. The Emperor travelled with a modest retinue of two attendants, Gustavus with twelve. Among the latter was Count Axel Fersen, 'the King's great favourite'. Bess's casual comment that she 'saw a great deal' of Gustavus – one of Europe's most fascinating and enlightened monarchs – masks the fact that she all but fell in love with Fersen.

Axel Fersen was divinely handsome. Born into one of Sweden's most illustrious families, heir to vast estates, fluent in four languages and an experienced soldier, in December 1783 he was acting as Captain of the King's Bodyguard. He was also fatally attractive to women. He had spent several years in Paris, and there is ample evidence that Marie-Antoinette was in love with him, though no actual proof that they were lovers. (In certain circles, however, it was an accepted fact: in 1797, when Fersen was sent as Swedish ambassador to the Congress of Rastatt, Napoleon declined to see him, on the grounds that 'he refused to deal with a man who had slept with the Queen of France'.)

Bess probably met Fersen at the house of an old friend of her father, Cardinal Bernis, the French ambassador at Rome. As one of the leading figures in Roman society the Cardinal had entertained Gustavus and his suite to dinner, an occasion described by another guest, Miss Cornelia Knight, as being 'like the East Indies – all heat and diamonds'. She was shocked to see Gustavus 'scratch his head with his fork, and also with his knife, and afterwards to go on eating with them'.

Given Bess's connection, through Georgiana, with the French royal family, and her recent visit to Versailles, she was surely aware of the rumour linking Marie-Antoinette with Fersen. But a letter to Georgiana in January 1784 from Naples – whither she had retreated to escape the Roman winter – reveals other, darker aspects of the French connection. Though the letter is frustratingly opaque in its allusions to past events, it appears Georgiana had been warned that her friendship with Bess was attracting salacious gossip, and that Marie-Antoinette and Madame de Polignac were jealous of their relationship.

Bess opens her letter with a lyrical description of the hills around Naples, 'the fields enammelled with flowers, & the air perfum'd with myrtle & every aromatick Plant & Herb . . .', followed by a plea that Georgiana and the Duke should join her – 'for that lazy creature Canis it would be just the thing'. Then suddenly she changes tack:

> Am I then to be attack'd on every side & must you too be tired & griev'd for this our friendship? . . . Why are excuses to be made for its sharpness and its fervency . . . & why is our union to be prophaned by having a lie told about it? . . . No my drst Love, let spite & jealousy & envy take its fill, I am proof against its sharpest arrows . . . Does the warm impulse then of two feeling hearts want an excuse & to be accounted for, & must your partiality to me be usher'd in by another connection? If the Queen were Jealous of me I . . . will do all that is for your care & comfort . . . & shall give Madame P. no cause for jealousy. I will try to gain her friendship, & shall ever do all I can to prove to you mine.

Though the charge of lesbianism – and such a relationship might be considered implicit in this letter – is impossible to prove or refute, it would be wise to see both the letter and the friendship which prompted it in context. In the atmosphere of overcharged emotion inspired by Rousseau and prevalent in the 1770s and 1780s, passionate friendships between women were not uncommon, and from time to time attracted such rumours. Bess and Georgiana may have expressed their feelings for each other in a manner alien to modern readers, but it was one which reflected the language used by popular novelists of the day. Nor were men afraid of displaying emotion. Goethe's immensely successful novel *The Sorrows of Young Werther* (published in 1774), which, like *Héloïse*, concerns a three-way friendship, opens with a declaration by Werther to his friend Wilhelm: 'To leave you, whom I love so, from whom I was inseparable . . .' Numerous references to his heart, his soul, and his frequent shedding of a *thousand* tears proclaim Werther to be a man of feeling, though he was clearly no less a man because of it. Bess had almost certainly read *Werther*, even though her father had condemned it as being 'a totally immoral and damnable book' because it appeared to condone suicide. The Earl-Bishop had gone so far as to challenge Goethe on the subject but had, surprisingly, lost the argument.

By coincidence or design, Bess was in Naples at the same time as Gustavus and his suite. She was invited by the King to join an expedition to Vesuvius. 'I was carried up, & almost all the way down,' she told Georgiana. 'The Crata was full of smoke, but scarcely a flame perceptible, the noise was considerable like bursting cannons & boiling water . . .' This expedition was followed by another, to the ruins of Pompeii (discovered in 1748) to see the most recent excavations. 'The Comte F. drove me in a Phaeton,' she told Georgiana in February, 'the day was fine, the Party numerous for we went with the King.' But the letter also contains an admission that Fersen had come alone one morning, and that being very low she had confided in him her concern over the part her father played in politics and his 'unfortunate uncertainty of Character'. She had also told him about her children in Ireland, and how she was forbidden to write to them, whereupon 'He burst into tears . . . kissed my hand repeatedly . . . [and said] that "he should feel more at leaving me when he left Italy than he could express" . . . & my sweet Love what touches me in him, he never address'd a word in praise of my appearance, nor utter'd a syllable that expressed other sentiments than those of tenderness.' She then compares Fersen's conduct with the 'wildest expressions of the most violent passion' to which she had been subjected by the mysterious 'H.' referred to by her mother the previous April.

A few days later Bess told Georgiana that there had been a *moment critique* with Fersen, but she had survived it. The Count had been alone with her, had kissed her hands and then her cheek. She had checked him, saying: 'This must never be again.' He had acquiesced. 'Pray forgive me,' she implored Georgiana, 'I think better of him than any

body I have seen, but your claims & Canis's on me can never lessen
. . . I do not pretend that I shall not regret him, he is in every respect
amiable and estimable' – to find someone 'amiable' meant far more in
the eighteenth century than it does now – 'but', Bess concluded, 'you
live in my heart, & if I confess my weaknesses to you, teach me to
correct them . . . Oh G., are you angry with me!'

The letter also refers to Georgiana as a 'safe harbour' and her 'guardian Angel'. Bess's choice of words is not random but instinctive, evidence of her belief that without Georgiana's guidance she was in danger of capitulating to Fersen. Since she was not free to marry him, capitulation meant becoming his mistress, and that only for so long as he remained in Italy: thus she had narrowly escaped scandal and eventual disgrace. In view of Georgiana's alarm over the Vevey incident, no wonder she feared her friend's disapproval.

Over a year later Bess confessed in her journal that she *had* been attached to Fersen, 'yet nothing could efface the impression the other [the Duke] had made'. For his part, Fersen noted in his Correspondence Book that he had written to Bess on 25 April to know how his portrait (which she had asked for) should be sent to her, and had requested her portrait in exchange. But Fersen was a philanderer; quite apart from his relationship with Marie-Antoinette, while in Florence he had embarked on a flirtation with Emily Cowper, the daughter of old friends of Bess's parents. In December he noted that he had written to Bess and 'Declared everything', which could mean that he had confessed his liaison with the Queen. His Correspondence Book also records that he had written to 'Josephine' (his code name for the Queen) twenty-seven times since leaving Paris the previous September.

In late March Bess returned to Rome, where she resumed her study of the city, describing every painting and antiquity with a diligence which is tedious, but truly impressive. The reluctant Charlotte was obliged to trail about in her wake. Though she is so seldom mentioned, in January Georgiana had declared to Bess that she now had great hopes 'since you have drawn from her the load that must have opprest her'. Yet a month later Bess reported that, despite a rigorous daily programme of study, Charlotte 'does not in any respect improve as I hope she would have done', and that her character was 'very difficult to manage.' Mrs Garner, Charlotte's keeper, was also proving difficult. A report from Bess on her conduct so enraged Georgiana that she briefly contemplated stopping the 'hateful woman's' allowance.

Having to devote time to Charlotte when the upbringing of her own children was denied her was very painful for Bess. Although there were perhaps times when she used the loss of her sons as a means of arousing sympathy, it caused her genuine and continuous distress. In January she had told Georgiana that she had heard from Mrs Marshall, who looked after the boys in Ireland, that Frederick was to begin learning Latin. 'Oh My Angel, am I to have no share in the education & cultivation of these dear Boys' minds!' Mrs Marshall was to arrange for their portraits to be painted, 'for I felt I needed the comfort of their Pictures'. Would Georgiana, she begged, pay Mrs Marshall, and 'will you add this to the numberless obligations I have to you . . . ?' until she returned to England.

Indebtedness was a recurring theme in their correspondence. Georgiana had told Bess in January that she had been 'part of this year in great adversity, but nobody shall ever know this but you'. It seems the Duke's agent was still pressing her to disclose her debts to the Duke. Bess replied by return of post: 'My sweetest angel, perhaps you have had disputes with him [the Duke] about money; perhaps this odious journey, added to all other expences has been distressing. Oh, dearest dearest G., and would you not tell me if it was so? Oh, do not let me be a source of any pain or disquiet to you . . .' Georgiana hastened to assure her that 'the little expence you are at is like a drop of water in the sea . . .' In March, Georgiana revealed that she had incurred 'a very, very large debt', and that she had at last confessed it to the Duke: 'What had I to offer for the kind of ruin I brought on him (for ev'ry year of my life I have cost him immense sums) – a mind he could not trust in, a person faded, and 26 years of folly and indiscretion. And how do you think he has receiv'd the avowal – with the utmost generosity, goodness and kindness.' Shortly after writing this letter, Georgiana suffered yet another miscarriage. In April her problems multiplied when she became involved in the 1784 Westminster election, canvassing for Charles James Fox. Admired by some but viciously attacked in the press, she felt that the notoriety this brought had 'lowered' her in the eyes of the world.

In the midst of this tumult, in April, Georgiana wrote Bess a letter of extraordinary immediacy. 'Oh let me be Eloquent to you my ever Dst Dst Dst Bess, may my heart my head my expressions speak forcibly to you & may you hear me & comply with my request. As much as I long to see you it is not for me I write. I am certain poor Canis's health and spirits depend upon your soothing friendship. Just now he said to me – write to Bess, tell her I never have heard from her, won't she come? Why won't she?'

Bess had been contemplating remaining abroad another year, and had admitted to Georgiana that she dreaded lest her return should 'renew all remarks & observations & conjectures, our tender friendship makes me an object of envy, & of course of the malice of others . . .' But Georgiana's plea, or perhaps the Duke's, was irresistible, and she sailed from Genoa to Nice in early June, then travelled north to Lausanne. On 2 July Gibbon reported her progress to Lord Sheffield: 'She passed through Lausanne . . . poorly in health, but still adorable (nay, do not frown!) and I enjoyed some delightful hours by her bedside.' On her arrival in Paris she again encountered Gustavus and Axel Fersen, but her journal refers only to an invitation to join the French Court at La Muette, a small château on the edge of the Bois de Boulogne. 'The Queen came to me in the most agreeable manner; her manner is delightfull. Her countenance animated. Her complexion brilliant.'

Bess had already left Rome before a mysterious letter from her mother could reach her. In the interests of speed, Lady Bristol had posted it to Devonshire House, to be sent on by courier. 'There are many reasons', she explained in a covering letter to Georgiana, 'to operate against her return at present, for besides the fatigue & heat of a summer journey, the situation of her Family at this moment would be death to her.'

4

Children of the mist
1784–1786

'Emily, does it never strike you the vices are wonderfully
prolific among Whigs? There are such countless
illegitimates, such a tribe of children of the mist.'

Miss Pamela Fitzgerald, 1816, from Lord David Cecil,
The Young Melbourne

BESS HAD BEEN abroad for eighteen months. In that time she had
successfully conducted her little party round Europe, filled poor
Charlotte with enough culture to last her a lifetime, received far more
admiration than was good for her, behaved imprudently towards
numerous admirers, fallen half in love with Axel Fersen, and proved
herself a redoubtable traveller and passionate student of the arts. The
heights, however, had been interspersed with frequent depths, when
she suffered from periods of guilt, self-doubt, loneliness and despair.

On her return to Devonshire House in late July 1784 she found
Georgiana sadly chastened by recent events. 'I am cross, miserable and
unhappy,' she had confessed to her mother a month before Bess's
arrival. 'I hate myself. I find my debts are much talk'd of . . . It seems
to me that this year, when I wd have ventur'd my life that I should have
lead a much quieter life from my angel child . . . and that I should have
recover'd more dignity and good opinion in the eyes of the world, it
seems to me worse than ever.' And this letter pre-dates Georgiana's
latest 'scrape' – her unwilling involvement in the Prince of Wales's

melodramatic attempt at suicide as a means of persuading Mrs Fitz-herbert to marry him (a marriage which, as he well knew, was forbid-den by both the Royal Marriages Act and the Act of Settlement). Though the birth of her daughter had satisfied a profound need in Georgiana, it had not lessened her dependence on Bess. Through the medium of their correspondence their friendship had intensified while Bess was abroad. They had committed to paper their most inti-mate thoughts, sworn undying love, and made plans for their future together – and with the Duke. Most immediately, Bess was to visit her mother at Ickworth; then, accompanied by Charlotte, she would join the Devonshires at Chatsworth. Georgiana seemed impressed by the improvement in Charlotte. 'You never saw so ridiculous and clever a little witch,' she told Lady Spencer. 'She speaks perfect French and Italian & is vastly clever.'

Bess's health had not improved, however; she was still coughing and painfully thin, and it was assumed she would return to the Con-tinent before winter set in. Lady Spencer clearly hoped so: 'I am sorry Ly E. Foster's cough is worse,' she wrote to Georgiana with unblink-ing hypocrisy. 'Indeed,' she continued, neatly sidestepping the fact that it was high summer, 'she should not stay in such a climate as this, every hour may be of the utmost consequence to her . . .' To Lady Spencer's disapproval of Georgiana's friendship with Bess were now added dark suspicions: was the Duke 'very much in love' with Lady E., as she had been told by her friend Lady Clermont, who had heard it from the Duchess of Rutland?

Lady Bristol's fears that Bess would find the situation at home 'death to her' were not unfounded. The family had virtually disinte-grated, and there was no longer any pretence that Lord Bristol would return to the conjugal home. By letting Bristol House he had deprived Lady Bristol and Louisa (now sixteen and ready to enter society) of the customary London season. He next demanded that his youngest son Frederick should live with him in Ireland, a terrible wrench for his mother. Mary, still living apart from Lord Erne, had moved to France with her daughter; Jack had quarrelled with his father; and Lady Bristol was so short of money that she could not afford the upkeep of Ickworth Lodge – the poor woman could not even go riding, as the Earl-Bishop had taken her horse. 'One must make of it what one can,' she told Bess with saintly resignation, 'and live from day to day.'

There is no doubt that Bess's sympathy for her mother's plight created a breach between herself and her father, but she had her own reasons for feeling injured by his conduct. His political views and the scandal over Mrs Mussenden had caused her embarrassment in Italy – where he was so well known – and, having quarrelled with John Foster, he had refused to register the settlement agreed between himself and the Fosters following her separation. He had even interfered over the two boys: 'I dread the Pansey's trying to reconcile me to Mr F.,' Bess had told Georgiana from Naples, 'which I think influences him to approve the children being kept from me.'

From the gloom of Ickworth Bess travelled north to Chatsworth, spending one night on the way. Beyond the village of Beeley the public road crosses the River Derwent and enters what Walpole described as a vale 'rich in corn and verdure'; today it is a magnificent park, grazed by sheep and deer. Bess would have caught her first glimpse of the house across the valley to her right, the golden stone luminous against the wooded hill beyond. The original Elizabethan house begun in 1552 by Bess of Hardwick had been remodelled by the first Duke of Devonshire. Described as a 'stupendous Pile' by one early eighteenth-century visitor, the house is baroque in style, with each façade differing from the other three. When it was completed in 1707, it was one of the first houses in England to have sash windows. The domestic plumbing arrangements, however, were sufficiently meagre, even eighty years later, for Miss Lloyd, a friend of Lady Spencer, to write delightedly to a friend that her room was 'near the Water Closet, so I am quite at my ease!'

What today's visitor sees as he approaches Chatsworth is the great rectangle of the first Duke's house and the long North Wing added by Georgiana's son, the sixth Duke, in the early nineteenth century. When Bess first stayed with them in 1784, Georgiana and the Duke had just completed alterations to the principal rooms of their private apartments on the first floor. One, the Music Room, was described years later by the sixth Duke as being 'the most joyous and frequented of all the rooms at Chatsworth'. The state apartments, which were seldom used, occupied the second floor, facing south towards the Canal Pond, a sheet of water stretching serenely into the middle distance.

When Bess arrived, she found the house already full of guests, all enjoying the relaxed, haphazard atmosphere created by Georgiana. During the day the Duke would take the men shooting on the moors or fishing on the Derwent. If it was fine, the ladies drove out in open carriages or strolled in the grounds, Georgiana walking beside her daughter in her little chintz-lined pram – which can still be seen on the

Great Staircase at Chatsworth. In the evening everyone played whist, billiards or commerce (a primitive form of poker). On one occasion they were entertained by a company of strolling players who erected a stage in the echoing vastness of the Painted Hall. 'It was very bad,' Georgiana told her mother, 'but amus'd us.'

Twice a week there was a Public Day when the house was thrown open to all-comers. These were clearly painful for Georgiana and the Duke, especially the dinners, which began at three o'clock and lasted for several hours. Some of the men became extremely drunk. On one Public Day in September they received a visit from Dr Samuel Johnson. 'He look'd ill,' Georgiana told her mother, 'but, they say, is wonderfully recovered. [He had suffered a paralytic stroke in June the previous year.] He was in great good humour and vastly entertaining ... Ly Eliz and me were very sorry to leave him for the public day. He din'd here and does not shine quite so much in eating as in conversing, for he eat much and nastily.' After dinner the Duke took his distinguished guest into the garden, where they sat and discoursed in the shade of the lime trees. Though pressed to stay, Johnson declined 'on account of his bodily infirmities'; he was suffering from gout and dropsy, and died three months later.

In an attempt to fill the pages of the daily letters demanded by her mother, Georgiana regaled her with the day's events, including – much to Lady Spencer's irritation – delightful cameos of Bess. One of the guests had been saying 'all manner of fine things to Ly Eliz, so the Duke threw her whip down the steepest part of the hill that he might fetch it, but his gallantry did not reach so far for he would not go.' Lord Jersey had also 'quite fallen in love' with Bess. A week later, Georgiana wrote, 'Sr Wm [unidentified] has succeeded Lord Jersey in being a lover of Ly Eliz, he is quite desperate. I tell her she is like Susannah tempted by the Elders.' The following Sunday Georgiana reported that the vicar had preached an 'excellent sermon upon the text of the serpent tempting Eve'.

'When does Ly E. go?' Lady Spencer enquired hopefully of Georgiana in September. 'She should not delay for she will not bear a winter in England with that cough.' The arrival at Chatsworth of her son George and his evil-tongued wife Lavinia supplied Lady Spencer with a fresh source of information. It was the first time George had met Bess. Though he admitted to his mother that she was 'very pretty and sometimes very engaging in her manners', he was irritated by her affectation, but detected nothing amiss in her behaviour to the Duke.

Lady Spencer at last had her wish: it was decided that Bess, accompanied by Charlotte, should again winter abroad. As Bess had ceased keeping her journal when she arrived in England in July 1784 and no letters for this period survive, how she felt about returning to the Continent after only five months at home is unknown. When the house party at Chatsworth broke up in late October, the Devonshires returned to London while Bess went to Ickworth to take leave of her mother. She then went to Devonshire House for a few weeks. When she left England on 2 December she was – although unaware of it – already pregnant by the Duke.

It is impossible to establish exactly when Bess and the Duke became lovers. When she began her journal again on 25 March 1785, she speaks of 'love so lately given and proven to the D. of D——e'. As the baby cannot have been conceived later than mid November 1784, her use of the phrase 'lately given' may have been precise. But the Duke, writing to her in nostalgic mood after she had been abroad for nine months, recalled the 'blue bed you slept in' at Chatsworth, which could be taken to imply a more than passing knowledge of its blueness. Georgiana and the Duke – unusually for the time – appear to have shared a suite of rooms at Chatsworth, a bedroom flanked either side by dressing-rooms, and this suite had a convenient feature – a narrow passage running behind it, probably with doors to these and other rooms. Such passages, for the use of servants going about their business, facilitated privacy at a time when they were everywhere, equipped with long ears, sharp eyes and, frequently, loose tongues (the key witnesses at trials for adultery among the aristocracy in the eighteenth century were always servants). That they were also convenient for discreet use by other members of the household cannot be discounted.

But another entry in Bess's journal gives rise to further speculation; on 6 April 1785 she recorded that while 'attached' to Count Fersen, she was never 'led an instant to what even now I wish I had not done. I then thought D.D. indifferent to me, that his former love had only been a sensual one.' This could mean that she and the Duke had become lovers *before* she went on her Grand Tour and met Fersen – that is, within months of her first meeting the Devonshires. Pregnancy was, naturally, a frequent outcome of a liaison. Contraceptives were a rare commodity. A shop off Piccadilly sold them – handy for Devonshire House – but the chances of being able to procure one in the wilds of Derbyshire were remote. Besides, they were French, and wickedly expensive. Made of sheep gut, they were nine and a half inches long, and held in place by a red ribbon round the scrotum.

And what of Georgiana? Had she noticed any change in Bess's attitude towards the Duke while she was in England? 'I was not well,' she told her mother in September 1784, '& felt more nervous, unhappy & uncomfortable than I ever did almost in all my Life!' But this confession comes out of the blue, in a letter otherwise devoted to daily life at Chatsworth. It is perhaps Bess who casts the most light on Georgiana's behaviour during those months, recording in her journal on 6 April 1785 that Georgiana's 'unthinking kindness has hurried me down the precipice. Perhaps she thought I was still attached to Comte Fersen . . .' Georgiana was neither suspicious nor jealous by nature, and would probably have despised herself for suspecting a liaison; instead, she would have preferred to cling to the belief that Bess and the Duke loved each other in just the way she had described to Bess in February 1784: 'What a happiness it is to me that my dearest loveliest friend and the man whom I love so much and to whom I owe everything, are united like brother and sister, that they will ensure one another's happiness till I hope a very great old age, that I am equally loved by both and that we three may pass our lives in making one another happy.' It was the second time Georgiana had expressed this idealized view of the relationship, and in very similar terms.

It has been suggested that Bess aroused the Duke and increased his potency, thus enhancing Georgiana's chances of producing an heir, but this hypothesis ignores the fact that she had frequently conceived, only for each pregnancy to end in miscarriage. That Bess's presence raised the emotional temperature is entirely possible: far from being an intrusion, it was the catalyst which brought husband and wife together. Once they were united, she acted as both a foil and a focus. What the Duke craved was to be left in peace, and the freedom to retire to his apartments with his dogs and his books. Georgiana's sprawling, indiscriminate benevolence filled his life with noise and clamour; Bess, with her natural coquetry, teased the Duke from his lethargy, while her soft caressing ways soothed and beguiled him. She provided an alternative target for Georgiana's lavish affections, and to Georgiana, whose own need for affection and approbation was infinite, she gave loyalty and devotion. And the Duke could hardly be accused of neglecting his wife for his mistress, since the two women conceived within a few days of each other.

To pretend that Bess's adoption by the Devonshires was not greatly to her advantage would be naïve. She had gained financial security, an elevated social position, and a series of luxurious roofs over her head. Had she begun an affair with someone outside Devonshire House, even a close friend of the Devonshires, and as long as she obeyed the cardinal rule of discretion, society would have turned a blind eye. Particularly at this level of society, infidelity was an accepted fact in the later decades of the eighteenth century, perhaps a consequence of the custom of arranged marriages, which could tempt both men and women to seek romantic love elsewhere. The Earl of Carlisle once remarked that his friend Charles James Fox spent his youth in a London presided over by '37 Ladies . . . who would have all been affronted, had you supposed their [*sic*] had been a grain of conjugal fidelity among them.' It was Bess's misfortune – and Georgiana's – that she fell in love with the Duke.

When Bess left England it was without Charlotte, who had been packed off to a fashionable London school to continue her education. Though there is no proof, the impression persists that she disliked the child. If that was the case, Miss Lloyd's view perhaps justifies her feeling: 'I don't like this Charlotte much,' she told Lady Spencer after meeting her at Chatsworth, 'I fear there is something bad in her . . .' Bess was accompanied instead by her brother Jack's wife, the sweet and gentle Lady Hervey, and their five-year-old daughter Eliza, her beloved godchild. Jack was to join them in Paris, from where they would all travel together to Italy. Had Bess had her way, her eldest son Frederick would have been of the party. She had begged her husband to let her take the boy, now aged seven, but he had refused on the grounds that it was 'Full time to place him among Boys of his own years' as he was 'backward and timid'. Foster's letters demonstrate a wish to meet Bess half way, but also a determination to do what he deemed was right for the boy.

Bess resumed her journal when she reached Turin in late March. The version that has survived is not the original, but a copy made by the daughter whose journey into life fills its pages. That it is a copy naturally raises questions. What happened to the original? Was it destroyed, either accidentally or on purpose, after the copy was made? If so, why? After Bess's death in 1824 her daughter Caro was the first to go through her papers, writing to her brother Clifford: 'You may imagine the extreme interest that her early letters and journal are of to me and will be to you dearest. How she suffered, poor angel, and how much she went through for our sakes.' But as it was Caroline who made the copy (possibly altering it in the process), it seems odd that she should have retained the names of both the Duke of Devonshire and the Duke of Dorset, or revealing passages such as those recounting Jack's infidelities – surely better expunged if the intention of the copyist was to sanitize the journal.

Bess's motives for keeping this particular journal can only be guessed at. Was it intended, as has been suggested by Amanda Foreman in a footnote to her recent biography of Georgiana, 'In the main . . . [as] a self-justification for stealing her friend's husband, and to that end her other lovers are either excised completely or their existence glossed over'? If this was the case, why did Bess herself not omit all reference to the Duke of Dorset, to Axel Fersen, and to her inability to resist flattery? Was it rather that, afraid she might die in childbirth, she wanted a record of her ordeal and her feelings for the Duke to survive her? Or did the journal become a much-needed friend during months when she was often alone, ill and afraid?

It has been alleged, too, that Bess rewrote all her journals, but this is not supported by the evidence of the journals themselves. Except for the journal covering the birth of the Duke's children and one other, all are in Bess's hand and contain numerous pen-and-ink sketches, little watercolours, and the occasional pressed flower. That she reread them is clear from the pencilled notes added later. For example, 'Bonaparte has built them bridges. E.D. [Elizabeth Devonshire] 1813' is added after an entry in 1783 describing a river crossing by barge. Next to an entry critical of Michelangelo's *Last Judgement* in the Sistine Chapel, written during her Grand Tour, she later added: 'A young rash judgement of mine on this painter – for the paintings are certainly admirable. E.D. 1815.' Her son Clifford also added corrections to the later journals, but these were purely historical and probably made with a view to publication. In 1863, thirty-nine years after his mother's death, Clifford had excerpts from the journals privately printed, as *Anecdotes and Biographical Sketches by Elizabeth, Duchess of Devonshire*, but these are simply an edited version of the originals and very limited in scope.

By the time Bess took up her journal again she knew for certain that she was carrying the Duke's child. 'After four months spent at Paris in all the amusements which the best society & the gayest Court could afford us, how does my situation hang over me like impending ruin! And how have I spent these four months? In shutting my eyes on all that could reveal what I apprehended . . .'

The 'best society' had included the third Duke of Dorset, ambassador at Paris since 1783 – though not a very good one, according to Walpole, who pronounced him a 'proverb of insufficience'. But the Duke excelled in another field: he was a womanizer of some repute. In 1783 there had been a rumour, put about by Georgiana's sister-in-law, Lady George Cavendish, that Bess was, or had contemplated becoming, his mistress. Bess's association with Dorset during the early months of 1785 rekindled the talk, and she obviously felt some guilt since she admitted in her journal that while declaring that she 'could not love him otherwise than as a friend', she had allowed him 'to cherish a warmer sentiment' for her. She added regretfully: 'I suppose that woman's vanity requires more fortitude than we like to exert to resist it . . .' As the journal later reveals, she was far too in love with the Duke of Devonshire to have an affair with Dorset. Besides, as all the world knew, Dorset already had a mistress, the famous dancer Giovanna Bacelli. They had been together since 1779 and she had her own apartments at Knole in Kent, the Duke's country seat.

But something occurred while Bess was in Paris which briefly marred relations between her and Georgiana. It seems Bess wrote Georgiana a letter which upset her; Georgiana's reply upset Bess in its turn. Both have since been lost, but another of the same period from Bess to Georgiana, which has in part survived, gives some clue to the cause of the trouble. Bess begins by describing the warmth of her reception at Versailles by the Duchesse de Polignac and the Queen, but adds that the latter's attentions had created 'much spite & jealousy, as I saw by being placed next her at the play to night'. Then, in a sudden rush of emotion, she exclaims: 'Oh God! Can you do yourself & me the injustice to doubt that knowing you & Loving you as I have done my heart can ever alter towards you! No, never, never never . . . I cannot read your letter without a trembling heart that Paris or anything, or anybody . . .' Unfortunately, the rest of the letter is missing. Subsequently the Duke seems to have stepped in, writing to assure Bess that Georgiana's letter had 'proceeded only from her love for you being as great as ever, and from an apprehension that yours for her might be diminished, by your new acquaintance in Paris'.

Peace was thus restored, and in her next letter Bess asked Georgiana to tell the Duke she was reading Cook's *Voyages* 'in order to be a wise little thing, & that no novels bear to be read after the *Héloïse*'. She also recounted a dream in which she had been carrying Georgiana's daughter but let her fall. 'I never felt or suffer'd so much.

And then I thought I was holding her & my own poor little boy who had hurt himself & I woke in the attitude I should have been in had it really been so. How solitary did I then feel, & how my heart ached; how many bitter tears have I shed since that *miserable day* I first married!' Unaware of Bess's pregnancy, Georgiana would have seen no significance in the dream; Bess, however, knew Georgiana was with child. 'With what delight I told Madame de P[olignac] yesterday of your dear & precious secret . . .'

Soon after Jack's arrival in Paris the Herveys and Bess left for Italy. Relations between Jack and his wife were difficult; Bess had hoped her 'unhappy sister-in-law, would be eased of the uneasiness my Brother's infidelities had caused her'. Yet despite her brother's transgressions, Bess was too ashamed of her own to take him into her confidence; male immorality was to be expected, but female immorality was less readily forgiven. Bess was so terrified of discovery that she even contemplated trying to abort the child 'by exercise' (she does not seem to have considered either Farrer's 'Catholic Pills' or Velno's 'Vegetable Syrup', two other popular nostrums which allegedly induced abortion). 'I weighed the criminality of the act with the great object of saving my mother, family, & friends from the sorrow I should bring on them . . .' At the town of Lapalisse, near Lyons, she fainted. 'I thought fatigue had operated what I could not voluntarily do, but my misfortune was but ripening – & from the moment my babe had life, tho' sorrow did not forsake me, yet tenderness often blunted the sting.' Her passionate attachment to the Duke's baby, even while it was still in the womb, is in stark contrast to her apparent reluctance to bear John Foster's children.

When they reached Lyons, Bess engaged 'Miss A.' as her maid; this was almost certainly the tiresome Mrs Ashburner who had been with her during her Grand Tour until Bess lost patience and abandoned her in that city. From Lyons they crossed the Alps by way of the Mont Cenis pass. That Bess arrived at Turin 'heated, ill, and exhausted' is hardly surprising; she was now four months into her pregnancy, and crossing Mont Cenis was arduous at the best of times. Coaches had to be dismantled down to the last screw and loaded on to pack-mules (the erstwhile occupants no doubt anxiously hoping that every screw had been safely accounted for). More robust travellers crossed on foot, but the majority were carried over the snow-covered pass in a contraption like a sedan chair but open to the elements. The pass was unfit for carriage traffic until the nineteenth century.

At Turin Bess was blooded, the standard response by the medical profession to virtually every ailment; the aim was to evacuate evil 'humours' from the blood. 'It was a miracle so copious a bleeding did not occasion a miscarriage,' Bess wrote. 'I half hoped, half dreaded it. Nature as if to torture me more, spoke all a Mother's language within me . . . Could I be forgot by the world I would nurse thee, my child, and bless thy birth, and he who gave it thee: but to have thee born to Heaven knows what fate, a misfortune perhaps to thyself and others, nay, not daring to own thee, yet anxious for thy safety – oh till this hour I knew not what misfortune was. Oh, may thy too dear, too beloved Father never know the pangs which rend my heart.' Bess's adoption of a biblical tone is not the only evidence of her belief in God, of whose existence a quiet assumption permeates the journals; but her piety was perhaps given an added boost by the perils of her situation.

During the *longueurs* of the journey south Bess turned for comfort to her journal, which had become a confessional as well as a record of events: 'I have felt less vanity since my love for the D. of D——e & I think if I know my own heart, had I been his, or could I live near him, I should feel no desire of conquest, but my isolated situation & continual absence from him, my privation of all the ties so natural to a heart like mine, particularly the loss of my Children . . . all have exposed me at times to give way to the pernicious desire of attaching people to me, yet even this desire whilst I was with the D. of D——e was quite annihilated within me so totally did I love him . . .'

By the time she reached Florence on 6 April, Bess was becoming desperate: 'Every day increases my torment and misery. I know not how to bear up under such oppressive circumstances.' She was ashamed of 'the esteem & consideration' shown her by the friends she had made during her Grand Tour. 'They know not how I have fallen . . . I dread a confinement I may not be able to conceal, yet my soul yearns to cherish the dear Babe I bear . . . Oh, God pity me. How could I bear to let the D. of Dorset be attach'd to me, to think me virtuous! I shall write to tell him I don't deserve his love . . . Would I could fly the face of human kind – yet I could not bear not to see my lov'd friend [Georgiana] again. She has been my comfort and happiness . . .'

Though Bess acknowledges her debt to Georgiana, at no time – even in this, the most self-revealing of her journals – does she confess to a sense of guilt for betraying her. This is surprising, since the journal is suffused with the sentiments and moral philosophy of Jean-Jacques Rousseau. In *Mes Confessions* (profoundly admired by Bess,

Georgiana and the Duke when it was published in 1782) Rousseau not only condemns adultery but bitterly reproaches himself for 'the abuse of a trust I owed to friendship' when he falls passionately in love with a friend's mistress.

In the journal Bess returns again and again to her loss of virtue and the pain it caused her. 'What can be greater misery to a feeling and delicate mind than to lose the Virtue it cannot cease to love? . . . My God, my God assist me, help me to hide my shame and sorrow from the friends it would afflict.' This shame is again an echo of Julie, the heroine of Rousseau's *Héloïse*, who struggles to retain her virtue despite her love for Saint-Preux; having failed, Julie descends into a welter of remorse: 'Thus, one unguarded moment has ruined me forever. I have fallen into the abyss of shame from which a girl never returns, and if I live, it is only to be more wretched.'

Bess's candid self-assessment continued after the party moved on to Rome in mid April. 'Sometimes I look at myself in the glass with pity. Youth, beauty, I see I have; friends I know I have; reputation I still have; and perhaps in two months, friends, fame, life and all future peace may be destroyed and lost for ever to me. If so, my proud soul will never, never return to England. Cruel friend, when I could not stay to be supported and comforted by you, should you have plunged me in such misery? But it was not his fault. Oh no, his nature is noble, kind, tender, honourable, and affectionate. Passion has led us both away . . .' This is the closest Bess comes to laying any blame for her plight on the Duke. Yet, given that the adultery took place under his roof, and that the first approach would almost certainly have come from him, surely he was equally, if not principally, responsible?

At Naples Bess received letters by courier from the Devonshires. The Duke's was 'mysterious from necessity – my heart wanted the comfort of reading the expressions of his tenderness, but prudence forbid his writing them. Patience, oh, my soul, he tries to encourage and support me.' Georgiana's letter showed, 'more than ever, the goodness & nobleness of her mind by ingenuous confessions regarding herself. She asks me an entire confidence about the Duke of Dorset. I have nothing to conceal and the recital costs me nothing. Would it were so on all subjects.' On 16 May Bess wrote: 'I can no longer calm the agitation of my mind – dangers seem to multiply around me – my shape increases every day – my health grows weaker . . . How I long for the solitude of Ischia.'

While dining out at Naples, Bess found herself obliged to listen to her fellow guests discussing 'the cleverness of some women in concealing their being with child . . .' That she was able to conceal her own pregnancy even from Jack and his wife was largely due to the current female fashions. Gone were the rigid bodices of the early 1780s; instead, all was billowing softness, gossamer-thin muslins and gauzy scarfs. A downy shawl, artfully draped, supplied added camouflage, and a large wide-brimmed hat, trimmed with ribbons, flowers or ostrich feathers, completed the picture.

Taking leave of Lady Hervey and her daughter Eliza, on 20 June Bess, Jack, her maid 'Miss A.' and her servant Louis sailed to Ischia. 'The Place seems pretty,' Bess wrote to Georgiana, just after her brother had left to go back to Naples. 'I could like it, had I health or even tolerable spirits. If you was here, oh how we would ramble about . . . Think of me my Love set down alone in this little Island, my heart full of sorrow & head of anxiety, but ever inexpressibly attached to you . . .' In her situation, all this misery is understandable; but since neither Georgiana nor the Herveys knew she was pregnant, what reason had Bess given them either for her depressed state of mind or for her urgent need to seek solitude in Ischia?

A thousand miles away, Georgiana's problems were multiplying. In Lady Spencer's opinion she was living a 'wild scrambling life', gambling obsessively and ever more deeply in debt. She had also become briefly entangled with Charles James Fox, but felt able to tell Bess in June: 'I think I have got out of all my *messes*. The Eyebrow [their code name for Fox] is going & I have left off my playing & extravagance – in short I hope Canis will tell you your Rat is not *very naughty*. As for Canis he is the best of Dogs . . . Oh Bess you must come very soon & make your Dog and Rat happy.' The letter is continued by the Duke, who hoped Bess was in better spirits than when she last wrote. He ends on a surprisingly tentative note: 'I hope you are not out of humour with, or forgetfull of C , who loves you as much if not more than ever.'

Bess was now within a month of her expected confinement, which she had intended should take place on Ischia. But early in July she heard that people from Naples were to visit the island. 'I am not safe here. I must expose myself to new fatigues and dangers . . . For I must go near 100 miles at sea and in an open boat.' For such a journey she needed her brother's help and, confessing the true nature of her predicament to Louis, she sent him with a letter to Jack at Naples. He hastened back to Ischia, and 'We were a long time without speaking,

63

clasped in each other's arms ... I could not – dared not name the dear Author of my child's existence.' It was arranged that he would return in a week and conduct her to a place where she could give birth in secrecy. While she waited for Jack's return, she again sought solace in her journal. 'A year today that I was restored to my beloved friends. Oh, I felt that the D.D. had ever influenced my conduct. 'Tis true I thought myself attached, I *was* attached to Count Fersen: yet nothing could efface the impression the other had made. My return proved it too well. Could I have foreseen the ills that awaited me, I believe I should have avoided those dear friends, tho' so tenderly lov'd ...'

On 22 July Bess left the island, accompanied by her brother and Louis, and at this point the journal ceases. On 4 September it was resumed with a restrospective account of the intervening weeks, written in French. 'We set sail ... I am on the open sea, expecting the final moment of pregnancy. We touched at the Island of Procida to deceive the crew.' But the wind rose and they were forced to alter their plans. Bess would go on alone with Louis. 'I had to part from this dear brother of mine not knowing whether I should ever see him again. I had to pass myself off as the wife of Louis and, in a condition which needed so much care, I had to submit to a thousand discomforts ... I gave my beloved medallion to my brother and parted from him with despair in my heart.'

This medallion was almost certainly the jewelled oval miniature of Georgiana which Bess is wearing in her portrait by Angelica Kauffmann. Kauffmann painted the head during her stay in Naples in 1784, completing the picture – with its hazy view of Ischia in the background – when Bess returned to Rome in 1786.

The boat put in at Salerno, from where Bess and Louis drove west to the little town of Vietri. As Louis conducted her through stinking, dimly-lit alleyways to the house of the 'Archi-Prêtre des Amoureux', she must have thought herself descending into hell. That her brother should have known of such a place casts an interesting light on his connections; that he should have seen fit to consign his frail, highly-strung sister to what was, in essence, little more than a brothel seems reprehensible, but may indicate his awareness of the lengths to which she was prepared to go to preserve her anonymity.

Weak, and encumbered by the weight of her child, Bess mounted a squalid stair to the Archi-Prêtre's apartment to find herself surrounded by his family. The 'seraglio', as she called it, included such grotesques as the 'wicked, vulgar and horrible' wife, a 'coarse, ugly and filthy' servant, two weeping daughters, and an unspecified number of babies who cried from morning till night. Also present was the doctor, 'an honest man', and the nurse who would take charge of the baby. Guessing at once that Bess was not Louis' wife, they later assumed her instead to be Jack's mistress – a perfectly reasonable conclusion since brother and sister made a striking couple. For Bess, caught as she was between these cross-currents of deception, the indignities of her position intensified: to maintain the pretence, she was obliged to share a room (perhaps even a bed) with Louis. 'My faithful servant wept for me and wept that he was compelled to forget that he was my servant in the familiar terms upon which we had to live.'

Bess's misery lasted not for the few days she had expected but for fifteen, only briefly alleviated by a visit from her brother. Together they concocted letters to Naples 'full of imaginary incidents', which included a story that they had been shipwrecked. When Jack left, Bess was alone except for the faithful Louis. 'I waited patiently for death, regretting only my child, and its father, and my friend.'

To describe herself as waiting 'patiently for death' was no hyperbole. With none of today's methods of easing childbirth, prolonged and unspeakable labour was not uncommon in the eighteenth century, and death a distinct possibility. Denied the support of family or friends, ogled by 'the seraglio', her days and nights filled with the sounds and smells of the back streets of Vietri, Bess had no choice but to consign herself to her fate. It must have required Christian stoicism and great courage.

On 16 August, 'after strong but short pains', she gave birth to a daughter. 'The moment I took her in my arms I felt only a mother's tenderness. With tears in my eyes I commended her to God. I kissed her – I examined her features – weak as I was, I took her into the bed and tended her myself, seeing the ignorance of those about me.' Though desperate to keep her baby, fear of her mother's distress and an awareness of her own disgrace gave Bess the strength to part with her. History was repeating itself: she had been forced to give up her second son when he was only eighteen months old; the little girl born in Dublin in 1778 had died within days of her birth; now she must surrender her second daughter. The baby would be encased in swaddling clothes and suckled at the breast of a stranger.

Within three weeks, in what Amanda Foreman describes as a 'vast bed decked with enormous paper flowers and silver ribbons, and crowned at the top by a gold canopy, embellished by ducal ornaments inside and out', Georgiana was showing off her second daughter, named Harriet Elizabeth after her sister and her friend.

Dispensing with the traditional lying-in period of four weeks, Bess left Vietri for her brother's house in Naples within six days of giving birth, heartbroken at leaving her child. In two weeks, Louis was to collect the little girl from Vietri and bring her to Naples, where she would be cared for by foster-parents of his acquaintance. Bess's return to civilization reawakened her dread of discovery, but Lady Hervey's warm reception put her mind at rest. 'I felt ashamed', she wrote, 'of playing my role so well . . . Each day my valet . . . brought flannels for my breasts, everything I need to hide my condition.' Considering Bess's feeble health and the unhygienic conditions of the birth, it is a miracle that she escaped the numerous perils – such as puerperal fever, haemorrhage, thrombosis and milk-fever – associated with the post-natal period.

To her surprise, Bess found that the shipwreck story she and Jack had concocted was believed by everyone. To spread it further afield, she wrote to Lord Sheffield describing with Rousseauesque fervour how she had been 'born away by a storm' and 'passed a month amidst mountains and forests, on the borders of the sea, or on rocky cliffs', but had now returned to Naples, where '*Vesuvius threatens hard*, the lava is burst out & runs down the side with violence . . .'

The Duke of Devonshire, unaware of Bess's precipitate departure from Ischia, was no doubt still addressing his letters to the island, which would explain why Bess received none until her return to Naples. On 12 July he had written that it was 'impossible to express to you how impatient I am to hear how Ischia agrees with you' – obviously a code agreed between them before her departure. On 4 August he wrote again: 'I have not had a letter from you this great while, Mrs Bess . . .' In her isolation Bess seems to have been tormented by insecurity and suspicion, as he also hastened to assure her that she was much mistaken about his flirtations, 'for I have had none at all, and don't desire to have any.' On 11 August – he was alone at Chatsworth, and Bess within five days of giving birth – he wrote her a full-blown love letter.

> I am terribly in want of you here, Mrs Bess, and am every minute reminded of the misfortune of your not being here by things that I see, such as the couch you us'd to sit on in the drawing room, amidst all your sighing lovers. The blue bed you slept in, and little Mr Phaon [her pony] who is at grass in

the park. I have some thoughts – if I have time – of going to Bolton [Abbey, one of his properties] to shoot upon the moors, and to prepare the place for you against next summer, for I intend to take you there whether you like it or not, let the consequences be what it [*sic*] will; so don't talk any more nonsense about not returning to England . . .

Aware that the baby was due in early August, by the 29th he was becoming increasingly anxious: 'I am very much surpriz'd and impatient at not having heard from you . . .' He went on to respond to a concern evidently raised by Bess in an earlier letter – that things had been said about her in England of a 'contrary nature'. While admitting there had been reports 'concerning yourself and me', he advised her to have 'philosophy enough not to be disturbed with it'. A letter of 23 September shows that the Duke was by then fully aware of her recent ordeal, and also how well he understood her. 'You have sometimes reproach'd me, Mrs Bess, with being too much at my ease about your situation, but now you are so well again I'll confess to you that my ease was entirely counterfeited, for it was impossible for anybody to be more uneasy than I was about you for many months, but knowing that you are apt to think every thing worse than it really is, I thought it best not to assist you in magnifying your disagreeable circumstances . . .'

On 6 September the little girl was installed with foster-parents in Naples, but Bess was horrified to hear from Louis how badly she had been neglected. Four days later she 'went by stealth' to visit the baby, whom she had named Caroline Rosalie Adelaide, Caro for short. 'My darling daughter grows more beautiful every day. Sometimes I go to see her as her protectress . . . sometimes I arrange for her to be taken for solitary walks where I myself go on horseback, and where I dismount and gather her into my arms . . . How I suffer, how I am punished by not being able to have her near me.' Distressed afresh by signs of neglect, she ordered finer linen for the child's 'dainty limbs', and arranged that henceforth she should be cared for by Louis' parents. Bess makes no mention in her journal of what she intended for Caro's long-term future. She apparently never considered adoption.

Unaware of her recent ordeal, Neapolitan society received Bess back with open arms. Punctuated by frequent references to her 'beloved child', her journal also records her success at Court and the attention shown her by the Queen of Naples, Marie-Antoinette's sister. 'A succession of Balls, Operas, Dinners, Concerts with a crowd of flatterers, Lovers, and admirers,' she writes, then adds: 'Vanity always gratified, and the heart never interested.' Various sighing lovers make brief appearances: the Russian ambassador is followed by the Duke of Cumberland, brother of George III: 'The D. of C——d seems to be in love with me – one cannot be suspected of encouraging him' (his wife certainly thought she had). Then there was a charming Captain B., and a brace of little Neapolitans. 'Do any please me? – No.'

It is tempting to assume that Bess exaggerated both the number of her lovers and the intensity of their sighs, but such temptation must be set against a retrospective view of her effect on men given years later in the memoirs of Charles Greville: 'Lady Elizabeth, without great talents or great beauty, seems to have been one of those women (of whom there are rare instances) who are gifted with an undefinable attraction – or perhaps attractiveness is the word – which none can resist. Everybody was in love with her, and She exercised an influence of one sort or another up to the end of her life.'

At the house of her father's old friend Sir William Hamilton, Bess encountered Georgiana's brother George and his wife Lavinia. George lost no time reporting to his mother that the 'very extraordinary being' – as he called Bess – 'seems very well but has always the same languid appearance that she has in England. She is not very well liked by the Italians on account of her want of facility in speaking their language, and her wearing perfume which is here an unpardonable offence . . . a great many things I have heard, many of which are certainly not true but some must be, I don't know what to make of her.' Bess told Georgiana that George's conduct towards her had been impeccable, but not so Lavinia's: 'Lady S. seem'd to raise herself three feet in order to look down with contempt on me.'

Her success in Naples was not everything. As Bess told Georgiana on 2 December, 'It is a year today that I left you – even you can scarcely conceive how much unhappiness to me is comprised in that reflection . . . I think every thing grows worse & worse, my Brother is more low than ever [he had become infatuated with the beautiful, but married, Princess Roccafionta] . . . & of course Lady H[ervey] is expressing her unhappiness from morning till night . . . My dear Love, I am quite oppressed by all these things, & dread of Pansey.'

Bess's 'dread of Pansey' was no mere affectation: the Earl-Bishop was on his way to Rome. Not only was Bess terrified he would learn about the baby, but he was accompanied by her sister Mary and her youngest brother Frederick, thus bringing the whole unhappy family situation to her door. In an attempt to heal the breach between himself and Jack, the Earl-Bishop – using Frederick as mediator – had invited his eldest son to meet him in Rome for Holy Week. Bess, also invited, was anxious they should both accept. As she told Georgiana, she saw the family reunion as a 'trial of Pansey's feelings towards us all'.

As Bess again gave up keeping her journal in April 1786 there is no contemporary record of this meeting, but when she resumed her entries two years later she described it retrospectively. It had not been a success: her father's 'strange conduct which made him censured' had distressed her, her attempts to make peace between him and Jack had failed, and she had been 'vexed' by Mary's 'jealousies'. An independent view of Lord Bristol appears in a letter from Horace Mann, the British envoy at Florence, to his friend Horace Walpole: 'He moves from place to place to avoid his eldest son whom he leaves in absolute distress [financially], at a time when he himself squanders vast sums in what he calls the Beaux Arts, though he only purchases the dregs of them.' 'Nothing you tell me of the Episcopal Count surprises me,' Walpole replied, 'he is horrible!'

After six weeks in Rome, the family party dispersed. Lady Hervey and Mary left for Switzerland, while Jack hurried back to his princess in Naples. Bess set out for Venice accompanied by Anne Seymour Damer, a friend of Georgiana and well known in society. Mrs Damer's marriage had ended abruptly when her husband, having gambled away his fortune, shot himself in a public house in Covent Garden. Mrs Damer had survived this disaster with great courage, and was now a celebrated sculptress. 'I cannot tell you how much I am struck with her,' Bess wrote to Georgiana from Ferrara in June, 'her soul seems to be on a greater scale than other people's, her feelings finer, unimpaired by the world . . .' Mrs Damer later modelled a bust of Bess, which has since been lost.

On her way to Venice Bess stopped at Cento, near Ferrara, to see her father and brother Frederick. Lord Bristol was recovering from an illness, but despite Bess's pleadings refused to see her. She told Georgiana that he was in bed, 'saying he is dying, seeing no body but Frederick, yet very likely issuing forth some of his terrible letters to my Mother . . . I never was so distrest.'

Though enraptured by Venice, Bess was distraught to find no letters from either the Duke or Georgiana waiting for her, a disappointment which precipitated a passionate outburst:

My Angel dear love I cannot live away from you . . . our hearts are formed
for each other, & we lose the most precious time of our lives being away &
separate – each day you are dearer to me – time, mutual confidence, our
different sufferings, & equal sentiments, my obligations to you, & adoration
of you . . . all, all in short heightens our sentiments for each other . . . All,
all my hopes of possible comfort, pleasure or happiness are concentrated
in you – without you the world is nothing to me. If you should forsake me
I would not bear to live – or living would never never think of any other
creature.

This is the letter of a woman close to breaking-point. She had
undergone an upsetting and humiliating experience at Vietri; she had
been forced to abandon her child; her relations with her father and
sister were abysmal; and her brother's reckless behaviour threatened to
break up his marriage and disgrace the family – as she herself had so
narrowly avoided doing. Now, simply being at the mercy of the erratic
postal services was almost more than she could bear. Her letter, though
hectic and confused, states her case exactly: without Georgiana, she
was lost. What is so remarkable is that the relationship worked both
ways: without Bess, Georgiana was also lost. Though it may have varied
in intensity over the years, this extraordinary interdependence held
firm until Georgiana's death. On the Duke, however, Bess could not –
dared not – rely to the same extent.

The Duke *had* been writing to Bess, but a number of his letters had
miscarried. In a letter of 16 May 1786 he promises to write more often
in future, counsels her not to 'despond about every thing', and again
assures her of his attachment. His last sentence confirms that
Georgiana remained in ignorance of Bess's baby. 'The Rat does not
know the chief cause of your uneasiness, and I, of course, shall never
mention it to her, unless you desire me, but I am certain that if she
did, she would not think you had been to blame about it, particularly
after I had explain'd to her how the thing happen'd.' It would be fascinating to know in what way the Duke proposed to explain to his wife
how it was he came to make love to her best friend. It is also interesting that he was apparently not only prepared to do so, but confident
of her reaction.

From Venice Bess travelled to Spa, where she expected to meet
the Devonshires; but Georgiana, persuaded against the trip by her
mother, had instead taken her children to the seaside at Southampton.
She wrote to Bess at Spa, begging her to hurry back as '*je ne vie pas sans
toi*'. She then described meeting Axel Fersen, who had visited London

on his way to Sweden after nine months at Paris. 'He has delightful eyes, the finest countenance that can be, and the most gentlemanlike air . . . Canis has peep'd at him and he peep'd thro' the *jalousie* to see Canis riding, but they have not met yet. I am sure he still thinks about the Scimia [another code name for Bess] as he us'd, but thinks it better for both to stifle it . . .' Fersen had been taken to Devonshire House by the Duke of Dorset, on leave from Paris.

Dorset corresponded regularly with Georgiana during his years in Paris, and his letters provide a fascinating insight into the byzantine intrigues of the French Court. He and Georgiana frequently exchanged news about Bess, Dorset referring to her fondly as 'the dear little Scimia' – hardly the language of a jilted lover. 'The Queen enquired about her the other day. I believe she would not wish her to come, till the *Roman* [code name for Fersen] is gone . . .', which appears to imply that Marie Antoinette knew of Fersen's involvement with Bess two years earlier.

To be at Spa without the Devonshires seemed pointless, and Bess hurried home. 'My friend [Georgiana] was at Southampton. I fear I was glad. I arrive – he [the Duke] had dined out but left a note. He came. Oh, Heavens, such moments do indeed efface past sorrows! Yet it was happiness mixed with fear and agitation. My friend came next day – new joy and delight for I loved her "passing the love of women".' This biblical quote appears to have had a profound significance for Bess, since she repeats it no fewer than three times in her journal. It is from the Second Book of Samuel, which contains David's beautiful lament for the death of his friend Jonathan: 'I am distressed for thee, my brother Jonathan: very pleasant hast thou been to me: thy love to me was wonderful, passing the love of women.'

5

Devonshire House
1786–1788

'I will cease to live in error with him, tho' with shame and
blushes I confess it, one moment passed in his arms, one
instant pressed to his heart, effaces every sorrow, every
fear, every thought but him.'

Bess in her journal, 26 April 1788

———————————◆———————————

IT IS A curious fact that in the four years Bess had known the
Devonshires, she had passed barely nine months in their company;
the rest of the time she had been abroad. When she returned in July
1786, it was to spend eighteen months in England. Not that she settled
comfortably in one place; instead, she was constantly on the move. In
the north she travelled between the Duke's various properties –
Chatsworth, Hardwick Hall, Bolton Abbey; in the south it was to the
spas of Bath, Tunbridge Wells and Cheltenham, or to Ickworth to visit
her mother. And these were journeys which often took up to two days,
the coach lurching for hour upon hour along rutted and pot-holed
unmetalled highways. In the intervals between such peregrinations,
she came to rest at Devonshire House in London.

Bess's first journey was to see her mother and sister Louisa, who were
taking the waters at Tunbridge Wells. In early 1785 Louisa had suffered
from a nervous collapse, brought on by the frustrations of her dull and
isolated existence alone at Ickworth with her mother. Now, eighteen
months later, Bess found her sister 'grown very handsome', and her

mother 'kind'. (These comments may seem perfunctory, but come from the short summary of the events of the past two years with which she opened her journal when she began to keep it again in February 1788.) From Tunbridge Wells she joined the Devonshires in London. Despite her long absence, it appears that she slipped easily into her old intimacy with Georgiana and the Duke, and that Georgiana's plan for Bess to occupy her own little house nearby had been forgotten. Thus Bess found herself living in luxury at the very heart of fashionable London. Friends, theatres, the elegant shops in Covent Garden, the print-sellers and galleries in the Strand – all lay within easy reach by sedan chair, the chairmen picking their way round the puddles and the mounds of horse dung. The Houses of Parliament were half an hour by chair from Devonshire House; Brooks's, the Duke's club, was a five-minute stroll along Piccadilly to St James's Street.

Seen from Piccadilly Devonshire House looked like a barracks, the high walls that surrounded it creating a defensive barrier against the clamorous and noisome city beyond. Designed by William Kent to replace a late-seventeenth-century house destroyed by fire in 1733, inside it was magnificent. On the first floor, reached by a double outer staircase, a suite of splendid reception rooms led off a cavernous hall, their walls hung with one of England's finest collections of pictures by the Italian masters. To the south the rooms looked over the great walls on to Green Park, and to the north on to a peaceful, shaded garden which extended the length of Stratton Street.

A number of new personalities now make their appearance in Bess's life, members of what had come to be known as the Devonshire House Circle, a social and political élite composed of some of the most brilliant figures of the day. Many, like James Hare, 'Fish' Craufurd, Lord John Townshend and Charles James Fox, were old friends of the Duke, but it was Georgiana's warmth and charm, and the heady atmosphere she created, that drew them to the great mansion on Piccadilly. As they grew to recognize that Bess's presence at Devonshire House was essential to Georgiana and desirable to the Duke, they began to accept her. With some she even forged friendships which were almost – but never quite – independent of Georgiana. The benefits of living in the shadow of a woman so beloved as the Duchess were incalculable, but there must have been times when Bess wondered whether she existed in her own right.

The most outstanding member of the Circle, both in charm and in intellect, was Charles James Fox. Portraits depict him as raffish, blue-chinned and corpulent, with heavy black eyebrows like out-stretched wings – a gift to caricaturists like Gillray. An engaging and precocious child (he was a regular theatre-goer from the age of five), he was famously indulged by his father, Lord Holland, who declared: 'Let nothing be done to break his spirit. The world will do that business fast enough.' But the world, despite its endeavours, failed to break such an original, and Fox remained a man governed by his appetites and his generosity of spirit. Blessed with the stamina of an ox, he could gamble for eighteen hours, then rise to his feet in the House of Commons and deliver a speech of rhetorical brilliance. Yet for all his learning, his gift of oratory and his passion for liberty, Fox retained a child-like quality that was infinitely endearing to his friends. 'Perhaps no human being', Gibbon wrote in 1788, 'was ever more perfectly exempt from the taint of malevolence, vanity, or falsehood . . .'

The friendship between Fox and the Duke, begun at Eton, was continued at Brooks's, where they spent the greater part of their waking hours gambling with their fellow Whigs. They shared, too, a profound love and knowledge of the Classics and of Shakespeare. Georgiana's ardent admiration for Fox, meanwhile, had matured into close political alliance and intimate friendship.

If Fox was the Circle's greatest leader, James Hare was regarded as its most brilliant wit. Snatches of his quaint humour illuminate Georgiana's letters to her mother. 'I can remember no jokes except Hare's saying if he betted to kill a hare he not only would fire at it sitting, but have it tied first . . .' Years later he was described by Bess's son as 'the tallest, thinnest man I ever saw, his face like a surprised cockatoo, and as white', a description borne out by the portrait after Reynolds in which he seems on the point of delivering one of his famous quips. His letters to Bess and Georgiana are whimsical, intensely personal and instantly recognizable. He wrote what he thought, without equivocation or artifice. His perceptiveness and honesty, but above all his profound humanity, took him unfailingly to the heart of any matter. While frequently exasperated by Georgiana's apparent desire to destroy herself and bankrupt the Duke – to whom he owed his seat in Parliament – his affection for her never wavered. His friendship once given was unquestioning, his discretion and loyalty limitless. Perhaps alone of all the men in the inner circle at Devonshire House, he extended genuine friendship to Bess.

When Bess became an intimate of Devonshire House, the dramatist Richard Brinsley Sheridan was already, by virtue of talent rather than birth, an established member of the Circle. His plays *The Rivals* and *The School for Scandal* (the latter based on life at Devonshire House) had made him famous. He was devious, dissolute, and persistently unfaithful to his beautiful wife, but he possessed enormous charm and a brilliant mind. His legendary eloquence never left him, even after drink had taken a permanent hold. In her memoirs, the notorious courtesan Harriette Wilson claims that Sheridan was rebuked by his physician for drinking a lethal combination of 'brandy, Arquebusade, and Eau de Cologne', on the grounds that it would 'burn off the coat of his stomach'; 'then', Sheridan blithely replied, 'my stomach must digest in its waistcoat; for I cannot help it.'

While not strictly a member of the Circle, the Prince of Wales was another frequent visitor at Devonshire House. To a young man brought up with Teutonic severity, the attraction of free spirits like Fox and Sheridan was irresistible. Georgiana described him as 'inclined to be too fat and looks too much like a woman in men's cloaths', but he possessed undoubted grace and charm of manner. Capricious, petulant and given to histrionics, he was none the less capable of strong attachments, such as he felt for Fox and Georgiana, and later for Bess. The possessor, poor man, of an unfashionably florid complexion, he was obliged to whiten it by the regular application of leeches, followed by a liberal dusting of face powder.

'Lady Melbourne and I became acquainted,' Bess wrote in her journal. 'I like her much.' This dispassionate comment marks the beginning of a friendship which was to play an important part in Bess's life. One of the leading Whig hostesses, Lady Melbourne was a clever, ambitious woman who perfectly understood the rules of society. She married Sir Peniston Lamb, a shy, dull man but exceedingly rich, supplied him with a legitimate son and heir, and then produced four more children all of whom – except possibly the last – were bastards. The second son, William (the future prime minister), once described his mother as 'a remarkable woman, a devoted mother, an excellent wife – but not chaste, not chaste.' If her husband objected to her infidelities, he gave no sign of it, although it was said the ribbon of black velvet she wore around her throat (featured in some of her portraits) was to hide the marks he made trying to strangle her. One of her sons, George, whose likeness to the Prince of Wales apparently left little doubt as to his paternity, later became Bess's son-in-law. Lady Melbourne presided over these unruly Lambs at Melbourne House (now the apartments known as Albany), a handsome mansion richly decorated with Classical statues and Venetian art which lay to the east of Devonshire House along Piccadilly.

If Bess once cherished ambitions of moving in more brilliant society than was offered by Dublin, they were realized beyond her wildest expectations. In England at that time there *was* no society more brilliant than that to be found within the walls of Devonshire House. As the separated wife of an obscure Irish MP Bess, though an earl's daughter, was privileged to join it. But there was a price to pay. 'The private (for *secret* it never was) history of Devonshire House would be curious and amusing as a scandalous chronicle – an exhibition of vice in its most refined and attractive form, full of grace, dignity, and splendour, but I fancy full of misery and sorrow also.' This view, given years later by Charles Greville in his memoirs, followed a conversation between himself and Georgiana's son, Hart. Greville had given Hart four boxes of letters to read, letters written by Georgiana to her mother (they are now at Chatsworth), and had talked to him of 'Devonshire House in the old time, and the strange connexion of the Duke, the Duchess and Lady Elizabeth Foster . . . the latter at the same time the Mistress of the Duke and the bosom friend of the Duchess, and the wife passionately attached to the mistress and dreading nothing so much as the loss of her society.' This summing-up of the complex situation undoubtedly reflects the view generally held by Bess's contemporaries.

The emotional dynamics of this *ménage à trois* can only be guessed at. The Duke, it would seem, had the easier time of it. Rising late, he spent what remained of the day and half the night at his club. On his return, he was able to enjoy the attentions of two women – utterly dissimilar in looks and demeanour – in bed and out of it. Just how different they were is neatly captured by Richard Cosway's delightful drawing of them dancing with the Duke: Georgiana, bountiful in body and mind and heedless of her appearance, abandons herself to the dance; Bess, slim and delicate, her head coyly tilted, remains watchful and self-aware. What is so surprising is Cosway's rendering of the Duke. Can the skipping grinning figure, pigtail swinging, be the aloof, lethargic figure depicted in print? 'His Grace is an amiable and respectable character,' once observed the *Morning Herald and Daily Advertiser*, 'but *dancing* is not his forte.' (Cosway shows the Duke as small of stature, whereas Wraxall describes him as tall and manly.)

For Bess the strain of living a double life is evident from several entries in her retrospective journal. 'I am capricious, jealous and quarrelsome with the Duke,' she wrote in February 1788. 'Made me wretched, but he forgave me.' And again: 'I go for a week to Tunbridge – return and am foolish and capricious because they dined out, but suffered severely by the D. taking it very ill of me.' When roused from his lethargy the Duke was not to be trifled with, and perfectly capable of keeping Bess in her place. She in turn regarded him with the deepest respect, and accepted without question that behind the impassive façade lay not a void but a man whose actions were governed by integrity, kindness, and a powerful sense of duty.

Bess was often called upon to play a somewhat tortuous role inside the three-cornered relationship. 'Depository of both their thoughts, I have sought, when her imprudences have alienated him, to restore him to her . . .' Having mediated successfully between husband and wife, she then had to suffer the consequences: 'And when my full heart has mourned over her avowal of his returning caresses, I have checked and corrected the sensation.' It could be argued that Bess had only herself to blame for her situation; that her long absence abroad should have been taken as a perfect opportunity to cut the ties that bound her to the Devonshires – or at least to distance herself from Devonshire House, something that would only have been achieved if she had begun the process while she was abroad. But the ardent letters from both Georgiana and the Duke that pursued her round Europe, and to which she responded in kind, had made that course impossible. Besides, there was now a new tie: the little girl hidden away in Naples, whose existence remained unknown to everyone except herself, the Duke, her brother Jack, and one other.

When the Devonshires went north for the summer, Bess remained in London: Lady Spencer was staying at Chatsworth, and Georgiana did her best to keep the two apart, for a while at least. Bess was to follow later. A letter from the Devonshires to Bess in August 1786, written from Hardwick, illustrates their easy intimacy. Georgiana begins the letter: 'Your Ca[nis] is as drunk as a piper & as imprudent as you ever saw him. He however misses the Marchioness [a nickname for Bess] tho' he is half seas over.' The letter has then been appropriated by the Duke. What follows provides a glimpse into an aspect of his character hitherto unseen, except possibly in the drawing by Cosway.

Dearest Bess, I have interrupted the Rat's letter because I find she is going to be deuced saucy. It is true that C. misses the Marchioness, but not that he is half seas over, only a little tired with shooting, and heavy from having had too little sleep and too much ale. We are much pleased with the idea of seeing the Racoon at this place in the Autumn, and can venture to assure her that it will be worth her while to come, as she is a lover and a judge of the arts. There are some very capital paintings here, but I have only time at present to give you an account of one of them, which is a portrait of Lilly the Lill [Bess's dog, a pointer] by C—s [Canis]. It is indeed a *chef d'œuvre*, and in the very best manner of that Master, the expression striking, the colour rich and glowing, and the *tout ensemble* full of spirit, and costume! The Rat wants to have her letter back again but she must not, so I am going to seal it up. Good night Mrs Racky. C.

Soon after Bess arrived at Chatsworth, Georgiana was plunged into a fresh crisis over her gambling debts. 'There passed the sad scene of telling the Duke she had again lost an immense sum,' Bess recorded. 'How nobly, kindly, touchingly did he behave, but what a time of misery! The house, too, full of company. She kept her rooms sometimes.' The 'company' included Lady Spencer, James Hare, General Richard Fitzpatrick ('Mr Fitzpatrick inclined to make love to me'), Sheridan and his wife ('Mr S. accuses me of being in love with the Duke'), the Duke of Dorset, Harriet, and her husband Lord Duncannon. With Lady Spencer resentful of Bess's presence, Bess trying to remain loyal to husband and wife simultaneously, the Duke still convalescent after a serious attack of the gout, Sheridan's dark hints, and the Duke of Dorset flirting now with her, it is little wonder that Georgiana periodically went to ground in her rooms.

On this occasion, Georgiana's debt was too large to be simply paid and forgotten; the Duke demanded a separation. Georgiana must live in one of his other houses, or with her mother. Lord Spencer proposed that Georgiana should live with him and his wife at Althorp, but much as Georgiana loved her brother, she knew she could not live for long in the same house as Lavinia. As Heaton, the Cavendish agent, wrestled with the problem of paying her debts, the battle raged as to what should be done with Georgiana.

Since Bess's journal at this point is merely a brief retrospective summary of these months and none of her own letters survive from this period, frustratingly little is known of her reaction to the crisis. That it was 'a time of misery' is undoubtedly true, for if the Duke insisted on an official separation from Georgiana, where could *she* go? Though society might accept Bess's continued presence at Devonshire House while she was there as Georgiana's friend, it would not countenance her living there alone with the Duke. She could not possibly accompany Georgiana to her mother or brother, nor could she afford to set up house on her own. She would have to retreat to her own mother, at Ickworth. For a few weeks during that summer it must have seemed to Bess that her brilliant world was about to come crashing down around her.

Georgiana, however, still held the trump card: only she could produce a legitimate heir. And to do so, she must live with the Duke as his wife. This fact, and no doubt the prospect of suddenly finding himself without any women at all, seems to have gradually cooled the Duke's ire. In early November, while Bess was with the Devonshires at Hardwick, Georgiana was able to tell her mother that when the Duke allowed himself to forget the cause of the crisis, 'he is, at times, very comfortable, and now that he is alone with us amuses himself by conversation and reading with us with a great degree of cheerfulness'. Bess's journal confirms this: 'We passed 7 weeks at Hardwick in happiness, tranquillity and comfort. Every day my tenderness for him increased, so I think did his confidence and affection for me. Oh, he is everything that is amiable and noble. We wish for Caroline – but we know not what to do.'

Built by the formidable Bess of Hardwick in the late seventeenth century, Hardwick Hall in Derbyshire was an ideal refuge from the world. A visit in 1789 inspired John Byng to call it 'a great old castle of romance . . .' The house clearly had a beneficial effect on the Devonshires; according to Georgiana's son Hart, his father used to dine 'as he supped at Brooks's, with his hat on, which his friends gave as the reason for his being so fond of Hardwick', while his mother spent there 'the happy part of a harassed life'. But the world invaded their seclusion: rumours that the Devonshires were 'parted' reached them through Lady Spencer, whose letters to Georgiana at this time were full of love and encouragement, even if her belief that reading novels had weakened her daughter's mind was hardly constructive. More useful were Heaton's proposals: a small reduction in staff and horses to meet the debt, and the Duchess to be kept away from London at all costs. 'The Duke wishes it to be a *permanent reform*,' she told her mother, 'not a violent and painful one for a year, or two, but one that may go on.' James Hare was less sanguine about her ability to reform. In a somewhat peevish letter written to Bess at Ickworth in early January 1787, he declared: 'She must co-operate – and you must keep watch and guard; if you are, as I am persuaded you are, her real friend. I do not mean it as a compliment when I say that the whole depends upon you, but in order that I may have lied [*sic*] in my chair for abusing you if you make feeble or unintellectual efforts – the devil take you all; I almost wish I had never seen any of your faces.' James Hare was an impartial observer, and his endorsement of Bess's sincerity is a most convincing rebuttal of the belief that her friendship with Georgiana was largely self-serving.

This letter is typical of Hare's style, the abrasive tone masking his deep concern for Georgiana. In another, undated, letter from this period he begs Bess to assure Georgiana 'that no person living can take a greater interest in all that concerns her than I do', and that her interests will be best served if 'left entirely to his [the Duke's] kindness and generosity'.

'Came to town towards the end of February 1788,' Bess wrote in her journal, 'but oh what misery follows – she contracts another debt – the Duke again forgives her.' It may have been this debt which prompted a pathetic letter from Georgiana to Bess, written some time during 1787 and discovered slipped between the leaves of a little blue notebook containing her poems. 'My dearest dr Bess,' it begins, 'This is the last time perhaps you will ever speak to or love me – I really am unworthy of you and Canis . . .' She then admits that when confessing her latest debt to the Duke, she withheld information about another debt (in fact, she withheld information about many more) in the hope that she could regain some of her losses by 'reserving £500' which she 'had agreed to insure' in the Lottery. 'Oh God Bess, I have gone on and lost an immense sum . . . It is madness and I ought not to live on with Canis – but what am I to do? You must not tell him this – and you shall advise me when I return what I am to do – whether to tell him or not – it could be settled without and so that it should never come to him – you know he *could* not forgive me. My Bess, I am desperate . . . You see that doating on Ca how I have used him . . . Oh Bess!'

Bess's own finances are a mystery: by rights, she should have been receiving the agreed annual allowances from her father and husband, but the Duke must have supplemented her income to enable her to dress in the height of fashion and pay for Caro's upkeep in Naples. There is no evidence that she lost money at the gaming tables, or that she even gambled, which she once condemned to Lord Sheffield as a 'pernicious amusement'. In March 1787, Georgiana placed the administration of her finances in the hands of the banker Thomas Coutts.

While she believed herself thereby saved from ruin, Coutts presumed that his association with a duchess would raise him in the world; the poor man was to pay highly for his social ambition.

In 1787 Bess was painted by Sir Joshua Reynolds, the greatest portraitist of his day. The Duke paid the bill – fifty guineas for a head and shoulders. Reynolds's eyesight was failing, but the result was simple, direct, and incredibly alive. Exhibited a year later at the Royal Academy, it was seen by Lady Bristol, who pronounced it the 'best in the room, but it is evidently fading'. (This is not surprising: Reynolds persisted in certain techniques, notably the use of bitumen, despite knowing they would shorten the life of his pictures.) In the delicate features and wistful, vulnerable expression, Reynolds has captured that fatal allure.

It seems odd that Bess should have left no record of sitting for this portrait, for it is easy to imagine her quizzing the great Sir Joshua about his techniques, and enjoying an exchange of views on Italian art. His house in Leicester Fields contained an elegant room for his sitters, and a gallery where prospective clients, artist's models (such as the notorious courtesan Kitty Fisher, one of his favourites) or the merely curious might mingle freely while inspecting his work.

During the early months of 1787 Bess divided her time between Ickworth and London. Her presence at Devonshire House had the effect of excluding Lady Spencer, who felt that if she stayed there while 'the obstacle' (Bess) was in residence, she would appear to sanction what she scathingly referred to as 'that incomprehensibe connexion'. The skilful diplomacy which served Bess well in her other relationships completely deserted her when it came to Lady Spencer, and her frequent attempts to woo the dowager were clumsy and ill-chosen. Seldom did seed fall on stonier ground.

The London season began in late October with the opening of Parliament and ended in June with the summer recess. At its height, life was a continuous round of balls, routs, masquerades and gambling parties, and the Great Court at Devonshire House thronged with arriving and departing carriages. As women of fashion, Georgiana and Bess had to keep up appearances. Rising late, they breakfasted on hot chocolate, coffee or tea while their hair was dressed, by a professional coiffeur or their personal maids – a much simplified process by the late 1780s, when the lofty edifices popularized by Georgiana in the early years of her marriage had given way to frothy curls. The result was more natural, as can be seen in Reynolds's portrait of Bess, but still hair required artful frizzing and powdering; it was not washed for weeks, sometimes months. In her portrait Bess appears to be wearing lipstick, and she certainly applied a little rouge, but there is no evidence that she daubed her face with the white powder which, as it contained lead, was ruinous to the complexion. The beautiful Gunning sisters not only lost their looks through powdering; one became ill from lead poisoning, and the other died of it before she was thirty.

The Devonshire House ladies spent mornings and early afternoons paying or receiving calls, or walking in Kensington Gardens with Georgiana's children. Though there were some who passed contented hours at their needlework, it is hard to imagine either Bess or Georgiana thus occupied. There were also tradesmen to be received: booksellers with the newest novels; mercers with French or Italian silks; lacemen; shoemakers; milliners with the latest fashion dolls from France (called 'Jointed Babies' by *The Spectator*) from which the design for a new gown might be chosen. An outfit ordered in the morning could be worn the same evening. Alternatively, the ladies might take a chair to the Strand or Covent Garden, and there browse through the shops themselves. With their large families and vast acquaintance, they devoted at least an hour a day to writing letters, a practice delightfully satirized by James Hare, who described them writing 'long letters on all subjects, and to every sort of correspondent; standing, walking, and even running, and without the least interruption of conversation . . .'

Dinner, the main meal of the day, began any time between three and six o'clock – the more fashionable you were, the later you dined. A vast array of meat or fish dishes was succeeded by confections such as syllabubs, sorbets, trifles and meringues, the various courses accompanied by white wine and port, followed by claret, burgundy and cherry brandy. In the evening, the tempo quickened; although Georgiana once insisted to her mother that she had gone out 'sparingly', over four days she had attended 'Cumberland House on Thursday, on Friday the rehearsal at Ly Aylesbury of Mrs Damer's play . . . and then to Mrs St John, Saturday the Opera, Sunday I had Morteloni here for Ly Bristol . . . and afterwards to D'Adhémar's [the French ambassador].' The hectic comings and goings of the fashionable *ton* filled the cobbled streets of London's West End with the sound of hooves and iron-wheeled carriages, the thunderous din likened by one bemused French visitor to the sound of Niagara Falls 'heard at two miles' distance!' London society finally crept into bed shortly before dawn. 'We sleep with the Sun, and wake with the Moon,' complained Evelina, the heroine of Fanny Burney's first novel.

The appearance and location of Bess's apartments at Devonshire House are unknown, but a description of some of the contents has survived. It is written as if by Bess herself, but almost certainly comes from the satirical pen of James Hare, and includes:

> Johnson's Poets, Tasso, Ariosto, Danté, Petrarch and other bound books on tables and chairs all over the room . . .
> 42 locks of hair of my most intimate friends in the drawer of the Ink Stand; the Poker, Tongs and Shovel upon the Pianoforte . . .
> Miniatures of the Polignac family . . .
> Attorneys' Letters made into allumettes on the chimney-piece . . .
> Shawls, handkerchiefs, a Bottle containing Magnesia . . . in the wicker basket . . .
> My Night things in the brass coal-scuttle.

Even Hare would not have presumed to include the portable water-closet and mahogany 'biddett and pan' which are listed in a later inventory of Bess's Devonshire House apartments.

When in need of peace and tranquillity, the Devonshires went to Chiswick House, their route taking them through the turnpikes along the Bath Road and past mile upon mile of the market gardens which stretched from Kensington to Twickenham. The house, a masterpiece of Palladian architecture built by the third Earl of Burlington between about 1727 and 1729, had once been condemned by Bess's grandfather, Lord Hervey, as 'too small to live in, and too big to hang to a watch'. But in 1788 the Duke demolished the old Jacobean house Burlington had left standing and added flanking wings to his villa, thereby creating a house large enough for his growing family. The grounds were an enchanting mixture of wilderness with formal avenues of lofty yew and lime; there were four magnificent cedars (which are still standing), a cascade which never worked properly, temples, antique statues, and an ornamental lake. It was a rural paradise within an hour's drive of Piccadilly.

Except on Public Days, life at Chatsworth moved at a slower, gentler pace than it did at Devonshire House. None of the ladies appeared until early afternoon, when they fluttered about the great house like brightly-plumaged parakeets, settling briefly to coo and murmur to each other before flying off to perch elsewhere. They even had their own language, known as the Devonshire House drawl: 'Dearest one, how do oo do?' 'As oo do, so does poor little I . . .' Lavinia Spencer, however, claimed that they never actually spoke, as 'their method of conveying their ideas is by their eyes & the motion of the muscles of their face'. According to a description – this time certainly by James Hare – their choice of attire was nothing if not perverse: '. . . when the Ladies first come down to a small Room with a large fire they are wrapped up with furs and waddings of various sorts', but when they ventured out for a walk, they donned 'a lighter drapery . . . such as gauze or muslin shawls [and] thin silk sandals'. On inclement days, they took a turn in the gallery instead.

The Duke of Richmond now made the first of many appearances in Bess's life: 'I am fortunate enough to have my Brother nam'd Minister to Florence,' she wrote in her retrospective journal, 'but unfortunate enough to have the Duke of Richmond fall in love with me. It is impossible I should like him, but gratitude for the service he has done my Brother, joined to esteem for his good qualities, make me treat him with friendship.' Two weeks later she added: 'My friend [the Duke] jealous of the Duke of Richmond – indeed, without cause.' At fifty-three, Charles, third Duke of Richmond was twenty-three years older than Bess, had been married for thirty years and had allegedly enjoyed numerous liaisons. Bess's gratitude was genuine: by helping to secure for Jack the Florence post (in succession to Walpole's friend Sir Horace Mann) Richmond had simultaneously found employment for her improvident brother and removed him from the passionate embrace of the beautiful Princess Roccafionta. Georgiana told her mother that Bess was 'wild with joy' over Jack's appointment, adding that the 'Duke & Dss of Richmond are very kind to Bess'. Georgiana's inclusion of the Duchess makes Richmond sound harmless, but according to Lady Augusta Murray he was so in love with Bess 'that they say he has made a ridiculous figure of himself, and it is due to his infatuation that Lord Hervey owes his new employment'.

Jack's elevation did not however heal the breach with his father. The Earl-Bishop, now bored with Downhill, had begun to build a new 'villa', called Ballyscullion, in an impossibly remote and mountainous region overlooking Lough Beg in County Derry.

In August 1787, Bess was with the Devonshires at Bolton Abbey for the grouse shooting. 'We are all happy and contented – but oh I fear it was a fatal journey to me.' As this entry appears in Bess's retrospective journal, it can mean only one thing: she knew by the dates that it was at Bolton she had conceived the Duke's second child.

Did she recall the letter the Duke had written her exactly two years earlier, when she was in Italy about to give birth to Caro, in which he told her he was going to Bolton to shoot and would prepare the place for her '. . . for I intend to take you there whether you like it or not, let the consequences be what it [*sic*] will . . .'

To avoid clashing with a proposed descent by Lady Spencer on Chatsworth, Bess visited her mother. 'I soon had cause to apprehend my misfortune. I grew very ill. We came to town – still ill – was forced to reveal to the Physician my fears.' At about this time, she received a tenderly solicitous letter from the Duke: 'Your room here is very warm, and I believe you will be much safer from catching cold here than in London, especially as I hear you go to plays. Take care you do not catch cold by going with the coach-glasses down.'

As soon as Lady Spencer's visit was over, Bess returned to Chatsworth. 'Found only a few people there. Mr S[heridan] still observing to the Duchess how attach'd I seem'd to the Duke . . . The Duke hardly knew the ill I had hinted to him, and asked me if it really was so. I confirm'd it. We regret this new anxiety, but as yet I felt a kind of pleasure that supported me. Yet would it had not been . . . How kind he was to me – how soothing and endearing his manner.'

Chatsworth was followed by two months spent at Bath in the hope that the waters might alleviate the Duke's gout, which was growing increasingly troublesome. During their stay, Bess suffered what was almost certainly – though she does not say so – a return of her bronchial trouble. 'Their kindness redoubled to me,' she recorded, 'but I dreaded my friend and being exposed to her remarks.' This reference to 'remarks' may indicate that Georgiana, aware of some extra ingredient in the supposed sibling relationship between the Duke and Bess, found herself unable to suppress an occasional display of jealousy. The journal continues: 'It was decided, as if for my health, I was to go abroad.' Georgiana was so concerned for Bess that she wanted to accompany her 'part of her road' with the Duke, and spend a month with her in France. But it was now early February, and Bess was due to come to term in late May: had Georgiana accompanied her, and the proposed stay of a month been prolonged – this was a time when a trip abroad could be a very open-ended affair – there was a danger that Bess's pregnancy would become apparent. As there is no clear evidence that at this juncture Georgiana knew of the *first* baby's existence, Bess would have been especially anxious that she remain in ignorance of this second pregnancy.

In the event, the Devonshires did not accompany Bess: the Duke was required to attend the trial of Warren Hastings, and Lady Spencer, exercising as usual a sort of divine right over her daughter, forbade Georgiana to go on her own; perhaps she feared a renewal of her flirtation with the Duke of Dorset. Georgiana was reduced to a muted protest: 'I don't know how I shall be able to bear my parting with Bess.' In early February 1788, the Devonshires escorted her to Dover. At Lyons, Bess continued her retrospective journal:

> We staid two days [at Dover]. We walked on the beach. We seem'd actuated by the same sentiments. Oh, my God, what I suffer'd when the sad morning came . . . I thought I could not bear the agonies of parting from him. When she embraced me, it was bitterness of grief to lose her – but him – his last embrace – his last look drew my soul after him. I remain'd motionless – even now, it is present to me. I see him – he is fixed in my heart. This guilty heart – oh, why could I not love him without crime? Why cannot I be his without sin? My soul was made for virtue and not for vice . . . *I have told nobody yet* [author's emphasis]. Shame ties my tongue . . . I live retir'd, for I fear all eyes – my little dog [Lilli] all my comfort.

The Duke of Dorset, writing to Georgiana from Paris, was full of sympathy. 'I feel for you very much, dearest Duchess, at parting with poor Bess. In reading your letter I sincerely wished myself at Dover. I hope she got safe over, I think the *monkey* ought to have written me word of her arrival at Calais, but I forgive her for her mind must have been too much taken up with you to have thought of any body else.' In fact, Bess had no intention of going anywhere near Dorset.

From this point Bess's journal ceases to be a restrospective summary and becomes contemporaneous with the events described, very similar in tone to the one she kept during the months preceding the birth of Caro; the biblical idiom is resumed; she resigns herself to God and implores his forgiveness; she blames herself repeatedly for her errors; she even resolves to have 'no further connection' with the Duke of Devonshire on her return.

At Lyons at the end of February 1788 Bess took her maid Lucille into her confidence. 'Why, why, have I put myself in such situations, why reduce myself to esteem my own servant more than myself?' At Marseilles she writes, 'The letters I have from England, tho' not immediately from *him*, yet hers assure me so much of his affection that I feel supported beyond my expectations.' One of Georgiana's letters contains a curious sentence which could be taken to imply an awareness and acceptance that she came second to the Duke in Bess's affections: 'Dear Bess, I know you are safe and therefore am not hurt; always write to him if you have not time for both.'

After five weeks at Marseilles Bess travelled south to Toulon, where she found her former servant Louis awaiting her. It was arranged that he would go at once to Naples to collect Caro from his parents and return with her to France, where she was to be installed with the family of a 'Monsieur B.' at Sorèze, a small town north of Carcassonne. 'He [Monsieur B.] only knows her as a Protestant child my friends and I wish to educate, and who is to be removed in September to Paris.' Bess possibly told the same story to a certain Comte St Jules, whom she had managed to persuade (it would be fascinating to know how) to give Caro his surname. He lived near Aix-en-Provence, so it was perhaps during her travels between Toulon and Carcassonne that Bess made, or renewed, his acquaintance.

On 26 April, after a separation of nearly three years, Bess at last saw her daughter. 'She is gentle, lovely, and like her dear, too dear father. It was by stealth I saw her – such are the consequences of errors . . . Oh, how dear she is to my heart – how I gazed on her dear little innocent face and pressed her in my arms. She looked at me with an enquiring eye and did not shew any fear . . . Sweet Innocent – may the plan I have formed prove to thy advantage, as it promises.'

Bess gives no details of 'the plan', but there are various possibilities. It may be that Georgiana already knew Caro was the Duke's child with Bess, and had agreed that she should be brought up with her two half-sisters at Devonshire House. If she did not already know, Bess may have felt confident that if she were told, she would act with her usual humanity, a conjecture borne out by Bess's comment that 'My darling friend will be kind to her. Oh, I know the generous goodness of her heart . . . and if I am to be taken from her, she will be a Mother to my innocent Child.' A further possiblity, and perhaps the most likely, is that Bess had fed Monsieur B., the Comte St Jules *and* Georgiana the same story – that she had taken Caro under her protection – and Georgiana, believing it, had agreed that she and the Duke should contribute to the child's education. That Caro herself believed she was an orphan is revealed by a prayer – it is undated – found in a notebook of Georgiana's at Chatsworth: 'I, an orphan in a foreign country, without thy goodness might long ago have fallen a victim to my fate, but thy ever watchful mercy has given me parents, ah yes let me call them by so dear a name, for they have been to me the tenderest best of parents.'

Bess's joy at seeing her daughter supported her for two days. 'I felt nothing, neither fatigue, nor apprehension, nor even the sorrow of having left her, so glad was I to have seen and removed her – dear, dear little Angel.' From Sorèze she travelled west and north for four days to Bordeaux, an arduous journey for a frail woman only a month from giving birth. She arrived 'so tired and full of pain, I begin to fear I never can reach London'. Demoralized and ill, she poured out her feelings in her journal:

> Oh, may I see my beloved friends again, for they are dearer still to me than all else in the world! – She is the kindest, dearest, best most beloved of friends – and he is and must be ever the very soul of my existence. I will cease to live in error with him, tho' with shame and blushes I confess it, one moment passed in his arms, one instant pressed to his heart, effaces every sorrow, every fear, every thought but him – but this must not be, shall not be – no, I'll live for him, but as his friend; still will I share, if he will let me, his every thought, his cares, and his anxieties, or his happiness, still will he find my heart adopt and make its own whatever can interest him, still will his pursuits be mine, whatever he dislikes, will be pleasing or otherwise to me, for not only are my natural inclinations like his, but the instant his are known they become mine without a thought to make them so. May he never doubt, therefore, the strength of my affection, because I may alter the tie which unites us, for him and him alone I love, can love, or ever have truly and fondly loved.

At Rouen on 25 May she wrote: 'This is the day on which I expected to be confined, yet I do not think I shall, and my anxiety and apprehensions of discovery increase with the length of time that I pass thus in secret.' The Duke, well aware of the horrors to which Bess had been exposed during the birth of Caro, had sent a 'Dr G.' to meet her, and with him a letter for Bess which restored her courage: 'Such is his influence over my mind, a kind expression makes me forget everything but him.' Dr G. found her a French doctor and an apartment which, though in 'a close confined street on one part and a stinking court at the other', was a great improvement on the brothel with its leering occupants at Vietri.

As she waited for the birth, with only her maid and little dog for company, Bess worried that the Duke might suspect Richmond to be the father. 'For should I pass the 28th, what will the D. think, when that is the last day I was with him . . . Yet I could as much set about clearing myself of murder, as of clearing myself of an infidelity to him, to

whom my faith and love is pure and unspotted as the love of angels.'
But her fears proved groundless; on 26 May 'at 3 in the morning I was
taken ill and brought to bed of a son at six – a dear, dear little boy
whom I pray to God to preserve and bless with his father's virtues and
merits . . . I suckle my darling child who is loveliness itself. Erring as I
have been, yet my heart can feel nothing but tenderness and joy at the
sight of this dear child.' She adds, significantly, 'I only wish that my dear
friend had a son also.' She named the baby Augustus William James
Clifford: Augustus was a standard Hervey name and William the
Duke's Christian name, while the Duke's mother had been Baroness
Clifford in her own right. He was always known as Clifford.

The Duke of Dorset, who was still expecting Bess to turn up in
Paris, wrote with unconscious prescience to Georgiana on 19 June: 'I
have heard nothing of that abominable *Scimia*, she is playing her
monkey tricks somewhere, *perdue dans quelque coin* . . .' Though she
dreaded separation from her son, Bess made arrangements for him to
be placed in the care of foster-parents in Rouen. At the end of June
she was back in England.

6

Alarms and excursions
July 1788 – August 1790

'Your poor little boy is quite well, he is an amazing child
. . . If he does not recover his own friends very soon I
shall begin to think he belongs to me . . .'

James Hare to Bess, 18 December 1789

———————◆———————

CLIFFORD'S BIRTH ADDED yet another dimension to Bess's secret
life. To have borne one illegitimate child without detection was
itself an achievement, but to have produced two was altogether more
remarkable. It seems incredible that someone so slightly-built should
have been able to conceal her pregnancies from those around her,
especially from her mother and Georgiana. Her last visit to Ickworth
had been made when she was six months pregnant; surely a perceptive woman like Lady Bristol would have noticed, if not the bulge,
then something ungainly in her daughter's movements, a reluctance to
stoop to retrieve a fallen book, a slight puffiness in the face? (Yet her
sister-in-law Lady Hervey had remained ignorant of her pregnancy
despite living with her until a month before she gave birth to Caro.)
And did no one wonder why someone going abroad for her health
should delay her departure until February, when winter was almost
over? There is, however, a world of difference between suspicion and
certainty.

Furthermore, if Lady Bristol had allowed herself even to suspect a
pregnancy, she would have had to face the fact that her daughter

was involved in an illicit and scandalous liaison. To judge from her cheerful correspondence with Georgiana, and her occasional visits to Devonshire House, however, she was either genuinely ignorant of her daughter's conduct, or deliberately so. If the latter, she found support in the attitude of Georgiana and the Duke: since they treated Bess's presence under their roof as entirely normal, society was obliged to follow suit. It was a nice example of the emperor's new clothes.

As for Bess's father, though he was eminently a man of the world there is no evidence that he suspected the true nature of Bess's position at Devonshire House. His estrangement from all his family except Mary persisted: in a letter to her of March 1787 he had complained of Bess asking for fifty pounds to pay for two pictures by a Mr Day, and of Louisa selling a gown he had given her because she thought the shape unfashionable. 'But I am inured to it all,' he added bitterly. 'I strike against my heart and it hurts my hand, all but a corner of it which will not petrify. In the meantime I am stoick enough to find adopted children . . . and can smile with ineffable contempt at the injuries and revilements I incur.' By 'adopted children' he meant Henry Hervey Bruce, his kinsman in Ireland, the brother of Mrs Mussenden, and his wife Letitia. Bruce had been too poor to marry until Lord Bristol provided him with four hundred pounds a year – a hundred more than he had settled on either Mary or Bess. He acted as the Earl-Bishop's agent while he was abroad, and Lord Bristol in his will of 1791 left all his Irish property, which included both Downhill and Ballyscullion, to Bruce.

On her return to England after the birth of Clifford, Bess resumed her life at Devonshire House. Whether she succeeded in keeping her vow to 'cease to live in error' with the Duke it is impossible to tell, but the ties of profound affection and mutual need which united the three were as strong as ever, if apparently less intense. When the Devonshires went north in August, Bess was content to remain at Devonshire House. That she now clearly regarded it as home and held court there to numerous gentlemen callers is evident from her chatty letters to Georgiana: 'Here has been Lord Frederick [the Duke's uncle] & I as thick as possible – hand in glove – in vulgarer terms hail fellow well met – in more refined language the inseparable inimitables . . . Lord Macartney came in for a smile – Craufurd had a squeeze of the hand at coming away, but Dutan – poor hideous Dutan [Louis Dutens, the historian] – no nothing could make me leer, smile or attend to him. Well, dear Rat, you think I am still a wild little thing . . .' Yet even such a confident letter ends on a plaintive note: 'Let nothing surprise you that I say do or write – I am not myself, & have but one fixed constant and consolatory sentiment, the inexpressible love I bear to you & Canis.'

Society might have become reconciled to Bess living with the Devonshires, but Lady Spencer remained implacable. To Georgiana she complained of scenes she had witnessed at Chatsworth which had 'deeply affected' her, but said she would continue to 'behave civilly to Ly E. F. whenever I meet her . . .' She also said she would 'listen candidly to him,' should the Duke wish to discuss his sentiments on the subject – an offer it can be assumed the Duke actively failed to take up.

Though Bess was oblivious of the danger at the time, an addition made to the Devonshire household this year was to prove a persistent thorn in her side; it comes as no surprise that this thorn was lodged by Lady Spencer. Little G. now required a governess, and Lady Spencer suggested Georgiana should employ Miss Selina Trimmer, daughter of Mrs Sarah Trimmer, a celebrated children's author and educationist. She clearly hoped a young woman of such impeccable moral and religious principles as Miss Trimmer would bring order into the somewhat irregular lives of her granddaughters. It took Georgiana a long time to realize that Miss Trimmer kept Lady Spencer minutely informed of what went on at Devonshire House, particularly with regard to 'Lady E. F.' But in the autumn of 1788 Georgiana was preoccupied: she was again deeply in debt, borrowing money from Coutts and also from France's recently dismissed Finance Minister Charles de Calonne, who had become a friend of the Devonshires. Even Georgiana's debts, however, were eclipsed by the crisis precipitated by the illness of George III.

The King's health had been giving concern since the summer; by October he was seriously ill, both in body and mind. The Queen was driven frantic by his 'great hurry of spirits and incessant loquacity' (he once talked for nineteen hours with barely a pause) and terrified by his eyes, which she said reminded her of blackcurrant jelly. But he was still sufficiently sane to fear that he was going mad. The doctors were baffled. (Understandably; only recently has it been suggested that he was suffering from a rare hereditary disorder of the blood known as porphyria.) On 5 November the King suddenly attacked the Prince of Wales during dinner, hurling him against the wall; the Queen had hysterics and the Prince burst into tears. The King was hurriedly moved from Windsor to the summer palace at Kew, which was comfortless and freezing. The doctors dosed him with laudanum, quinine and digitalis and administered emetics and purgatives; he was bled, cupped and blistered until he prayed for death. Yet he grew progressively worse.

The unfortunate King's descent into apparent madness posed a dilemma for Pitt's government: was the madness permanent and if so, should a Regent be appointed? As heir-apparent, the Prince of Wales naturally assumed himself to be the obvious, indeed only, candidate. Charles James Fox and his associates agreed, and expected that the Prince, as Regent, would ask Fox to form a new government. Out of office since 1783, the Whigs were avid for power. Casting decency and caution aside, they began to jostle for Cabinet places.

The Devonshires and Bess were in Derbyshire celebrating the Glorious Revolution of 1688 when Georgiana received a letter informing her of the King's illness, and of the Prince's wish that Fox should be sent for. Fox's absence – he was in Italy with his mistress Mrs Armistead – at such a critical moment had long-term repercussions for his supporters, plunged into the crisis without their leader. Fox returned on 24 November, exhausted by the speed of his journey and suffering from dysentery, to find the Whigs in utter disarray. Sheridan and Grey were at loggerheads; the Duke of Portland (nominal leader of the party) was ineffectual; the Prince, still only twenty-six, was over-excited, politically naïve, and plotting with Sheridan.

Bess had been abroad during the 1784 Westminster election, so this was her first experience of Devonshire House as the centre of a political drama. While Georgiana took an active role as intermediary and strategist, Bess responded like a true journalist, recording every rumour and counter-rumour, who had fallen out with whom, and who was to be minister of what when the Prince became Regent. The entries in her journal are often in note form, written in haste in the early hours of the morning when peace had at last descended on Devonshire House; none the less, they demonstrate an astute grasp of the convolutions of the crisis and her remarkable ability to memorize facts and assemble them into a coherent narrative.

The first entry of the crisis records that the Duke, although he had been offered *carte blanche*, had declined a place in the new government. Two days later the Prince tried to persuade him to accept the Privy Seal, as 'his name was necessary to give weight to their measures, not only as being one of the first names in England, but as that of the most respectable Man in the Kingdom'. Expressing a similar view in

1783, the Prince had then added with youthful perception that the Duke would be the ideal man to govern the country provided 'his indolence did not get the better of him'.

Bess's gift for recalling conversations seemingly verbatim came into its own during the Regency Crisis.

The Prince [she wrote on 2 December] ask'd Mr Grey if C. Fox had spoke to him – & said, you must have something indeed, & mentioned to him the place as one of the Lords of the Treasury. Grey who aspired much higher [the Chancellorship, no less] thank'd the Prince & said he wish'd for nothing. 'Oh yes,' replied the Prince, 'you must indeed, don't be so diffident, you are a young man and full of talents, and should be encouraged . . .' Grey kept bowing, ready to sink all the time, and refusing all places that could be offered him. 'Sheridan,' said the Prince, 'Grey should not be so diffident.' 'Sir,' replied Sheridan, 'it may be diffidence, or it may be ambition.' 'Oh,' said the Prince, 'perhaps he don't think this good enough. Come to me Grey, and we will talk it over.' Grey bowed and said that he was at his Royal Highness's command. This scene Sheridan told with infinite humour.

Though Pitt had come to accept the necessity of the Prince's Regency – with certain restrictions attached – his insistence that it could be established only by Act of Parliament enabled him to play for time, hoping for the King's recovery. Impatient at the delay, on 10 December Fox made a disastrous speech in the House of Commons. He had been a devout advocate for limiting the power of the monarchy; his declaration now of the Prince's hereditary *right* to the Regency was a complete reversal of his Whig principles. Bess reported that 'Pitt got up & said that what C. F. had then said was treason to the constitution . . . that he [the Prince] had no real *right*, no more than any other subject.'

Throughout December the ferment increased. James Hare, writing to Bess from France, complained that he had not once heard from her since the drama began. 'Devonshire House, of course, must have been the centre of negotiation and cabal. You must have known all that has been plotting, as you have had all the principal conspirators about you, and probably most of them at your feet.' His surmise was correct: Devonshire House was in a constant bustle as the Whig leaders arrived with parliamentary news and rumours from Brooks's, or to discuss tactics. Sheridan and Grey often came for supper before going on to the Commons. While debates were in progress, Bess and

Georgiana were kept informed of their course in notes sent by messenger. Bess copied these into her journal, piecing together detailed accounts of the proceedings. If there had been a vote, Sheridan or Grey would call in on his way home with the result. 'After an evening of the utmost anxiety', Bess noted on 16 December, 'we went to bed tir'd and dejected at quarter past four in the morning.'

Had women been admitted to the Strangers' Gallery of the House of Commons, Bess and Georgiana would have been among the most regular visitors. Rebuilt by Wren after the Great Fire, the House was small and cramped, and according to one critic 'could just as well serve as a village chapel or house an assembly of grocers'. A German visitor in 1782 had been astonished by the casual behaviour of MPs: 'The members have nothing particular in their dress; they even come into the House in their great coats and with boots and spurs. It is not at all uncommon to see a member lying stretched out on one of the benches, while others are debating. Some crack nuts, others eat oranges . . .'

Since early December the King had been in the hands of Dr Francis Willis, whose draconian methods included imprisoning his patient in a strait-jacket or a restraining chair; at night he was tied to his bed. The wretched monarch had become an emaciated, shambling wreck, while the Queen was so thin 'her stays would wrap twice over'. Neither the Prince of Wales nor his younger brother, the Duke of York, behaved tactfully during the crisis, the Prince leaving few in any doubt that he wanted to be Regent, even though it would confirm his father's loss of sanity. 'The Prince came to D.H.,' Bess noted on 16 December, 'said he must crush Pitt, or Pitt him.'

With the same diligence with which she had described works of art on her Grand Tour, Bess charted events during the critical months of December and January, her entries seasoned with such comments as 'Sheridan out of spirits', 'Grey very angry with Sheridan' (or with Fox, or Fitzpatrick, or Pitt). A revealing remark of Sheridan's was that the Prince was 'chicken-hearted'. Hare's absence throughout the crisis deprived the party of his gentle satire, which might have diffused some of the quarrels. Opinion was canvassed from the other Whig centres – Carlton House, Melbourne House, Burlington House (the Duke of Portland's residence) and, that fount of all rumour and intrigue, Brooks's. From the Duke of Richmond, once a Whig but now in Pitt's Cabinet, they gleaned intelligence of the enemy camp. On 14 December Bess noted that he was 'in great spirits and said they [the Government] had caught them [the Opposition] on the hook & would keep them to it.' Richmond was right.

Despite losing every debate, the Foxites were still fighting over places well into February 1789, when it was clear the King was on the mend. On 24 February he was declared completely cured. Prayers of thanksgiving were said in churches throughout the land, and the nation rejoiced that the King was himself again. George III had never been more popular, the Whigs never less. Bruised and disunited, they retired from the contest.

On 23 April Bess and Georgiana attended the thanksgiving service in St Paul's, taking their places in the peeresses' seats in the choir. 'About 12 the signal was given, the Tower guns fir'd, the Soldiers in the church were drawn up, the band struck up, & as the King enter'd the organ play'd & the 6000 children sung the 100th Psalm. The effect was finer & more touching to the feelings than any thing I ever experienc'd . . . During the Thanksgiving prayer, the King seem'd extremely affected, tears roll'd down his cheeks which he tried to hide, but which being oblig'd to wipe, were easily perceiv'd.'

For the Whigs, the aftermath of the crisis was unpleasant and prolonged. Their sense of failure was exacerbated by the general mood of celebration. When the Duke announced that he was taking Georgiana and Bess across to Spa, they greeted the prospect of escaping London with relief. It was hoped the Spa waters would improve the Duke's gout and increase Georgiana's fertility. Her need for a son was now acute: under the terms of the Cavendish estate settlement, the birth of an heir would enable the Duke to raise a mortgage to pay off her astronomical debts. The Cavendish children were to remain with Lady Spencer and the already indispensable Miss Trimmer. Charlotte, now fifteen, would accompany the party to Paris, where she was to lodge with a family named Nagel to improve her French. It was obviously no coincidence, for when Caro St Jules had been moved from Sorèze to Paris the previous September, she was installed with the same family.

Matters having been so arranged that the Duke might visit both his illegitimate daughters under one roof, the question of what Georgiana did or did not know about Caro again arises. Proof that she at least knew of the existence of a child of this name occurs, incongruously, in a letter from her to Lady Spencer written in July, after the party had left Paris on their way to Spa: 'We have established Charlotte with Mr and Mme Nagel . . . Luckily there is only one other pensioner, Mlle de

St Jules, a young Ly from the provinces, and as she is very young [Caro was now four] Mme Nagel will attend entirely to little Charlotte.' Georgiana had therefore met Caro in Paris – but did she know any more about her than she told her mother? Either she knew everything, or she believed – or chose to believe – Bess's story that Caro was a child whom she had taken under her protection during her travels in France between 1785 (the year of her birth) and 1786. Four months later, there is a fresh surprise. Writing again to her mother, Georgiana returns to the subject of Caro: 'I wish I could send you over the little St Jules, she is [a] sweet child . . . Some time or other I will shew you a letter of Mme de Polignac's about her, who protects her; which will interest you much for her, but she is too young to send over at present . . .' The most likely explanation for Madame de Polignac's involvement is that Bess had asked her to act as Caro's 'protectress' while the child was in France and Bess in England – further evidence that where her daughter was concerned, Bess could be immensely resourceful. She would stop at nothing to keep her child.

In this she found an ally in James Hare, who had been in Paris for several months. The convolutions of Hare's family are impenetrable: Georgiana noted that he 'entirely supports 9 children of his sisters & 5 of his B's [?brother's] besides some children of his own', some of whom were almost certainly illegitimate – a considerable financial burden for a relatively poor man. One daughter, Sophie, seems either to have had a French mother, or to have been brought up, like Caro, in France.

It is not clear at what stage Hare became intimately involved in Bess's life, nor is there any evidence either way to show whether he believed, or chose to believe, Bess's story that Caro was a motherless child whom she had taken under her protection. The impression remains that he was perfectly aware of her imprudences, as she was of his, and that their love for their illegitimate children was one of the bonds which united them. 'The constant anxiety I feel for my own children', he told her, 'would of itself sufficiently dispose me to assist almost anybody when children are concerned, but I hope you will believe that I do not put my offer of serving you on so general a ground.'

Not only did Hare know of Caro's existence: he had known of it for some time. When travelling in France in late 1788, he had asked Bess to advise him on the best route from Toulouse to Montpellier ('I have found you so excellent a guide that I would not be willing to trust any other'), and had gone out of his way to visit Caro at Sorèze during his journey. 'I was very much struck with her,' he had reported. He had continued to visit 'the little Huguenot', as he called her, when she was moved to Paris, declaring her to be 'excessively improved'. Later his interest in Caro took a more concrete form, when he actively encouraged Georgiana to accept her into Devonshire House.

For the Duke to have chosen to travel to Spa by way of Paris in June 1789 seems, in retrospect, an act of folly. As early as the previous June the Duke of Dorset had warned Georgiana that the situation in France was very unstable. His offical despatches trace the perilous state of the nation's finances, the disastrous harvest of 1788, the growing condemnation of royal absolutism, and the increasingly frequent outbreaks of violence in both Paris and the provinces. On the other hand, even an objective observer like Dorset could not have known that in the summer of 1789 France was on the verge of one of the most fundamental upheavals Western Europe had ever experienced. 'Never was any such event so inevitable,' declared Alexis de Tocqueville, the nineteenth-century French historian, 'yet so completely unforeseen.'

Typically, the Earl-Bishop had his own colourful view of the state of the French nation. '*This* Frippery Country is still the same,' he grumbled to Mary in March from Montpellier, 'a skipping dancing tribe – they are fit only for themselves – and when the circling glass goes round they talk of Beauties which they never saw, & Fancy raptures which they never felt. All now is commotion, & all soon will be sing-song, in the meantime the hot heads let one another's blood, the Clergy rise against the Bishops, & the laity against the Nobles . . .'

At Versailles in the weeks preceding the Devonshires' departure for France, Louis XVI had convened the old Estates General, which had last met in 1614, consisting of the clergy (First Estate), nobility (Second Estate) and commons (Third Estate). On the grounds that it represented 96 per cent of the population, the Third Estate declared itself a National Assembly, and on 20 June took an oath not to disperse until a new constitution had been established. The King was forced to call a *séance royale* of all the Estates.

The Devonshires and Bess left London in mid June. They had barely crossed the Channel before they received reports that Paris and Versailles were in turmoil. They were undeterred: Londoners were accustomed to spasmodic civil unrest. Bread riots were frequent, if brief, and even the Gordon Riots of 1780, Britain's longest and deadliest urban disquiet, had only lasted a week. But within hours of their arrival in Paris on 23 June Bess had recorded that 'civil war was every hour expected', and that at the *séance royale* the King had told the Estates 'he disapproved of their measures, annull'd them and dissolv'd the meeting'. He had no sooner left the hall than the Third Estate defiantly declared the *séance* null and void.

Bess entered into this new political crisis: in exhaustive detail she chronicled events, consuming page after page of her journal with gossip, rumour and fact (she was conscientious about rumours, always correcting any that later proved false). She had seldom set forth her own views in recording the Regency crisis, but the horror and indignation provoked in her by events in France are expressed with clarity and force. An aristocrat herself, her attention was naturally focused on the French nobility, especially on the royal family and the Queen's intimate friend, Madame de Polignac.

On 25 June Bess and Georgiana made the two hour journey along the broad, tree-lined road to the Palace of Versailles, where the Court was in mourning for the Dauphin, who had died on the 4th. They found their hosts, the Polignacs, 'the same kind and affectionate friends', but 'dejected and agitated' by the news that most of the clergy and forty-seven of the nobles, led by the King's cousin the Duc d'Orléans, had gone over to the Third Estate (d'Orléans had openly espoused revolutionary policies from the outset). The Estates General were in session, and the Polignacs' apartments were thronged with an anxious crowd discussing the proceedings.

Bess and Georgiana returned to Versailles two days later, this time with the Duke. At the Polignacs' they were told that the King, threatened by a mob invasion of the palace, had written to the remaining clergy and nobility asking them to join the Third Estate. The Polignacs and their guests waited in the 'greatest anxiety' for the answer. When news came of their capitulation, 'scarcely a person in the room could refrain from tears. It was a confusion of sentiment, a mixture of Joy & grief, of regret & content that quite overpower'd them . . .' Dinner was 'silent & thoughtfull, such as I had never seen before at Versailles'. The aristocrat in Bess rebelled against this triumph of the Third Estate, 'who seem'd insatiable in their desires who having nothing to lose there was everything to fear from. In short, it was the first nobility in the world yielding to & joining themselves to a sett of people without family & without an inch of landed property . . .' The mob later surged into the gardens and demanded to see the Dauphin, and Madame de Polignac, as Governess to the Royal Children, held up at the window the boy who had become Louis XVI's heir on the death of his brother. The mob then entered the court of the palace. The King and Queen appeared on the balcony and, according to Bess, the Queen 'burst into tears'. The King, aware that he was losing control of events, ordered troops to occupy strategic positions around Paris and on the road to Versailles.

At the King's Mass on 29 June, Bess and Georgiana spoke at some length with the King and his two brothers, Monsieur and the Comte d'Artois. After dinner they were 'received very graciously' by the Queen. 'She took me by the hand', Bess wrote, 'and said how low her spirits were & how terrible the times. I told her if she had courage I hop'd all would go well. She shook her head & I don't believe she took my meaning which was that she ought not to abandon Madame de Polignac – & this I fear she will do . . . The Queen shew'd us the Dauphin . . . [who] . . . is a Beautiful Boy. The D. of Dorset told the Queen she ought to have another son. "And why?" she replied, "so that the Duc d'Orléans can have him killed?"'

Despite occasional outbreaks of violence, the Duke and his ladies enjoyed their weeks in Paris. Georgiana wrote delightedly of being 'overwhelm'd with stay makers', and told her sister Harriet that 'the hair is drest narrow, high – long curls on the chinion – light crape caps'. They attended the theatre and the opera, strolled in the Champs Élysées, made an expedition to the Bois de Boulogne, and twice visited the Palais-Royal. As the Duc d'Orléans's private residence, the Palais-Royal enjoyed immunity from the police; already a centre of vice and gambling, it was rapidly becoming the focus of the revolution, and many of the acts of mob violence recorded by Bess occurred within its confines. 'We heard that they had tied an Abbé to a tree at the Palais-Royal & then beat him. They next forc'd him to kiss the ground & the shoes of the Man with whom he had disputed . . .'

Pursued by rumours that Versailles was already ablaze and that 'in two days Paris would be no more', on 12 July the ducal cavalcade set out for Spa. 'As we drove thro' the streets great crowds were running towards the Palais-Royal,' Bess wrote. At Senlis they were told 'the Tocsin had rung, the Bell always rung at Paris in time of great distress'. On reaching the frontier town of Valenciennes they were met by Count Fersen, whose regiment was stationed nearby. It was a strange encounter for Bess; she had not seen him since their romantic episode in Italy in 1784, and he had recently returned from Versailles where he had gone to comfort the Queen for the loss of her eldest son. (Apart from a brief encounter in Paris in 1790, Bess never met Fersen again, but they continued to correspond until a month before his death in 1810.) From Fersen they learnt that Jacques Necker, France's popular Finance Minister, had been dismissed by the King; that on 11 July he and his wife had fled France, crossing into the Austrian Netherlands at dead of night without baggage and still in Court dress. The Neckers were only the first of many who were to gallop through the frontier towns under cover of darkness during the weeks to come, many of them leaving France for ever (some 300,000 emigrated between 1789 and 1795).

At Brussels the Duke and his party found Germaine de Staël, Necker's daughter, newly arrived from France to join her parents. It was Bess's first encounter with this remarkable woman, but their lives were already strangely linked. In his youth, Gibbon had fallen in love with Germaine's mother, Suzanne Curchod, but his father had forbidden him to marry her. Germaine herself had briefly contemplated marriage with Axel Fersen but had chosen instead one of his close friends, Baron de Staël-Holstein, Sweden's ambassador to France. In 1784 Gibbon had described her as 'one of the greatest heiresses in Europe . . . wild, vain but good natured and with a much larger provision of wit than beauty'. Still only twenty-three, she had recently published *Lettres sur Rousseau*, which earned her Bess's immediate admiration.

It was not until the Devonshires and Bess arrived at Spa on 18 July that they heard of the fall of the Bastille. 'The very night we left Paris', Bess recorded, 'the firing began & for several days nothing was to be heard but the beating of drums, the cry of arms, the firing of guns, for they took the Hôtel des Invalides, the Bastille & pillag'd several convents for corn.' This news was followed by alarming accounts of Madame de Polignac's narrow escape from Versailles disguised as a chambermaid. Reviled by the mob as the Queen's favourite, she was one of the first to leave; hard on her heels went the Comte d'Artois and other members of the French royal family. A number of acquaintances last seen by Bess and Georgiana amid the splendours of Versailles began to arrive at Spa, distraught and exhausted. Among them was the Baron de Breteuil, who had fled with a price on his head but was not too exhausted to flirt with Bess. Every day brought fresh reports of the persecution and humiliation of aristocrats, and of the 'greatest fermentation' in Paris. When from the safety of England Walpole exclaimed 'In what a combustion is

France! I understand nothing I hear or read', he spoke for a bewildered Europe.

While Bess spared neither pen nor paper in recording events in France, her journal is strangely mute on the subject of Caro. She says nothing about seeing the child at the Nagels', nor of the Duke's feelings on meeting his daughter for the first time. But as the news from Paris became increasingly ominous, concern for the safety of Caro and Charlotte became acute. Hare, who was rather enjoying the 'tumults' in the city, wrote on 18 July to assure them that all danger was over. Lest he should prove mistaken, however, 'the Duke seems inclin'd to engage the Nagels to take a small house near London for a year,' Georgiana told Lady Spencer. 'This would be an advantage to their own children and their little pensioner, Mlle St Jules.' Such a painless transfer of Caro across the Channel was an unlooked-for benefit of the unrest in France: for all her resource, Bess could not have planned it better. However, Hare's comments that Nagel was an 'odious beast' and his house smelt 'like a Painter's Shop' spurred the Duke – who was convinced that paint damaged the health – into action. It was arranged, probably through Hare, that Charlotte and Caro should be despatched with Madame Nagel to the Austrian Netherlands. 'I am really very glad to hear that you intend taking Charlotte and the little girl from Nagel's,' Hare told Georgiana, adding intriguingly: 'It is a pity that there should be any obstacle to your taking little Caroline more immediately under your own care, for she is the prettiest child I ever saw.'

Bess, though at last in possession of her precious daughter, had begun to lose her nerve. To bolster her courage, on 15 September Hare wrote her a letter remarkable for its humanity and wisdom:

It would be dealing insincerely with you if I were to say that I think her [Caro's] introduction at D. House will occasion no surmises or scandal, but this consideration is in my mind infinitely over ballanced by your having her under your own care, whether one thinks of her advantage or your amusement. As to the difficulties which seem to terrify the Dss so much, I guess that they must be . . . but they cannot last long, and when once the little woman has gained a footing, I am not afraid of her being disturbed. As to any scruples that you may entertain about imposing on people whom you ought to love, and do, I confess it would be pleasanter if no deceit were necessary, but when things have gone so far as they have, there is no choice left, and it becomes a duty to consult the interest of the poor little helpless wretches, even at the expence of feelings, which may be sometimes distressing . . .

Thus, as far as Hare was concerned, deceiving Georgiana as to Caro's true identity was justifiable for the sake of the child. This same letter discloses that he also knew about Clifford, who had been moved from his birthplace, Rouen in Normandy, to Paris: 'It was not necessary to desire me to make a visit to the little Norman. I had seen him before I received your last letter, and found him perfectly well. He promises to be a giant. He is uncommonly shy (how happens this?) and would not take much notice of me. The woman [the foster mother] seems to be very fond of him . . . She enquired how my friend did, when she should see him, and whether the little boy's mother would return at the same time.' (If Hare's 'friend' was the Duke, it seems that Clifford had also met his father.) 'I was so surprized, confounded and puzzled that I said yes, and am now as much surprized at my answer as I was at her question.' This last sentence is baffling.

Whatever Georgiana may have known, or suspected, about Caro, she knew nothing about Clifford. For Bess to have to confess to the birth of a daughter by the Duke would be bad enough; to have to confess to the birth of his son when Georgiana had yet to produce one herself was too much even for Bess's courage and ingenuity. The silence about Clifford was to persist for several years.

Hare's letters to Bess also provide glimpses of her life with the Devonshires at Spa. 'I wish I could see your Baron [de Breteuil] in his dress Coat and Boots making love to you,' he teased her. A month later he was in sardonic mood: 'Perhaps you & the Dss have not remarked that I do not need give into your accounts of Barons & Bishops dying for love, for to say the truth I hold it that you both carry on a most abominable Plot against all poor people that come near you, all of whom You are trying to make fools of, and some of whom probably you make miserable. [But] my scolding will not reform either of You . . .' Despite the flirting of his ladies, the Duke was in high spirits, and by late September he had good reason: Georgiana was pregnant. At thirty-two, and with her previous history, this was probably her last chance to produce a Cavendish heir. Fearful that a sea crossing might precipitate a miscarriage, the Duke decreed that they would remain on the Continent for the birth. In early October he moved his entourage to Brussels.

On the day of their arrival they received the shocking news that on 5 October a mob of some six thousand market women had marched on Versailles, invaded the palace, and forced the King and Queen to return with them to Paris. The royal family were now shut up in the

Tuileries, prisoners in all but name. There is a sense of Bess's horror in her account of the death of one of the King's bodyguards when the mob engulfed the palace: 'His blood ran into the King's apartment. The Queen, half-dressed, had fled to the King's room . . . [and] fainted when she heard that she was to go to Paris . . .' In a letter to her old friend Lord Sheffield, she poured out her feelings towards the French people: 'I hate them for their conduct to their sovereign, their useless wanton barbarous humiliation of them, & their injustice to my dear banish'd friends [the Polignacs] . . .' This passionate defence of the royal family did not however blind her to the King's conduct; while pitying him, she admitted to Sheffield that she could not 'forgive his want of courage & resolution'.

Revolutionary fever had spread from France to the Austrian Netherlands, inspiring an uprising against the high-handed policies of Marie-Antoinette's brother, Emperor Joseph II. 'Here we are shut up in the town,' Bess wrote to Lady Sheffield, 'surrounded by Batteries, hearing & talking of nothing but engagements, battles & sieges – I hope we shall grow inur'd to it, but it is a strange situation is it not?' Several times the ducal party found itself caught up in the disturbances. On one occasion, they were startled by a man jumping on to their carriage. 'The postilion', Bess recorded, 'very imprudently struck at him with his whip . . . the man levelled his pistol at him, swearing and threatening very much . . . I was much alarm'd at seeing the pistol, but I concealed the motive of my fear from the Dss of D. till we were out of his reach, for she was with child . . .' To her brother, Georgiana praised her friend's conduct. She had been unaware of the danger until it was over, she said, as Bess had placed herself in front of the coach windows. The Duke, with typical Cavendish phlegm, had walked on ahead, blithely ignoring the commotion behind him.

As friends of both Bess and John Foster, the Sheffields had become involved in Bess's continued attempts to see her two boys. John Foster had resisted her latest scheme for them to be educated in England, explaining to Lord Sheffield that he dreaded the boys 'acquiring high Family Notions which they will not have Fortune or Situation to support, & above all, that refined Hereditery Sensibility [he was too polite to call it Hervey Eccentricity], which is certainly amiable, but too often leads the Possessor into error & misfortune.' 'How eternally he disappoints me!' Bess wailed to Lord Sheffield.

In December 1789 the Duke returned to England, ostensibly on business but in reality to try to prevent Harriet's husband, Lord

Duncannon, from divorcing her for her affair with Sheridan, which had been going on since late 1788. Georgiana, meanwhile, was still fighting a rearguard action over her debts, now grown byzantine in their complexity. Hare urged her to confess everything to the Duke, 'or let Ly Elizabeth or let me tell him'. A letter from him to Bess of 18 December shows how much faith he placed in her ability to control Georgiana's 'excesses'. Neither of them could have known they were dealing with an addiction, for which there was neither understanding nor cure in the eighteenth century.

> I can give you no advice [he wrote] for I have no hopes of her ever being more prudent . . . Unless some method is designed to prevent her going on at this rate he will be terribly distressed. She ought to consider that his estate is so encumbered already that he can borrow very little more on mortgage, and all other ways of raising more are doubly ruinous . . . She ought to be restricted from these ceaseless and odious excesses in any way . . . If ever I hear that you give any advice that tends to leaving her at liberty to eschew these indiscretions I shall join your worst enemies and far exceed them in rancour, everything depends on you . . .

Under pressure Georgiana confessed to some of her debts, but again shrank from a full disclosure, exploiting her delicate state to prevent the Duke from pressing her further. As the baby was not due until May it was decided that the Cavendish children (Little G. and Harriet, known as Haryo, to distinguish her from her aunt) and the Duncannons should join them at Brussels in March. This sudden exodus of Cavendish relations from England caused fevered speculation: why had the Duke chosen a country in the throes of a revolt for the birth of his heir? Why was Georgiana's usual *accoucheur* not to be in attendance? Was some dark plot afoot, involving a pregnant Bess whose baby, should it prove to be a boy, would be passed off as Georgiana's?

Georgiana was so anxious that her children, who would be in charge of Miss Trimmer, should have a trouble-free journey that she bombarded her mother – who was to follow in May – with letters of instruction. One letter sought to reassure Lady Spencer that Little G. and Haryo would be enchanted by Miss St Jules, who was, 'tho' very lively, a remarkably orderly little creature and will be of great assistance to their French'. Bess, however, must have wondered whether Caro's camouflage as 'the little pensioner' would survive close inspection by Lady Spencer, who would be only too pleased to find some tangible proof of her treachery to Georgiana.

In April a batch of the ducal party's letters was intercepted, and some were found to contain information on the political situation in the Austrian Netherlands. The authorities were indignant; there was even talk of Georgiana, now eight months pregnant, being arrested. With a fresh uprising expected, it was thought prudent to leave Brussels. The Duke marshalled his party, numbering about a hundred altogether – one mother-in-law, one wife, one mistress, one sister-in-law and her husband, two legitimate children, two illegitimate children, Miss Trimmer, numerous nurses, maids, couriers, grooms and footmen – and conducted them south to Paris.

As they entered France, Bess noted that all seemed quiet. 'One would never think that it was a country without King or Law – and that [it] had been for the last 8 months the scene of discord and bloodshed.' After five nights in the Hôtel de l'Université, they were lent a large house on the outskirts of Paris at Passy. During the move, Bess noted: 'The Dss has *felt herself* ill.' That evening Bess attended the opera with the specific purpose of dispelling the rumour that it was she who was pregnant. Lord St Helens, who invited her to share his box, later confirmed that Lady Elizabeth was 'as thin as a Wrayle'. By the time she returned to Passy, Georgiana was in labour. Bess's entry for 21 May reads simply: 'The Dss of Devonshire was brought to bed of a Son to our inexpressible Joy.' As the Duke's heir the child would be known as the Marquess of Hartington, but was called Hart for short.

Hare, who had returned to England the previous August, wrote Bess a mischievous letter expressing his hope that important personages such as the Mayor of Paris had been invited to witness the birth, and were thus able to contradict the rumours. 'People arrange the circumstances according to their own fancy,' he went on, 'some suppose that You are the person to whom the World was to owe a new Inhabitant . . . Some who are of a more sociable turn place You both in the same situation, others are very niggardly, and will not allow either of You the least merit with regard to population, but ascertain that the Child had been bought, begged or stolen, and was to be introduced into the Dss's room in a Warmingpan . . .' Hare also thanked Bess for visiting his son and daughter in Paris. 'I love my poor little Girl so much, that I am delighted with what you say of her, even tho' I know you are likely to commit your Good nature more than your Judgement.' Bess was clearly as diligent about visiting Hare's children as he had been about visting hers.

Georgiana took some weeks to recover from Hart's birth. No

sooner had she done so than Little G. contracted a mysterious and dangerous illness. 'We have pass'd many days in the greatest anxiety,' Bess wrote on 14 June. She took her turn to sit through the night at Little G's bedside. Their departure for England was delayed until August, but too much was going on in Paris for time to lie heavy on their hands. There were no fine carriages to be seen in the streets, but the cafés, theatres and opera were crowded and aristocrats, provided they wore the tricolour cockade, were relatively safe. Bess records the heroism of a woman who saved a young man not wearing a cockade from being lynched by the mob. She begged them on her knees

to spare her son (so she called him to interest them) but they only replied, 'All the better – we shall rid ourselves of two of you.' She continued however entreating them to spare his life till she got him into a coffee house, when seeing that he was safe, she turned round & said, 'Now that my son is safe, I hold my own life of no account. Let us see if you dare kill me. You are all cowards, murderers unworthy to be called Frenchmen, you are hired assassins, you are cannibals greedy for human blood.' In speaking thus she traversed the Tuileries and got into her coach, no one daring to strike her. I must add that this extraordinary woman is about 6 feet in height & proportionately large.

On the day the National Assembly revoked all aristocratic privileges and titles, Bess gave full rein to her disgust: 'Can this Assembly be compar'd as they compare themselves to the Roman Senate, or do they inspire a single sentiment of respect & admiration, or conviction that their subject is the publick good? Have they even the right . . . to rob these families of the long possess'd inheritance of Nobility . . .? It really is affecting and distressing to be with some of the great families, to hear them giving orders for effacing the arms on their carriages, relinquishing the respected names they have borne . . . If we read of these extraordinary events ten years hence, we shall scarcely believe that we have been witness to them.'

On 2 July Bess and Georgiana met the Queen at Saint-Cloud. 'She was visibly agitated and affected at seeing people she had known in her happier days; but with her usual dignity sweetness & affability shew'd attention to every one . . .' Turning to Bess's sister Mary Erne (who had just arrived from Italy) the Queen enquired about Madame de Polignac, but 'her voice falter'd so that she could scarcely pronounce the name, her eyes fill'd with tears, & when I told her that I was to write next day to Madame de P. she said in a low trembling voice, "Tell her that you have seen someone who will love her all her life."' The Queen 'caress'd & kiss'd' Hart and enquired after Little G., then took them to see the Dauphin. 'We left Saint-Cloud, our minds impress'd with admiration & fill'd with pity for this amiable & unhappy Queen . . . In the short space of two years she has lost two children, a beloved Brother in the Emperor, her life has been attempted, she is a Prisoner in her own Palace, & she lives in the constant expectation of being dethron'd or assassinated – so great a fall from happiness has scarcely its parallel in history.' The Queen was, however, being consoled by Axel Fersen, who visited her in secret both at Saint-Cloud and the Tuileries.

The day after the Devonshire ladies visited Saint-Cloud the Queen held a clandestine meeting with Comte Mirabeau, a man she detested for his dominant role in the revolution. But Mirabeau's aim was to save the monarchy, and towards this end he was prepared to play a double game. When Bess met him later, in August, she remarked upon his 'quick & daring spirit . . . bold & hideous countenance' (his face was pitted with smallpox scars), and while she conceded that his conversation was 'lively & interesting', she felt he sought 'to surprise his hearers by the boldness of his principles, the profligacy of his character & his gigantic expressions'. He also 'spoke of Charles Fox & Pitt with great admiration, & I could not perceive which he admir'd most . . .'

When the ducal entourage left for England on 14 August, Paris was calm. Though anticipated with some trepidation, the anniversary of the storming of the Bastille had 'pass'd off with the greatest peace & order'. The revolution appeared to have run its course.

7

A sacrifice to friendship
August 1790 – September 1793

'Bess has very generously promised to go with us, I urg'd
her to it almost as much on her own account as my
sister's. It must have been ruin to her to stay behind . . .'

Lady Duncannon to Lady Melbourne, 15 October 1791

———————◆———————

THE DUKE AND his party landed at Dover on 18 August 1790 after
'a sick passage' from Ostend. Possibly they should have adopted
the Earl-Bishop's curious method of avoiding seasickness: 'Lash your
carriage to the mast & in the center you know is little or no motion.
Then let down the Glass on the Windward for fresh air, but above all
clothe your self in a Pelisse as if it were winter, & keep yourself in a
perpetual Sweat . . . 'Tis the stoppage of perspiration is one of the
chief causes of our Sickness . . .'

The Earl-Bishop featured in Bess's journal soon after her return:
'My father came to England & was very kind to me.' This is the first
sign of a possible reconciliation between Bess and her father since the
breakdown of her parents' marriage in 1782 and the unhappy week she
spent in Rome in 1786. Yet there remains no record of a regular correspondence for another four years, nor is Bess ever mentioned in her
father's letters to either of her sisters. In the will he made in 1791 Lord
Bristol left nothing to either Mary or Bess, on the grounds that they
had already received their marriage portions. To 'his affectionate and
dutiful daughter' Louisa he left five thousand pounds, but a derisory

thousand to his 'ungrateful and undutyful' youngest son Frederick. Why poor gentle Frederick, recently graduated from Oxford with honours, should have been thus designated is unknown. Perhaps, like Bess, he had shown too clearly that his sympathies lay not with his ego-centric father but with his long-suffering mother.

The Earl-Bishop had not seen his ancestral home for ten years, but in 1792, while Lady Bristol was absent, he paid a short visit to Ickworth to make arrangements for building the house which stands there today – referred to by its creator as an 'impudent house' but dismissed by Lady Bristol as 'a stupendous monument of folly'. The Earl-Bishop never saw so much of it as the laying of the foundation stone: shortly after this visit he left for the Continent, never to return.

On the political front, the Foxite Whigs, still in disarray following the Regency Crisis, were ill-prepared for the turmoil provoked by the French Revolution, and their leaders differed wildly in their reactions. As an advocate of the end of the old order in France, Fox had greeted the revolution ecstatically; Edmund Burke passionately opposed it; Sheridan defended it.

A note from Sheridan to Georgiana and Bess strikes a cheerful tone sadly at odds with the mood that autumn at Devonshire House: 'I don't know whether you are all out giddy gay and chirriping like Linnets and yellow-Hammers or sitting at home soberly like pretty Bantams and Peafowl on your Perches.' Georgiana, despite her triumphant return bearing the Cavendish heir, was already fending off her creditors and complaining that she was 'vex'd and perplex'd to death'. When she begged Lady Spencer to join them all at Eastbourne, her mother refused: 'You would not, I am sure, wish me to go if you could know what torture it is to me to endure all I have so long done . . .' – in other words, she refused to sleep under the same roof as Bess. Georgiana's response was immediate and wildly out of character. In a letter of 9 September 1790 which covered fifteen sides of paper she began by attacking Selina Trimmer for colluding with her mother, for showing a lack of respect to Bess, and for presuming to know more of her plans than she herself did. She then turned the attack on her mother, saying that the Duke could

not help thinking it a most extraordinary circumstance that when a man and his wife both agree in living with a person, that you should be persuaded to imagine that there was a cause of complaint . . . I can only add, Dst M., that I am born to a most complicated misery. I had run into errors, that would have made any other man discard me; he forgave me; my friend who had likewise stood between him and my ruin, was likewise his friend; her society was delightful to us, and her gentleness and affection sooth'd the bitterness that [my] many misfortunes had brought on us. And the mother whom I adore . . . sets herself up in the opposite scale, forgets all the affection her son-in-law has shewn her, and only says: I will deprive them of their friend or of my countenance . . .

Lady Spencer's reply was immediate and emollient, but Georgiana's blood was up. There is a sense throughout this exchange of letters that she was at the end of her tether, that the long years of her mother's interference in her life – aided and abetted now by Miss Trimmer – had finally become insupportable. Her second letter reiterated her first, adding for good measure that the Duke's health and frayed nerves required 'quiet & gentle society . . . and that he meets with & I will pledge my Life, with perfect Innocency, in her . . .' To claim Bess's innocence was either a magnificent bluff by Georgiana, a pathetic attempt to convince herself of it, or a tragic lack of awareness. Presumably Lady Spencer, who suspected everything but could prove nothing, never called Georgiana to account for this breathtaking assertion; she was certainly left in no doubt as to how the *ménage à trois* operated.

Bess apparently never criticized Miss Trimmer, though she did once liken her to the north-east wind, 'which in the brightest sun shine has still some chill in it'. But Georgiana's sister Harriet once said that Miss Trimmer's fault was a want of *'graciousness* in every thing she does; rigidly right, she forgets that one may do right without making oneself disagreeable to every one around . . .' Miss Trimmer nevertheless became utterly indispensable to Georgiana, and much loved not only by the Cavendish children but by all the other progeny, including Bess's, who came and went at Devonshire House.

Georgiana's confrontation with her mother was but a prelude to two further crises which followed one upon another and became inextricably entwined: her sister Harriet became dangerously ill, and she herself began an affair with Charles Grey.

Harriet had been unwell for some time, and in March 1791 she suffered what appears to have been a stroke, which paralysed her down one side. Bronchial pneumonia followed, leaving her with a racking cough, and spitting blood. Rumours suggested a variety of dramatic reasons for her collapse: she had suffered a miscarriage, attempted suicide, or bungled an abortion. As soon as she showed signs of improvement the Duke took a house in Bath and Harriet, Georgiana and all their children moved there in May, accompanied by Bess and her daughter Caro.

Bess and Harriet had initially been brought together by their love for Georgiana, and the friendship between them remained close. Still only thirty, Harriet had led a life as eventful and as crisis-ridden as her sister's. Her marriage to Lord Duncannon had been unhappy from the outset – he was suspected of abusing her, she was known to have had numerous affairs – but despite periods of open warfare they had managed to produce four children. Faced now with the possibility of his wife dying or becoming a permanent invalid, Duncannon began to behave surprisingly well.

Georgiana had been attracted to Charles Grey since their first meeting in 1785, confiding to Bess that while she admired the handsome young politician, she was not in love with him – though she thought him 'a very dangerous man, from being a very amiable one'. During the heady months of the Regency Crisis he had been one of the most frequent callers at Devonshire House. Now, having fulfilled her principal duty of providing the Duke with an heir, Georgiana succumbed: passionate and demanding, Grey was a difficult man to resist. Harriet and Bess knew of the affair from the first and foresaw its consequences, but were powerless to prevent it. In their distress, all three women turned for advice to an acknowleged expert on affairs of the heart: Lady Melbourne. Bess told her that Georgiana was 'working herself up to think she is more attach'd to him than I know she can be'. But she was wrong: this was the love of Georgiana's life, and she gave herself to Grey without discretion or restraint, first at Devonshire House and then at Bath. Lady Melbourne urged Georgiana to give him up before either the Duke or Lady Spencer – it is hard to know which they all feared most – came to hear of the affair. But in May Bess told Lady Melbourne all their attempts to save Georgiana had failed; Lady Spencer 'had receiv'd an anonymous letter & her commands are [as] you know absolute & her vigilance extreme'. Dread of Lady Spencer was enough to persuade Grey to leave Bath. Bess reported optimistically that at least Georgiana had not 'entangled herself further, & his present absence must set all things right . . .'

Everyone except the thwarted lovers heaved a sigh of relief. It was to be hoped that one of Beau Nash's 'Rules to be observ'd at Bath' – 'that all whisperers of lies and scandals be taken for their authors' –

would prove a sufficient deterrent to protect Georgiana's reputation. Clearly, not a whisper of the affair had reached the sharp ears of the novelist Fanny Burney when she met them all at Bath in August. Miss Burney had only recently resigned her post as Second Keeper of the Queen's Robes, and five years spent in the atmosphere of austere rectitude which characterized the Hanoverian Court predisposed her to 'unconquerable repugnance' in encountering the notorious Spencer sisters. Their beauty, warmth and sweetness conquered her with ease; Bess, however, was apparently fair game for censure since she had, in Fanny's view, inherited 'all the wit, all the subtlety, all *les agréments*, & all the wickedness of The Herveys' – a judgement which shows how relentlessly the stigma of being a Hervey pursued Bess.

As for the *'little French lady'*, as Fanny referred to Caro, 'to the tales about *her, scandal* is nothing – INFAMY enwraps them'. She also declared the child to be 'fat and full of mincing little affectations and airs'. Already suspicious regarding Caro's parentage, Fanny sought confirmation from Sarah Holroyd, sister of Bess's friend Lord Sheffield. The lady proved well informed: 'If I answer you what they say of her themselves . . . I shall tell you she is a little french orphan, to whom the Duchess took a fancy when last abroad, but if I answer what my Brother would say – I shall tell you she is a little orphan between the Duke & Lady Elizabeth!' Suitably shocked, Fanny vowed to avoid Bess at all costs. 'She has the character of being so alluring that, Mrs [*sic*] Holroyd told me, it was the opinion of Mr Gibbon NO MAN could withstand her,' Fanny says, and goes on to repeat Gibbon's quip about Bess being able to 'beckon the Lord Chancellor from his woolsack'. Then, on the basis of her very brief acquaintance, Fanny has the presumption to assert that Georgiana only put up with Bess because of her liaison with the Duke, and that she was forced to submit, 'with the best grace in her power, to save her *own* character by affecting to have no doubt of Lady Elizabeth's, but that, in her inmost mind, she detested such a Companion . . .' Fanny may have been correct in thinking Georgiana only pretended to believe in Bess's innocence, but for all her supposed perception she utterly failed to appreciate the depth and complexity of the relationship between the two women.

Lord Sheffield's awareness of the origins of Caro St Jules, as disclosed by his sister, appears to have had little effect on his fondness for Bess; indeed, her wicked reputation probably added a spice to their relationship. In early 1791 he was once more pressing John Foster, on her behalf, to keep his promise that the two boys should finish their education in England. A 'congress' was convened at Devonshire House, attended by Georgiana and by Bess's mother, her two sisters and her youngest brother Fred – the first indication for some time of her family acting in concert. John Foster came very close to capitulating to the family's demands, but at the last minute refused to let the boys leave Ireland. General consternation ensued. John Foster was backed by his cousin, another John Foster (known as Lord Oriel in right of his wife's barony, and Speaker of the Irish House of Commons), acting in his capacity as the boys' guardian. Lord Sheffield accused Foster of breach of promise. When informed of his cousin's duplicity, Lord Oriel expressed shocked surprise. Even the Duke of Richmond added his voice to the chorus of disapproval. Foster was actually in London, but wisely kept his whereabouts a secret. His nerve seemed to have held, because the boys did *not* come to England; the heated correspondence between the various parties either ceased, or has not survived. Bess, overtaken by a more serious crisis, may have temporarily lost heart: Georgiana was pregnant with Grey's child.

Bess's journal studiously ignores this new calamity, concentrating instead on events in France. An attempt to smuggle the French royal family out of the Tuileries and transport them in secret to the Luxembourg border had gone disastrously wrong; Bess's former admirers Baron de Breteuil and Count Axel Fersen had been among the principal conspirators. The escape took place on the night of 20 June 1791 when Fersen, disguised as a hackney coachman, spirited the royal family out of the palace and drove them the first stage of their journey. As the result of a series of tragic errors, delays and misunderstandings, the royal party were stopped at Varennes – only a few miles from safety – and forced to return to Paris under guard, entering the capital surrounded by an exultant mob. The attempted escape, later known as the Flight to Varennes, sent shock waves through Paris and sealed the fate of the monarchy. In her journal Bess paid tribute to Marie-Antoinette's courage during these terrible days, then added: 'When I turn back a few years to all that splendor of situation, that brilliancy, life & Joy that was always around her . . . her figure in this bright prosperity is so present to me, that it requires all the horror of the present moment to make me feel that it is not a fiction.' Of Fersen she says: 'He was considered as the Lover and was certainly the intimate friend of the Queen for these last 8 years, but he was so unassuming in his great favour, so modest and unpretending in his manners, so brave & loyal in his conduct that he was the only one of the Queen's friends who had escaped the persecutions of malice . . .'

For a while, there was peace at Bath. At the end of July the Duke left for Chatsworth, and Georgiana's state remained undetected until October. That the current fashions were seemingly designed for women with something to hide can be seen in the charming but absurdly flattering miniature of Georgiana and Bess painted in Paris by Jean-Urbain Guérin in November, when Georgiana was nearly six months pregnant. In early October the Duke, apprised of the situation and in a rage, arrived unannounced at Bath. There was a stormy interview with Georgiana and Bess, after which Georgiana retired to bed with a headache. 'Bess', Harriet told Lady Melbourne, 'looks grave & out of spirits', while the Duke 'walks up and down his room without speaking, & I dare ask no questions'. A little later Harriet again took up her pen: 'My mother is come and our difficulties encrease. Vexation and unhappiness surround me . . . I never felt so frightened about her [Georgiana] as now. Wherever she goes I will go with her.' The following day, the Duke delivered an ultimatum: Harriet and Georgiana were to go abroad immediately, Georgiana without her children. Harriet's health would provide the excuse. If they refused to go, he and Georgiana must separate. Bess could do as she pleased.

Once again, the ambiguity of Bess's position at Devonshire House was exposed. In 1786, when Georgiana was threatened with separation on account of her gambling debts, she had faced the same dilemma: she could neither live alone with the Duke, nor live with Georgiana at Lady Spencer's. This time, however, there was a third possibility: she could go abroad with Georgiana and Harriet. To have to part from the Duke through no fault of her own was painful, but she was left with no alternative. Harriet lost no time reporting Bess's decision to Lady Melbourne: 'Bess has very generously promised to go with us. I urg'd her to it almost as much on her own account as my sister's, it must have been ruin to her to stay behind' – which puts Bess's situation in a nutshell. Unlike Georgiana, however, she was able to take her daughter Caro with her.

But there was more grief to come. 'If the Duke had purposely intended to perplex and torment us, he could not have done it better,' Harriet told Lady Melbourne. 'His only excuse is his being himself excessively unhappy, which indeed poor fellow I am afraid he is . . .' Following yet another exchange with her irate brother-in-law, Harriet confessed herself shocked to hear him 'speak in a manner so unlike the cold & reserved man he generally is . . .' Yet she had great hopes that he would find life so uncomfortable without Georgiana and Bess that he would relent. 'Bess really behaves like an angel to her always . . . & I am certain will do whatever she thinks best for her, but she says she feels it impossible for her to press him much on a subject in which she is herself so much concerned as he might attribute every thing she says to interested motives.' The Duke, having taken his position on the moral high ground, would lose face were he to retract his ultimatum. The die was cast.

To Bess's consternation, Lady Spencer was to accompany them. The Dowager, far from being grateful for her loyalty to Georgiana or seeing her desertion of the Duke as a potential end to their liaison, tried to prevent Bess going. 'Lady S. has begun as bad as possible about me – even so as to say I should not travel with them . . . [but] if the Dss goes I will.' Lady Spencer made things so unpleasant that, briefly, Bess's resolution faltered. 'Bess and I had a long conversation and a half quarrel last night,' Harriet told Lady Melbourne, 'but I think I have [fixed] it . . . I really believe it is nothing but the fear she has of my mother and the mistrust she feels when with her that makes her hesitate.'

By confiding as they did in Lady Melbourne, Harriet and Bess were flouting the Duke's express wish that no one outside the family should be told the real reason for their banishment. Harriet believed his wish for secrecy to be a good sign, for 'if he never meant to live with her again why should he care what was said'. Georgiana's letters to Lady Melbourne never mention that she is pregnant, but their incoherence demonstrates her anguish at having to part from both Grey and her children. Lady Melbourne agreed to act as a conduit for her correspondence with Grey.

Initially under the happy impression that their destination was Penzance, Lord Duncannon survived the revelation that it was to be France and agreed to take charge of the party. Harriet was still partially paralysed and could only walk with the aid of crutches; moving her about would add to the usual vicissitudes of Continental travel. The Duncannons were to leave their three boys in England but take their daughter Caroline Ponsonby as a companion for Caro St Jules (they were exactly the same age). The Cavendish children were to remain with the Duke under the care of Miss Trimmer.

It is a measure of the love Georgiana inspired that Harriet was prepared to leave her three boys, Lady Spencer her peaceful retirement at

St Albans, Lord Duncannon his beloved print collection and ailing father, all to take to the road like gipsies. Had Georgiana known her exile was to last for more than two years, would she have refused to go? *Could* she have refused? Either way, she stood to lose. Formal separation from the Duke – which might end in divorce and social ruin – meant permanent separation from her children. But if she fulfilled the Duke's demands and gave up both Grey and, when it was born, the baby, there was still hope that he would relent and take her back. And he might be more prepared to take her back if it was the only way of restoring Bess to Devonshire House; as Harriet pointed out to Lady Melbourne, Bess was their only security.

While the Duke's initial anger and sense of betrayal command sympathy and understanding, as the period of exile grew from months into years, his behaviour began to resemble nothing so much as a vindictive sulk. Georgiana was to be made to pay for her transgression, and Bess for taking her part against him: fair enough. But that so many innocent people – principally the children – should also be required to suffer is little to his credit. Nor does he appear to have cared what happened to them, choosing to disregard the hazards of a Europe seething with unrest, as he chose also to ignore the fact that they were all desperately short of money. (Oddly, it may be that Bess was the least impoverished of them all, thanks to the small income she received from her husband and father.)

The main party left for France in November. Bess was to follow a few days later, accompanied by the two Carolines and her dog Lilli. But first she went to London to see the Duke. By so closely allying herself with Georgiana, she had jeopardized not only her own future but Caro's and Clifford's. If the children were brought up under the Duke's protection and within Georgiana's loving orbit, their future was assured; but if she was forced to sever all connection with the Duke, what then? Besides, her plan to insinuate Clifford into Devonshire House had lately moved a stage nearer realization: at some time during 1791 the child had been brought over from Paris with his foster mother and established in Somerset with a couple named Marshall (it seems too much of a coincidence that Bess's two Foster sons had also spent much of their childhood with people named Marshall).

Bess left no record of what passed between her and the Duke, only an inconclusive reference in a much later letter to Lady Melbourne, where she says that knowing what Georgiana was suffering had made her 'give way in some things in London, perhaps foolishly . . .' Her journal contains only two brief personal comments: that her journey 'was a sacrifice to friendship', and that she had left the Duke 'God knows with what sorrow'. Delayed six days at Dover by contrary winds, she and the two Carolines eventually sailed for France. Relieved, Harriet reported her arrival in Paris to Lady Melbourne, in a letter which reveals that she at least never doubted Bess's love for the Duke.

> She was excessively low when she first came. Poor little soul, I felt for her from my heart, for I am certain the effort was as much as she could bear; but she is better now . . . I don't think she will go back without us now she is come, though I had very great doubts that she would have [the] resolution to tear herself away, but that once over, I think the natural generosity of her character, and her friendship for my sister will have the leisure to act.

However much she might have tried to prevent Bess accompanying the exiles, her 'sacrifice' signalled a remarkable if short-lived alteration in Lady Spencer's attitude. 'My Mother is very good humour'd & civil to Bess,' Harriet told Lady Melbourne, 'more so than I ever saw her; she seems pleas'd and touch'd with the proof of her friendship for us.' But Lady Spencer, seemingly bent on punishing Georgiana, never let her out of her sight, even insisting that they sleep in the same room – as if her daughter were not unhappy enough. Separated from Grey and her beloved children, about to have a baby which would be taken from her, she had apparently been entirely abandoned by the Duke, who had not written to her once since her departure.

Paris was quiet, the streets full of *fiacres* and carts, scarcely a gentleman's equipage in evidence. Bess saw 'a vast number of people' of her acquaintance, 'all of whom appear'd fearfull & apprehensive of future events'. Following their attempted escape, the royal family had been allowed to return to the Tuileries, but it was said the Queen was never without a guard except when she was in bed. After a week in the capital, the party left for Nice, making the journey in short stages to avoid tiring Harriet.

Bess's journal now ceases to be 'a recital of publick events' and becomes a record of their journey addressed to her daughter, written in French – Caro's first language. Bess was, however, incapable of confining herself to descriptions of *'jolie villages'* and olive groves; instead the poor child, not yet seven, was treated to a detailed history of every town they passed, with special emphasis on the glories of

Ancient Rome. Unless many of these details were taken from a guide book, Bess's erudition is remarkable, as is her diligence and her instructive zeal. She seems to have had a special affection for Hannibal, who trudges doggedly through the journal on his way to Rome. Charming little drawings and watercolours illuminate the text. Watercolour was the preferred medium of amateur artists, especially since little slabs of colour had replaced the messy powders. Lady Palmerston, who encountered the party at Naples, duly admired the ladies' artistic endeavours, and declared that 'Lady Elizabeth draws in a most capital style'. Harriet and Georgiana also kept instructive journals, Harriet for her two sons at Harrow and Georgiana for her eldest daughter. Georgiana's letters to Little G. contain glimpses of Caro St Jules: 'She has great good sence; attention like yours; and sweetness of disposition & manner like you – and has wonderful piety for such a little creature. I wish your cousin Caroline was as good . . . your grandmama is the only person she minds at all.' ('Cousin Caroline' Ponsonby was to prove more troublesome than everyone else put together.) Bess also wrote to Little G. with news of Caro. Little G. replied, and on one occasion sent Bess a beautiful box. 'I have ever loved you so much as if you were mine,' Bess responded.

At Marseilles, the party divided: Lady Spencer and the Duncannons continued on to Hyères, south of Toulon, while Georgiana, Bess and Caro spent a month at Aix-en-Provence and then journeyed to Aigues-Mortes in the Languedoc to see Comte St Jules, the 'old man' as Georgiana called him, who had so unaccountably agreed to give Caro his name. Referring to the Count as the child's grandfather, Georgiana explained to Lady Melbourne that the purpose of their visit was to secure Caro's 'little income' before the ailing gentleman died. Harriet, on the other hand, believed it was to obtain 'proofs that may silence all reports' about the child's birth, although she herself, as she told Lady Melbourne, had 'not the smallest shadow of a doubt . . .' Clearly – despite the 'mystery that has always been thrown over Caroline's birth' – Harriet had drawn her own conclusions (unfortunately, her writing is appalling – even her mother complained about it – and sections of this revealing letter are illegible). Georgiana, writing to Lady Melbourne from Aix, adds yet another layer to the mystery: 'Mme de N. has sent her [Caro] her Mother's picture which is very pretty and delights her as you may imagine.' What mother? And who is 'Madame de N.'? It would seem that Bess's fabrication of Caro's origins was so thorough that she had not only found a woman to impersonate the child's mother but arranged for her portrait to be painted as a proof of her existence. This is deception practised on a grand scale, and was to have unfortunate repercussions. Caro has left a memoir-cum-journal, apparently begun in late adolescence, which includes retrospective comments on her life from the age of eleven; it is from this perspective that she mentions having been given a picture

as of my mother; it was a miniature of a beautiful woman with a wreath of roses on her head and a heavenly expression. I used to kiss it and say my prayers before it and address her as a saint in heaven looking down on her child. When I found it was all an error and that it was an imaginary picture I took a dislike to it and don't know what became of it. I feel hurt at having thrown away my best, my warmest feelings upon it. When we were travelling in France an old man was dressed up to personate my grandfather who gave me this miniature and other presents. I don't know if it was meant to deceive others as well as me, but it seems a great deal of trouble to take to mislead a child.

Having constructed this elaborate fiction, Bess was careful to promote it. In a letter to Lady Melbourne written from Brussels in April 1790, she had complained of people spreading rumours about 'poor little Madlle St Jules . . . They would be ashamed of their malice when they saw her innocent little beautiful countenance and knew how unfortunate she was – nothing shall ever make me change my manner towards her . . . If fortune ever favours her friends again, she may laugh at the world & its ill nature – till then we will shelter her from it!' By 'her friends', Bess might have meant the Polignacs; Madame de Polignac's role as Caro's protectress while the child was in France had ceased abruptly when she fled to Switzerland following the fall of the Bastille. Bess's pretended indignation maintains the fiction that she too was acting purely as Caro's protectress, the child's real mother having died. (The delicious twist to this correspondence with Lady Melbourne is that she later became Caro's mother-in-law.)

Georgiana was now approaching her confinement. Fearful that she might not survive, three weeks before the birth she drafted a will. Addressed to the Duke, it begins: 'Every thing I have is yours, therefore I can leave you nothing as a remembrance but a green antique ring which was given me by Bess . . .' Following a list of small bequests to her family, she says: 'To Bess, I beg your leave to give the Prints of the Vatican & Raphaels given me by my Brother, the picture of you in my pocket; To Caroline [St Jules] the Emerald picture of Bess in a ring, &

the picture of Bess by Hamilton' – and a hundred pounds. One name is missing from this list: Clifford's. If she had known of his existence, it is inconceivable that Georgiana – who had not a vindictive, ungenerous bone in her body – would have failed to leave him some little memento. Nor is he mentioned in the letter she wrote at the same time to her son Hart, to be given to him in the case of her death. Written in her own blood, it expresses her anguish at being separated from her children and her fear that she might never see them again. Counselling Hart to obey his father and be kind to his sisters, she adds, 'Love always dear Ly Elizabeth and Caroline.'

Georgiana's mention of Caro St Jules in her will and in the letter to Hart is possible evidence that she now knew Bess and the Duke to be the child's parents. The weeks the two women spent together without Lady Spencer and Harriet had surely presented Bess with an ideal opportunity to confess: Georgiana was consumed with guilt over Grey's child and her abandonment of her other children, apprehensive about the birth, and entirely dependent on her friend. Besides, she could scarcely have taken part in the negotiations to secure Caro's 'little income', as apparently she did, if Bess was still maintaining the fiction of the child's birth.

On 20 February Georgiana gave birth to Charles Grey's child. The little girl, named Eliza Courtney, was immediately handed over to a foster mother and was later taken to England, where she was brought up by Grey's parents – effectively as his sister. There is no record of Grey's reaction, although there is evidence that he wrote seldom, and then often unkindly, to Georgiana. 'Black [code name for Grey] has been again very cruel . . . ,' she told Lady Melbourne. 'Why will people be harsh at such a distance?' Georgiana, Bess and Caro did not join the rest of the party at Nice until mid March; Bess's journal neatly skips this awkward interlude, sliding over two eventful months without a hiccup.

They had now been abroad nearly four months. The post, their only link with home, had been disrupted by terrible weather, and by the general unrest in southern France. Apart from an occasional letter to Bess, the Duke ignored them. Thomas Coutts, however, did not; Georgiana was pursued by a stream of plaintive missives in which he complained that his own family's welfare was endangered by the sums of money she owed him and that his appeals directly to the Duke to honour his wife's debts had gone unheeded. Their most faithful correspondent was Miss Trimmer, who reported regularly to Lady

Spencer on the Cavendish children. The Dowager's replies are surprisingly intimate and reveal her despair over Harriet's Caroline, who was 'captious, fretful & obstinate beyond imagination'. (This tempestuous behaviour was an early indication of the mental instability which was to overwhelm her in later life, blight her marriage to William Lamb, and lead to her notorious affair with Byron.) But for Caro St Jules – so unkindly judged by Fanny Burney – Lady Spencer had nothing but praise, confessing to Miss Trimmer that it was impossible to say too much of the child's 'sweetness of temper & docility. One cannot live with her & not love her.' It is a mark of Lady Spencer's capacity for love – so mistakenly applied to her daughters – that, almost despite herself it seems, her dislike of the mother did not extend to the child.

Another correspondent was Sheridan. His wife was dying, and during her final months his letters to Harriet and Georgiana were suffused with regrets for 'the restless contriving Temper with which I have persevered in wrong Pursuits and Passions . . .' The grief of their old friend added to the exiles' sense of abandonment and isolation. But at Nice they made a new friend, Lady Webster. Still only twenty-one, she had been married at fifteen to a rich but gloomy man more than twice her age. In a letter to the Sheffields, who had met Lady Webster while staying with Gibbon in 1791, Bess described her as 'clever, good humour'd & very original'. The Sheffields' daughter Maria had been less complimentary: 'If anybody ever offends you so grievously that you do not recollect any punishment bad enough for them, only wish them on a party of pleasure with Lady Webster!' Such was the complex character of this unusual woman. She later married Lord Holland, Charles Fox's nephew, and became Georgiana's successor as London's most celebrated society hostess.

By April Bess was agitating to return to England, but the Duke made it clear that he had no intention of recalling Georgiana in the immediate future, and hinted at a formal separation if she disobeyed. What Bess should do was left to her; uncertain perhaps of her reception, she elected to stay.

When Nice grew too hot the party made its way by sea to Genoa, then north towards Switzerland. Their progress was charted by Gibbon, who told Lord Sheffield that 'the good Dutchess of Devonshire, and the wicked Lady Elizabeth Foster are on their march'. Gibbon's great affection for Bess ensured a joyous reception for the nomads on their arrival at Lausanne. They moved into a small house set among vineyards by the lake at Ouchy, close to Gibbon's villa. For

Gibbon, depressed as he was by the death of his old friend Deyverdun with whom he had shared the villa, and secretly afflicted by a swollen testicle (later diagnosed as a hydrocele, a form of dropsy), their presence was a tonic. 'To take tea with three women,' he told Bess, 'the most amiable in Europe (I speak with the religious accuracy of an historian), is the perfection of human society . . . Goodnight! . . . but I do not dare tell you how much I love you.'

At Ouchy they passed a carefree summer picnicking with the two Carolines, studying German, attending lectures on chemistry and mineralogy, and playing charades. One of these charades may be the origin of the oft-quoted story that Gibbon once threw himself at Bess's feet and proposed to her, whereupon she burst out laughing; too stout to rise by himself, he had to be helped up by his servants. The same tale had been told before, but with other ladies as recipients of the proposal. Gibbon's own version, given to the son of his adopted family the de Séverys, firmly states that it was a courtly charade, and that it was Georgiana he knelt before, not Bess; Bess had then presented a sword to Georgiana, with which she knighted him. Gibbon's version fails to mention his inability to get up afterwards. Bess later wrote to him, 'Pray think kindly of the time spent at the petit Ouchi, forget neither its Philosophy nor its folly.'

Gibbon was not their only companion; the three graces – Harriet, Georgiana and Bess – could never be anywhere for long before their beauty, charm and notoriety attracted a circle of admirers. English expatriates, summer visitors and French *émigrés* flocked to the house at Ouchy to exchange gossip, read aloud from letters and newspapers, and discuss the latest news from France.

Already officially at war with Austria and Prussia, by August France was menaced with invasion by their combined armies. With the publication of the Brunswick Manifesto, which threatened the destruction of Paris should the royal family come to any harm, the monarchy was doomed. On 10 August an enraged mob invaded the Tuileries and massacred more than five hundred of the Swiss Guard. The royal family were rescued, but imprisoned in the Temple. The consternation at Ouchy as news of these horrific events began to filter through may be imagined: with the closing of the city gates, friends and relatives were trapped in Paris, and in mortal danger. For weeks the little house became a forum, with a constant stream of visitors and couriers arriving at all hours. In the heat of the moment Bess forgot that her journal was addressed to a child and recorded every shocking and bloody detail which came her way of the atrocities taking place at Paris. Accounts of the September massacres, however, proved too much for her. 'This is the first day I do not wish to see letters from France, the horror of their crimes exceeds my curiosity.' Although Bess recorded that the Queen's great friend the Princesse de Lamballe – a woman she had met on several occasions – had been among the murdered prisoners, she could not bring herself to give the details: the princess had been raped, her body dismembered and her head, stuck on a pike, paraded beneath the Queen's prison window.

By September a French invasion of Switzerland seemed inevitable. Gibbon prepared for flight by purchasing two strong horses and keeping a bag of gold in readiness. In the fervent hope that Italy might be safer, Lady Spencer and the Duncannons left in early October. Letters from the Duke showed him still opposed to Georgiana's return to England, although he spoke vaguely of meeting her somewhere in Europe the following spring. James Hare, finding himself subjected to questioning as to the truth of the rumour that the Devonshires had separated, confessed to Georgiana that while he frequently dined alone with the Duke, 'as he never entered upon the subject of your situation I never suggested it'. His silence was wrongly assumed by friends to arise from discretion, rather than ignorance.

Proving yet again what a good friend he was to Bess, Hare visited Clifford at Clewer in Somerset.

> The Boy is very much grown, & improved, but so shy, that he will scarcely speak, & when he does, that old Norman Hag [his foster mother] never fails to accompany him with an explanatory Speech, that gives one no chance of guessing what the poor boy says . . . However, she seems very good to him, and I believe takes all possible care of him. It would be an advantage to him to mix with other children . . . I have therefore proposed to send for him sometime to my Villa where Mercy [another of Hare's daughters] will do the honours with perfect cordiality, and amuse him . . .

Hare kept his word, and had the boy to stay:

> He came here with all his household, except the young man who waits on him, and staid a day or two; it is impossible to be more amiable & interesting than he was thought by every body here, and as for Mercy & Charlotte they were eternally disputing & fighting about him. His health seems very good, and he is strong & active, but I think you mistake in bringing him up with so much delicacy, both to cloathing and Diet. I told the old Lady so, and she appeared to agree with me, but pleaded positive Orders . . .

Hare was concerned that the child's diet – 'no bread, never beef, scarce ever mutton' – would have to change when he went to school, which might upset him. He also disclosed that the Duke had been present during the visit. 'A friend of yours & mine had apprehensions about his speech, in which he seems to have some difficulty.' Hare was reassured when he overheard the boy speak to one of his daughters 'very plainly & distinctly'. He ended with a description of the boy which must have delighted Bess: 'He is one of the finest children I ever saw, & the most striking likeness of one of his Ancestors, not only in features, but in manner, winking of his eyes [a habit of Bess's when agitated], & many other particulars, that is quite unaccountable as there can be nothing of imitation in it.'

Were it not for these occasional nuggets from Hare, Clifford's early life would be a complete mystery. But the extent to which Bess supervised the boy's upbringing indicates her determination to remain involved with him. In the meantime she had Caro, and that in itself must have seemed little short of miraculous when Georgiana's anguish at having to surrender Grey's baby was still so fresh in her mind. Today a divorce or separation requiring the permanent estrangement of mother and children is inconceivable. Few women of Georgiana's day had the courage of Lady Webster: she, apparently foreseeing that her marriage would end in divorce, was so determined to keep at least one of her children that she tricked her husband into believing it had died.

In late October Georgiana and Bess finally abandoned all hope of the Duke recalling them, and set off to join the rest of the party in Italy. Since Savoy was overrun with French troops, they were advised to take the less frequented route over the St Bernhard pass. Travelling by carriage into the mountains required the passengers to walk from time to time to relieve the horses – but walking had its compensations. There was time to pause to drink from a mountain stream, contemplate the view, or dash off a quick sketch. Bess had been indoctrinated with the benefits of exercise by her father, who stressed that 'movement is above all things essential to the human frame, which for want of it must be loaded with obstructions, bad secretions, redundant bile, & the inevitable consequences of all, bad humour, discontent, pining &c. &c.'

Bess was clearly missing Gibbon. Perhaps fearing, too, that he was fatally ill, she wrote him a series of letters, beginning the first within hours of their departure from Lausanne: 'I would fain have written from the top of St Bernhard but we are still in all humility at the bottom.' Italy proved no safer than Switzerland, and from Turin Bess told Gibbon they were hastening to Rome before it was destroyed by 'Goths and Vandals'. From Milan she informed him that crossing the St Bernhard pass was nothing to the dangers of 'traversing the once peaceful country of Italy – troops dispers'd every where, anxious and fearful countenances, sudden alarms, bold attempts & strange successes are what characterize each day's experience'. When she found no letter from Gibbon at Bologna (where they caught up with Harriet and Lady Spencer), she pretended outrage, vowing that she would write to him no more: 'You may hear from others of Rome being pillag'd, Italy conquered & us made prisoners, but not a syllable from me!' At Florence she relented, describing Georgiana's delight in the city (it was her first visit), especially in the Cabinet d'Histoire Naturelle. 'I own my passion for mineralogy & botany is sunk into something like indifference,' she confessed, '& Raphael & Praxitiles have an undisputed power over me.'

At last she was rewarded by a letter from Gibbon: 'I remember it has been observed of Augustus and Cromwell, that they should never have been born, or never have died; and I am sometimes tempted to apply the same remark to certain beings of a softer nature, who, after a short residence on the banks of the Leman Lake, are now flown far away over the Alps and Apennines, and have abandoned their votaries to the insipidity of common life.' After this tremendous opening, he dwells lovingly on the 'pleasures of the summer', then turns to the political situation: 'I begin to feel that I shall have been expelled [from Switzerland] by the power and not seduced by the arts of the blackest demon in hell, the demon of democracy. Where indeed will this tremendous inundation, this conspiracy of numbers against rank and property be finally stopped. Europe seems to be universally tainted, and wherever the French can light a match they may blow up a mine. Our only hope is now in their devouring one another.'

Gibbon's letters to Bess are no mere *billets doux*, but lengthy and considered appraisals of current affairs addressed to a woman whose intelligence he respected. Her correspondence with him and with other men of distinction – Lord Sheffield, Cardinal de Bernis (scholar, diplomat, and Louis XVI's ambassador at Rome), the renowned Swiss physician Tissot and, later, Cardinal Consalvi – is a gauge of her powers of fascination. Most were twice her age, yet all treated her as an intellectual equal. Nor does this list include other correspondents such as Axel Fersen and James Hare, whose lives and personalities were hardly commonplace. At this stage in Bess's life, female correspondents were notable by their absence. Apart from Georgiana and Harriet (and Lady Melbourne, to a lesser degree), her most intimate and enduring friendships were with men.

In early February 1793 Bess recorded the execution of the French king. Her journal entry reads simply: 'I am so overcome I can say no more.' A letter from Gibbon contains a fitting epitaph: 'Louis had given and suffered every thing. The cruelty of the French was aggravated by ingratitude, and a life of innocence was crowned by the death of a saint, or, what is far better, of a virtuous Prince, who deserves our pity and esteem.' The letter ends: 'Adieu, ingenious and amiable little creature, as the wise Duke of Cumberland used to call you.'

At Florence Bess's brother Jack, Britain's envoy to the Tuscan Court, entertained the party royally. It was something of a family reunion for Bess since her brother Frederick was also in Florence. Both brothers fell heavily under Georgiana's spell, Jack because he was addicted to women and Frederick because he was a sensitive youth who perceived the sadness beneath the charm. As soon as he returned to England he did what he knew would please her most: he visited her children. 'Ld Hartington is in the most perfect Health & amazingly grown,' he told her. 'You will find Lady Harriet's *Cheeks* a good deal diminish'd ...' Further visits disclosed a great improvement in Haryo's skill at the pianoforte, and that Hart spoke exactly like the Duke. The boy had stuffed Frederick 'with applepye & made me wheel him about in a Wheel barrow', a view of her son which must have delighted Georgiana. Frederick also showed concern for his older brother, begging her to 'keep up dr Hervey's Spirits, & make him ride every day which is good for his 5 fat sides ...' (Jack feared he would be recalled as a consequence of certain imprudences in his dealings with the Tuscan Court).

Florence was followed by a sojourn in Rome, where Bess continued her indefatigable survey of the city, this time ostensibly for Caro's benefit. The poor child was trailed about, much as Charlotte had been ten years earlier, her little head crammed with a steady stream of knowledge. In mid April the party moved to Naples, where they were taken under the wings of Sir William Hamilton and his new bride, Emma. Bess also went to Vietri, a curious pilgrimage, noting in her journal that the town was 'famous for its clean air and its beautiful location' but making no reference to its squalid backstreets or the house of the Archi-Prêtre where Caro was born. 'I sketched, you picked flowers. I was so pleased to see you so happy . . .'

It was at Naples that Georgiana at last received the Duke's permission to return home. As far as difficulty and danger went, the party could hardly have been further from England. Planning their route with care to avoid the fighting along France's northern frontiers, they began the long trek home. At Pisa, they realized Harriet (Lady Bessborough, since the death of her father-in-law in March) was too ill to continue the journey. After an emotional parting, Georgiana, Bess and Caro set off alone, often travelling before dawn or in the late evening to avoid the summer heat. Their crossing of the St Gothard Pass inspired Georgiana to write a poem thirty stanzas long. (It was published in 1802, and Bess later published a special edition which she illustrated herself.)

The ladies reached Ostend safely in early September, only to find themselves caught up in the chaotic retreat of British forces through the Low Countries following their defeat by the French at Hondschoote. The Channel crossing took twenty-two hours, much of it in dense fog. They arrived exhausted at Dover, apprehensive of their reception after being virtually ignored by the Duke for two years.

8

Change and decay
1793–1800

'The Duchess of Richmond is dying and Mr Forster [*sic*]
is just dead, so that the Duke has been already given to
Lady Elizth, by the chattering world.'

Mrs Matthew to Mrs Montagu, October 1796

———————◆———————

SHORTLY AFTER BESS returned to England in September 1793, her
mother Lady Bristol wrote to her daughter Mary: 'Bess's coming
here will be some [expence], but I think it is essential to her. All is to
pieces at D.H. and no plan settled. I expect her tomorrow to stay a
month. I think she looks well tho' she is very thin indeed.' It may be a
mistake to read too much into Lady Bristol's remark that 'all is to
pieces at D.H.' or into the fact that Bess, having not seen the Duke for
two years, was to go at once to stay with her mother, but the suspicion
remains that some fundamental change had taken place at Devonshire House.

Their years in exile had profoundly affected both Georgiana and
Bess. That the Duke had been able to dispense with their presence with
such apparent ease and had shown so little concern for their welfare during their often hazardous peregrinations around Europe must
have gravely undermined their self-esteem. No matter that Hare had
reported Devonshire House to be 'incredibly dismal and dirty' in their
absence, and that the severity of the Duke's gout bespoke time spent
largely at Brooks's; on the face of it, he had managed perfectly well

without them (whether he had remained celibate during their absence is unknown). He did, however, arrange a great welcome for Georgiana, meeting her with the three children at Dartford, and turning out the household staff in force to greet her on her arrival at Devonshire House. 'There was never anything equal to the attention I have met with from him – to the generosity and kindness,' Georgiana wrote to Lady Spencer in Italy. But it is perhaps significant that Bess spent the first evening with her mother. This may indicate a tactful acceptance on her part that the Duke must be seen to celebrate the return of his wife and duchess, and that his mistress had no place in such a public homecoming. Alternatively, it may be that she felt excluded, even that she felt her future with the Devonshires to be in doubt.

Another possible interpretation of Lady Bristol's remark is that either choice or some force of circumstance had caused Bess and the Duke to at last confess to Georgiana the existence of Clifford, and her initial reaction made it difficult for Bess to remain under her roof. But Georgiana, generous and loving to a fault, would have found it impossible to banish her for long; she could not live without her. When Bess tells Georgiana a few months later that she is going to Clewer – where Clifford lived with his foster parents, the Marshalls – it is clear from the tone of her letter that the subject is entirely open: up to that point, the boy had never been mentioned between them. (Oddly, there is no evidence that Bess had felt it necessary to invent an elaborate cover story for him, as she had for Caro.)

After so long an estrangement, the *ménage à trois* required time to find a new level. The years had altered all three, but the change in Georgiana was the most extreme. A letter to Little G., written after her first year of exile, shows it taking place: 'My sweet Love, when I do see you, oh may we never be parted again; I shall never leave you if I can help it for a day . . . I am grown a very different creature I believe . . . I only wish for quiet with you my Dst children . . .' Georgiana had had a severe fright: she had suffered unbearably through being parted from her children, and had the Duke insisted on divorce or separation she might never have seen them again. That this would have been the result of her abandonment to Grey only intensified her sense of guilt. Never again would she take such a risk. She became at once less independent of and more submissive to the Duke; her energies were now focused not on pleasure and dissipation but on her husband and her children. For a man of the Duke's retiring nature, the change in his wife can only have come as a relief.

His health had visibly declined. Gout had become a major factor in his life, as it was in those of so many of his contemporaries. Lord Chesterfield's view that 'Gout is the distemper of a gentleman, whereas the rheumatism is the distemper of a hackney coachman' reflected the general assumption among male members of the aristocracy that it was a question of when – rather than whether – they too would join the ranks of the afflicted. The obese Georgian gentleman slumped in a chair with one hugely bandaged foot supported on a gout stool was a favourite humorous image of caricaturists like Hogarth and Rowlandson, but the complaint was exquisitely painful. While it was well known to be caused by over-indulgence and lack of exercise, everyone gorged and guzzled, kept irregular hours, and seldom walked further than the few steps between a front door and a waiting carriage. Gout was a favourite topic of conversation, and a constant theme in letters of the period. 'I have been in bed these four weeks with what is called a flying gout,' complained the Earl-Bishop, 'but, were it such, it would have gone long ago, & it hovers round me like a ghost round its sepulchre.' Gout incapacitated its sufferers and shaped their lives, obliging them to spend several months a year purging their digestive systems at one of the English or Continental spas. The Duke was no exception: within six weeks of the ladies' return from abroad the Devonshires and Bess were comfortably established among the wheelchairs and swollen extremities at Bath.

Illness in various forms dogged people's lives. Neither Bess nor any of her acquaintance escaped frequent and often severe health crises. Even a mild indisposition was treated with care; given the relative lack of medical expertise, what began as a chill at dawn might prove a killer by nightfall. Tapping, bleeding, blistering and purging – plus a plethora of largely useless pills and potions – were the standard responses to most ailments, with liberal doses of laudanum (opium dissolved in alcohol) to quell the pain. Bess was once nearly 'destroy'd' (Georgiana's word) by too strong a draught of laudanum, and the many such incidents lent colour to the view, ascribed to Voltaire, that 'doctors poured drugs of which they knew little to cure diseases of which they knew less into human beings of whom they knew nothing'. In late eighteenth-century terms, the Devonshires and their circle were now well past the prime of life, and could expect to be struck down at any moment. Despite his reputation for killing more of his patients than he cured, the fashionable physician Dr Walter Farquhar began to play an ever-increasing part in their lives.

On 16 October 1793 Marie-Antoinette went to the guillotine. Appalled, Bess left a blank page in her journal on the day she received the news. Next day she wrote: 'Her sorrows it is true are at [an] end . . . but yet it is by a deed shocking to Nature & to humanity.' The execution of Marie-Antoinette cannot have been unexpected: Bess's journal is full of accounts of the death or imprisonment of friends and acquaintances in France – 'One has to fear for every body one knows and cares about' – and there was little reason to suppose the Queen would be spared. But the image of the woman she had known in 'bright prosperity' being driven to her death through the streets of Paris, dressed in a threadbare shift, with her hands bound behind her back, was a terrible one. (It was some time before Bess learnt that the Queen's corpse had been thrown into a common grave in the cemetery of La Madeleine. She may never have known that a young woman named Marie Grosholtz, acting under orders from the National Convention, had waited secretly in the graveyard to receive the head, then made a plaster death mask of it – as she had of the King's head ten months earlier. When Miss Grosholtz, by then Madame Tussaud, moved to England in 1802, the two heads were among those she took with her.) Shortly after the Queen's execution, Bess received a letter from Axel Fersen informing her that Madame de Polignac had 'surviv'd but a few days [the death] of the Queen. She press'd her hands to her heart & died.'

The next loss was Bess's old admirer, Edward Gibbon. Although his hydrocele had grown 'almost as big as a small child', news of the unexpected death of Lady Sheffield none the less prompted him to undertake the six-hundred-mile journey from Lausanne to England to comfort his friend. In November he was at Devonshire House: 'The Dutchess is as good and Lady Eliz. as seducing as ever,' he told Lord Sheffield. Despite surgery to 'tap' liquid from the massive swelling, Gibbon died on 15 January 1794. 'I regret him much,' Bess recorded sadly. It would seem from Gibbon's comment that at the age of thirty-five Bess had lost none of her allure, but had remained for him 'a bewitching animal' who also amused him, flirted with him, and helped him briefly forget his ugliness, his affliction and his advancing years.

Bess had other sorrows: after six years as British Envoy to the Tuscan Court, her brother Jack had finally proved himself too eccentric and too undiplomatic to be allowed to continue at his post, and was to be recalled. Lady Webster, still in Florence, claimed that since he had called the Grand Duke a fool and the Prime Minister a knave, he could hardly expect to remain. (Lady Webster had her own reasons for wishing Jack out of Italy: 'Oh! what vile animals men are . . .', she confided to her journal after he tried to make passionate, unsolicited love to her in the back of a carriage.) To soften the blow of his dismissal, it was agreed that his brother Frederick should personally carry the bad news to Florence. Lady Bristol, who dreaded her eldest son's 'warmth of temper', confessed to Mary: 'I will not tell you how many things I fear & how few I hope.'

To avoid the 'hurry' of London, and seemingly undeterred by the logistical nightmare of transporting children, dogs and numerous servants long distances by coach, during 1794 the Devonshires and Bess spent the winter at Bath, spring at the Duke of Bedford's hunting seat at Oakley, summer at Chatsworth, and the next winter at Teignmouth; in the intervals they returned briefly to London. Much of the practical planning for such visits fell to Georgiana: amid all the dramas of her emotional life it is easy to overlook the work involved in her role as mistress of a large household.

Their arrival at Chatsworth elicited Bess's first written response to the great house and reaffirms her feelings for the Devonshires; yet her words somehow convey the impression that she was no longer confident her future lay with them.

> It is with unspeakable pleasure that I find myself again at this beautifull place; the woods, the hills, the valley, river & magnificent house all remind me of past times, all bring back recollections to which the destiny of my life is annex'd, whether future good or ill await me I know not, but amidst the various trials I have known of is a blessing which fills my heart with gratitude, to find in the owners of Chatsworth the same warm & tender friendship as united us ten years ago. Bless'd in them, I feel as if I could meet & support almost any trial.

Bess's journal for this year reveals that in May 1794 she took Caro with her on one of her visits to Clewer to see Clifford, but there is no evidence that at this stage Caro knew the boy was her brother. Nor is much known about this part of Clifford's childhood, apart from a letter to the Marshalls' daughter in which Bess discusses what books the five-year-old should be reading. She adds that she had 'observ'd in him an extreme sensibility to what is good & great', a sensibility also enjoyed by his sister, who by all accounts – even Lady Spencer's – was the gentlest, sweetest child imaginable. Had she not been, her life at the hands of the Cavendish children and their mercurial and unstable cousin Caroline Ponsonby (Harriet's daughter) would have been unbearable.

Returning from her exile, Georgiana was enchanted by her two daughters. Little G. was 'all soul and heart'; Haryo was too fat, but had the 'most winning & comical little countenance' in which reposed two small but watchful eyes. The comical exterior concealed a bright and perceptive mind, and what later became a razor-sharp tongue. Neither girl had inherited her mother's exceptional looks and charm. Both had been old enough when Georgiana went away to accept her when she returned, but her son Hart fiercely rejected her, refusing to obey anyone but Miss Trimmer, who for more than half his short life had been the only mother he knew. It took Georgiana months to woo him back, and it was longer still before anyone realized that he was partially deaf.

For five years Miss Trimmer had represented the one fixed and immovable object in the lives of the Cavendish children. Parents could disappear for months – years – at a time, but Miss Trimmer never deserted them. Her firmness, piety and strict moral principles made a foil for Georgiana's intensely loving but erratic mothering, anchoring the children to reality. But her alliance with Lady Spencer often brought her into conflict with Georgiana, and was fatal for Bess. Not all Bess's loyalty and devotion to Georgiana could alter the fact that Miss Trimmer and Lady Spencer heartily disapproved of her as a person, and of her presence at Devonshire House. To their eternal credit, they never took out their dislike on Caro.

Caro, however, was painfully aware of the animosity between Miss Trimmer and Bess. 'I tried in vain to make them better friends,' she recorded in her memoirs, 'but was obliged to give up in despair. I became reserved myself; the strangeness of my situation in that house, the not knowing who I was, the not having a human being to whom I could speak, made me so. Everything seemed full of secrets. I did not know the natural ties that bound me to my M, but I loved her as my protectress, my adopted mother, yet with a mixture of fear.' If Bess ever read Caro's verdict on her childhood, it must have upset her. While a strict moralist might argue that Caro should never have been born, she was at least conceived in genuine love. And though adoption would have been far the safest course, given her dread of discovery, Bess had instead placed her with foster parents. Despite all the risks, she had hung on to her daughter, and by dint of skilful manipulation had eventually grafted her onto the Cavendish family.

That she had managed to do the same for her son would remain unknown were it not for a letter from Clifford himself to Heaton, the Duke's agent, written in 1827, three years after Bess's death: 'You know who I am and it is perhaps only necessary to say that I was brought up at D. House from the time I was nine years old & I was frequently there before, & always spent my Holydays there, & also whenever I came home from Sea.' So Clifford had made visits to Devonshire House while still under the care of the Marshalls, and it had become his home in 1797, the year before he went to Harrow and two years before he joined the navy. Thus yet another fledgling cuckoo was accepted into the Cavendish nest.

In August 1794 the Bessboroughs and Lady Spencer returned from Italy. Harriet was still lame, though her general health had improved. In Naples, however, she had fallen in love with the supremely handsome Lord Granville Leveson Gower. He was barely twenty, she thirty-two. By frequently reminding him – and herself – of the difference in their ages, Harriet perhaps hoped to avert eventual disaster. But Granville was the love of her life, as Grey had been of Georgiana's. Posterity has reason to bless their liaison, as Harriet's brilliant letters to Granville form an invaluable record of public and private events over a period of twenty-seven years, years during which she remained very close to Bess. 'I believe there never existed a stricter confidence and friendship than there has for many years between my sister, Ly Elizabeth, and myself . . . ,' she once told Granville.

Bess's journal for 1794 ends with a succinct but depressing summary of the international situation as she saw it: 'Poland subdued – France triumphant – Holland inclin'd to peace – Austria tir'd of war – Prussia false – Russia indifferent to everything but her own aggrandisement – Spain frighten'd & not to be trusted – England alone firm & resolute – ruin or success will pronounce this courage or obstinacy.' Nor was the political scene at home any comfort; following the split between Fox and Burke in 1791, first Burke and then the majority of Whigs deserted Fox and joined Pitt's government. Hare, Sheridan and Grey remained loyal to Fox and against war with France – as did Georgiana. Bess herself believed that Britain should resist the French, and when the Duke gave his support to the government, she felt his conduct to be 'noble & great'. She admitted, however, that 'when we differ from J. Hare or Charles Fox how difficult it is to think one is right. Perhaps the horrors of the French Revolution, which I have seen so much of, and the persons I love who have suffered in it, influence me. The Dss regrets the Duke voting for the War . . . but I feel implicit faith in D.D's judgement.' Isolated from the bulk of his party, Fox increasingly distanced himself from Parliament, spending his time peacefully at St Anne's Hill, his villa in Surrey, with his devoted mistress Mrs Armistead. Devonshire House, once a bastion of Whiggery, had lost its political heart.

Politics were a matter of the utmost importance to Bess and her circle. Much to a biographer's frustration, her journals and correspondence often contain little else – which is hardly surprising, since the majority of her male friends and acquaintances were, if not actually Members of Parliament, then involved in some way in running the country. When in 1795 her sister Louisa married the Tory MP Robert Banks Jenkinson, and then in 1801 her brother Frederick joined Addington's government, Bess as a passionate Whig found her political loyalties painfully at war with her family feelings. Georgiana had faced the same dilemma in 1794 when her brother Lord Spencer became First Lord of the Admiralty under Pitt.

In February 1795 Georgiana told Coutts that Bess had been very ill. She often exaggerated illness within the family as an excuse for not having responded to Coutts's desperate pleas for repayment, but a letter to Lady Spencer carries more conviction: Bess had a violent fever, and could all the children remain with her mother at Holywell until she was out of danger? Lady Spencer, despite her moralizing and spying, was a devoted grandmother. In her memoirs Caro recalls her frequent visits to Holywell: 'The cloistered house and quiet garden . . . Lady Spencer herself so good and kind and venerable, uniting such simplicity and sweetness by so much sense and gentleness.'

Bess convalesced at Bognor with the Devonshires, and in September they were all guests of the Duke and Duchess of Richmond at Goodwood House in Sussex. The two dukes went sailing, but Georgiana complained of the 'early and regular' hours and longed to be back at Bognor. In October Bess was again at Goodwood, this time with her mother. It was now eight years since the Duke of Richmond had become infatuated with her. At the outset she hotly denied any attachment, but they had remained friends and corresponded regularly, and he had been a frequent visitor to Devonshire House since her return from abroad. Twice she had solicited his advice, during her campaign to have her sons educated in England and again when her brother was recalled from Florence – a post the Duke had partly engineered. In January 1795 Richmond himself had been relieved of his post, as Master-General of the Ordnance. His dismissal came as no surprise to Bess: 'One truth must be confess'd, that he is so obstinate & has so perverted a judgement that it is almost impossible for people to act with him.' This is an opinion she repeats several times in her journal, and it is odd that, holding this view, she should later have contemplated marrying him. Mortified by his fall from grace, Richmond retired to Goodwood to look after his sick wife and to build a race track.

The new year, 1796, began with the news that Bess's brother Jack was dead – unheroically, on board a man-of-war, some said from catching cold by going on deck scantily clad, though Clifford later claimed it was from the effects of sleeping in a newly-painted cabin. For Bess, it was an irreparable loss. Jack was a kindred spirit, the only one of her siblings who did not censure her association with the Devonshires. He was wild (he had recently been involved in a duel), imprudent, dissolute and a philanderer, but she adored him. It was Jack who had given her the courage to leave John Foster, and Jack who had supported her through the horrors of Caro's birth. 'Grief . . . confin'd me a long time to the house,' she wrote. In Naples, her father collapsed on hearing the news and remained dangerously ill for several weeks.

Scarcely had Bess recovered from this blow when Georgiana was struck down with a hideous eye infection. She had been plagued for years by agonizing headaches – the majority almost certainly caused by what would today be called stress – but when one eye swelled to the size of a fist the surgeons had to operate. Initially leeches were applied to the eye to reduce the inflammation, but an ulcer formed on the cornea and then burst, causing permanent damage. 'After hearing what I did tonight,' Harriet told Granville, 'I can bear anything. If you could but see how well she bears the greatest tortures, tho' hopeless, you would admire and love her more than ever.' The 'tortures' inflicted by the surgeons were not of a kind to enhance the reputation of late-eighteenth-century medical science in the eyes of later generations, and did nothing to save Georgiana's sight, which remained blurred in one eye for the rest of her life. Harriet, her mother and Bess took turns at Georgiana's bedside, Lady Spencer reluctantly pronouncing Bess 'a most tender nurse'. Caro, the only child in the house at the time, was alarmed to see Bess faint 'from fatigue and anxiety'. The Cavendish children remained at Worthing throughout their mother's ordeal; to prepare them against the shock of seeing her, Bess wrote Little G. a carefully-worded letter in which she made light of the whole appalling episode, assuring her that though the eye had 'certainly been in some danger', it was 'now nearly its proper size again'. Georgiana had to undergo two more operations before the year was out.

Debilitated, disfigured and partly blind, Georgiana turned her back on the world. Her letters show her at her most contented when at home with the Duke, her children and Bess. Her reliance on Bess she made painfully clear in a sad little poem written when she was fearful of losing her sight entirely.

> I regret not the freedom of will,
> Or sigh, as uncertain I tread;
> I am freer and happier still,
> When by thee I am carefully led.
>
> Ere my Sight I was doomed to resign,
> My heart I surrendered to thee;
> Not a Thought or an Action was mine,
> But I saw as thou badst me to see.
>
> Thy watchful affection I wait,
> And hang with Delight on Thy voice;
> And Dependance is softened by fate,
> Since Dependance on Thee is my Choice.

In October 1796 Bess received the news that John Foster had died. It may be that she was prepared for it, as the previous year he had come to London for a major operation; Lord Sheffield, as a friend of the Foster family, had kept Bess informed of his progress. Anxious 'to exchange mutual forgiveness' with her husband, she asked to see him, but Georgiana intervened on the grounds that Bess was not well enough for such an ordeal. Foster recovered from the operation, but it prompted him to make a will. By law, a widow had no rights over her children unless her husband's will made her a guardian: Bess urged Lord Sheffield to find out if she was named. 'Now that his danger is over it really will not affect me . . .' Her anxiety is understandable, in view of the ample evidence that John Foster had for years prevented her from either seeing or communicating with her sons. (For a while she had secretly written to Fred, the eldest boy, but Foster found out and put a stop to it.) There is no record of Lord Sheffield's response, and when Foster died Bess was told that he had left her nothing in his will, not even a memento. A certain Mrs Elizabeth Casey, however, was generously provided for – as were her two daughters. Bess complained to Lord Sheffield that she had not seen the will, assuming it was because 'there was Mrs Casey nam'd in it'. She added, 'poor Soul, my first hope was that she was provided for', which implies that she had known about her. With a generosity worthy of Georgiana, she also hoped that if there were any children, 'something may be done for them'. John Foster had left the bulk of his estate to his own sons.

As Bess was not named in the will, she had to await a decision by the boys' guardians as to whether she would be allowed to see them. In the event, they were allowed to make only a brief visit to London. While Bess waited nervously for the day of their arrival, she wrote Fred an intensely loving letter sympathising with him over the death of his father and expressing her longing to see him and his brother. 'My friends the Devonshires', she added, 'beg you would accept of an apartment both at Chiswick & in their house in Town.' Georgiana also wrote to Fred, urging him to make haste as any 'disappointment or delay' would be fatal to their mother's health. Bess had been suffering from a 'hemicrania', a pain affecting one side of the head, generally brought on by nerves and anxiety. (She claimed to have cured it with 'an extract of bark in pills with ginger tea'. 'Bark' – 'Peruvian bark' – cinchona bark – was an eighteenth-century cure-all, recommended for everything from fevers to scrofula. Unlike many such popular remedies, it had genuine value as a tonic and febrifuge.)

'I have seen, I have embraced, I have then recovered my children!' Bess exulted in her journal on 29 December 1796. Georgiana described the reunion to Little G.: 'They clung about poor Bess, who cried terribly . . . They are interesting creatures . . . Augustus is a very fine pretty boy [he was tall and blue-eyed], but I like the entertaining affectionate looks of Fred. They have very little brogue & seem to adore her.' Bess's letter to Little G., written later that night, is surprisingly calm: 'You will conceive my happiness my dearest G. at having *my sons* with me . . . I know Fred is not handsome, but Augustus is charming, & the manners of both are very engaging.' Lady Bristol, too, delighted in her daughter's joy, remarking significantly, 'You happy will be a novelty indeed', then adding, 'but you have been patient under your sufferings as a wife, you have done your utmost to perform your duty as a mother, and I doubt not but that Providence has in store a reward for you, *more especially* as you think yourself undeserving of it.' Ten days into the boys' visit, Bess recorded: 'As to the Duke & my dear G. they behave to them with their usual kindness & attention to all that belongs to me – and they are as *enfants de famille.*'

It was one thing for Georgiana and the Duke to welcome the Foster boys as members of the family, but the Cavendish children probably eyed the two large youths of nineteen and sixteen – with their provincial manners and 'very little' brogue – in some bewilderment. Since there was no rational explanation for Bess's presence in their midst, how could they possibly make sense of this fresh invasion? For Fred and Augustus the effect of being transplanted from their Irish backwater to one of London's most magnificent houses must have been overwhelming. The Duke was impossibly grand, Georgiana unbelievably glamorous, the two Cavendish girls (now aged thirteen and eleven) unnervingly clever and sophisticated, and Caro St Jules sweetness itself (Bess had told them that Caro was adopted, not that she was their half-sister). Most remarkable of all, living as of right amid all this splendour, was the mother they had not seen for fourteen years and, in Augustus's case, did not remember.

No sooner had the boys returned to Ireland than Bess renewed her attempts to persuade their guardians to allow them to complete their education in England. Lord Sheffield again acted as her intermediary, supporting her in her shrill complaints against them for keeping her sons from her. She finally succeeded: both boys went up to Oxford in 1797, and two years later Augustus joined the Horse Guards.

Bess's affectionate correspondence with Little G. continued for some years, but as the Cavendish girls matured, their acceptance of Bess turned to a sharper assessment of her role within the family, especially on Haryo's part. 'Dear Lady Liz' became 'a certain lady', and descriptions by Little G. of comfortable hours spent in Bess's room 'talking and drawing till dinner time' are succeeded by such sneering remarks from Haryo as '*my dear 'ady 'iz may chance* to give us a *spinkum spankum over her knee*'. (That so-called Devonshire House drawl irritated Haryo when Bess used it, but not when her mother did.) There were other causes for their resentment: her intimacy with their mother, which at times must have seemed to exclude them; her horrid little dogs; the fuss everyone made when she was ill. Nor can it have helped that Bess had retained her beauty while Georgiana was losing hers. And why did they have to put up with so many of her relations? Jack's widow was a particular target of Haryo's. 'Lady Hervey was here last night,' she told Little G., 'more odious than ever in a bright purple gown . . .' But even Haryo could find no fault with Lady Hervey's daughter, Bess's adored niece Eliza.

If Bess found the hostility of Haryo and Miss Trimmer intimidating, she could not afford to show it. To set up house on her own and educate her children was way beyond her means; nor would separation from the Devonshires have been conceivable on emotional grounds. But while the essential cosiness of the *ménage à trois* remained unchanged, subtle shifts of balance had occurred since the exiles' return. As Georgiana's closeness to her elder daughter grew, her dependence on Bess declined. Little G. was shortly to make her debut in society, and launching her successfully on the marriage market would take all Georgiana's time and energy. There was no place for Bess in this operation, or in Georgiana's other activities and interests – her studies in mineralogy (begun while she was at Lausanne and continued in Italy), the redecoration of Devonshire House, and the development of the garden and dairy at Chiswick. In early 1797 Georgiana suspected that she had miscarried, so it would seem that another of her activities was sleeping with her husband. By the end of that year, Lady Spencer was able to tell Miss Trimmer: 'I have not for many years seen the D. and Dss so happy in each other . . . he listens often with attention to her conversation with other people, and I often see a cheerful whisper between them . . . and in her last headache he was in and out of her room perpetually to know how she did . . .' The Duke was also taking a more active interest in his children.

So where did all this conjugal and familial felicity leave Bess? Not out in the cold, exactly, but perhaps she felt less necessary to either Georgiana or the Duke than at any time since their first meeting in 1782. When John Foster died and Richmond's wife looked as if she were about to follow suit, society was quick to tie the knot between Bess and Richmond. The Duchess's frail health had given rise to speculation before: 'I know when she was ill last year,' Georgiana wrote to her mother in late 1795, 'every body thought he would marry again but I think not. He is so fond of Charles [his nephew], & besides so wrapp'd up in Miss le Clerc . . .' Henriette le Clerc was Richmond's daughter by his French mistress; though she was never openly acknowledged as such, from an early age she had lived with him and the childless Duchess as an adopted orphan.

It has been suggested that Bess set her cap at Richmond because it had long been her ambition to be a duchess in her own right – that she was jealous of Georgiana and tired of living in her shadow. While it cannot be denied that Bess seems to have had a partiality for dukes (counting Dorset, Richmond made her third), it is far more likely that she was running *away* from the situation at Devonshire House rather than specifically *to* the Duke of Richmond. Marriage to Richmond would provide her with the status and long-term security she lacked with the Devonshires. And despite the difference in age between herself and Richmond (he was twenty-three years her senior), there were numerous reasons why the match made sense. Richmond had been a member of the Devonshire House Circle for years; Bess's family, especially her mother, were often guests at Goodwood; like Bess, he was 'prodigiously' fond of dogs, and a keen patron of literature and the arts (of Romney in particular, who painted Bess sometime in the 1790s). And, yes, the prospect of being mistress of Goodwood House and an estate at Aubigny in France – though not of his house in London, which had been destroyed by fire in 1791 – was not wholly without charm.

It would have been unthinkable for Bess to marry Richmond without the approval of Georgiana and the Duke, and by early 1798 such a marriage was clearly seen as a real possibility. Harriet, however, viewed it with 'great anxiety'. To Granville she confided that while nothing had been settled between Bess and Richmond, 'It seems quite a separation from us all, and changing the habits of fifteen years' standing is always a serious thing, especially at our age . . .' But a year later Lady Webster (now Lady Holland) noted in her journal: 'He [Richmond] is a strange, odd man. His conduct to Ly E. Foster is very unaccountable. He is always talking and writing as if he intended to marry her, and yet the marriage is not more advanced than it was two years ago.' James Hare was also frustrated by Richmond's delay. 'I wish the Duke of Richmond would make a wise use of the new house he is building,' he told Georgiana in September 1800 (Richmond was adding two wings to Goodwood House). Georgiana, however, told Little G. that Richmond had not only satisfactorily explained his conduct to Bess, but also reassured her of his 'friendship and esteem and attachment'. Bess, her doubts dispelled, hung on, though she admitted to her son Augustus that at times she felt 'very uncomfortable'. Her life with the Devonshires continued as before, the only difference being that she made a number of visits to Goodwood.

What either of Bess's parents thought of the proposed match is unknown. For some time her father had been pursuing an erratic course around the Continent, dodging the various warring armies, hobnobbing with Frederick II, King of Prussia (whom he later dismissed as a 'lump of inert matter'), and furiously denouncing the French republicans as baboons and orang-outangs. 'Nothing can equal the Déroute [overthrow] of the damned Blackguard, pilfering, plundering, pillaging Republicans,' he ranted to Bess, recommending that France should be rendered harmless by cutting it in two: a republic north of the Loire, a monarchy south of it. Immediately on his arrival in Italy, he embarked on another of his lavish shopping sprees, buying works of art and antiquities for the house at Ickworth. Though still a figment of his imagination, it had become an obsession, and his desire for Bess's aesthetic advice appears to have eased relations between them. Despite his respect for her taste, they did not always agree; to her plea for the house to be built of white stone brick, he exclaimed: 'What, child, build my house of a *brick* that looks like sick, pale, *jaundiced* red brick, that would be red brick if it could . . .' Certainly not; he would cover the house with 'Palladio's *stucco*'.

The house at Ickworth was not her father's only obsession: in 1796 he wrote Bess a series of letters pressing her to encourage her brother Frederick to marry 'the beautiful, elegant, important, and interesting object I have proposed to him'. The 'object' in question was the illegitimate daughter of the Prussian king by his long-term mistress Madame Ritz – a lady of bountiful charms with whom the Earl-Bishop had formed a friendship considered by many to be rather too warm. The marriage, he declared, would bring Frederick '£5,000 down, £5,000 more in reversion, an English Dukedom' and numerous royal connections. At the start of his campaign, Lord Bristol blithely forgot his designation of his son as 'ungrateful and undutyful', and credited him instead with every noble and superior quality known to man; that Frederick had already bestowed his affections on another, one Elizabeth Albana Upton, was immaterial. As he accuses Bess of being a 'nasty little Imp of Silence', it would seem that she disapproved of his mad plan, as did Frederick, who stuck stoutly to his guns and married Miss Upton. Whereupon Lord Bristol – the supreme egoist – accused poor Frederick of sacrificing a life of unimaginable riches to indolence and 'mere Egoism'.

In March 1798 there was a fresh eruption from the Earl-Bishop: Bess received a frantic letter informing her that part of his priceless collection of art treasures – which included 'pictures, statues, busts and marbles without end, first-rate Titians and Raphaels, dear Guidos, and three old Carraccis . . .' – had been seized by the French, and that he would be 'on thorns' if she did not pull every string available to her, from Pitt to the Duke, to secure its release. 'As to the Duke of Richmond,' he added darkly, 'I do not suppose he has now any interest, else he could refuse you nothing.' Bess must have wished her father's letter at the bottom of the English Channel. But it was the last she received for some time; shortly after it was written he was arrested by the French and confined in the citadel at Milan for nine months. For a man who believed himself to be utterly above the law, it must have been a shock to find himself in prison. The specific charge is unknown, but as he made no secret of his hatred of Napoleon and the republican 'orang-outangs', and actively spied on them for the British, the French authorities probably felt his confinement was long overdue.

The Earl-Bishop's view of Napoleon was not shared by Bess. In spite of herself, her admiration for him was growing. 'Bonaparte shews himself a great man, much too great for the enemies of France.' But she admitted that she admired him more 'amidst the Pyramids of Egypt' than when he was trampling through her beloved Italy.

At the end of 1796 Britain had stood alone against Republican France. Fears of an invasion were rife, and when the French made a brief landing in Wales in March 1797, Bess – who was at Bath with her younger sister – told Georgiana, 'Louisa and I feel as if we were going to be carried off!' Visiting the dying Edmund Burke the same year, she had found him so frightened that he had 'contriv'd hiding places in the cellar'. She had also been alarmed by the naval mutinies at Spithead and the Nore: 'This is the moment of the greatest danger that we have known, for if our Navy fails us, what is to protect England against French invasion.' But the Royal Navy did not fail; news of Nelson's great victory at the Battle of the Nile in August 1798 restored the nation's confidence. 'Nelson has turned all our heads,' Georgiana told her mother. The head most turned was Bess's, whose regard for Nelson increased over the years until it verged on hero-worship. Invited by Lady Hamilton, in late 1800 she took Caro and Clifford to meet him during one of his brief spells ashore. 'His countenance is interesting & animated,' she wrote in her journal, 'his manner simple & unaffected. He is cover'd with wounds and is of a slight rather delicate make . . .' Tactfully, she makes no mention of either his diminutive stature or his dearth of upper teeth. Emma Hamilton had a knack of turning up in Bess's life. They had first met at Bath in 1791, when Bess, though impressed by her 'attitudes', had thought her 'coarse and

1. Lady Elizabeth Foster, by Joshua Reynolds. By 1787, when the portrait was exhibited at the Royal Academy, Bess was already established at Devonshire House and had given birth to her first illegitimate child by the Duke

2. Frederick, 4th Earl of Bristol, Bess's volatile and eccentric father, painted in 1790 by the celebrated society portraitist Élisabeth Vigée Le Brun. Vesuvius, seen smoking in the distance, was one of the Earl-Bishop's many obsessions

3. Elizabeth, Countess of Bristol, Bess's mother, painted in Rome in 1779 by Anton von Maron. Lady Bristol has begun to show signs of the fatigue and melancholy which prompted the Earl-Bishop to cease calling her his 'Excellent' and refer to her instead as a 'majestic ruin'

4. John Augustus, Lord Hervey, depicted in naval uniform by Gainsborough. Bess adored her volatile and philandering brother Jack, and continued to grieve for him for years after his death at the age of thirty-nine

5. Bess's first husband, John Thomas Foster, miniature by John Downman. Temperamentally unsuited, the couple separated after five years of marriage. By law, Bess had to surrender her two children to their father, and did not see them again for fourteen years

6. Georgiana, Duchess of Devonshire, depicted as the goddess Diana by Maria Cosway (detail). Painted in 1782, the year Georgiana and the Duke first met Bess, it was considered to be the only portrait to capture her extraordinary charm

7. William Cavendish, 5th Duke of Devonshire, miniature by Hone after Reynolds. His remoteness and lethargy were legendary, yet Bess was devoted to him: 'For him and him alone I love, can love, or ever have truly and fondly loved'

8. This drawing by Richard Cosway of Bess (*right*) and Georgiana dancing highlights the difference between the two women in both personality and appearance. Cosway depicts the Duke, habitually dignified and reserved, gaily cavorting with his wife and mistress

9. Devonshire House in Piccadilly, the London home of the Duke and Duchess of Devonshire, where Bess spent many years of her life

10. Lady Georgiana (Little G), and her younger sister Lady Harriet (Haryo) Cavendish, brought up at Devonshire House together with Bess's two illegitimate children by the Duke

11. Edward Gibbon, from a portrait by Reynolds. His masterpiece, *The Decline and Fall of the Roman Empire*, inspired Bess's love of Rome and its Classical past. Though twenty years her senior, Gibbon was captivated by Bess, and shortly before his death found her 'as seducing as ever'

12. James Hare, after Reynolds. Witty, mischievous but unfailingly humane, he was one of the leading personalities in the Devonshire House Circle. To Bess he was a 'bright star', a much-loved friend and confidant until his death in 1804

13 and 14. A sketch of Georgiana by Bess, found pinned inside her journal for 1793.
When Georgiana was banished abroad by the Duke for becoming pregnant by Charles
Grey, Bess accompanied her, with her daughter Caro, into exile. Returning in 1793,
their crossing of the St Gothard Pass inspired Georgiana to write an epic poem, later
published by Bess and illustrated with lithographs, such as this one (*below*) of Tesino,
made from her own watercolours

gros, et tu eus un peu peur
mais enfin nous arrivâmes
de l'autre coté, ou 2de gdady
Duncannon et ta petite
amie Caroline Ponsonby nous
attendoit, ce fut un moment
heureux — L'approche de
Nice est très jolie, La Ville
est situé au bord de la
mer, et aux pieds des Alpes
des montagnes très hautes
s'élèvent derrière la Ville,

Nice 1793

15. A page from Bess's journal for 1793, adorned with one of her jewel-like watercolours. This journal, kept during her period of exile abroad with Georgiana, is written in French and addressed to her daughter Caro St Jules, whose early childhood was spent in France

16. Frederick Foster, Bess's idle but endearing eldest son. A *bon viveur* and bibliophile, he shared his mother's passion for Rome and its antiquities

17. Augustus, Bess's second son by John Foster. Reunited with his mother at the age of sixteen, he later became a diplomat and spent many years abroad. His letters to Bess, the majority of them previously unpublished, supply clues to her life and character not found elsewhere

18. Harriet, Countess of Bessborough, Georgiana's sister and a close friend of Bess. The three women were inseparable. 'I believe there never existed a stricter confidence and friendship than there has for many years between my sister, Ly Elizabeth and myself,' Harriet wrote

19. The French writer Madame Germaine de Staël first met Bess in 1789. Though they corresponded from time to time, it was not until Germaine's visit to England in 1813 that they became friends. 'The greatest of all pleasures', she told Bess, 'is to pass an hour *tête-à-tête* with you'

20. Clifford, Bess's illegitimate son by the Duke. A devoted son, husband and father, he rose to the rank of admiral in the navy. 'It is not his brother Officers alone,' Nelson told Bess in 1805, 'but all the Sailors, all love him who come near him'

21. Bess's daughter Caro with her husband George Lamb (*right*) and brother-in-law William (*left*), later Lord Melbourne, painted by an unknown artist in the drawing-room of the Lambs' home, Melbourne Hall in Derbyshire

22. William Cavendish (Hart), 6th Duke of Devonshire, drawn by Filippo Agricola in Rome in 1823, a year before Bess's death. As the acknowledged 'queen' of Roman society and a notable patroness of the arts, Bess introduced her stepson to numerous leading figures, including the great neo-classical sculptor Antonio Canova

23. Marble bust of Cardinal Ercole Consalvi, modelled by Bess's friend, the Danish sculptor Bertel Thorwaldsen. In profile, the bust clearly shows the strength of the man hailed by many as one of the century's greatest statesmen

24. The Roman Forum, detail from an engraving in Bess's de luxe edition of Virgil's *Aeneid*. The figure of a woman holding a book, a small dog at her heels, is almost certainly Bess visiting her excavation of the base of the Column of Phocas, seen in the centre

25. The Column of Phocas, illustrated in Giuseppe Valadier's book on the most outstanding buildings of ancient Rome. The drawing shows the pyramid of eleven marble steps which were uncovered by Bess's excavation

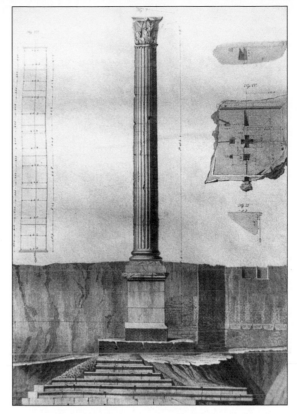

26. Clifford's three eldest children, William, Spencer and Bella, with Vesuvius in the distance. This delightful picture was painted during the months Bess spent at Naples with Clifford and his family in 1822

27. Bess, drawn by Thomas Lawrence in 1819 during the months he spent in Rome painting portraits of Pius VII and Consalvi for the Waterloo Chamber at Windsor Castle. Bess had known Lawrence since 1782, when she asked him to make a drawing of the two Foster boys shortly before they were taken back to Ireland to live with their father

vulgar'. At that time Emma was Sir William Hamilton's mistress; when their paths crossed in 1793 at Naples she was his wife; by the time they met again, in London, she was Nelson's mistress. (Perhaps unknown to Bess, she had also been the recipient of skittish letters from the Earl-Bishop who, tiring of his *amitié amoureuse* with Madame Ritz, had transferred his attentions to his old friend's lovely young wife.)

The war with revolutionary France brought civil strife, inflation, increased taxes, and a revolution in fashion. Women dressed in high-waisted gowns of Classical simplicity, while men abandoned pow-dered hair and gorgeous silks for simple riding-coats, breeches and top-boots. In the army, powdering – which consumed one pound of precious flour per head per week – was abolished in 1804; liveried footmen were among the few who still wore powdered hair. By some oversight, Harriet Bessborough failed to pay the new tax on powder for her servants and was fined. Granville, going against the trend, cut off his hair altogether and took to wearing a wig; Harriet begged him not to wear it too tight, as 'it will incline your nose to bleed'. A pro-posed tax on watches provoked an anxious letter from Hart to his father, asking him to pay it for him, for 'if not I must give my watch away I do not care much about it but all I know of the matter is that I cannot pay taxes without Money'.

In May 1797 Bess had noted that 'Ireland continues in a wretched and turbulent state...' A year later, United Irishmen and Catholic Irish nationalists rebelled against British rule. On a personal level, the rebel-lion threatened the Duke's Irish estates; on a political level, the Whigs, as the party pledged to Catholic emancipation, were opposed to the use of repressive measures against the largely Catholic population. Georgiana and Bess urged the Duke to make a speech in the House of Lords supporting the Duke of Leinster's motion for an inquiry into the state of Ireland. The Duke reluctantly agreed. 'This has satisfied us all,' Bess wrote, 'but the Dss and I, though confident of his speak-ing well . . . yet feel nervous about it.' The speech, however, was a success. 'The Dss & I are so pleas'd & happy.'

The personality of the Duke of Devonshire remains tantalisingly obscure. He left little of himself on paper, others only occasional glimpses of him. His apathy and reserve seem beyond dispute; George Selwyn once described him at a dinner at Devonshire House sitting like a statue, 'never changing a muscle of his face'. But this was his public persona; those close to him, like Fox and James Hare, loved and respected him for his learning, benevolence, and passion for justice. 'Mr Hare', Bess wrote, 'often says that he thinks the D.D. has the best sense & Judgement of any body he knows – & added to that good taste & much real humour.' Caro's description of him, written before she knew he was her father, is perhaps the most endearing: 'I have often remarked that folly & untruth are the two things that amuse him most from being so totally foreign to his nature; that he examines a liar & a fool with the sort of curiosity, interest & entertainment that any other person would a savage from some distant unknown country.'

Georgiana's years of retreat had gradually restored her confidence. The French writer Chateaubriand described her as 'still fashionable & beautiful, though deprived of an eye, which she covered with a lock of her hair'. In May 1800 Little G., now eighteen, was presented at Court, gowned in white crêpe and dripping with the Cavendish diamonds, and in June there followed a great ball at Devonshire House, triumphantly stage-managed by Georgiana. One of the guests, the Earl of Carlisle's son and heir Lord Morpeth, was already showing an interest in Little G. A month later at Chiswick Georgiana gave one of her breakfasts, charming, informal affairs typical of her light touch and sense of style. 'Several Bands of Musick were very well placed in the garden,' Lady Jerningham told a friend, 'so that as soon as you were out of the hearing of one Band, you began to catch the notes of another; thus Harmony always met your ears.' For Bess, the chief object of interest was Monsieur, the late King's youngest brother, whom she had last seen at Versailles three weeks before the fall of the Bastille and who was now living in exile in Britain. She was impressed by the change in him: there were no signs of the previous dissipation; instead, dignity in his misfortune and a quiet optimism for the future.

Periods of calm in Georgiana's life always seemed to end with a spectacular crisis: in August 1800, Harriet gave birth to Granville's child. She had somehow contrived to hide the pregnancy from her husband and mother; to mask the actual birth, she claimed to have fallen downstairs (and may, indeed, have done so). The baby, a girl, was immediately handed over to foster parents. Bess, who had been in on the secret from the first, was at Bognor with Caro and Fred. Desperate for news of Harriet, she wrote to Little G. (who had also known of her aunt's pregnancy) at Devonshire House: 'Oh my G. write me what you know & how you think your dear M[other] & poor dear aunt are in health, and how your aunt bears all this . . .' Bess, about to visit the

Duke of Richmond at Goodwood, added that she was glad Little G. liked him, as 'he is deserving of love & esteem'.

The visit to Goodwood was marred by Richmond's gout, and Bess was in any case impatient to return to London in order to welcome to England the late Madame de Polignac's family – her son Jules, daughter the Duchesse de Grammont and granddaughter Corisande. Georgiana, at Chatsworth with the Duke, asked Bess to escort the French trio north. 'This will prevent my going round by Ickworth,' Bess wrote in her journal, 'which I had intended doing to see my dear Mother, but on my return I mean to stop there.'

Bess arrived at Chatsworth with the French contingent in late November 1800. 'With what delight I enter'd the park gates, & through the snow frozen on our windows shew'd [them] the gardens, then the House with its cheerfull lights & blazing fires . . . Then the Dss came flying down to the Library to see us.' Bess found 'D.D. uncommonly well; my dear G. calmer & happier, & much wit is going on with Ld John & her [and] Mr Hare (who is wit personified).' Georgiana told her mother that with twenty-three people in the house, not counting the children, they were consuming '15 sheep and 2 oxen in the week . . . Our great deficiency is in eggs.' The Duke played billiards with his children, and 'Every night we have musicals.' To the delight of all, Lord Morpeth proposed to Little G. and was accepted. Jules de Polignac flirted with Caro, and one day kissed her. 'I thought it right to resent this', she wrote in her memoirs, 'as an amazing liberty, and wrote to him, I believe, a very vindictive letter about English girls and English manners. He took it good humouredly, we made it up and remained friends.'

In the midst of all this gaiety, Bess received the shocking news of her mother's death. For five days her journal remained silent, then on 24 December she wrote: 'I still keep my room. I cannot talk or write of my sad, sad loss. My angel Mother – Oh God – never did Parent so absolutely possess the love & respect . . . & adoration of her children.' On 1 January she at last explained how she had heard the news: 'It was quite sudden, and sudden was my hearing of it. A letter from my sister Louisa said, "our sad loss" – I knew not what it was – turned the page – saw, "our Mother" – I could no more. I lost my reason – almost my life.' A letter of 31 December from her brother Frederick described how Lady Bristol had suffered 'a Violent Spasm in her stomach'. Brandy and water had been administered, but to no avail. She had died 'without a struggle'. Georgiana told the Duke of

Richmond that the shock 'very nearly deprived me of my Dearest friend. Her convulsions were dreadful . . . We keep her quite quiet & under the influence of Laudanum.' Bess poured out her grief and regrets to Richmond, writing him five letters in January alone. Reduced to a 'mere creature of feeling & affection', she refers to the 'unreserv'd kindness of all around me . . .' Her only consolation was that one of her mother's last letters had stressed what a comfort Bess had always been to her. At her most maudlin she vows to Richmond that she will leave 'this dear country for ever. Caroline will [have] abler protection from the D. & Georgiana than I could give her.' (Clifford was now living at Devonshire House, so it is odd that Bess mentions only Caro.) Apparently a letter had been left for her father which she wanted to deliver to him personally: 'I would if I could be with him when he receives it.' Her words hint at an element of retribution: she undoubtedly believed that his treatment of her mother had caused her endless suffering.

Little G. was to be married to Lord Morpeth in March and Georgiana wished to return to London to make the arrangements; but who would look after the Duke, too ill with gout to travel? Bess offered to remain at Chatsworth, although she admitted to Richmond that she was 'aware how much it may renew old stories, and he [the Duke] has been uneasy about it, but I have told him how little I mind if it does so . . .' Then, in a sentence which suggests a readiness to relinquish the past and move on, she adds: 'For myself I feel a gratification in having an opportunity of shewing how deep I feel the excessive kindness of all his conduct to me.' Apparently she was still looking to Richmond for her future.

9

A fragile peace
1801–1805

'I had always the fear of this separation, & now you see
how it prolongs itself – yet you will not let it continue
beyond my bearing. I am sure you will not.'

Georgiana to Bess, 18 February 1803

Bess was correct in her assumption that her remaining alone with the Duke would 'renew old stories'. But in her absence from London, her interests were ably championed by James Hare:

> You will not be surprised to hear that your staying at Chatsworth gives rise to many illnatured remarks [he wrote in February]. I always defend you by saying, that if there was any grounds for the stories one has heard so often about you & D. of D. nobody could blame you, who had been his mistress, for now being his Companion, or if necessary his Nurse; that if all these reports were mere scandal, it was not likely that anything should pass . . . now, which had not happened 16 or 17 years ago. This Argument has generally been triumphant.

It was Hare who broke the news that Pitt, after leading the country for seventeen years, had resigned over the King's refusal to grant Catholic emancipation. 'Never were times so extraordinary as the present,' Harriet wrote to Bess, thrilled by the prospect of months of political chaos and intrigue. 'I long for your coming & to tell you fifty thousand anecdotes.' The Duke was now well enough to travel, and he

149

and Bess hastened to London. To complicate matters, the King again showed signs of madness – 'whimsicality', as Hare put it. Was the country on the verge of another Regency Crisis? Fox, Bess noted in March, remained at St Anne's, 'more eager about the blossoms in his garden or a literary dispute than about Politicks'. Speculation was rife for three weeks, then the King recovered; Addington became leader of the government, and the ship of state was back on course. It had been exciting while it lasted, and Georgiana had enjoyed her return to the political fray in her old role of adviser and confidante.

In March Little G. married Lord Morpeth, and went to live with his family at Castle Howard in Yorkshire. Georgiana's loss of her daughter's close companionship was in no way replaced by any similar closeness with Haryo. Haryo, too, was miserable, and wrote to her sister constantly. Intent on making her letters amusing, she perhaps spiced her remarks with more malice than she actually felt. She was critical of everyone, but for Bess she began to reveal an increasing dislike. What irked Haryo most was her affectation, a fault admitted by Hare though excused on the grounds that it had become 'quite natural'. In a particularly waspish letter to Little G. from Bath in 1803, Haryo portrays Bess fussing over her little dog Sidney, feeding him scraps of chicken and debating whether she should fashion a little shawl for him in the 'Grecian' style. 'After all, my love,' Haryo concludes, 'why should not a silly affected dog be draped like a silly affected woman?' But it is when comparing Bess and Georgiana that Haryo's tongue is at its sharpest: 'Lady Eliz. and Sidney both unwell, both whining and both finally as agreeable as you know I always think them. Mama . . . kinder, more indulgent and more unlike the Lady or the Dog, than I can express.' Haryo's perception of Bess as being false should however be balanced against Hare's praise of her sincerity. 'If I were to say you are the best person alive,' he wrote to her, 'perhaps you would mistake my meaning, for I should not mean that you are better than all, but better than most; my reason for this explanation is, that when I asked you whether any particular kindness was intended when you said "dear" and "dearest", or whether there was any difference in your use of the words, you told me that you never confounded them, & that they had a very distinct meaning.' Haryo's view is laced with all the prejudices of a prickly eighteen-year-old, Hare's with the deep affection of an old friend.

There is no evidence that Bess ever acknowledged Haryo's dislike, still less that she complained of it to anyone; her response to a concern

expressed by Georgiana about Haryo's untidy appearance is not, however, devoid of implied criticism: 'Above all I think you should . . .
regulate her hours a little more – it is the extreme liberty she is allow'd
in every thing that also tends to the negligence of her person which
you lament.' Echoing the Earl-Bishop's views on the benefits of physical exercise, she recommends a programme of early rising, equitation
and a daily turn round the park – advice which would have caused
Haryo to snort with disgust.

To her own children Bess was loving, understanding and ceaselessly
encouraging – and they adored her. Fred once described her as having
'the most warm, kind and feeling heart that ever human being possessed'. Affectionate and very amusing, Fred showed a reluctance to
go into society or to take up a career. He went everywhere with Bess,
who referred to him fondly but a little sadly as 'my poor Fred'.
Augustus left the army when the Peace of Amiens was signed in 1802
and was preparing for entry into the diplomatic service by travelling
on the Continent. His letters show a young man groping towards
maturity, and developing a feeling for antiquity equal to his mother's.
They also show him to be in love with Corisande de Grammont,
Madame de Polignac's granddaughter, who had been given a home by
Georgiana when her mother contracted tuberculosis. Clifford was
proving exceptional. After two years at Harrow with Hart, at the age
of twelve he had entered the Royal Navy as a midshipman (a place
obtained by Georgiana's brother Earl Spencer, who may have been a
Tory but whose position as First Lord of the Admiralty was undeniably useful), and had already been to sea. In February 1801 Bess
received warm praise of him from Admiral Lord St Vincent: 'He has
considerable abilities, a heavenly temper and the most generous disposition I ever met with. He is beloved by every Officer in the Fleet,
justly so, & be assured that he will make a great man . . . His attention
to and his love of his profession are remarkable; in short in body &
mind he is a glorious Boy.' The combination of Cavendish and Hervey
genes had, it seemed, produced children who may have lacked fire and
brilliance but were remarkable for their sweetness of disposition.

Bess's life was not entirely devoted to children and politics: as a
woman of refined taste she enjoyed a rich diet of what Burke called
'works of the imagination and the elegant arts'. London in the latter
part of the eighteenth century had become one of Europe's most
exciting cultural centres, a mecca for foreign artists and musicians
attracted by the high fees and artistic freedom. Cultural delights were

no longer the preserve of the gentry and nobility: 'In London, every-thing is easy to him who has money and is not afraid of spending it,' Casanova had observed during a visit in 1763. The British Museum first opened its doors in 1759, the Royal Academy ten years later. Private picture galleries flourished along Pall Mall, booksellers and print-shops in the Strand. Music, once the glory of the private salon, could now be heard at public concerts or in the pleasure gardens of Vauxhall and Ranelagh. Georgiana and Bess regularly attended the Italian Opera at the King's Theatre in the Haymarket. The London theatre had been revitalized, first by Garrick with his reintroduction of Shakespeare, then by Goldsmith and Sheridan. Actors like Sarah Siddons and John Philip Kemble dazzled huge audiences at London's two main theatres, Covent Garden and the Theatre Royal, Drury Lane. When Sheridan's *Pizarro* was staged in 1799 at Drury Lane, it played to a capacity audience of 3,600.

The late eighteenth century also saw a remarkable increase in the range of literature available; novels (usually in two or three volumes) and pamphlets poured from the publishers, and were made more widely available by the new circulating libraries. Bess's letters and jour-nals contain frequent comments on the books she was reading. She admired Rousseau's *Mes Confessions*; the Duke read it, and 'mark'd it all through'. Choderlos de La Clos's scandalous and amoral *Les Liaisons dangereuses* was read hot off the press, as Georgiana foolishly confessed to Lady Spencer, who was horrified. Fanny Burney's three-volume novel *Evelina* and five-volume *Cecilia* were substantial companions on a long journey. 'Gothic' novels like Walpole's lurid *Castle of Otranto*, and Ann Radcliffe's tales of persecuted heroines, such as *The Mysteries of Udolpho*, were hugely popular among the ladies of Bess's circle. But novels were by no means her only form of reading; she was steeped in Shakespeare, Dante, Virgil, Horace, Herodotus and Homer; the first summer she spent with Georgiana they read together (in the orig-inal French, of course) the letters of Madame de Sévigné, the *Mémoires* of Madame de Maintenon and Pascal's *Lettres provinciales*. During long winter evenings at Hardwick they studied a Life of Mary Queen of Scots, then cheerfully embarked on an Italian translation of Caesar's Commentaries. When the Duke was laid up with gout, Bess soothed him with *The Dunciad*, Pope's satire on dullness.

Some time in 1801, Sir Thomas Lawrence began a large portrait of Bess. For some unknown reason the picture was not finished until 1805, when it was exhibited at the Royal Academy. (Bess's long association with Lawrence had begun in 1782 when the artist, still only thirteen years old, made a drawing of her two sons just before they were returned to their father in Ireland; it has since disappeared.) Lawrence depicted Bess as the Tiburtine Sibyl, resident pythoness of the temple at Tivoli. A magnet for the eighteenth-century tourist, these picturesque ruins held a special significance for Bess: she believed them to be the most beautiful in Italy, and in his endless quest for art and antiquities her father had actually bought the Temple of the Sibyl, intending to re-erect it in Ireland; the Papal authorities, however, in an early instance of export control, had prohibited its removal. The portrait has a theatrical quality, with none of the spontaneous charm achieved by Reynolds in 1787. Bess herself was unhappy about it, complaining to Augustus that Lawrence had painted her 'in such a tragedy queen dress, that . . . I have begg'd of [him] to change it, & am to go to him for that purpose'. Augustus replied: 'I am quite angry at Lawrence for having changed the Plan agreed about your Dress & shall write to him on the matter. I am surprized he has not written to me long ago to announce its being finished.' From Augustus's tone it would seem that he had either commissioned the portrait himself, or been involved in discussions about its content.

Had Bess not abandoned her journal between May and September 1801, there might be more clues to the unravelling of her relationship with the Duke of Richmond. Other entries for that year make no mention of him, but Haryo had an odd encounter which she described to Little G.: rushing into Bess's room expecting to find Caro, she surprised 'his grace erect with both arms stretched out and a little thin taylor running round and round him with a measure, and Lady E. with a look of agitated interest, unfolding a book of patterns. Taking it *all in all*, it was the most ridiculous thing I ever saw.' The final break with Richmond came in October. To Lady Melbourne, Bess explained her reasons for ending the affair: 'I am sorry that any part of my conduct makes D.R. unhappy, but he has himself alone to reproach for it, for certainly there was a time when his happiness was an object very essential to mine . . . His perverted way of seeing every thing, & the alienating systems he acted upon' had altered her feelings, however, and she had 'felt call'd upon to break thro' a situation which exposed me to much censure without in fact encreasing his comfort . . . *D.D. says I ought never to have gone there* [to Goodwood], *till he propos'd.* I could not bear however to do any thing that seem'd to urge this.'

Her next letter to Lady Melbourne lays the blame more precisely:

Richmond, she wrote, was 'so subdued by Henrietta . . . as not to dare to show me the marks of confidence & attachment which he really feels for me. He must be conscious of how wrong his conduct has been to me, tho' had he not luckily for me, broke thro' my romance by shewing me he had to a certain degree not only resisted but subdued his attachment to me, I might have long gone on as I did these four years.' Four months later she told Lady Melbourne she was quite certain Richmond now regretted his conduct, and that he confessed himself to be 'a helpless wretched Man'. She added revealingly: 'Lady C[harlotte] L[ennox] is an odious being & I should like to be certain of never seeing her again.' So it would seem that Lady Charlotte (wife of the future fourth Duke of Richmond) and the Duke's illegitimate daughter, Henriette le Clerc – whose winning ways apparently enslaved him from the moment he took her in as a child – had finally done for Bess.

At this stage Bess makes no mention of Richmond's mistress, his housekeeper Mrs Bennett. But a letter from Harriet to Granville, written a year later, shows that Mrs Bennett had almost certainly been a factor in the equation: 'The D. of Richmond was driving his housekeeper from Titensor . . . and was overturn'd, but luckily the Lady was fat, fell out first, and receiv'd him on her bosom, by which means he escap'd unhurt and she only a little bruiz'd. I hope this will be an argument for taking me in your Curricle. See how useful it is to chuse a plump companion that may prove a soft Cushion in case of accidents.' Mrs Bennett had the last laugh: in his will Richmond left her an annuity of £450 – a handsome bequest for a housekeeper – which must have come in useful in providing for the three daughters she had had by the Duke.

In October the Devonshires, the Bessboroughs, Bess, and all their various offspring travelled north to Hardwick. Perched on a lofty eminence, its great windows facing boldly into the westerly gales, the house was arctic in winter. Harriet, however, took a perverse delight 'in its gloom, its black velvet furniture, casements grown over with Ivy [and] floating Arras . . .' Caro recalled the deep snow, and the games they played in the Long Gallery, while Hart turned the Dining Room recess into a 'kind of menagerie', where he kept everything from rabbits to white mice. As he later recalled in his *Handbook*, 'The smell caused by these quadrupeds and their vegetable diet was overpowering . . . A tree stood in the middle for the unhappy birds . . . and an owl made its melancholy hooting in one of the corners.'

The whole party moved for Christmas to Chatsworth, where they were joined by numerous guests. Unknown to them all, this was to be the last of the great house parties assembled there by Georgiana and the Duke. It was a time of much wit and merriment, of continuous heavy snowfalls, of masquerades, of skating on the Canal Pond. Often confined to the house by the weather, the company huddled as near the fires as possible. Harriet described the scene to Granville: 'Sol [Lord Morpeth] and Jules playing at Chess, [Little] G. and John talking on the couch, Augustus asleep in the corner, Mr Hare in the great chair reading Dryden and discussing on *Alexander's Feast*, Bess by the fire reading Chénier . . . I am writing to you near the fire, and at times disputing with the whole room in turn. The rest of the family are variously dispos'd of; my Sister shut up with Gurdon; the Duke, tho' well, not up (at past five); Ld B[essborough] in his room, and Frederick hard at Euclid.'

The background for this scene was probably the Billiard Room, later described by Hart as a place where 'so many recollections crowd upon me, that I know not how to begin'. It contained a number of bookcases, the contents of which Georgiana did her best to keep in order – efforts which were mercilessly satirized by Hare:

> The Duchess is sorry to be obliged to request that no lady will appropriate to her own use more than twenty volumes at one time, as considerable inconvenience has arisen from the want of this limitation . . . N.B. Books written on serious subjects, and of use for the guidance of female conduct in all concerns of life, such as plays, romances, novels, familiar letters, and so forth, are not to remain in the possession of the same lady more than twenty-four hours. With respect to publications of a more frivolous nature, such as Newtons, Lockes, Paleys, and others of that stamp, the same strictness has not been found necessary . . . The Duchess takes this opportunity of acknowledging the great attention of all the gentlemen now at Chatsworth to the arrangement of the library, and observes with gratitude that not one of them ever looks into a book.

In her journal Bess pays tribute to Hare's unequalled wit, unerring judgement and 'exquisite sensibility . . . In his friendships he is [as] steady as he is warm & passionate in his attachments.' She was fortunate that this singular man counted her among his 'attachments'. To judge from his numerous letters to her, their friendship had intensified over the years. With her he discussed everything freely: politics, his neurotic wife Hannah, rascally son Charles and beloved daughters, and his rapidly declining health. His little daughter Sophie idolized Bess, calling her 'Lilibess Foster', a sobriquet occasionally adopted by her father.

In May 1802 Bess fell victim to one of her periodic fevers, and her journal entries ceased. The Duke succumbed to his most serious fit of gout to date and Hare, desperately anxious, made daily visits to Devonshire House. His cry that 'if any thing were to happen to him, we had better all hang or drown ourselves' is an indication of how much the Duke was valued by those close to him. Georgiana, though sympathetic to her husband, complained to Lady Melbourne that she was 'vex'd to see a man throw away such a constitution' by imprudence and mismanagement.

When Bess resumed her journal it was to continue her customarily lucid exposition of political events. Though her role in politics might not have been as active as Georgiana's, her extraordinary memory enabled her to record what passed, both inside Parliament and out, in a way which combined in some degree the accuracy of Hansard and the intimacy of Pepys. Trusted implicitly by the leading Whigs, she was frequently present at political discussions at Devonshire House. Not only discreet but loyal, she was a fierce defender of all members of the circle – except, latterly, Sheridan: 'Sheridan clouds his talents by a mean & pitifull love of tricks & by way of influence. His want of truth, his jealousy of Fox, & his total want of integrity about money have really lower'd him in [my] estimation.' She does not mention that he was now seldom sober, or that he persecuted Harriet with unwanted attentions.

After Addington succeeded Pitt in 1801 Fox had ended his self-imposed 'exile' from the House of Commons, and had once more become a frequent visitor at Devonshire House. He would go up to see the Duke 'with his hat on as usual', or settle down for a comfortable chat with Georgiana and Bess. 'We talked of novels,' she recorded. 'He said, "I don't read as many now as I us'd to do". "Oh Fie," said the Dss. "I only read them," said C. Fox, "in two cases – when Mrs Armistead is ill, & when I am in Town – but I am far from thinking that there is no good in the modern novels as most people do."' Bess had a profound regard for Fox, declaring that 'Never was human mind so truly great & magnanimous as his, so open & so undisguis'd.' Despite his openness, Fox had contrived to keep at least one important secret. Her account of its revelation is one of Bess's most vivid anecdotes:

A few days ago whilst Mr Hare was sitting with me, Dss D. came in & ask'd him if there was any news. 'I know such news,' he said, 'but I'll give you to guess. You,' he said to the Dss, 'who guesses well, now guess.' 'Is it a marriage? Your son, your daughter?' 'No, but you are near. The deed is done. I shall only tell D.D. – yes I will tell you both. I know both you & Lady E. are full of every right feeling.' 'Oh, is it C. F[Fox]?' I said. 'He is married,' continued Mr H., 'to Mrs Armistead.' We were silent a moment. I don't know rightly what was the feel – it was something of surprise – of regret, yet a hope that it was not of consequence. 'But how extraordinary', Hare said, 'it is – they were married 8 years ago!'

Society was stunned. Until she met Fox, Mrs Armistead had been one of the most sought-after courtesans in London, with a clientele which included the Prince of Wales. 'I suppose the jokes are endless,' Lady Holland remarked drily.

In March 1802 the Peace of Amiens had been signed between Britain and France. In reality it was more of a truce than a peace, simply a recognition that France controlled the land and Britain the seas. The Peace was the signal for a rush of Francophiles across the Channel, all eager (though loath to admit it) to catch a glimpse of Napoleon. Fox and his wife sailed in July, Hare in September. The Devonshires and Bess were to follow, but the Duke baulked at the last moment. He had become obsessed by his health, and instead of breasting each wave of illness now sank feebly beneath it. Bess had not been abroad for nine years, too long for such an inveterate traveller, and she was anxious to be within easier reach of her beloved niece Eliza, her brother Jack's only child, who had married Charles Rose Ellis in 1798 and borne him a second son in 1800; now, already in the last stages of consumption, she was wintering with her family and her mother, Lady Hervey, at Nice. Bess decided to go without the Devonshires, but accompanied by Fred and Caro. Augustus had gone to Paris in April, had met Napoleon – reporting to Bess that the first Consul had 'the air of a gentleman, and certainly the manners of one' – but had since left on his travels to Italy, Greece and Asia Minor. Clifford, now fourteen, had received orders to join his ship, the *Argo*: 'The dear Boy is in transports of Joy,' she told Augustus, 'tho' his eyes fill with Tears whenever he talks of leaving me.' Bess set off for Paris in October. Hare warned her that the city was 'much changed for the worse' and very expensive, and that 'the indecency of women's dress is shocking'. Poor Hare had been ill and depressed since his arrival, in no mood to appreciate the latest fashions.

Within hours of seeing Bess off at Dover, Georgiana wrote her the first of what became a series of despondent letters. 'Do you perfectly understand what it is to be once more separated by the sea? Since 87 we have breath'd the same atmosphere, and our separations have been always within the power of our own will to be reunited in a very few hours . . .' With Harriet's departure to join Bess in early December, and Little G's and Lord Morpeth's in January, Georgiana was bereft of all those on whom she most depended for love and support. Her health declined, she was crippled by headaches and suffered bouts of giddiness. Creditors beat at her door. Her eyesight was now so bad that her writing, Bess found, was often illegible. Some of the letters have been heavily censored, probably by Bess herself: the secrets remain secret, but Georgiana's despair is exposed to the world. 'Do you hear the voice of my heart crying to you? Do you feel what it is for me to be separated from you, or do new scenes and occupations obliterate the image of a poor, dull, useless, insignificant being such as myself? I never did feel more lonely.' A contributory factor to her unhappiness – and possibly one of the secrets later censored by Bess – is disclosed by Hare in a letter to the Duke from Paris: 'If the pursuit in which I am told you are engaged serves to amuse you . . . I shall rejoice in it as a proof of compleat recovery of health and spirits, and an excellent way of passing your time; but "if when the darling nymph is gone" &c &c . . . in short, if you are seriously in love, I am not sure that I shall enter into all your lovesick feelings.' The Duke, it seems, was having a fling, but with whom remains a mystery.

Bess did her utmost to respond to Georgiana's misery, and her replies were often couched in their special language. 'My dearest, dear G., we do indeed see by your letters that things have gone wrong but cannot guess what it has been. My heart aches when yours does & I grieve when oo do.' She worried about Georgiana's health: 'I don't like this nasty giddiness, yet I know Farquhar will make oo well, if oo will but mind him.' In an effort to cheer Georgiana, she filled her letters with Paris gossip and descriptions of the latest fashions. 'Gowns', she told her, 'are all round breasted, short waists, very often white sleeves to a coloured gown, of patent[?] lace or embroider'd muslin.' 'Oh my dear love,' Georgiana replied, 'what dear, dear letters. I am so happy when I receive them.' She kept them in a special book, arranged in date order. 'I only wish I had always kept them so . . .'

On her arrival in Paris, Bess took up residence in the Hôtel de l'Empire in the rue Cerutti. On her last visit in 1791 the royal family had been alive but imprisoned in the Tuileries. She was now shocked to see the republican tricolour flying above the palace, and a wooden frame marking the site of the guillotine in the Place de la Concorde. The gaunt ruins of La Madeleine, where the bodies of Louis and Marie-Antoinette had been consumed by quicklime, provoked morbid reflections. But she was delighted by the Grande Galérie in the Louvre. Opened to the public in 1801, the gallery contained the great master-pieces the Vatican and the Papal States had been forced to cede to Napoleon following his occupation of Italy. These included the *Apollo Belvedere* and the *Laocoön*, both of which Bess eulogized. (The reloca-tion of the centre of prostitution from the Tuileries to the gallery's entrance was a measure of its success.)

Bess soon began to revive old social connections and make new ones. The beautiful Madame Récamier, whose visit to London in June had caused a sensation, was among the first to ask her to dine, with Caro, receiving them – as was her custom – in bed. 'It was pleasant', Bess told Georgiana, '*mais un peu farce* . . . I sat down on the bed. She was very coaxing, & is I am afraid on the eve of some mess . . . After dinner she called me to her, and whilst she said in a very pretty voice, "My dear, I love you", the Gentlemen were kneeling, standing by and leaning over the bed.' Juliette Récamier's marriage to a wealthy banker twice her age had raised her from a bourgeois background to the heights of Parisian society. Habitually dressed in a cloud of white muslin, at once virginal and seductive, she remained tantalizingly elusive to countless aspiring lovers, who had included both Napoleon and his brother Lucien.

It was at Madame Récamier's that Bess first met Antonio Canova, the celebrated Venetian sculptor. 'His Statues may be placed with Grecian sculpture & not lose their merit,' she noted. He was in Paris to model Napoleon, a delicate assignment since he bitterly resented the First Consul's 'appropriation' of Italian art, particularly the four great bronze horses from St Mark's in Venice.

At a great dinner given by Talleyrand, Bess renewed her acquain-tance with Dominique de Denon, the inventor of the science of Egyptology and now director of the Louvre. He 'is our constant visitor', she told her sister Mary, 'and with his book open [*Voyage dans la Haute et Basse Egypte*] it is delightful to talk to and question him.' In her journal Bess ignores the dinner, devoting her entire entry to Denon. Intellectual stimulation now meant more to her than admira-tion and flattery, and she increasingly sought out personalities with an interesting tale to tell. While she clearly did not subcribe to the notion that women should pretend ignorance in order to flatter male egotism, she did not hesitate to use her charm to persuade men to talk. Several of the leading figures of the day – the royalist Camille Jordan ('delightfull, so natural & so full of feeling'), Adrien and Mathieu Montmorency, the Comte de Narbonne (once Madame de Staël's lover) and the generals Lafayette, Berthier and Moreau – willingly succumbed to her arts. Moreau joked about a half-hour call on Bess and Harriet that lasted until one in the morning.

Sadly for Bess, Madame de Staël was absent in Switzerland throughout her stay in Paris. Bess had just read her latest novel, *Delphine* ('I read it till I cried'). Augustus, dining with the leader of French intellectual society before she left the capital, had not been impressed. 'I was the only Englishman, we had a bad Dinner at a little low table – many of the men had boots. I don't admire Mad. de Staël much, she may have a vast deal of Esprit, but shews a vast deal too much of it I think, or in other words is a great *Bavarde* & in my humble opinion is a very disgusting woman.' Bess had replied: 'I agree with you in most things about Madame de Staël except that I don't think the word *bavarde* can apply to her; she talks too much, has not much pretension, but *bavarde* applys more to a person who talks a great deal without much sense or meaning – she talks too much, but yet talks well. Her ugliness too is against her.'

A report of the impact made on Parisian society by the Devonshire House ladies reached Haryo in London, who relayed it back to Little G. in Paris. 'Camille Jourdain [*sic*] says that you, Lady E. and my aunt, have all the *cleverness, vivacity* and *piquante charms* of what he fancies the ancienne noblesse of France to have possessed in their perfection, united to all the *truth, candour* and *solidity* of the English character.' A certain Madame de Cazenove d'Arlens paid Bess a similar compliment: 'Lady Foster is very popular here; it is true that nothing becomes a woman so much as a combination of English grace and French charm: the men in particular love her to distraction.' Such comments demonstrate the ease with which Bess mixed in Continental society. A true European, she flourished in the Parisian salons, where she found – in the view of Chateaubriand – 'that charming, swift, easy commerce of thought, that utter absence of arrogance and prejudice, that heedlessness of fortune and names, that natural level of all ranks, that equality of mind which makes French society incomparable . . .'

But it was her sightings of Napoleon that made the deepest impression on Bess. The first was at a parade. 'Our eyes were rivetted on him, who in plain uniform, attended & surrounded by his Generals . . . rode along the lines . . . He came under our windows. I could see the animation of his countenance tho' not the sweetness of his smile.' (To Augustus, however, she wrote: 'I wish Bonaparte would comb his hair.') She was able to observe him more closely one night at the theatre: 'I never saw a face it would be more impossible to overlook. I never saw one which bore a stronger stamp of thought, penetration & a daring mind.' Her last sighting was again at a parade. Berthier had promised to ask Napoleon to turn towards her. 'Caro and I caught his eye, & his smile is agreeable.' In her journal she admits that 'when he came up to where I was, I only thought of him as a Conqueror amidst his Troops & forgot the Tyrant.'

Though fascinated by the First Consul, at heart Bess was a royalist. In an attempt to recapture the past, she obtained a permit from Denon to visit Versailles with Caro and Fred. 'We drove in thro' the Court as I us'd to do, the noise of the wheels so powerfully recall'd those times that it made me quite shudder . . . The grass was growing every where in the Courts, half of the windows were boarded. The passage which led to Madame de Polignac's apartment was [as] silent & dark as the Cloister in a Convent. We heard only the echo of our own steps.' She was taken to see portraits of the royal family hidden away in a lumber room of the palace, and was overcome with nostalgia as she gazed upon Vigée Le Brun's resplendent painting of the Queen and her children. 'I left Versailles, my mind, heart & memory crowded & oppress'd with the variety of feelings, thoughts, recollections & regrets which a place so remarkable & a contrast so extraordinary occasion'd.'

In early February 1803 Bess received the news from Nice she had been dreading: 'All, all is over – on the second we had letters which told us of my almost insufferable loss. Oh, my Angel Eliza.' To Georgiana she wrote: 'It is losing my dear brother all over again.' There were other anxieties: she was worried by Hare's crippling asthma, and his daughter (in Paris with him) and Little G. were both ill. Bess nursed the girls devotedly. 'I thank you from the bottom of my heart my own dear Bess,' Georgiana wrote, 'but you have the best & most generous of hearts . . .' She was also running short of money, complaining that it 'melted like sugar'. An appeal to the Duke elicited the favourable yet convoluted response that 'whatever sum you may want will be paid by me with as much pleasure, and I may truly say with more, than I should advance it to answer any purpose of my own.'

At the end of February the Bessboroughs and Morpeths returned to England, while Fred left for Italy with Harriet's son, Duncannon. Bess was tempted to follow suit, having received a request from her father (plus money for the journey) to join him at Rome. But she lingered on in Paris, half hoping to receive a summons to go to Lady Hervey in Nice. No such summons came, but she received a pathetic plea from Georgiana: 'Come to us, come to the hearts that want you, that call you to bring comfort and pleasure to them by your presence . . . I do not mind it, as you may well imagine, but people want to persuade me you will not return, and I believe it is very much put about that we have quarrel'd.' A letter from the Duke was probably decisive: he expressed complete faith in her judgement as to what she should do, and assured her 'that the love and friendship that I have so long had for you, are firmly fixed and unalterable'. Such proof of the Duke's attachment was irresistible. Bess and Caro left Paris – accompanied by a young hairdresser named Rose, disguised as a woman, whom Bess wished to save from conscription into the French army – and arrived at Devonshire House on 25 April 1803.

Three weeks later the Peace of Amiens collapsed; war with France was resumed, and some ten thousand English tourists on the Continent were interned as 'spies'. In Paris, James Hare was placed under house arrest; Duncannon and Fred were arrested near Fréjus. Bess at once wrote to General Berthier asking for his help, and while all at Devonshire House waited anxiously for news, she sent Hare parcels containing 'Iceland Drops, Chocolate & Lozenges', and the English newspapers. 'It is impossible to thank you sufficiently for all your goodnature,' Hare replied. Despite his wretched health he admitted to Bess that he had not 'felt the slightest inconvenience from being a Prisoner'. Six weeks later all three 'spies' arrived safely in England; poor Berthier was 'shockingly scolded' by Napoleon for obtaining passports for Fred and Duncannon. The war had severed once again Bess's connection with a society in which she excelled. In June she received a sympathetic letter from Camille Jordan: 'You give me the impression of being the most conciliatory person in the world and I cannot conceive of your being capable of uttering the word *war* when your expression always seems to say: peace to all sensitive souls, tranquillity to those in love, comfort to those that suffer, succour to those in need.'

In August 1803 came news that Bess's father was dead. It was twelve years since she had seen him, years in which his behaviour had become increasingly bizarre. Catherine Wilmot, a young Irish girl who glimpsed him from the windows of her hotel in Rome, described his face as 'very sharp and wicked' as he sat 'in his carriage between two Italian women, dress'd in white Bed-gown & Night-cap like a witch & giving himself the airs of an Adonis'. The *Gentleman's Magazine* was less colourful, but probably more accurate: 'He wore a white hat edged with purple, a coat of crimson silk or velvet (according to the season), a black sash spangled with silver, and purple stockings.' One of his last letters to Bess demanded that she should despatch her son Fred to Paris to recover some of his valuable property, including fifty thousand livres 'swindled from me for a passport I never got', a superb painting by Claude 'filched' from him by Berthier, and his 'magnificent double barrell'd Gun'. Augustus, visiting his grandfather while on his travels in late 1802, had reported him to be surrounded by a pack of rascally servants and 'purchasing pictures by the dozen', some of them 'execrable'.

Death had come suddenly to the Earl-Bishop on the road from Rome to Albano: seized by a fit of his old enemy gout, and carried to a cottage, he was refused entry when the occupants realized he was a heretic bishop; he died a lonely death in a nearby outhouse. 'His kindness & affection to me I shall ever remember that was constant,' was Bess's only comment, a response markedly in contrast to the profound grief which had followed the deaths of her mother, her brother Jack and her niece Eliza. The father who had dissipated the family fortune on works of art and grandiose palaces, flirted with women half his age and emptied a tureen of pasta over a religious procession (he had an aversion to tinkling bells) was not the quirky and delightful parent of her youth but an embarrassment. Nor could she forgive his cruelty to her mother. Yet it was to him she owed her passion for art and her love of travel, two gifts which were to prove her greatest resource in years to come. Perhaps, too, she reread his vivid letters in her old age and recalled that, despite his egotism, volatility and erratic behaviour, he had possessed the courage to obey no rules but his own.

Arrangements were made to bury the Earl-Bishop at Ickworth, but the captain of the ship chosen to bring the body home had the seamen's superstitious dread of sailing with a corpse on board to contend with. His Lordship's mortal remains were therefore cunningly (and appropriately) concealed in a box marked 'antique statue'.

An obelisk was erected to his memory at Ickworth, the cost partly borne by his parishioners in Derry; the inscription recorded that 'he had endeared himself to all Denominations of Christians resident in that extensive Diocese', and that 'hostile sects which had long entertained feelings of deep animosity towards each other were gradually soften'd & reconciled by his Influence & Example'.

With the resumption of war, the threat of invasion returned to haunt Britain, and all things French were regarded with suspicion. Bess was summoned to the Aliens' Office and questioned by a Mr Reeves about her French servants, Laure and Rose – the young man she had smuggled to England. Mr Reeves was reproachful: Devonshire House, he told her, 'was consider'd as an asylum for all foreigners'. Bess was indignant. 'I said it was – for all whom we had known in prosperity & had now found in adversity . . .' Mr Reeves was didactic: ladies of high rank and fashion should not, he declared, protect foreigners who might be hostile to England. 'Certainly,' Bess countered, 'but that it also belong'd to Women of birth & education to protect those who were wronged & to set an example of justice . . .' Mr Reeves foundered, and 'I came off with flying colours,' Bess noted proudly. She was an excellent employer and generally kept her servants for many years. 'There never was so indulgent and good a mistress as Lady E.' was the verdict of the staff at Devonshire House.

In September Georgiana became seriously ill. For a week she was in agony. Harriet and Bess were at their wits' end; the surgeons, as usual, were baffled. Relief came when she passed a gallstone 'of a most extraordinary size'. Within a month she was back at the hub of political life, but her constitution, weakened by years of physical and psychological trauma, could not long withstand the pace of London. To aid her recovery, the Devonshires, Bess and their children spent the winter at Bath.

Bess's journals reveal a strong sense of the passage of time. The entries for each New Year's Day frequently open with an exclamatory sentence in Italian, the language in which she expressed extreme emotion or commemorated the death of a loved one; on 1 January 1804 it was her niece Eliza – not her father – she mourned. Her habit was to continue with a brief summary of the past year, and 1803 had been 'A year of anxiety, of hope & of many tears, yet soften'd & temper'd by kindness . . .' – a summary which might indeed have been applied to almost any year of her adult life. This time she added: 'Now is 22 years since these dear friends I am with were at Bath together . . .

& when first began our strong & unalterable friendship.' It would seem that factors which might have divided them – Georgiana's debts and her profound melancholy, the Duke's dalliance with the 'nymph' referred to so mysteriously by James Hare, and Bess's hopes of becoming Duchess of Richmond – had not caused any lasting damage, and they were content to sink back on to the safe and familiar ground of friendship and mutual need.

When Hare arrived at Bath in January, it was clear that he was desperately ill. By late February, when the Devonshires and Bess returned to London, he had rallied, but within three weeks he was dead. Bess was distraught. 'Never did a private loss excite more general sorrow and regret; but to those who really were his friends . . . the loss of such a Man & such a friend must ever be felt deep in the heart.' For Bess he had been a 'bright star', a friend from whom few secrets were hidden. He had loved and admired Georgiana, but his friendship with Bess was earthier, more intimate, and wholly without reserve. One of his last letters to her to have survived contains an enigmatic passage – made more so by the eradication of the sentence preceding it – which displays a remarkable blend of rough candour and deep affection: '. . . it cannot be necessary that I should abuse you, that I am interested about you as much as I can be about any one, & that I shall always be so, unless I should find that I have mistaken your character & that you are false, & deceitful, which would include (in your case) almost every other bad quality.'

In the midst of this private grief, the King went mad again. Devonshire House throbbed with the convulsions usual to it when a Regency seemed imminent, Georgiana wielding her influence to keep the Prince of Wales under control and the leading Whigs from tearing each other apart. As self-appointed chronicler of Whig politics, Bess sat up late into the night covering page after page of her journal. 'I am sick of politicks,' she exclaimed wearily, 'yet must write the story of today.' With the King's recovery, the crisis passed.

In October 1804 Augustus, still not cured of his love for Corisande de Grammont, left to join the British embassy at Washington. His letters to Bess reveal a genuine disdain for America and its society. 'Even you,' he told her, 'with all your resources and powers of self-amusement, would absolutely be puzzled here. You can bear many things, but you cannot bear vulgarity.' His way of remaining sane was to live on a diet of Shakespeare and Virgil. Bess fed his cultural starvation by regaling him with accounts of the latest phenomenon to hit

London, the thirteen-year-old actor William Betty, billed as 'the Young Roscius'. 'He has changed the habits of Life,' she told him, 'people dine at four, go to the Theatre at six, & meet to talk of him & him alone.' On the night he first played Hamlet, the House of Commons adjourned to enable members to attend. The Devonshire House party required four carriages to convey it to the theatre; Bess travelled with the Duke while Georgiana went with the Morpeths – surely an indication of how inured society had become to the sight of the Duke with Bess on his arm. In the Duke's box, the 'Boy's' performance was minutely analysed, scene by scene. 'The one with the Ghost,' Bess recorded, 'fine beyond all description. When in the most touching tone of voice, he kneels & pronounces "Father", never did I feel any thing like the emotion it gave, or hear so immediate a burst of enthusiastic applause.'

Such glittering occasions give a misleading impression of life at Devonshire House, however. 'We have had several things to make us low & nervous,' Bess wrote on 24 February 1805. 'Affairs perplex my dear G. . . . There is no saying the gloom & lownesss which I sometimes feel, yet were ever friends so united as we three.' That they were still united is a tribute to the resilience of the friendship, since Georgiana had just admitted to the Duke that she owed her creditors some fifty thousand pounds (perhaps three million today), and Bess had played a major part in extracting the confession.

There had, of course, been numerous other crises over Georgiana's debts, but nothing like this. Already aware that it was brewing, Bess had consulted Hare before he left for Paris in 1802. His reply had been pessimistic: he neither believed Georgiana capable of making 'a compleat & entire disclosure' of her debts, nor trusted her not to 'repeat the same indiscretions'. But were she by some miracle to do both, he was confident the Duke would 'engage to pay off her whole debt gradually . . . provided it falls within the limits of his Fortune'. Two years later Bess was still urging Georgiana to cease temporizing and 'make but one effort and tell dear Ca'. But Georgiana, terrified both of the Duke and of what a comprehensive list of her creditors might reveal, could not bring herself to do so. As the only one able to approach the Duke, Bess tried to prepare him for the shock to come. 'I am sure she [Bess] will use all her influence in trying to determine him . . . ,' Harriet told Granville. But Bess's role as confidante to both husband and wife – so much an advantage at other times – now backfired. 'If you knew how terrible it is to have dear Ca say sometimes that I do not check you enough,' she wrote to Georgiana, 'that I know every thing & could control you, & this when I know how little I do know & how impossible to prevent things, & how much happier you would be if I could; you would not be hurt if I force myself sometimes to hold your hand when a kind or a generous action makes you ready to pour out all it holds.'

Georgiana's distress became so evident that Fox and his close friend and colleague Robert Adair, both constant visitors to Devonshire House, divined the cause and beseeched her to make a full confession. Adair's letter is full of apocalyptic phrases: 'Remember that you are now drawing out your last stake . . . that you are, in a manner, at *your world's end . . .*' Such sentiments were no exaggeration; nor was Harriet's contention that it was 'literally a concern of life and death'. Georgiana's debts – the feelings of guilt attached to them – were slowly killing her, and those close to her sensed it. When the Duke was presented with the final bill he behaved, according to Bess, angelically, and arranged to pay off everything. If further proof were needed of the vulnerability of Georgiana's health to emotional and mental strain, in March she was seriously ill with another gallstone, and in June suffered fresh agonies from her damaged eye.

In May Harriet's daughter Caroline became engaged to William Lamb. The news caused little rejoicing in either family, but Caroline was so in love that to thwart her wishes would, in Georgiana's view, 'be productive of madness or death'. No one was prepared for Hart's violent reaction: secretly in love with his cousin for years, he had planned to marry her when he came of age. In June, however, the girl Bess once described as a 'wild, delicate, odd, delightful person, unlike anything' was married. Bess told Clifford that the ceremony had passed off tolerably well, although Caroline collapsed in a fit of hysteria which was promptly followed by Harriet and Caro giving way 'to tears and sobs, & dear Sir Walter [Farquhar, the doctor] was oblig'd to throw cold water on them'.

Clifford, on board the *Tigre,* a 74-gun ship captured in 1795 and commissioned into the Royal Navy, was somewhere in the Atlantic in pursuit of the French. Bess had heard nothing from him since March, though this was not unusual as their letters frequently fell foul of wind and weather or the erratic movements of the British fleet. But for Clifford, Bess's letters were a vital lifeline. Written when he was alone in his cabin, her miniature on the table before him, his own reveal an almost excessive adoration of the woman he believed to be his adoptive mother. 'My dearest dearest Liz,' he wrote, 'the one who is Dearer to me than all the world': such expressions bespeak a love of an intensity unusual for a seventeen-year-old midshipman, even in an age when men were allowed 'to feel'.

Bess's anxiety for Clifford's welfare was at last relieved by Lord Nelson himself, making a brief visit to England in August 1805. Emma Hamilton invited Bess to her house in Clarges Street so that Nelson could deliver his news in person. Bess recorded his words in her journal: '"I cannot say too much, I cannot praise him beyond what he deserves . . . never yet have I seen a Boy like him – but he is not a Boy now, he is a fine Young Man & he will be an honour to the Country." I ask'd him if he was much grown. He said, "Yes" & added, "that beautifull delicate face of his is now form'd into a handsome manly countenance . . . It is not his brother Officers alone, but all the Sailors, all love him who come near him."' Bess, understandably, was 'affected to the greatest degree' by such generous plaudits for her darling Clifford. She had a parcel for him, which Nelson promised to deliver.

Two days later, she and the Duke were invited to dine. Nelson asked Bess 'to drink a glass of wine with him that he might tell Clifford I had done so & after dinner I ask'd to put into his own hand the letter I gave him for Clifford. "Kiss it then," he said, "& I will take that Kiss to him."' Such delicacy of feeling goes a long way to explain Bess's extravagant expressions of grief when news reached England on 6 November of Nelson's death at Trafalgar (Clifford's ship had taken no part in the action). Haryo failed to take account of Nelson's exceptional kindness to both Bess and Clifford when she told Little G.: 'Lady Elizabeth is still in despair for Lord Nelson . . . She sobs and she sighs and she grunts and she groans and she is dressed in black cockades, with his name embroidered on every drapery she wears . . . and whilst she is regretting that she could not "have died in his defence", her peevish hearers almost wish she had.'

Bess was not alone in her hero-worship of Nelson: the whole nation was plunged into the deepest mourning. Even the phlegmatic Duke talked 'of nothing but Nelson', and composed a short poem in his honour. Harriet, too, admitted to Granville that she 'hardly imagin'd it possible to feel so much grief for a Man I did not know', adding that 'Almost every body wears a black crape scarf or cockade with Nelson written on it.' There were some who took the cult of hero-worship still further; in 1814 Lavinia Spencer, Georgiana's sister-in-law, wishing to commemorate the valour of the Duke of Wellington, launched a public subscription – aimed at women only – for a huge statue of a nude Achilles to be erected in his honour in London's Hyde Park. Lady Holland, sharp as ever, remarked that 'a difficulty had arisen' as to whether the statue 'should preserve its antique nudity or should be garnished with a fig leaf. It was carried for the leaf by a majority . . . The names of the *minority* have not transpired.'

On 22 November Bess called on Lady Hamilton. 'I found her in bed; she had the appearance of a person stunn'd & scarcely as yet able to comprehend the certainty of her loss.' Emma read her some of Nelson's letters written from the *Victory*, one of which contained a message for Bess: 'If you see Lady Eliz. Foster, tell her that Clifford dines with me to day & that I have kept my promise to her & given him myself the parcel.' Bess asked whether Nelson had had any presentiment of his fate. 'She said "No, not till their parting, that he had come back four different times & the last time, he had kneel'd down & holding up his hand had pray'd God to bless her."' When Bess called again, Emma was still in bed, weeping over accounts she had just received of Nelson's last moments before he died. She related them to Bess. 'I never felt more affected,' Bess wrote, adding revealingly, ' . . . but oh what it must be to lose one whom one so dearly loves – oh what should I do – what could I do – oh, friend of my life, beloved – .'

10

A year of sorrow 1806

'This dreadful year is to be marked by the loss of all that
is brilliant, great or noble.'

Harriet to Lord Granville Leveson Gower, 27 June 1806

VICTORY AT TRAFALGAR had secured Britain's supremacy at sea and
her safety from invasion, but in the closing months of 1805
Napoleon tightened his grip on Europe with his victories at Ulm and
Austerlitz. On 9 January 1806 the war was briefly forgotten while the
British nation honoured its greatest sailor; Lord Nelson's funeral was
to set the tone for a year of public and private sorrow.

Strangely out of keeping with the nation's mourning, London on
the day of the funeral was bathed in brilliant sunshine, the dome of St
Paul's silhouetted against a sky of cloudless blue. Women did not customarily attend public funerals at that time, but Bess watched from
Charing Cross as the procession wound its way from the Admiralty to
the Cathedral. Knowing how much it would mean to Clifford, at sea
somewhere off Cádiz, she wrote some of her account as the funeral
cortège passed. 'All London is pour'd out . . . nothing can be finer, but
it is heart rending.' The huge crowd waited in profound silence. 'When
the [funeral] Car pass'd "hats off" was repeated on all sides, & in an
instant all heads were uncover'd.' The Duke and Hart, riding together
in the ducal carriage, took part in the procession. Hart later wrote to
Clifford that he had found it 'by far the grandest and most awful sight
I had ever beheld'.

On 20 January Bess wrote in her journal: 'D.H. looked tonight as it used to do in the Regency winter. Many people came to discuss Pitt's illness . . .' Three days later Pitt was dead. Devonshire House was shocked: the principal focus of Whig opposition for the last twenty-two years had suddenly ceased to exist. Bess expressed the general feeling: 'Even his enemies must lament the loss of a Man whose wonderfull abilities & beautifull eloquence have so long been the admiration, not only of England, but of Europe.' During the political hiatus that followed, Bess made frequent visits to her sister Louisa in the hope of eliciting information about the new government. Louisa's husband, now Lord Hawkesbury, was tipped to become First Lord of the Treasury but, having been Home Secretary since 1804, hoped for a less exhausting post. Bess's relations with Louisa were delicate; though they had been close as children, in recent years their paths had diverged both politically and socially. Prudish, sanctimonious and neurotic, Louisa disapproved of Bess's position at Devonshire House and of her glamorous and hedonistic Foxite friends. She also resented Bess's current probings, rightly suspecting that everything she said went straight back to Devonshire House. For her part, Bess complained that Louisa either prevaricated, or pretended to an ignorance she knew to be false. 'I often say to myself, why not take people as they are, & as often relapse into my usual regrets of her reserve and coldness.' This was an unusually candid comment for Bess to make about a member of her family, and reveals as much about her as about Louisa. There was not much sympathy between Bess and her strait-laced sisters, and she continually mourned the loss of her dissolute but much loved brother Jack.

With Pitt gone, the King was left with little alternative but to send for Lord Grenville (once referred to by the Earl-Bishop as an 'impenetrable and unpenetrating blockhead'). Grenville formed the 'Ministry of all the Talents', with Fox as Secretary for Foreign Affairs. Fox, who had once expressed to Georgiana a wish that the Duke would 'bestir himself', offered him on Grenville's behalf any post he chose; the Duke assured Fox of his full support, but declined. His diffidence – or indolence – was not matched by others: 'What a scene of rapacity, self interest, discontent, envy, rancour and heart burnings, this change of Administration has occasion'd,' Harriet stormed to Granville, who was safely out of the way in St Petersburg. Bess was equally disenchanted by the behaviour of the Foxites, but well able to extract some humour from a conversation at a supper given for 'all our friends the new Ministers' at Devonshire House. The Prince of Wales, she wrote, was very amusing on the subject of Erskine's impatience to be Chancellor in form, & his joy now he is so. 'Fox & I (he said) were talking seriously & Erskine interrupted: "But are you sure I am to be Chancellor?" "Yes, yes," said Fox. Presently, "but is the patent made out?" "Yes . . ." said Fox, "don't interrupt us." A pause. "Fox, by Gad, we shall save the Country." Another pause. "By G. the Country shall be sav'd." Then, "By G. I will save the Country."'

Though continually harrassed by the demands of his friends and colleagues, Fox still found time to promise Bess that he would try to relieve Augustus of his post in Washington. Augustus had found much to interest him in America, but his overall verdict of its people and society remained savage: 'There is neither Honour nor Generosity nor Taste nor, least of all, Delicacy in the whole Nation.' As to Washington itself: 'It is an absolute Sepulchre, this Hole.' He was none the less acute enough to recognize that America was the land of the future. Yet he longed to return to England, the land of 'Liberty & Greatness', and to his 'dearest Ma'. Bess and Augustus wrote to one another constantly, their letters revealing deep affection and a shared passion for literature, the arts – and dogs. 'I tell you all the Nonsense in the World', he told her, 'because I always have & shall always consider you as my Sister.' Eager to cut a dash in the 'Land of Swamps and Pawnbrokers', Augustus asked Bess to send out a fur cloak, a curricle and, less glamorously, '12 bottles of Tincture for the teeth . . . & a dozen or two Tooth Brushes'. In exchange, he sent the Duke some wild turkeys (which duly arrived 'fat & in excellent spirits' at Portsmouth: 'Indian corn is the favorite food of the Birds and gravel they must have,' Augustus instructed) and a 'large bull frog nearly the size of an owl'.

Clifford was now tired of his 'servitude as Midshipman' and agitating for promotion to first lieutenant. His friendship with Hart, which had blossomed at Harrow, was sustained during the long periods he spent at sea by an exchange of infrequent but jocular letters. Clifford sent Hart stones from the walls of Troy, and Hart offered Clifford his new horse to ride when he next had shore leave, and described the dogs at Devonshire House as 'multiplying amazingly'. 'When once we get you home again,' he wrote in June 1805, 'we shall keep you and send somebody else in your place.' Caro continued to be everyone's friend and confidante, and had already fended off a number of potential suitors. Her memoirs first mention George Lamb in December

1805, when a farce he had written, *Whistle for It*, in which he also took a leading part, proved a great success on its debut at the Priory, Lord Abercorn's house at Stanmore. 'He is the best comic actor I ever saw,' she declared.

The change of administration had breathed new life into Georgiana, but the renaissance was brief. Her letters during her last months make tragic reading. The relentless cycle of illness, headaches, and despair over her debts had reduced her life to a perpetual struggle. Yet there was one profound consolation in the closeness she had at last achieved with Hart and Haryo. No mother could have worked harder to repair the damage done to her children by years of separation. Little G. had been the first to respond, but was now married and producing a child a year with clockwork regularity (the final total was twelve). Haryo, truculent as a child, had grown into a surly and suspicious adolescent, critical of everyone but her sister. She even tormented Caro, her dearest and often her only companion, whose soft and yielding nature made her an easy target. As she matured, however, Haryo grew more tolerant of the faults and foibles of others, particularly her mother's. 'One cannot know till one has separated from you,' she wrote in 1804, 'how different you are from everybody else, how superior to all mothers, even good ones.'

Georgiana's problems with Hart had not been made easier by the boy's deafness, which had 'brought on him habits of reserve, seclusion and timidity'. Byron, who had known him at Harrow, described him to his half-sister Augusta Leigh as being 'of a soft milky disposition, and of a happy apathy of temper which defies the softer emotions, and is insensible of ill-treatment'. One of the few adults Hart trusted was Bess, who visited him at Harrow, took him to the theatre, and twice carried him off to the seaside (Margate and then Hastings, in 1804). Though few of Georgiana's early letters to Hart survive, those from mid 1805 show her increasingly able to express her feelings for him on paper. In an unbearably poignant letter of 9 March 1806 she reproached herself bitterly for the giddiness and vanity of her youth, expressed her deep love for him, and counselled him to emulate his father in everything but his idleness. One passage in the letter – '*I hope to live* to see you not only happy but the cause of happyness to others' – later haunted him.

On the day Georgiana wrote this letter, the entry in Bess's journal reads 'The Dss went to Court, but was sadly out of spirits'; the following day she noted 'She has some jaundice.' Georgiana still felt able, however, to write to her mother begging for the loan of a hundred pounds. On the 16th she was so ill that Farquhar spent the night at Devonshire House. On the 20th Bess wrote: 'Yesterday was a miserable day. We felt the greatest alarm about the Dss till three or four in the morning when the warm bath procur'd her the first sleep without moaning that she has had . . . Her dear countenance is more her own.' On the 23rd: 'I have had no courage to write. Yesterday the Dss was very ill, so much so that Blane [another doctor] advised me to send for dear Hartington.' That Bess should have been the one to recall Hart from his tutor's in Kent has been interpreted as unwonted interference, the responsibility for taking such a step being seen as the Duke's alone. But it was not the first instance of a doctor appealing directly to Bess, either out of fear of the Duke or because it was tacitly understood that if urgent action were required it was she who would best carry it out. It was also Bess who wrote to Little G. at Castle Howard with news of her mother's illness, even describing what she had eaten: calomel (used as a cathartic), arrow root, *crème de riz* and vermicelli broth.

That Georgiana was suffering from a gallstone was never in doubt; that she would – after periods of agonizing pain – eventually pass the stone was assumed. They had been through it before. This time, however, there was a terrible difference: it was not one stone, but many. Such an acute attack of gallstones could have been alleviated only by opening the abdominal cavity – which, in the early nineteenth century, was tantamount to signing the patient's death warrant.

On the 24th Georgiana saw Hart '& without alarm about herself'. Bess later told Clifford that Hart had 'staid almost to the last with *her*, returned each day to the room, & shew'd a feeling and manliness quite delightful'. Harriet Bessborough was also sleeping in the house, and she and Bess took turns to sit with Georgiana. 'The Duke hardly goes to bed,' Bess wrote, 'yet all will surely be well.' As news of the Duchess's illness spread, 'Crowds come to inquire, some we see but most of the day I am at her bed side.' The following night Georgiana had a fit lasting nearly eight hours. None of them slept. Georgiana's head was shaved and a blister applied. 'The lethargy was terrible . . . She has taken bark twice.' On the 27th she had another fit which was 'succeeded by a sort of hysterical sigh which lasts now . . .' Two more doctors were called in. 'She said to me, "They think me very ill then?" Oh, my G!'

The only direct evidence of the Duke's feelings during Georgiana's ordeal is a note to Miss Trimmer of the 29th. In its brevity and honesty, it is a strangely moving document: 'If the worst should happen I hope you will be so good as to stay at Devonshire House for the present, for I shall not be in a state of mind to attend to anybody, or to receive or give any comfort whatever.'

Bess's journal is blank for the next three days. On 31 March she wrote:

Saturday was a day of horror beyond any words to express – yesterday & today have passed, & we are alive – but stunned, not yet feeling or conceiving the fullness of our loss, scarce believing it true . . . The Duke is rather calmer – but we are a family of sufferers & my heart feels broken. My Angel friend! Angel I am sure she now is! – but can I live without her who was the life of my existence. Oh bitter, bitter and overwhelming loss! Friend, companion, farewell indeed – yet even the last day she knew me.

For five days Georgiana's body lay in state in the Great Hall of Devonshire House. Though there is no description of the scene, it is unlikely to have differed materially from the form usually adopted at that time for aristocratic funerals. The open coffin would have been placed on its catafalque beneath the appropriate heraldic escutcheons; the curtains would have been drawn throughout the house, the shutters closed, and the walls of the Hall hung from floor to ceiling with black cloth. The family, wearing deep mourning, would have assembled to receive the callers.

Thousands of mourners lined Piccadilly; many had never known Georgiana personally, but wanted to pay their respects to a woman who had captured their affection and whose exploits had illuminated their lives. Among the many who had loved her, Fox was inconsolable, the tears pouring down his cheeks. The Duke kept to his room. 'One night he was very hysterical,' Bess records. 'I staid late, very late, with him. I then went feebly and ill to my room – when I got there, on turning round, I saw in his anxiety he had follow'd me.'

In the early hours of Easter Day, with the coffin now closed, family and staff waited in the great sombre house for the arrival of the hearse which was to carry the body on its long journey to Derby. A scrap of paper found pinned inside a journal of a later date bears the following in Bess's hand, the words run together and barely legible:

3 a.m.: My Sister, my beloved, my darling Sister – the joy, the solace of all my life; she who gave life & animation to my peace, joy, delight & comfort; she with whom I shared every thought, every care & every pleasure – at this

moment lying cold in the room near me . . . Day after day I have held your poor unconscious body, kissed your cold lips & contrived to warm your stiffening hand in my bosom . . . and to night, Oh God, you are to be borne for ever from me . . .'

Later, Bess recorded that she and Harriet had again 'knelt by the Coffin, kissed it, prayed by it & we were calm, prayed to be a comfort to each other & I offered up prayers that my heart might be purified by the tears of agony I had shed.' But the finality of the closed coffin destroyed her brief calm. 'I traversed the Great Hall with horror, every noise makes me shudder, I feel cold & appalled – it is now that Death, death in all its terrors, seems to strike me – I had not lost her before. She was there, we could see her . . .' Two hours later, at 5 a.m., she scribbled: 'We have seen the Coffin pass! We have heard the deep sound of the hearse!' Surmounted by plumes of ostrich feathers and drawn by six black horses, the hearse led the line of mourning coaches into Piccadilly.

> We saw the long procession leave the Court & pass through the Gates that seemed to open but for kindness or to gaiety! It is done, it is over – and we have scarcely wept. Involuntarily we kneeled as it passed . . . Never shall I forget Hartington's look & figure as I saw him in the Great Hall as if to attend on his poor Mother there & then on the steps, fixed without his hat, his innocent interesting countenance & looks bent to the last on the Coffin as it was carried slowly down the steps & on the Hearse as it was placed within. He did not appear to weep, but his whole soul seemed absorbed by what was passing. The morning just began to dawn, all was reviving to light & life, but her, her! who was our light & life.

Following the departure of the coffin, Bess's journal remained closed for five weeks.

Those who suspect Bess of having perpetuated her friendship with Georgiana to maintain her position in society and stay close to the Duke have only to read her letters in the weeks following Georgiana's death to understand that her love for her friend was, and remained, the single most important element in her life. Any affectation or exaggerated sensibility she had displayed in the past gave way to genuine, crippling grief. In a letter to Clifford on 17 April she speaks of 'we poor who live to lament her, who adored her living & must ever, ever feel lost without her, we are not ill, but we feel stunned and overcome . . .' She adds pathetically, 'We all keep together and exert ourselves as well as we can.' To Augustus she wrote: 'The recollection alone remains, & regrets, never ceasing regrets . . . Oh, my dear Augustus, what a blank in my future life! I am & ought to be grateful for the friend that is preserved to me [the Duke], & for such affection-ate sons, but she was the only female friend I ever had.' Again to Augustus, on 3 July: 'The constant charm of my life is gone. She doubled every joy, lessened every grief. Her society had an attraction I never met with in any other being . . .' And on 9 July: 'Never, I believe, were two hearts and minds so united; never did two people think and feel so alike. She is so present to me, and I am so constantly occupied for her that I feel as if she was absent on a journey, and I catch myself saying "I'll tell her this" . . .'

References to her loss appear repeatedly in Bess's journals in the years that follow. Often it was a visit to one of the Devonshire prop-erties, particularly Chiswick House or Chatsworth, which released a flood of emotion. On such occasions her first entry, always written in Italian, would be devoted to Georgiana. As late as 1810, returning to Chatsworth for the first time as Duchess of Devonshire, she writes: 'How many, oh how many sweet and loving memories!'

Once the coffin had left for Derby, Harriet took Haryo and the Morpeths to her villa at Roehampton. The Duke, Bess, Caro, Hart and Lady Spencer remained at Devonshire House. 'Lady Spencer is staying on here for some weeks longer,' Bess told Clifford on 17 April, '& bears up most wonderfully.' (She was still there in late May. Though the house was vast enough for them to keep out of one another's way, it was only now that Lady Spencer and Bess found themselves able to live under the same roof.) Bess's letter to Clifford is the only record of how the five of them survived the immediate aftermath of Georgiana's death. 'The dear Duke, tho' wretched, is not ill, he has been twice to Chiswick, walk'd there – & I have walk'd in the garden here . . . Caroline is recovering her appetite & sleeps . . . Hart is well & going back to Mr Smith [his tutor] . . .' Even these brief glimpses have been given a gloss by Bess, who wished to shield her son from the reality of what they had all suffered: 'Any thing so horrible, so killing, as her [Georgiana's] three days' agony no human being ever witness'd,' Harriet wrote to Granville.

Bess's own estimate of the value to her of Georgiana's friendship is almost too comprehensive to require further elaboration. What she perhaps did not recognize, however, is that living with Georgiana had almost certainly made her a better person. A woman of her intelligence, ambition and self-confessed vanity might easily have become scheming and manipulative; Bess's circumstances might indeed have left her little choice. In 1782, when she met Georgiana, she had already made a mess of her life: she had married unwisely and the marriage had failed, condemning her to live out her days as a separated and 'childless' wife. Hovering on the fringes of a society in which such women were not 'received', she could have lived chastely, frugally, respectably and oh! so dully, like her sister Mary. What seems more probable, however, in view of her ability to attract men, is that she would have found herself a protector – or a succession of them.

Bess describes herself as 'incapable in those first days of all – but of fulfilling her wishes & directions left me in writing about her papers'. At what stage Georgiana had made Bess the sole guardian of her papers is unknown. That she took such a step as a means of protecting Bess's position at Devonshire House in the event of her own death is entirely possible: she must have known it would take months to sort out her thousands of letters, documents, and unpaid bills. It was certainly not a task she would have left to the Duke; the only other person she would have trusted was Harriet, and in the event it proved so distressing and so overwhelming that Bess enlisted her help. Writing to Granville, Harriet described her daily pilgrimage from Roehampton to Devonshire House: 'When you return [from St Petersburg] you will judge a little by your own feelings what mine must be at driving into that court, seeing her Windows, her room, all the places which from custom seemed incorporated with her, and seeing at the same time the sad escutcheon and the deep mourning of all around . . .' The house, its knocker swathed in black crêpe, remained shuttered for twelve weeks. The escutcheon displaying Georgiana's arms was later moved to the Cavendish family vault in All Saint's Church, Derby.

It presumably fell to Bess and Harriet to sort through the unpaid bills Georgiana left. Her debts were already a subject for gossip about town. Lady Jerningham told a friend she had heard it said that the Duchess had pleaded with the Duke to pay them, that he had refused, and that 'the Duchess in despair . . . fell ill'. When the Duke realized her danger, he had declared 'that He would purchase her Health with any thing she could command. But, poor thing, I suppose it was then too Late. I pity the duke who they say, is very much affected. And well He may!' This sort of talk was damaging to the Duke. According to Bess, he consulted her about paying the debts. 'I could only speak as my feelings prompted me,' she records. 'He said, with that angelick goodness & simplicity which so characterises his actions, "I should not feel comfortable, I think, if I did not pay these debts – & yet perhaps many may think it absurd in me to do so."' Bess concludes this entry with one of her fervent pleas to the Almighty: 'God Bless him & preserve him.' (The Duke's 'angelick goodness' notwithstanding, the bulk of the debts remained unpaid until Hart succeeded his father in 1811.)

That the Duke should seek Bess's advice about Georgiana's debts is an indication of the role she played in his life. And she not only advised him, but nursed him, soothed him, and protected him from anything she thought might distress him. She records that on the night that Georgiana's body was to leave for Derby, Hart had come to her room around midnight 'for some ink' (surely a pretext to be with her), and had told her the hearse would come at 4 a.m. 'Dear, dear D.D. I have kept it from him,' Bess wrote. 'He has not left his room.' For her to presume to spare him the distress of seeing his wife's coffin leave the house was licence indeed. But it was licence well-earned. She had lived with the Duke on terms of the closest intimacy for some twenty-two years; they had shared, with Georgiana, a long and eventful history.

In his remote way, the Duke had loved his wife. But life with Georgiana had been too hectic, too emotional, too full of dramas; as Haryo once remarked, she had 'little command over her feelings' and a 'most unfortunate knack at making every thing into a scene'. He now craved peace and tranquillity. He was nearly sixty, and plagued by gout; Bess was nearly fifty, still beautiful, even if the bloom had gone; though passion had mellowed into companionship, separation was inconceivable. For the Cavendish children, however, the situation was far less clear-cut. Bess had been part of their lives for as long as they could remember; they all knew how much, often to their cost, their mother had loved her. What they did not, could not, fully comprehend was just how much Bess loved their father. They also probably failed to appreciate how much she cared for them and how, therefore, since there was little hope of the Duke filling the void left by Georgiana, she felt able to justify remaining with the family on the grounds that she could go some way towards filling it herself (nor is it impossible that in her last agony Georgiana had begged Bess to 'take care' of her children). While they could love and respect their father, and learn to emulate his virtues, to expect him to be minutely involved in their lives would be fruitless.

There were other ways in which Bess was made to feel indispensable to the family; Georgiana, unwilling to charge the Duke with the simple task of distributing her most treasured possessions, had entrusted it instead to Bess – who carried out her written instructions to the letter. And in June, when Hart fell ill, it was left to Bess to call in Farquhar. When the boy's breathing became laboured, Sir Walter panicked and woke Bess. 'I come to you as a friend,' he explained. 'This is a thunderbolt from Heaven. I can't sit under it alone. Who shall be sent to?' Together, they decided which doctors should be called in. That Farquhar, when confronted by the possibility of the imminent demise of the Cavendish heir, should bypass the Duke to consult Bess only served to reinforce her belief that it was her *duty* to remain at Devonshire House. That it was essential to her own future happiness and security was, of course, undeniable.

There was one observer of Bess's delicate position at Devonshire House who thought she had the perfect solution: Lady Melbourne decided that now was the moment to revitalize Bess's relationship with the Duke of Richmond, and wrote urging him to call on Bess. The Duke's reply, though couched in the most diplomatic language, made it perfectly clear that, while he sympathized deeply with Lady Elizabeth's predicament, he was not about to do any such thing. (Richmond died in December, aged seventy-two. 'It is not known yet whether he married the Woman that liv'd with him & by whom he has three children,' Bess noted in her journal, indicating her perfect awareness of the housekeeper's role at Goodwood.)

Their mother's death brought the three Cavendish children closer. They began to write to one another regularly, and the two girls to take on Georgiana's role of advising and encouraging their young brother. 'I love you if possible better since our irreparable loss,' Haryo told him, 'and it wou'd be the pride and happiness of my life if I cou'd *in any degree* be to you what she was.' She was anxious that Hart should see more of his father. 'His manner is cold but his heart is noble & excellent and I am sure that he feels and values any little attentions from you.' Hart wanted to share with his sisters the letters Georgiana had written to him in the last months of her life. Part of his letter to Little G. enclosing them can only refer to Bess: 'Perhaps you understood more than I meant today about the person we talked of. I only think that as she *has* been calumniated, some little care ought to be taken and difference made, at a time when her enemies would talk more. If she does that I shall be the first to pay her every respect &

attention.' To plead for sympathy and clemency for the grief-stricken Bess shows remarkable maturity for a boy of sixteen, displayed again in his treatment of his grandmother, Lady Spencer, in writing her long newsy letters to make up for those she no longer received from Georgiana.

'I know not what is to restore me to any powers of the mind,' Bess wrote in her journal when she resumed it in early May, 'but I feel unequal to any exertion that has not to do with something for her! And thus the arrangement of her affairs is all that I have been able to occupy my mind with.' The discipline required to keep a daily record of events helped her to re-engage with the world beyond the walls of Devonshire House. With something of her old zeal, she detailed the long build-up to the trial of Lord Melville (for the misappropriation of public funds by one of his staff), and the tortuous affairs of the Prince of Wales and his allegedly adulterous wife, Princess Caroline. At the end of the month she records her joy at the return of Clifford, who was to be examined for promotion. Seeing him again after his two years' absence at sea brought a fresh burst of sorrow for Georgiana. 'Oh, how I want her to share my happiness in Clifford, how I want her every where & every hour!' His return had been eagerly anticipated by Hart: 'Among the few things that now make me happy will be your friendship and society,' he told him. 'It will make me able to bear D. House a little better & we will be as happy as it is possible after such a change. Above all dear Clifford let us be as perfectly acquainted and speak as freely as we did when we parted last.' (Clifford was promoted to first lieutenant in early June and ordered to join his new ship, the *Royal George*, on 23 July.)

Harriet, too, was struggling to return to life after her sister's death. 'No one knows, G. – not even you – how I suffer,' she told Granville. Caro, however, was quick to perceive Harriet's misery: 'I cannot tell you how much I think of her,' she told Caroline Lamb, 'she is for ever present to me, with that heartbreaking look which seems to say: "I have lost every thing"; for it has deadened her to every enjoyment of life.' From a letter Little G. wrote Hart in early 1807, it would seem that Harriet had made one room in her house into a shrine to Georgiana. 'Lady Bessboro shewed me her little room the other day & told me you had seen it & no one else. How melancholy it is. I think she indulges her grief even too much – yet I love her for it.' The room probably contained the death mask made by Joseph Nollekens, which Harriet, according to Joseph Farington, had appropriated.

Bess's journal reveals that despite the paralysis which seemed to grip all those who had been closest to Georgiana, life was gradually returning to normal. With very few exceptions, the names she notes of those who visited Devonshire House were little different after Georgiana's death. They came partly out of long habit, sometimes to see the Duke, but many can only have come to see Bess. The Morpeths and the Bessboroughs dined regularly; Charles Grey, Robert Adair, General Fitzpatrick, Lord John Townshend, the Hollands and the Melbournes appear time and again in the journals. Lord Bessborough and Lord Morpeth kept Bess in touch with parliamentary events, calling on her after sittings or sending her notes from the Lords. Their most constant visitor was the Earl of Tankerville's heir Lord Ossulston, who was engaged to Corisande de Grammont (thus putting an end to Augustus's hopes). The marriage took place in late July at Devonshire House; the Duke gave her away, and afterwards they sat down twelve to dinner.

Writing of this event later to Clifford, Bess gives the impression that she had presided over the ceremony. Such signs of her assumption of Georgiana's role incensed Haryo, who felt that as the Duke's daughter she was the rightful female head of the house. 'Lady E.F. is very disagreeable in doing the honours instead of me,' she raged to Little G., 'which for every reason in the world is painful to me.' What she failed to take into account was that Bess had been 'doing the honours' for years. So often was Georgiana incapacitated by illness or her terrible headaches that Bess had repeatedly been required to take her place at the last minute, even, on one occasion, when the Prince of Wales was to be entertained. Moreover, conversation around the dinner table almost invariably focused on politics, about which Bess knew a great deal while Haryo knew little, and cared less ('I care not a straw for politics,' she once admitted to Hart).

For Bess to act as hostess to the Duke's political friends and colleagues was one thing; for her to take over the running of Devonshire House was quite another. Yet since the Duke would certainly not have done so, and Haryo was too young, it must have been Bess. For this mammoth task her ability to command loyalty and respect from servants stood her in good stead. And she did try to carry it out with tact. When the Morpeths were due in September, Bess wrote to Little G: 'The Duke has given me a very pleasant commission which is to choose your rooms.' She then details the rooms which 'Ca and I' think would be best, but adds: 'If there is any change you want to make pray tell me.' In November, when Sheridan was elected MP for Westminster,

Bess received a request that the triumphal procession might pass through the Court of Devonshire House on its way along Piccadilly. 'I said I could not send any permission till the Duke was awake. About two I went to him & he said he thought it impossible to refuse.'

In late June a fresh tragedy had begun to unfold. The Duke, returning from a visit to Fox, told Bess that he was 'excessively alarmed about him. I hope I may be mistaken . . . but I think it is over with him.' He described him as 'thin in the face & swelled in the Body'. The Duke's prediction proved more accurate than the opinions delivered by the doctors. After weeks of optimistic blustering, they diagnosed Fox's illness as a 'dropsical complaint'. Dropsy, caused by an abnormal accumulation of watery fluid in the tissues or in a body cavity, frequently proved fatal in the early nineteenth century. Fox had scant regard for the skills of the medical profession and must have suspected that his chances of recovery were negligible. By a tragic paradox, after so long in Opposition, he at last had the power to promote the two causes in which he most profoundly believed. As he confided to his nephew, Lord Holland: 'the Slave Trade and Peace are two such glorious things, I can't give them up . . . If I can manage *them,* I will then retire.' But he meant retire from politics, not from life. On 10 June he had risen in the Commons, for what was to prove the last time, to propose the Bill for the Abolition of the Slave Trade. (The bill eventually became law in 1807; it was another twenty-six years before slavery itself was abolished.)

As the gravity of Fox's illness became known, his small house in Stable Yard, St James's was besieged by friends and well-wishers. Harriet and Bess often made the ten-minute walk through Green Park to call on him. Their visits were welcomed by Mrs Fox, still cold-shouldered by many of society's leading hostesses. Total strangers wrote recommending such pet remedies as 'the exterior application of snails'; that this one was actually tried gives an indication of the desperate lengths to which doctors were prepared to go to treat a complaint they so little understood. But years of hard living had so undermined Fox's constitution that he no longer had the reserves with which to combat the complaint. While his body failed him, his spirit did not, and many are the accounts of the patience and cheerfulness with which he bore his illness. As his aunt Lady Sarah Napier (one of the Duke of Richmond's sisters) reported to Lady Susan O'Brien: 'The Privy Council of his heart are Lord Holland & Mrs Fox; with these he indulges I hear in low or high spirits as he feels, sometimes crying, always tender & grateful to them for loving him so much, & never quite comfortable if they are not within call.'

In the months that followed, there is hardly an entry in Bess's journal which does not include an account of Fox's condition: 'This has been a day of anxiety about Mr Fox'; 'I have seen him this evening. The change is for the worse. It is really too shocking, such a Man & at such a time'; 'Fox is not quite so well, but Lord Robert [Spencer, a close friend of Fox] assured me it was only the sickness from Castor Oil & that the Physicians were satisfied. The Carrot seed had agreed so well that they meant to double the dose.' It was also suggested that 'the Fox-Glove' – digitalis – should be tried. Made from the leaves of the foxglove, this regulated the pulse and acted as a powerful diuretic; though it would surely have been more efficacious than carrot seed, Fox refused to allow it to be administered. On 7 August he was tapped. His secretary, Trotter, gives a graphic account of the operation, which entailed Fox being literally stabbed in the lower abdomen, upon which five gallons of foetid, bloody water gushed forth 'with great violence'. He bore the excruciating pain with amazing courage, even making bets on the likely quantity of fluid.

On her next visit Bess was struck by 'how thin he looked & it gave me a painfull nervous sensation'. Despite his appearance, there was a general improvement after the operation and it was decided that he was well enough to return to St Anne's Hill. To break the long journey, he was to stay at Chiswick House, and Bess went with Mrs Fox to choose the most suitable rooms. Bess and the Duke saw Fox the following day at Chiswick, where they found him 'eating chicken & mutton chops & in very great spirits. He said to the Duke "I'll tell you what I do, I eat my breakfast, dinner & supper & a luncheon between these – & sometimes something in the night."'

On 31 August, he was tapped again. When Bess returned to Chiswick she was told the 'discharge was prodigious'. Fox was asleep in bed 'with the door open. I could see him as he lay. He is quite a thin Man now. The windows & doors were open. The bed, to keep him as dry as they could, was only with its mattress. It looked melancholy – my heart sank. Perhaps I now fear too easily.' Again there was a brief reprieve, but when Bess arrived on 8 September she was told by Trotter that there had been a change for the worse. That Fox was dying was no longer in doubt. His friends and family gathered in the house to wait for the inevitable. Lord Holland and Mrs Fox never left his side. Bess, though careful not to intrude, haunted the house and gardens throughout Fox's last days. On the 9th she wrote: 'The whole scene was heart breaking . . . and to know that in that little room the greatest mind that ever animated the form of Man lay in a frame now in ruin!' For her it was an agonizing repetition of the scenes she had so recently lived through with Georgiana.

On 13 September Bess was in the garden at Chiswick, wandering about miserably in the late summer heat. A mountain ash grew outside Fox's window, and as August turned to September he had watched the berries ripen. Looking up, she now saw that both windows of his room had been thrown open and that those inside 'walked up and down the room, their handkerchiefs to their eyes. I knew then, I felt it must be so, that he was dead . . . It came like a blow on my heart.'

She returned to Devonshire House to comfort the Duke. She found him 'very pale & much affected' and she sat up with him until three in the morning, answering his questions about Fox's last hours. 'He went to his great arm chair & I could observe him wiping the tears away with his hand.' The following day she wrote: 'How terrible the stillness of this day has been! How dreadful the blank, the chasm & how irreparable is this loss!' In the space of eleven months, England had lost three of her greatest men: Nelson, Pitt and Fox. With Georgiana, Fox and James Hare gone, and Sheridan too often drunk and disagreeable, the heady, brilliant days of Devonshire House had vanished for ever.

Bess's entry for 25 December recalls the previous Christmas, which they had all spent together at Devonshire House:

Oh blindness to the future kindly given, could I have then thought that I was so near losing the dear, the idoliz'd, the sole real female friend of my youth, of my life! What sad, what bitter moments before the horrid ones I was doom'd by that loss to know, & what fearfull uncertainty for the future. How much it should make one try to look to that awfull moment which must come, how try to make oneself acceptable in the sight of God! How try to fulfill each duty & to correct each fault. Oh my God, assist me & enable me to do so. Bless & protect my lov'd children, my dearest friend, & teach me & them to be acceptable in thy sight! Bless, bless, oh bless him, my sole friend D.

11

Duchess of Devonshire
1807–1811

'I was married this day to Duke of Devonshire! So many
contradictory emotions agitate my heart & Soul . . . may I
be as gratefull as I ought & contribute to his happiness &
his children's as much as I wish.'

Bess in her journal, 19 October 1809

———————◆———————

B ESS BEGAN 1807 nervously: 'It is almost with trembling that I see
a new year begun! Pray God it may be more fortunate than the
past!' She had good reason to tremble, for her position at Devonshire
House had never been more insecure. It was now seven months since
Georgiana's death; she could hardly justify remaining because she
required still more time to sort out her friend's papers; nor could she
plead the seventeen-year-old Hart's need for a woman's care, since he
was touring his father's estates and was seldom in London. Society had
been perfectly aware of her liaison with the Duke; it was her friendship with Georgiana which had enabled her to live as part of the
family, however, and with her death Bess's cover was blown. A letter
to Augustus, written in late 1809, reveals how quick society had been
to unsheath its claws.

Our misfortune was so great a one, & we felt our loss [of Georgiana] so
deeply that had we liv'd retir'd from the world I do not know that ever my
situation would have chang'd, for all I wish'd was to be all the comfort I

186

could to the Duke, & for myself still to enjoy his friendship and society. He determined that nothing should ever separate him from me. The feelings of compassion in the World however soon subsided . . . & many not only horribly censur'd my situation, but shew'd me mark'd incivilities.

Her principal enemy, however, was not 'in the World' but living in Devonshire House, her small eyes watching Bess's every move. Haryo had been critical in the past, but in 1807 her letters begin to reveal the full extent of her hostility. Everything Bess said or did annoyed her, like sand in a wound. But since a veneer at least of respect and obedience to one's elders was expected, none of Haryo's resentment was ever openly expressed; instead, she unburdened herself to Little G. and to Hart in letters written without restraint, and on the assumption that they would be destroyed. Reading them today, it is easy to be seduced by the witty, needle-sharp prose, hard to resist its poison. Seen through Haryo's eyes, Bess was a silly, affected, interfering and tactless woman, forever adjusting her shawls and fussing over her little dogs. That Haryo exaggerated wildly in her criticisms – not only of Bess – does not lessen their impact, and it is impossible to deny an element of truth in much of what she said. The ambiguities of Bess's position did perhaps make her over-protective of her rights and quick to take offence if they were slighted. But what makes Haryo's letters such painful reading is their unintentional revelation of Bess's repeated attempts to please her. Clearly, for Bess to leave Devonshire House for ever was the only way to achieve this – and she was not about to do so.

Although as a perceptive and sensitive woman Bess was surely aware of Haryo's hostility, and hurt by it, never once, either in her journals or in her letters to her children, did she criticize her; it is always 'dear Harriet' this, and 'dear Harriet' that. And she continued to do what she felt Georgiana would have done for her daughter. Her attempts to encourage Haryo (now twenty-two) to go more into society prompted a furious response: 'Miss Trimmer being with me', Haryo complained to Little G., 'does not in the least prevent her [Bess] persecuting me from morning till night to go out with her to the park, play, etc.' Unable to refuse Bess's overtures outright, Haryo resorted to subterfuge, pleading illness. That Haryo might be embarrassed to be seen in public with her father's mistress apparently never occurred to Bess, who had, after all, gone everywhere with Georgiana.

The Duke, as always, contrived to remain detached from much of

what went on under his roof. As he seldom rose before five each afternoon and often did not return from Brooks's until the early hours, he
neatly avoided confronting the situation (and others: Hart's unfortunate tutor made two trips to London to consult the Duke about his
son, but both times found His Grace in bed). Bess once advised Little
G. that the only way of seeing the Duke was by going to his room and
'sitting up with him as I do'. This habit was ridiculed by Haryo, who
gleefully related to Little G. how Caroline Lamb had tried to dis-
concert Bess by reading aloud at supper 'a letter of Madame de
Maintenon, in which she excuses her conduct towards Louis [XIV]
and says, "If I did not go to his room, to whom could he confide his
secrets?" . . . describing, in short, scenes too like what we are so often
witnessing.' Haryo's malicious delight in this anecdote may have been
fuelled by jealousy, for she and her father were all but strangers.
Harriet blamed her niece for not exerting herself with him. 'It sounds
extraordinary,' she confided to Granville, 'but her Father certainly
does not know her . . .'

Hart too was estranged from the Duke. Endeavouring to bridge the
gulf between father and son was a pressing concern not only for Little
G. and Haryo, but for Bess. 'Think dearest Hart', Little G. wrote in
November 1807, 'how much *she* [Georgiana] always wished you to
shew our Father every respect & mark of affection . . . I think from
little things Ldy E. has said, of your not having written, & that surely
when so near you will come to see Papa – he might be really hurt with
you if you do not.' Both girls adored their brother, who had grown
into a tall young man with thick auburn hair, long oval face and blue
eyes. 'There is so much sweetness and affectionate attention in that
dearest boy's manner to any thing that belongs to him,' Haryo wrote
to Little G., 'such animation in all his feelings, and kindness in all his
intentions, that it is captivating to every body that comes near him.' It
was Hart's 'affectionate attention' and kindness that preserved his relationship with Bess despite constant infusions of Haryo's vitriol. He
never quite lost his childhood attachment to her.

The situation at Devonshire House was complicated by the friendships between Bess's children and the three Cavendishes. Little G's
marriage to Lord Morpeth and her move to Yorkshire had left Haryo
and Caro St Jules very dependent on one another. 'Caroline is the
greatest comfort to me,' Haryo told Little G. in November 1806, 'and
now that both Miss Trimmer and Hartington are gone, I do not know
what I should do without her.' Yet Caro was the 'adopted' daughter of

the very person Haryo wished anywhere but at Devonshire House. If Bess were to go, Caro would go, and Haryo would be left alone in the great house with a father she seldom saw, obliged to depend for company on the infrequent visits of her brother and sister. She could, and did, make extended visits to Little G. at Castle Howard, to her aunts Harriet Bessborough and Lavinia Spencer, and to her grandmother at St Albans, but Devonshire House remained her home.

Hart's close friendship with Clifford was yet another piece of the Devonshire House jigsaw, and Clifford was also both a friend and shipmate of Hart's cousin, Bob Spencer. This connection too had its paradoxes, since though Bob's mother Lavinia detested Bess, it was his father, Earl Spencer, who had obtained Clifford his place as a midshipman. Despite Clifford's touching assertion that the Spencers were his 'best and earliest friends', Lavinia did not hesitate to describe him as being 'as dull as a post', a remark reported to Hart by Haryo apparently out of pure malice.

Though he was often in Ireland attending to his own affairs, Bess's son Fred looked upon Devonshire House as home, which Haryo considered presumptuous. She nevertheless enjoyed his company, treating him as a sort of resident court jester. Her view of him as being 'so very unlike any thing else in the world' was one with which Bess would have concurred: 'You know as well as I do', she confided to Augustus, 'his excellent head & heart, but also his great peculiarities; they are such as would make it difficult for him to be happy as a Married Man, & would make me tremble for him in a public situation.' Among his 'peculiarities' were bibliomania, a large appetite, and a knack of making hilarious but tactless jokes. Generous to a fault, he had since the death of his father supplemented Bess's allowance – though she did not know it – from his own income.

Augustus was the least integrated into Devonshire House. His diplomatic posts kept him abroad for long periods, and beyond his unrequited passion for Corisande he never became attached to any member of the Cavendish family. He too gave Bess money. In 1802 he paid seven hundred pounds into her bank before leaving on his trip to the Continent; she responded with gratitude, but insisted she would only use it if 'in distress'. Both sons were certainly giving her money until 1805, and possibly afterwards. That they should have felt the need to support her financially suggests that she was not over-generously provided for by the Duke.

Bess might have found her situation there 'horribly censur'd' by the outside world, but Devonshire House continued to be almost as much of a political focus as in Georgiana's day. Whigs like Charles Grey, Lord Bessborough and Lord Lauderdale called almost daily while Parliament was in session. The younger generation was also well represented, by Corisande's husband Lord Ossulston, Lord Morpeth, William Lamb, his brother George, and Lady Bessborough's lover Granville. Bess's journal shows that on one day in particular she held court to no fewer than seven men. The 'undefinable attraction' commented on by Charles Greville had lost none of its power, despite the fact that she was nearly fifty. Her visitors came not just to gossip but to talk over the day's parliamentary debate and the progress of the war and, on occasion, to use her as a conduit to the Duke. The lively discussions that ensued – often over supper when the Duke was present – demonstrate that her opinion and judgement were valued. Little G. told Hart that a frequent visitor had reported Devonshire House to be the 'most delightful place in the world'.

Bess's political views had matured over the years, and she now expressed them more freely. 'Lord St Vincent . . . [though] great in command, is narrow minded in politicks & is guided by prejudices & party motives' she wrote in March 1807. She was also remarkably broad-minded; in her journal she recorded a delightful anecdote about one of George III's sons, the Duke of Clarence. The Duke had said to Lord Barrymore, '"Pray My Lord, was not your Mother very handsome?" To which Ld B. assented. The D. of C. then added, "I am told she was the greatest W. . . . in England." "Your Royal Highness's Mother would have been the same," said Ld Barrymore, "if she had not been so ugly." D.D. told me this & I think better of Ld Barrymore than I ever did before.' It was an anecdote her brother Jack would have relished, but would have shocked her prudish sisters.

In March 1807 the 'Ministry of All the Talents' resigned following a renewed clash with the King over the commissioning of Roman Catholics into the army: the Whigs had held office for only thirteen months. A new administration was formed under the ailing Duke of Portland, thus beginning a Tory domination of British politics which was to last some twenty years. Bess's brother-in-law Lord Hawkesbury returned to the Home Office, an appointment that elicited nothing but complaints from Louisa.

The relentless flow of politics in Bess's journal is only occasionally interrupted by brief glimpses of her personal life: Clifford returned from sea, Augustus from America; she had been impressed by the

Townley marbles and the Rosetta Stone at the British Museum; she had been to see the Sibozan (?) serpents from 'near Bengal' and thought the serpent had 'a very handsome countenance'. Every new edition of the quarterly *Edinburgh Review* was mentioned; founded in 1802, it had quickly become the most influential publication of its kind.

As the anniversary of Georgiana's death approached, Bess and the family braced themselves. 'Oh dearest what sad recollections every day awakens,' Little G. wrote to Hart. When the Duke developed ophthalmia in early March, Bess sat up with him night after night, applying ointment to the affected eye. He recovered, but the episode had shaken her. On 1 April, two days after Georgiana's death the previous year, she wrote: 'Thank God no new misfortune has mark'd this month, but many blessings still are ours: children, friends & tolerable health & perfect preservation of Eye sight to the Duke. On him, his, my dear children, all my remains of happiness depends, but what can ever fill up the blank my own lov'd G. has made in my life.' There were those who doubted Bess's love for Georgiana, and her commitment to the Duke and his children; had they been able to read her journal, they would have found much that was written from the heart, not for posterity.

The Duke was ill again in August, this time with pneumonia; Bess nursed him devotedly, treating him (on Farquhar's instructions) with ass's milk. In November she herself fell ill with her old bronchial complaint. For weeks she suffered from a crippling pain in her side, spat blood, and fainted continually. Her condition was such as to move even Haryo to some compassion. 'If I was to say the only moment in my life in which I had felt anything like affection for Lady E.,' she confessed to her sister, 'it would be during the last week and my conscience would be very uneasy and my heart very heavy, if joy at her danger or a wish for her death had ever for an instant come across my mind.' Bess was pathetically grateful for Haryo's solicitude during her illness; she would have been shocked and saddened, however, by the conclusions she came to, as confided to Little G.: 'Her illness and, of course, absence from our society have painfully convinced me that not only I, but my father would be much happier without her. I never saw him in such good spirits, so perfectly at his ease and talking so much and so cheerfully.' Even Caro, she said, had remarked on the change in him. 'Do not think from this', Haryo continued,

> that I mean to say it would be a good thing if she was *now* to leave the house . . . Her doing it would be attended with difficulties, reflections and

probably self-reproaches to him, that make it in my mind a thing never to be imagined practicable for a moment, but I only lament to find . . . that if she had not rooted herself by all the ties of habit and now almost a sense of duty in his home, he would be ten thousand times a happier person. I was always certain that her character and manners could not suit him . . .

Haryo had conveniently forgotten that only a week earlier she had attributed her father's high spirits to a marked improvement in his health. That aside, her case against Bess rests on her conviction that her father would have been – indeed, would always have been – happier without her. But was Haryo a fit person to judge what went to make a lasting bond between a man and a woman? Beyond an attachment to Harriet's son, Lord Duncannon, which had ended with his marriage to Lady Maria Fane, she had little experience of adult love. Her memories of her parents' marriage – already softened by time and grief – were of its last years, when Georgiana, her health, sight and beauty gone, had concentrated her remaining strength on her husband and children. Haryo perhaps never knew that the marriage had lurched from crisis to crisis, that her mother's name had been linked with that of Fox, that she had indulged in a passionate affair with Charles Grey. Nor was she unselfish enough – or imaginative enough – to look beyond the immediate future to her own almost certain marriage and permanent removal from Devonshire House. Who would care for her ailing father then?

To Bess's chagrin, her illness put an end to a long-cherished plan for herself, the Duke and Haryo to spend a month at Brighton, the most fashionable seaside resort in England since the Prince of Wales had taken up residence at the Pavilion (in 1807 the Pavilion was still a modest neo-classical structure; today's exotic edifice was not completed by John Nash until the early 1820s). Haryo had been appalled at the prospect of being seen in what she revealingly refers to as 'bad company', whether with the Prince at the Pavilion or at his latest mistress Lady Hertford's. Again, her memory is selective, for her mother and the Prince had been for years on terms of the closest intimacy. Bess's desire to go to Brighton baffled Haryo, and she cruelly pretended to believe that Bess had designs to succeed Lady Hertford as the Prince's mistress – were she 'old enough or fat enough to please him'. She then hit on another reason: Bess hoped the Prince would shower 'honours and dignities' on George Lamb, supposedly his son by Lady Melbourne. Though this was apparently another of Haryo's malicious jokes, if Bess believed the gossip about George's parentage there may have been some truth in her conjecture, since Caro St Jules was secretly engaged to him.

George Lamb certainly resembled the Prince of Wales in his red face and his tendency to run to fat. In character, where Caro was reserved, discreet and gentle, George was boisterous, witty and out-spoken. Lady Melbourne had brought up her children to think and speak for themselves but – in Caro's view – with rather too much 'freedom in religion & moral opinions'. *En masse* they were noisy and exhausting. 'It is like getting among savages,' Haryo told Little G., 'there is no knowing how far their vivacity may carry them.' But Haryo, who liked so few people, liked George. Besides, as she informed Caro, only half in jest, 'My maid told me that all the servants in the M[elbourne] family say George is worth the whole lot of them put together.'

Initially Caro refused George's proposal of marriage, confiding to her journals that she had no doubts other than 'his want of religion. I do not think it is quite like any other fault because I look upon it as the leading principle of life and which must influence the whole char-acter.' Once she had overcome her fears and accepted him, the mar-riage was delayed while George struggled to establish himself as a barrister. But since the success of his comic operas *Whistle for It* and *Who's the Dupe?* 'his heart', according to his sister Emily, 'is in Drury Lane and he thinks of nothing but plays and epilogues and prologues'. For Bess, the prospect of George as a son-in-law was delightful. Not only was he 'one of the most agreeable persons' she knew, but he was deeply in love with Caro. She was also very fond of Lady Melbourne. Indeed, everyone seemed delighted by the match – except George's brother Frederick. 'Think only', he wrote to his mother, 'what it would be for him at two and twenty to be set down with a great fubsy breeding wife to all eternity to be provided for by his own exertions' (Frederick himself did not marry until he was nearly sixty). This was written before the Duke announced his intention of giving Caro twenty thousand pounds as a marriage portion – a considerable fortune in those days – plus an allowance of five hundred pounds a year. George responded to the Duke's 'princely generosity' with frank astonishment. 'If ever man succeeded in life far beyond his merits', he wrote to Bess, 'and without owing anything to his own exertions, really it has fallen to my lot.' This letter is endorsed by Bess: 'I wish I had anybody I could talk to in my bliss.' The Duke's generosity to Caro has been taken as proving that he preferred her to Haryo, to whom he later gave only ten thousand pounds on her marriage; but Bess's references to the Duke's affection for his illegitimate daughter apart, there is little evidence to substantiate this claim. The Prince of Wales congratulated Bess on Caro's engagement 'to my friend George Lamb' and commended the Duke's generosity, but seems to have failed to fulfil any hope Bess might have had that he would show his approbation in some more tangible form.

Caro and George were married in the Great Salon at Devonshire House on 17 May 1809. Two of Little G's daughters were bridesmaids. To Clifford Bess described the wedding as 'brilliant' and Caro as looking 'as pretty as possible'. The wedding presents included jewellery from herself, the Duke and the Melbournes, and books from Fred Foster. From Caro at Brocket in Hertfordshire, where the couple were honeymooning, Bess received a contented letter. It is addressed, as usual, to 'Dear dear Liz', which seems to disprove Haryo's contention that Caro now knew Bess and the Duke to be her parents. 'I am in my own mind without a doubt that George has opened her eyes,' she had told Little G. in 1808, thereby revealing that she and her sister knew the truth – although who told them, and when, is a mystery. Certainly they had not been told by Bess.

It is typical of Bess that her journal entry for Caro's wedding day is brief: 'This evening my dear Caroline was married. They have gone to Brocket Hall!' (Both Caroline St Jules and Caroline Ponsonby having married Lambs, Bess's daughter was henceforth referred to as Caro George, Harriet's as Caro William.) She then resumed her record of public events, principally the progress of the war. 'What a brilliant & wonderfull career is Bonaparte's, & to what will all these conquests lead?' she had written in despair following Napoleon's victory at Friedland in June 1807.

Britain had been fighting France almost continuously since 1793, so that the generation born in the 1780s had grown up with the war, and many of the young men in the Devonshire House Circle were now old enough to take part. In March 1807 Clifford's ship had been involved in the capture of Alexandria; Clifford himself had narrowly escaped death when a shot fell among the officers on deck. The Duke's nephew George Cavendish was drowned when his transport was sunk returning after the retreat to Corunna. Harriet's son Frederick and Lord Morpeth's brother Fred Howard were both now fighting with the British forces in the Peninsula. That young men known personally to her were at risk brought the war into sharper perspective for Bess. From the first, she seemed to identify strongly with the Spanish people – referring to them as 'our dear Spaniards' – and their resistance to the French; she even began to learn Spanish. In December 1808, when Madrid surrendered to Napoleon, Bess wrote to Augustus (now chargé d'affaires at Stockholm): 'Oh, dear Augustus, what a sad reverse, and what reason one had to dread the arrival in Spain of that Tyrant . . .' But she still believed 'that a nation of brave peasants may yet check and withstand the disciplined barbarians of France'. Her faith in Sir Arthur Wellesley was confirmed in July 1809 by his victory at Talavera, but followed by an anxious pause while Harriet awaited news of Frederick, who had taken part in the battle.

The close relationship between Harriet and Bess remained unchanged following Georgiana's death. 'Lady Bessb. ever kind, consoling & a fellow sufferer is a true friend,' Bess noted in January 1808. But their friendship was about to be tested to breaking point by two marriages: Bess's own to the Duke, and Haryo's to Granville.

Society had long anticipated the first marriage. 'I should be more surprised at it *now* than I should have been a year or two ago,' was the response of Bess's niece Caroline Wortley, Mary's daughter, when told in October of the forthcoming event. Sheridan, with deplorable want of tact, had broached the subject barely five months after Georgiana's death, while Fox lay dying at Chiswick. 'Sheridan supp'd here & began by things personal to myself, saying how much he wish'd to see me married to D.D. I stopp'd him saying I was too unhappy yet to hear that language. He then went on talking of Fox', Bess had recorded, and 'cried so much I was oblig'd to make him drink Port Wine.' He became so intoxicated that she was 'glad to get him to go away'. Sheridan's version of this conversation, as related by Mrs Creevey to a friend two days later, was that Bess 'had *cried* to him . . . "because she felt it her severe duty to be Duchess of Devonshire"'. As one of Sheridan's greatest talents, drunk or sober, was for making mischief, Bess's version – confided to her private journal – seems more credible.

But if society had long taken this marriage for granted, Georgiana's family stubbornly refused to accept it, either as inevitable after all these years or as the Duke chivalrously making an honest woman of Bess; rather they assumed, as usual, that it was all Bess's doing, that the Duke was being led like a lamb to the slaughter, as if he had no will of his own. Nor did they pause to consider what Georgiana might have wanted; since she had surrendered her husband to Bess in life, she would surely not have begrudged their official union after her death, but would instead have seen it as the best solution for them both.

The decision taken, Bess informed her family, enjoining them to secrecy until she was actually married. To Augustus she explained that the Duke had resolved to silence the insidious talk for ever by giving her the sanction of his name. 'You my dearest Augustus who know how I lov'd her [Georgiana], will do justice to the motives which have influenc'd this conduct, & to the feelings which make me wish to avoid any publicity at present.' She had even suggested that the marriage should be kept secret 'as the revival of a name so dear is agitating to my own feelings as well as to her Children'. The Duke had sensibly insisted 'that we ought not to shrink from public knowledge of it, & besides he thought it would fail in advantage to me if not known'. Caro was told just before leaving with George for Chatsworth, to stay with Hart. 'It made her very happy tho' very nervous.' Fred too showed her 'great feeling & kindness'. Augustus's eventual response from Stockholm was a relief: 'A thousand, thousand thanks my dear child for your confidence in my conduct . . . and for the forbearance with which you have borne all the attacks which I knew well you must have heard made upon me.' Clifford's reaction has not survived, but it can be safely assumed that he too approved, since there is no evidence that any of Bess's children ever disapproved of anything she did. Instead, the record is one of boundless love given and reciprocated.

While Bess despatched letters hither and thither, the Duke wrote to no one. Bess herself eventually wrote to Lord Morpeth, asking him to prepare Little G. and Haryo for their father's letter and disclosing what it would contain. The Duke continued to procrastinate. Bess wrote again, this time on the Duke's behalf, authorizing Lord Morpeth to break the news. In the event, both girls seem to have been resigned: 'I am surprised and glad', Haryo told Hart, 'that I bear so well what I always expected to bear so ill.' The joint letter they sent 'Dearest Papa' successfully avoided any mention of either Bess or the marriage, but assured him of their 'most anxious wishes' for his happiness.

The first poor Hart had heard of the forthcoming marriage was from his cousin Caro William. It would be hard to imagine anyone more temperamentally unsuited to broaching such a delicate subject than Caroline. Her letter is a blistering attack on Bess; more woundingly, she charges Hart with hypocrisy, and with being so weak as to allow 'that old witch' to manipulate him: 'Oh she is a deep one! She has flummeried up a certain young Marquis from his cradle.' She even raged at Caro George, whom she accused of having been aware of the whole intrigue from the beginning (Caro did of course know before she went to Chatsworth, but had been sworn to secrecy by Bess on the assumption that the Duke would wish to tell his son himself). Hart's reply was indignant: 'When, I should like to know, have you seen me fawn upon that crocodile, as you have the cruelty to say I do in your wicked letter?' The Duke's letter finally reached his son four days after the wedding, when it had already been reported in the newspapers. Hart's reply was brief, formal and cold.

Two days before the wedding, the Duke at last wrote to Lady Spencer, informing her that he was marrying Lady Elizabeth – for whom he had 'the greatest friendship and regard' – because he had been told 'that in the opinion of the world there is an impropriety . . . in her being in my house upon any other terms'. He would, he added illogically, have done so sooner had he not felt that it might appear that he was not 'sufficiently grieved'. Lady Spencer reacted with surprising dignity and restraint, although she admitted to 'agitated spirits & an aching heart' and begged that she should not be required to visit Devonshire House. But her son George, inflamed by the shrewish Lavinia, began to talk of the Spencer family severing all connection with Devonshire House, and to suggest that Haryo should 'quit her Father'. For Bess, who had worked so hard to keep the peace, this would have been a disaster. Had it not been for Harriet Bessborough's intervention, a permanent rift might have taken place.

Harriet at this time was greatly to be pitied. Her grief for Georgiana had settled over her like a shroud, robbing her of any pleasure in life or hope for the future; she missed Granville desperately during his long absences abroad, yet the linking of his name with those of numerous eligible girls (most recently, with Haryo's) when he was in England caused her equal distress; her daughter Caroline's violent and irrational behaviour was endangering her marriage to William Lamb, and their only child Augustus was showing signs of mental deficiency; her son Frederick was in the thick of the fighting in Spain; Sheridan was still persecuting her; and – perhaps it was symptomatic of her wretchedness – she had grown 'immensely fat'. Faced with this fresh crisis, however, neither her compassion nor her courage deserted her. Rather than be unfair to Bess, she told Granville, she was prepared to stand alone against her own family *and* against Georgiana's children 'as favouring an event, which God knows pains me more than any, I believe, and taking part against them and against the memory of what

I lov'd best on earth . . .' Yet her support for Bess was qualified. 'I really love Bess, and think she has many more good and generous qualities than are allowed her, but I think she has the worst judgement of any body I ever met with; and I begin also to think she has more Calcul, and more power of concentrating her wishes and intentions, than I ever before believ'd.'

This view of Bess as manipulative and calculating is echoed by Lavinia's daughter Sarah in a letter to her brother Bob (Clifford's friend and shipmate): 'It is not an interesting *union de deux jeunes cœurs*, I must say, but rather the crowning of a perseverance in vice and artfulness, which is I fancy unheard of; Clifford of course knows, as it is no other than the long-expected wedding of his venerable parents.' (Sarah's assumption that Clifford knew the truth was incorrect, but reveals that yet another branch of the family was in on the secret.) Haryo, despite having resigned herself to the inevitable, fired a last devastating broadside: 'My mind was early opened to Lady Elizabeth's character,' she wrote to Hart, 'unparallelled I do believe for want of principle and delicacy, and more perverted than deceitful, for I really believe she hardly herself knows the difference between right and wrong now. Circumstances have altered her conduct and situation at different times but she has invariably been what even when a child I understood and despised.'

Such views are proof enough that many saw the marriage as the triumphant conclusion to a ruthless campaign by Bess to become Duchess of Devonshire. Had she been thirty years younger, it might have been true; the alliance of youth and beauty with the Duke's rank and position would have brought society to her feet. But at fifty-one, exhausted by years spent trying to placate the Cavendish children, soothing the Duke, braving the world's censure and bringing up her own children, marriage – and the security and respectability it gave her – was more a relief than a victory.

There was one person who wished her well, however, and from the very pinnacle of society: the Prince of Wales. In his elegant handwriting, the pen dipped in honey and the sentences so labyrinthine as to be barely comprehensible, he wrote to Bess the day before her marriage. Referring to himself as 'an old & dearest sincere Friend', he assured her of 'the lively & sincere interest which I have uniformly felt, & ever must feel, in whatever relates to your happiness & welfare', and hoped that she would 'long long enjoy the scene of happiness that awaits you, that no one in my mind, can be more entitled to it, than

Yourself, from the unremitting & disinterested attachment & affection you have invariably testified to One [Georgiana] that was so justly dear to us all, when living, as well as to Her memory, & ever since alas! she was taken from us, an event which can never be fogotten, by the circle of those who really knew her, (& of course could not fail to be devoted to Her,) while they have either a mind to think or a Heart to feel' . . . and so on, for five pages.

Bess and the Duke were married at Chiswick House on 19 October 1809. The only witness was a Mrs Spencer, a distant and impoverished relation of the Spencer family. In her journal, which had remained unopened during the difficult weeks leading up to the wedding, Bess wrote three lines of an Italian poem which had been a favourite of hers and Georgiana's some twenty years before. The poem refers to actions, thoughts and affections which they had shared in common; the last line, when translated, reads 'and at last the name also'. Bess adds: 'How little I thought when first we repeated them that they would be realis'd, & how my heart would have griev'd at the thought of surviving her, tho' its sole comfort & joy now is to belong to the Duke of Devonshire!'

Two days after the wedding, the Morpeths and Haryo dutifully visited the happy couple at Chiswick. 'Nothing could be kinder than their manner to me,' Bess recorded with her customary determination to think well of her step-children. 'The state of things here is better than I could have expected,' Haryo told Hart, adding astutely: 'Her manner is less offensive from no longer being a perpetual struggle to put forward claims and require attention to which henceforward nobody can dispute her right.' Fred had also 'shown good taste and what is better and natural to him, good feeling. He is neither elated nor significant, more attentive in his manner to us and exactly the same to her.' Caro George, as usual, was 'the best and most amiable of human beings but impenetrable as to what she thinks or feels'. Hart did not visit them until five weeks later. 'I have found everything here as I expected,' he wrote to his grandmother, Lady Spencer. 'Nothing at all offensive in the Dss's manner. On the contrary, her civility and kindness oppress us . . . and she really is behaving so well to Harriet [Haryo], that I feel some gratitude.'

Hart's gratitude sprang from Bess's support for Haryo's courtship by Lord Granville. Though Granville's interest in her seems to have come as a surprise to Haryo, Bess had been aware of her attraction to the handsome diplomat as early as 1807. Unwisely, she had indicated as much to Haryo, who scoffed at the idea to Little G. Bess had thought Harriet's son Duncannon 'wrong' for Haryo, but approved of Granville, possibly because she felt an older man more likely to command Haryo's respect and break down her reserve. 'She will never shew or feel a preference for any body who is not decided in their liking for her . . .', she told Augustus. Despite her fears for the effect it would have on Harriet Bessborough, she did her best to promote the match.

Granville had been the one great passion in Harriet's life. Their liaison had endured for thirteen years, survived his many flirtations and produced two illegitimate children (the second, a boy, had been born in 1804). To Granville, Harriet could say 'every thing from the very recesses of my Heart'. But she knew that he was too charming, too brilliant and too eligible not to marry. 'It is what I think you particularly form'd for,' she once told him. But to have to relinquish him to her niece was all but unbearable. Granville, too, was torn, later confessing to Haryo that 'there was scarcely a thought that passed through my mind, or a folly committed by me' which he had not felt able to share with Harriet. Always quick to judge, Haryo blamed Granville's vacillations on her aunt, accusing her of everything from duplicity to vanity. 'Lady B. is an awful example of what self-indulgence and yielding principles will end in,' she complained to Miss Trimmer, showing how little she understood the depth of Harriet's love for Granville.

Bess tried to calm the situation by assuring Little G. that in her view there were no 'insurmountable obstacles', and advising that she should counsel Haryo to be patient. 'I really have felt an anxiety about her happiness as great as if she were mine,' she adds. To Lord Morpeth she confided: 'Ly B. is nervous, but I *think* has determin'd on courageous conduct. She has a generous mind & will I hope exert it.' Granville finally proposed in November, and was accepted. With the generosity Bess had expected of her, Harriet wrote to Granville: 'God in Heaven bless and grant you every happiness . . .' The wedding took place at Chiswick on 24 December, two months after the Duke's to Bess.

The preceding months had been a bruising time for all concerned. But it was a polite and respectful society; the harsh judgements made, especially of Bess and Harriet, were committed to paper, not delivered face to face. Decorum was preserved, delicate sensibilities were spared. Haryo's marriage proved a great success. Georgiana would doubtless have been gratified, and perhaps a little surprised in view of the example she had set, to know that both her daughters were to lead exemplary married lives.

Bess's journal covering the first year of her marriage is fragmentary. There is no mention of Augustus's expulsion from the embassy in Stockholm when Sweden was forced to side with France, nor of the unspeakable death of her old flame Count Fersen, torn to pieces by a Stockholm mob in the mistaken belief that he had poisoned the Swedish heir-apparent. Only weeks before his terrible end, Fersen had written to Bess in praise of Augustus's conduct as chargé d'affaires in Stockholm.

In April 1810 Bess and the Duke returned from Chiswick to Devonshire House. 'It is not without regret that I quit this dear place, a place so full of strong regrets, endless recollections & present comforts. But still, to go to Town with D.D. free from all those unkind misconstructions of society . . . is a comfort for which I am most gratefull.' Her presentation at Court by her sister Louisa (now Lady Liverpool, since the death of her father-in-law) set the seal on her new respectability.

Augustus had returned from Sweden in time to join a large house party given by Bess and the Duke at Chiswick. Harriet Bessborough, who continued to correspond with Granville after his marriage, told him that 'nothing could be gayer or more brilliant . . . Each day we sat down 26 or 27 to table, waltzing every night and all night long.' (This is very early evidence of the waltz being danced in England. It was said to have originated in Germany, and people were initially shocked by the promiscuity of the 'close hold'.) Bess had again done her best to be tactful, discussing the guest list with Little G. beforehand. 'I think the Dss must have been highly gratified,' Little G. told Hart, 'the Duchess of Richmond and her daughters [the fourth Duke and his wife had seven altogether, and seven sons] came and most of the women she asked.' A brilliant assembly followed in June. According to Little G., Devonshire House 'looked beautifull and was excessively admired & tho' there were between 8 & 900 people there was no crowd'. Even Lady Spencer conceded that Bess's entry into society as Duchess of Devonshire had met with 'extraordinary success'. There remained one major challenge – to return to Chatsworth and Hardwick after an absence of seven years, and for the first time since Georgiana's death.

For Bess this was a double ordeal: not only were both houses suffused with memories of Georgiana, but any idea that she might be able to take the place of one so beloved by the staff and tenants was unthinkable. Yet it was Bess who urged the Duke to rouse himself to make the long-overdue journey north, even though 'should it disagree with him I shall be miserable'. On their arrival at Hardwick in October they were welcomed by Hart, who later told Little G. that 'the Duchess arrived here as if she had taken a morning drive, without the least sign of emotion of any sort'. Bess's journal gives a very different impression: '*Cento memorie e cento* crowded upon my mind & I was afraid to give them utterance, yet felt convinc'd that D.D. was affected in the same way . . . It was seven years since we had travell'd this road; what a fearfull change had death occasion'd, but humbly gratefull do I feel for what is preserved to me & for the incomparable blessing of being D.D's wife.' As for his father, Hart said he was 'as happy as possible and rides about all day'. Bess and the Duke celebrated their first wedding anniversary by giving dinner to nineteen poor children, an act of charity very much in the spirit of Georgiana.

A week later they transferred to Chatsworth. Moved by seeing the house after so long, Bess again took refuge in Italian: '*Quanto oh quanto rimembrance care dolci ed amari!*' Her journal is then taken up by an account of the King's illness and relapse into madness, exacerbated by the death of his favourite child, Princess Amelia. When a Regency became inevitable, the Duke set off in thick snow, travelling non-stop to reach London in time to vote on the restrictions to the Prince's powers contained in the Regency Bill. (He wrote to Bess on his arrival in London. 'God bless him – happy, happy me,' she wrote in her journal. Fragments of the Duke's letter, the last he ever wrote to her, were found in a minute envelope in her pocket when she died.) Bess followed, arriving in London on 5 January 1811, to become instantly embroiled in the now familiar sequence of events. Leading Whigs congregated at Devonshire House, where ministerial posts were bandied to and fro and plans hatched for an imminent return to power. On 6 February the Prince of Wales was sworn in as Regent. With his new status, however, came a swing in allegiance: the Prince turned his back on his old Whig friends, and retained his father's Government. Bess admitted to being 'thunderstruck', but was ready to believe the excuse given: the Prince had been warned that for his father to regain his sanity and find the Whigs in power might drive him mad again, or even kill him. Others were not so forgiving: 'The folly and villainy of this Prinney,' declared Mr Creevey to his wife, 'is certainly beyond anything.'

Within five days of becoming Regent, the Prince demonstrated his affection for Bess by obtaining Clifford's promotion to Master and Commander. Bess was ecstatic. She had been pulling every string she could muster to end three years of frustration, during which Clifford felt he had been passed over because of his Whig connections. He had even contemplated leaving the navy, a service he loved and for which he was ideally suited. His consideration of this course was based on a letter from Bess – dictated by the Duke – assuring him that he was free to do so if he chose, as he would be 'well provided for'.

Not content with one act of kindness, two days later the Regent informed Bess that he had assented to the nomination of Augustus as ambassador to the United States. 'But will my dear Augustus like this?' she wondered. To be made ambassador at thirty-one was a great achievement, but she knew how he had hated his previous term at Washington. She was also aware of his attachment to Annabella Milbanke, a cold-hearted young heiress from Durham with a passion for mathematics (dubbed the 'Princess of Parallelograms' by Lord Byron, who later married her). It was too early in the courtship for him to risk a proposal; in any case, as he had once expressed the view that 'a Woman of Education & feeling suffers dreadfully' in America, to do so would have taken courage. Beyond pointing out the advantages of such an important mission, Bess left the decision to her son. With great reluctance he left for America in June.

These were among the most tranquil and contented months of Bess's troubled life. Her situation at Devonshire House no longer ambiguous, liberated from Haryo's malevolent scrutiny, Caro married and two of her sons doing well in their professions, she was free at last to spend her days with the man she had loved for nearly thirty years. As she later told Augustus, 'there was not a day, scarcely an hour, I did not thank Heaven for the happiness of belonging to such a man'. The celebrations to mark Hart's coming of age in May set society's seal of approval on the new Duchess of Devonshire.

On 12 July Caro George noted in her journal, 'Duke of D. taken ill with a violent inflammatory attack on the chest'. The Duke had suffered such attacks before, and Caro left for Brighton with the Melbournes as planned. But a week later the Duke's health deteriorated, and the spasms on his chest became more frequent. For five nights he slept sitting upright in a chair to relieve his breathing. Bess never left him. On 28 July he felt better, and was able to walk on the terrace overlooking the garden at Devonshire House. He then ate a hearty dinner. Sometime on the afternoon of the 29th Bess scrawled a note to Lord Morpeth, who was in London: 'I am hardly able to write to you from anxiety and misery. D.D. has had a worse spasmodic attack than ever – but is something easier now, *much* as to pain.' At half-past six Granville, who was present in the house with Haryo, told Lord Morpeth the physicians considered the Duke 'to be in very great danger'. At nine his breathlessness increased, and the apothecary decided to open a vein in his arm. 'But just as he was preparing the lancet the head of the patient fell back and he expired without a groan in the arms of the Duchess.'

Late that night Hart sent a note to Lord Morpeth: 'I write in the greatest affliction and have to tell you that all is over . . . The poor Dss is in a dreadful state and our grief is overwhelmed in attempts to calm her.'

12

The dark years
1811–late 1815

'What a wreck in these last few years! All that is pre-
eminent is gone. To me it is as a desert, and but for my
children what an exile should I feel in this world . . .'

Bess to Augustus, 3 November 1811

Bess had been married for barely twenty-one months. 'It is a loss
& grief not to be conceiv'd almost – & so unexpected!' she wrote
in anguish to her brother, Lord Bristol. 'I thank God I was able to be
with him to the last, even to the feeling as I held him of the convul-
sive spasm that destroy'd him. I fix'd his last look. I felt the last
warmth. I remain'd till Hartington, who was weeping over him with
me, at last carried me in his arms to the next room.'

Devonshire House was once more engulfed in the paraphernalia of
death. Hatchments were put up, the coffin was laid on its catafalque in
the Great Hall. The family, dressed in deepest mourning, received relatives and friends. By ill luck Fred, like Caro, was away; they set out for
London immediately, she from Brighton, he from Ireland. The
Cavendish children, despite their own grief, behaved to Bess with the
greatest kindness and compassion in the grim days following their
father's death. 'The poor Dss has been in a sad state,' Hart wrote to the
Prince Regent on 3 August, 'our hearts bleed for her, and it is the greatest hope of my sisters and myself that we may by our attention in some
degree soothe and reconcile her to her cruel change of situation.'

The suddenness of the Duke's death was explained by a report in the *Morning Chronicle* of 3 August which stated that the 'body of the Duke of Devonshire has been opened . . . and upwards of three pints of water were found in his chest . . .' On 4 August, the night before the coffin left for Derbyshire, Little G. and Haryo took 'a last leave of all that was left us' (Bess told her sister Mary), then returned to their homes. Hart and Caro 'went again and again into the room' where the Duke's body lay. Five years earlier, when Georgiana's coffin left Devonshire House, Bess had watched the cortège as it swung through the gates into Piccadilly. This time her courage failed her, and she was put to bed with a sleeping draught by her maid, Madame Pallé. Twenty-one carriages, led by the Prince Regent's, attended the hearse on its journey as far as 'the stones' end' – the point where the cobbles ceased on the road leading north out of London.

On 9 August, accompanied by Caro and Fred, Bess left for Chiswick, which had been lent her by Hart. There she had spent much of her married life, the Duke pottering contentedly about in the garden 'planting & improving'. And there in the garden she had buried her beloved dog Lilli, beneath a large and handsome stone inscribed with a lengthy epitaph in Latin. From Chiswick she wrote to Augustus.

[I am] calmer now, but as wretched; less stunned, and therefore more competent to feel the full extent of my loss. I can only wonder that my life and intellect have lasted. What is it that enables one to survive such a shock, so sudden, so unexpected, so overwhelming? God has supported me, and given me dear children and kind friends, and I ought to be, and am, grateful for these blessings, but indeed, my dearest Augustus, the husband whom I have lost was the creature of my adoration, and long had been so. He was so eminent in all that is good, amiable, noble, and praiseworthy. I almost wondered at my own happiness in being united to him . . . Oh God, it is too, too much. This place, too, so full of him; his dear, his gracious form in every part of these gardens so present, so fully impressed on my mind, that all appears at times a fearful dream . . .

Bess's letters to her son are always written with this same candour and directness. 'God give you strength to bear this dreadful blow my poor Mother,' he replied. 'To one who knew how you were wrapt up in him it is dreadful to think of your loss . . .'

For once it was not left entirely to Bess to sing the Duke's praises. Two tributes, from very different sources, amply reinforce her view of her husband. 'My love and admiration for him was excessive,' Fred confided to Lord Morpeth, '& well it might be, for never I believe was there a nobler finer mind, or a kinder or purer heart. His goodness to me was unceasing. Never can I forget the great, the uncommon kindness I experienced . . . from him & the angelic being we lost before him.' From the Vicar of Edensor, the village which lies within the park at Chatsworth, there was equally sincere praise: 'He appeared to me to possess the kindest and gentlest heart, with the soundest & most extensive information, particularly on literary subjects; every soul in my parish appears to be struck with the deepest grief.'

Though she was never a real friend, Lady Holland's assessment of Bess's plight displays an astute understanding of her relationship with the Duke. 'The situation of the Duchess is deplorable,' she wrote to Charles Grey, 'for whatever faults she may have had they are expiated by this calamity, for to the Duke she was always affectionate, good, and grateful. And as he was the inducement and cause of her betraying and injuring others, so was he her protector, and now to be deprived of him her only support she becomes an object of very great compassion . . .'

Bess's letters in the weeks following the Duke's death are pitiful to read. To Lord Morpeth she wrote that she was 'very weak and little able to bear up under the weight of grief which oppresses me . . . My nights are bad, my waking worse . . .' Yet on the surface she supported herself, as Harriet Bessborough told Granville, 'with a degree of fortitude that is really quite wonderful. Her loss is one that, besides the tearing asunder every tie of long affection, touches her so in every point, that there can be no doubt of what she feels; indeed, her whole appearance bears testimony to it. Yet, so far from any display of grief, she quite surprizes me with the composure and even cheerfulness with which she mixes in society.'

Problems to do with his will surfaced before the poor Duke was in his grave. Bess was shocked to find that Clifford was not mentioned, nor was a codicil – which she believed existed – anywhere to be found. As Bess told Mary in October, the Duke had assured her that the codicil would provide Clifford with an 'independent' fortune which would enable him to leave the navy if he so chose. She appealed to Hart for some extra provision for Clifford; perplexed, Hart consulted his uncle, Lord George Cavendish, one of the Duke's executors, who clearly thought Bess had invented the codicil. So did Hart: 'I shall always feel for her what she deserves,' he told Lady Spencer, 'but I cannot bear to see art and falsehood employed at such a time.'

Clifford himself, in the Mediterranean, knew nothing of the dispute, but would have been gratified to learn that Hart was counselled by his sisters, his grandmother and even Miss Trimmer to correct the omission in his father's will. It was in Hart's nature to be generous, and he settled an annuity of two thousand pounds a year on his half-brother. This was not, he assured Lady Spencer, because he had been influenced by Bess: 'I only went by my idea of what *he* [the Duke] would have wished me to do and of what I think right to one to whom he gave existence . . .' He adds: 'The Dss to my surprise was delighted and satisfied with this.'

There was also trouble over Bess's settlement. She insisted, Harriet told Granville, that the Duke had promised to 'double her jointure, give her the choice of a House, and a large Sum of Money to dispose of; that the two latter . . . she would waive, but the jointure was a positive sum nam'd repeatedly, and that she looks upon it as much hers by right as if left by will . . . You cannot think how unpleasant all this is.' Unpleasant perhaps, but Bess was not going to give up now. She knew this was her last chance to secure her own and her children's future – a future which the Duke had painted *couleur de rose*. Given his positive gift for procrastination, who is to say that he had not indeed made such promises, fully intending to carry them out 'tomorrow' – but then died before tomorrow came. As there is nothing to suggest that Bess ever lied intentionally in her journal (that she may at times have deluded herself is another matter), her recorded view of events might clarify things, but either she had ceased keeping her journal in March 1811, or the notebooks covering the ensuing year have been lost.

Again Hart behaved with generosity, increasing Bess's jointure from four thousand to six thousand pounds a year. Again she was deeply grateful. There remained one major problem: where was she to live? By choosing a larger income, she had waived any claim to a house. When she showed no signs of removing herself from Chiswick, Hart 'very peremptorily' limited her stay there to a single week – despite her assertion that the Duke had intended it as her dower house. Bess thereupon rented 13 Piccadilly Terrace, overlooking Green Park and within a stone's throw of Devonshire House (the house is still there, a veritable mansion by today's standards, though a mere cottage compared to Devonshire House). Bess almost certainly received from Hart, at Haryo's instigation, an additional two thousand pounds with which to 'establish herself without encroaching upon her jointure' – a surprising and benevolent suggestion on the part of her severest critic.

The problems over the will upset the Cavendishes, but Haryo blamed much of Bess's assertiveness on the influence of Mrs Spencer. 'Disregard entirely that long German spider Mrs S.,' she advised Hart, 'she crawls amongst us all for no good purpose, and I suspect her to be the first amongst the Duchess's injudicious advisors.' Hart agreed: 'She makes me sick.' As Mr and Mrs Spencer first appear in Bess's journal in 1808, Mrs Spencer had been crawling among them for some time. Furthermore, Haryo claimed that her father's phaeton had been frequently observed standing outside Mrs Spencer's door at impru- dent times of the day, *after* his marriage to Bess. 'Can the Duchess like this?' she wondered. Even William Lamb suggested that Mrs Spencer was 'going to fill the [place] so lately made vacant by the promotion of Lady E. Foster'. (Yet her will shows that the Spencers' naval son William had been 'fitted out' by Bess and the Duke in 1809, and she left him an annuity of twenty pounds.)

Hart's conduct since becoming sixth Duke of Devonshire was remarkable for a young man only just turned twenty-one. Having dealt firmly and tactfully with his stepmother, he now displayed an unex- pectedly mature sagacity by insisting – against Bess's will – that he should reveal to Caro George the truth about her birth. Perhaps he felt that as everyone else knew, it was high time she did. (Presumably he also told Clifford.) Caro's reaction calls into question the wisdom of Bess's suppression of the facts for so many years: 'Oh how I regretted I had not known it during *his* life,' she wrote in her memoirs, 'most hon- oured! most beloved! now gone! gone, and I can never show what I feel! I should have been so different & so much happier!' Hart tried to comfort her: 'You never were wanting in affection and kindness to him, and perhaps an explanation might have been unpleasant to you and to him as he felt nothing to wish for in your conduct.'

In her confused and altered state, Caro wrote to Little G.:

You whom ignorantly I have always loved as a sister, you from whom I have not one secret thought concealed, to you I must write in this moment of agitation, anxiety, and yet of joy, to tell you I have learnt I am indeed your sister . . . You may imagine the various feelings this has caused in me. But love to you all, to my poor beloved *mother* (it is the first time I ever traced that endearing word) is uppermost. I am so happy to be no longer the unconnected being I thought myself.

Her words finally put an end to the persistent speculation that she already knew. She admitted to Little G. that there had been times when she had had her suspicions, but they were always dispelled 'by an odious picture which for many years I looked upon as my mother's' (the portrait of 'a beautiful woman with a wreath of roses on her head' which Bess, in her contortions to hide the truth, had arranged for Comte St Jules to present to Caro). Though Hart could not have known it, his revelation was ill-timed: the emotional upheaval which followed the shock of discovery may have precipitated Caro's confession to Bess that her marriage was in serious trouble.

It had begun so well. After their wedding Caro and George had moved into a small house near his chambers in Lincoln's Inn. In 1810 she accompanied him while he toiled around the Northern Circuit. A fellow barrister and friend, George Eden, was full of praise for the way Caro made 'the best of her dirty lodgings, attends the assize balls, sits half the day in court, makes up to all the lawyers, and appears as happy withal as if she were still living in Devonshire House'. But her memoirs contain a clue that all was not well: 'All this time while seeming so happy and gay a secret sorrow and warm corroding at the heart.' No wonder: after nearly three years, the marriage remained unconsummated.

Bess, for whom love and its expression had been the mainspring of existence, reacted almost hysterically. In her distress she turned for help to the Cavendish children, entreating them to be a support to Caro. Her letters are disjointed and emotional, her anxiety for Caro often submerged in her grief for the Duke; one shock had followed too quickly upon the other. Caro was 'the dear Angelick victim', George 'an unnatural being, a monster'. For Caro to be chained to a man who was 'insensible to joy and passion', for ever condemned to 'her solitary bed' and never to 'have the blessing of a child', tormented her. 'I feel by turns love, pity, sorrow & indignation against poor George,' she told Little G. Her stepchildren again behaved with compassion, not only to their half-sister but to Bess; she in her turn poured out her gratitude to them in numerous letters. In one to Little G. she adds that had the Duke been alive 'he would have tried to soothe and comfort' Caro, which casts new light on the Duke's relationship with his illegitimate daughter.

In the midst of this crisis Clifford returned, having acquitted himself with distinction in an action against the French in the Mediterranean and learnt while at sea both of the Duke's death and the truth about his parentage. 'Clifford and Caroline now know that they were his [the Duke's] children,' Bess told Augustus; what she does *not* tell him is that they were her children also. It was another seven months before she could bring herself to make this final confession. 'The love which you bear me has determin'd me not to delay till our meeting the asking of you to receive at my hands Caroline and Clifford as a Brother & Sister . . . How tenderly their dear Father loved them need not be told. For my own excuse I must plead his Virtues, & assure you as I can with truth, that as long as I lived with your Father, I was perfectly and strictly faithful to him.'

In early November 1811, Caro George wrote to Augustus from Devonshire House: 'The Duchess is come to town to pack up all her things and to leave this house for ever. It is a moment I have always dreaded for her.' To return to the house, which had stood virtually empty for three months, its shutters closed, the Great Hall still draped in mourning, was like entering a tomb. For Bess the act of packing up her possessions and saying farewell to the servants finally closed the door on the singular life she had led within its walls. 'What a wreck in these last few years!' she wrote to Augustus. 'All that is pre-eminent is gone. To me it is as a desert, and but for my children, what an exile I should feel in this world.'

From Devonshire House in November Bess, Fred and the George Lambs joined Clifford at Portsmouth, where he was waiting to take command of his first ship, the *Cephalus*. The port seethed with soldiers in transit to and from the Peninsular War, every hotel and lodging crammed with officers and anxious relatives. Harriet Bessborough, who was waiting for her son Frederick to sail for Portugal, thought Bess unwise to appear in such a 'gossiping' place. Her scandalous past had not been forgotten; nor had her negotiations over the Duke's will gone unremarked in the English press. But until her house was ready, where else should she go? Despite Clifford's prolonged absence at sea, he had been granted only a few weeks' leave; what was more natural than for her to want to spend those few precious weeks with her son?

Though he was normally a sensitive and modest young man, Clifford's recent promotion and the discovery that he was a duke's son went to his head. He took to walking out of rooms ahead of those he deemed his inferiors, and expected to take precedence at table. 'You have no Idea of the noise it makes here,' Harriet told Granville. Clifford's conduct was probably influenced by Bess, who briefly deluded herself that her marriage to the Duke in some way legitimized their children, even to the extent of entitling them to bear the Cavendish arms. (She may have been aware that an illegitimate son of her great-uncle Thomas Hervey had been allowed to use the family name and bear the family arms.) Clifford's foolish behaviour came to the notice of his admiral, who administered a sharp rebuke.

Clifford was also in trouble of another kind: he had fallen in love with Miss Mercer Elphinstone, confidante of the Princess Charlotte. 'She is a great coquette,' Harriet warned, 'and I am afraid poor Clifford will find her so.' Bess consulted Hart, already himself a target for ambitious mothers with marriageable daughters, and he confirmed Harriet's warning. The tentative courtship ended abruptly when Clifford received orders to sail. The Lambs returned to London while Bess remained at Portsmouth. 'How sad the house looks without you,' she wrote to Caro. 'I used to like it so in the morning to hear your dear brother calling you, then your soft voice answering, then to come and see the dear faces of each, and in both, kind inquiring anxious looks to know how I did. I had need of all the comfort and soothing which you both gave me.'

In early January 1812 Bess concluded 'an amicable controversy' with Hart over some of the Cavendish jewels in her possession by returning all but a few. 'Her chief reason for wishing to keep them', Harriet told Granville, 'was for the pleasure of giving them to Hart's wife whenever he married.' There now remained nothing except ties of friendship and good will to keep the two families together. Both Little G. and Haryo were taken up with their own growing families, and Hart was in the full flush of his dukedom. On paper he was now fabulously rich, but the debts left by his parents greatly reduced his income. He had nevertheless completed the purchase, begun by his father, of a house for Caro and George in Whitehall Yard. Bess moved in with them while Piccadilly Terrace was being prepared for her.

For nearly thirty years Bess had been borne along on the tide of Georgiana's popularity and the Duke's exalted rank; now she must paddle her small skiff by herself. The prospect filled her with dread. To Little G. she confessed she 'had a horror of society, a fixed determination never to mix in it again', that 'the poor remnants' of her life would be spent lamenting the loss of 'your dear Mother & Father . . . & in the sorrowfull conviction that nothing like happiness remains for me'. In this mood of morbid retrospection, she moved in February 1812 to Piccadilly Terrace.

Her journal, which she resumed keeping in March, and her correspondence reveal Bess's instability during this early period of her widowhood. She was restless, frequently ill, and subject to bouts of depression, often a burden to herself and to others. Her grief for the Duke was continuous. 'How is it possible to live without him?' she wrote in May 1812. In July, on the day preceding the anniversary of his death, she scribbled in Italian: 'This day last year was the last of my happiness. I feared nothing: and on the following day I was plunged into sorrow and agony so that I do not know how I find myself alive.' She evaded loneliness by visiting the Bessboroughs at Roehampton; July found her with Fred and Caro taking the waters at Tunbridge Wells. When Augustus finally returned from Washington, he joined her there. Clifford, still at sea and about to attack a French convoy, wrote to her in June: 'In case anything happens to me I leave this letter for you that you may know to the last moment that I loved and adored you more than any thing in the world.' In August he was made Post Captain, his promotion once again facilitated by the Prince Regent.

To judge by the entries in her journal, though Bess still did not go into society, she had numerous visitors. While Parliament was in session she was kept up to date with events by Granville, Lord Grey and Lord Morpeth. Hart (she now called him D.) occasionally dined with her before going to the House of Lords. 'D. has staid on comfortably talking to me till it is quite late, but I love to have him so, & he is so amiable & kind to me,' she told Clifford. On Hart's birthday she entertained him, Haryo, Granville and their children to tea. Haryo, blissfully happy in her marriage ('G., adored G., who would make a barren desert smile') could now look upon her stepmother with equanimity: Bess was no longer a threat, and compassion for her evident distress and Haryo's own sense of duty did the rest. Away from Devonshire House and all it had represented, Bess also now saw more of her sisters Mary and Louisa.

In March Lord Byron erupted on to the London scene when John Murray published *Childe Harold's Pilgrimage* and he embarked on his tempestuous and much publicized liaison with Caroline Lamb. Though Bess did not actually meet him until a year later – when she pronounced him to be 'nearly beautifull' – the affair wreaked havoc in the lives of several of those close to her. Typically, she makes no mention of this in her journal, confining her comments to Byron's admiration of Caro George's singing and to his prowess as a poet. As Caroline's life-long friend and William Lamb's sister-in-law, however, Caro could not help but become involved. She was also acquainted with Augustus's current obsession, Annabella Milbanke, who had caught Byron's eye at the same time as he met Caroline Lamb. Though flattered by him, Caro George did her best to warn both Caroline and Annabella against him. Byron was aware of her disapproval, yet pronounced her one of 'the three pleasantest persons' he knew, the other two being Lady Melbourne and her daughter Emily Cowper. The former, as mother-in-law to both Caros, Annabella's aunt and Byron's confidante, was not merely involved but in it up to her neck. Apart from Caroline herself – and poor William Lamb – Harriet was the person most grievously affected by the affair. Her daughter's scandalous conduct, the friction it caused between herself and the Melbournes, and Caroline's brief but alarming disappearance in August, culminated in Harriet being found by her maid, Mrs Petersen, unconscious on the floor of her carriage. Her collapse precipitated weeks of ill-health. In a furious letter, Mrs Petersen told Caroline that her 'cruel & unnatural' behaviour would be the death of her mother and that she had become the talk of 'every Groom & Footman about the Town'. The Bessboroughs, with Caroline and William firmly in tow, fled to Ireland.

Bess tried to console Augustus for his lack of progress with Annabella. 'She is really an icicle,' she wrote to him in Washington in May. 'We must look out for something better . . . Lord Byron makes up to her a little, but she don't seem to admire him except as a poet, nor he her, except for a wife.' By the autumn, Byron had had enough of Caroline's excesses and was trying to extricate himself. When Haryo saw the Bessboroughs and Lambs on their return from Ireland she reported to Little G. that Caroline looked 'worn to the Bone' and seemed to be in a state 'little short of insanity'.

The war continued to engross Bess, as Wellington reversed the French tide in Spain. In May her detailed exposition of events there was briefly interrupted by the murder of Spencer Perceval in the lobby of the House of Commons; he was succeeded as leader of the government by her brother-in-law, Lord Liverpool. In June 1812 Napoleon made the fatal decision to invade Russia with his Grande Armée and Bess later followed his terrible retreat from Moscow every step of the way.

Early in 1812 Bess had bought a secluded villa (which she renamed Devonshire Cottage) on the Thames at Richmond. A rough sketch by Caro depicts it as slightly Gothick in appearance and sheltered by tall trees. From the veranda Bess enjoyed an uninterrupted view across the river to lush meadows beyond. While the house was being altered, she often made the hour-long journey from Piccadilly to spend the day there. 'To you my love', she wrote to Caro in September, 'I must write my first letter from this lovely place. I came today alone . . . I walked into the meadow and sat by the side of the river a long time. You need not dread for me the solitude. You cannot conceive the calm it was to me to venture to give way to thoughts which the painful restraints of society continually prevent me daring to dwell upon. But here in the calm of this little retreat I can indulge in dwelling on the angelic mind and virtues and retrace all his fond affection for me, my own enthusiastic adoration of him.' She then added a significant sentence: 'I also dare hope that, in the bitterness and agony of his loss, that which was wrong in our attachment may be expiated.' In her journal she repeats many of these sentiments, but adds one that acknowledges her debt to Georgiana and the Duke, both while they were alive and since: 'All that could give happiness to life I ow'd to them; all that has extended comfort under the severity of their loss I still owe to them. O, dear, adored husband & friend, may Heaven grant my prayer & suffer me to be reunited to you both in another world.'

On Clifford's return from sea in November he moved into Piccadilly Terrace, and Fred gave up his Albany chambers to join his mother and half-brother. Caro and George, though in theory they shared the house in Whitehall Yard, in practice spent much of their time apart, the marriage remained unconsummated. While 1812 was a 'brilliant' year for Caro socially, in her journal she admits to endeavouring 'to drown care by dissipation'. This seems to have led her, reluctantly, to the brink of an affair, and on 1 January 1813 she wrote: 'God give me strength to keep the resolutions I have made this day, and that if I live through this year, I may look back to it without one feeling of remorse.' Her suitors were numerous, but the most prominent was Henry Brougham, a successful young lawyer and politician whom Bess believed to be 'clever, but a cold-blooded, mischievous and malicious man' – either because she suspected Caro's interest in him, or because he was Princess Caroline's principal adviser in her long-running battle with the Regent over their daughter Charlotte. The Regent, convinced of his wife's immorality, had tried to limit her access to their daughter, and when an investigation exonerated the Princess from any wrong-doing, Bess was indignant, claiming there was not 'one person there whom if he lay his hand on his heart would not say he had any doubt of the impropriety & even criminality of the Prs's conduct'.

In June 1813 Madame Germaine de Staël came to London,

accompanied by Baron de Rocca (with whom she had exchanged a secret promise to marry), her son and daughter. Exiled from France for her opposition to Napoleon, Germaine had since travelled restlessly around Europe. Her arrival in England marked the beginning of Bess's gradual renaissance. Following their first meeting, she noted: 'I had known Madame de Staël a little at Passy [in 1790] & since that she had sent me her works & often written to me so that I have felt still more acquainted with her than I might say in fact that I am . . . She is I think the cleverest Woman existing, if not the cleverest person & I think the most agreeable.' It was during Germaine's eleven months in England that the two women became intimate. Sadly, within ten days of her arrival Bess ceased keeping her journal (she did not resume it until September), and thus the early stages of the friendship remain unchronicled.

In her depleted state Bess was perhaps unprepared for the onslaught of Madame de Staël's personality. This extraordinary woman was celebrated not only for her books but for her courage during the Revolution and her defiance of Napoleon; her ugliness was eclipsed by 'the brilliancy of her eyes', her eloquence, and her emotional intensity. She was exhilarating, but exhausting. Requiring only a few hours' sleep, she spent the rest of her day in 'furious activity', a third of it in writing. Her three great passions in life were politics, literature and love. 'I have but one sorrow,' she told her great friend Madame Récamier, 'and it is a cruel one; it is the fear of not being loved.' This fear is apparent in her numerous letters to Bess. 'Let me have the opportunity of seeing you . . . and you will free my heart of that feeling of loneliness that only leaves me when I am with you.' When Bess spent time at Richmond, Germaine complained that being in London without her made her feel like 'a poor dog which has lost its master'. The emotional intensity of Germaine's letters to Bess (and to other close friends, like Madame Récamier) is a reminder that she too had been profoundly influenced by the writings of Jean-Jacques Rousseau, so much so that she had chosen him as the subject of her first book, *Lettres sur Rousseau*. Oddly enough, though Bess's letters were always affectionate and full of solicitude for Germaine, the language was far less highly-charged.

But there were those who were shocked by Madame de Staël's boldness, her notoriety, and her multiple love affairs. Lady Hertford, the Regent's mistress, said she 'ought to be made to leave the country'. Bess was outraged: 'I do hate ill-nature, and to a foreigner, too.' Fearful that Lady Hertford might ostracize Germaine from society, Bess wrote to the Regent. He called on her that night at Richmond and assured her that Madame de Staël would be invited to Carlton House. From then on, the doors of every notable house in town were flung wide to receive her. At Lord Lansdowne's the guests climbed onto chairs and tables to get a better view of her. She was regarded as the one person in France to have resisted Napoleon as energetically as England did. The publication by John Murray in November of her book *De l'Allemagne* – suppressed in France by Napoleon – ensured her success. Bess thought it a work of genius, though she suggested that page 166 of the third volume should be altered as it 'was unjust to the Germans'; Germaine agreed, and changed it.

Bess was drawn, despite her persistent melancholy, into Germaine's world. She found herself in the thick of intellectual discussion with old friends like Sheridan and new ones like the distinguished polymath Sir James Mackintosh. It was the heady, brilliant days of Devonshire House briefly revived. Sheridan, Germaine declared, 'was the remains of that race of giants when it comes to talent that you had a hundred years ago'. Sheridan thought her the 'most eloquent person he ever knew, Burke not excepted'. Piccadilly Terrace became the focus for those eager to meet the celebrated authoress and her family. After one such gathering, Bess noted in her journal that Germaine was 'the most natural person' she had ever met, '& never makes a parade of a feeling which she has not, nor indeed of those she has, tho' she expresses them eloquently & strongly'

In the summer of 1813 Clifford became engaged to Lizzy, daughter of Lord John Townshend, one of the original members of the Devonshire House Circle. Hart was delighted: 'I always liked & loved her extremely,' he told Bess. While Bess thought Lizzy 'so gentle and so amiable' that it was impossible not to love her, she was again worried about money. Clifford's income from the Devonshire estates was for his life only, so that, if he died before Lizzy, she (and any children) would be destitute. 'The little I can do', she told Little G., 'can only be after my death . . . I have a name I must act up to the dignity of & a rank that requires some things I can't well do properly without.' Bess was clearly determined that Hart should rectify the situation; he complained that she was 'barefaced' in her demands. (Underlying all Bess's wrangling over money was her contention that the Duke had made her various promises during his lifetime which his son, she thought, should feel himself duty-bound to honour.) Hart, of course, did everything and more for his half-brother, making a generous settlement on Lizzy in addition to a lump sum for them 'to set out with', a trousseau and a carriage.

The wedding was to take place on 20 October at Devonshire House, and Bess helped Hart with the preparations beforehand, though returning to Devonshire House was an ordeal: 'Ages to eternity could not enable me to enter those dear gates without a pang – those gates that never open'd to me but for happiness and kindness.' Hart told Little G. that 'She behaved as well and as amiably as possible. She staid till one o'clock looking at my books with the greatest interest, which I own is one way to my heart, and one which few women are in the habit of taking.' The ceremony went off perfectly. Bess pronounced the dinner 'magnificent' and 'my Cliff quite beautifull'. That night Hart wrote to Little G.: 'The company are gone and the candles put out, there's a smell of liquor and smoke and I am sleepy . . . They were married in the Hall and it looked very well full of white ladies . . . On my left [at dinner] the Dhs in beautiful pride all over white satin and necklaces and ridiculous.' (Writing to Little G. earlier that year Haryo too had ridiculed Bess's dress sense, in particular a 'white gauze bonnet with six pink roses in it and a shawl of all the colours of the rainbow'. The implication that Bess looked like mutton dressed as lamb is not reflected by her own contemporaries, such as Madame Récamier, who called her an 'elegant' woman.)

In October Wellington led his forces out of Spain and into France; Napoleon was heavily defeated at Leipzig. From her garden at Richmond Bess could hear the Tower guns signalling victory after victory. In January 1814 Britain was gripped by the hardest winter it had experienced for centuries. The Thames froze from London Bridge to Blackfriars; people crossed the river by way of 'Freezeland Street'; booths erected on the ice sold everything from gingerbread to oysters. Bess told Clifford – who was snowbound at Chatsworth with Lizzy and Hart – that the tide had brought great blocks of ice downriver, spilling them over the banks and onto her meadow. 'I never saw any thing of the kind before, it has a look of desolation & ruin that is really grand, almost awefull.'

When the Allied armies invaded France in January 1814, Germaine was torn between her desire for Napoleon's downfall and her anguish that it could only be achieved by the humiliation of France; when they entered her beloved Paris she was distraught. But Napoleon's abdication brought universal joy: two decades of war were over. With the restoration of the Bourbons, Louis XVIII (who had been living in exile in Buckinghamshire) could now return to France. On 20 April he made a public entry into London, driving through streets bedecked with *fleur de lys* and the white flag of the Bourbons. Bess had 'a large company' on her balcony to watch the procession pass along Piccadilly. A fortnight later, Germaine left for Paris. She and Bess parted with real regret. That Bess had survived and indeed bene-fited from close and prolonged contact with a woman of Germaine's power and intellect is a tribute to her own intelligence and ability to command affection. 'I feel to love as well as to admire her,' she wrote. It was not an outright declaration, but it was the closest Bess ever came to expressing so strong an emotion for any women other than Georgiana and Harriet.

In June the flags and crowds were out again for the state visit, stage-managed by the Regent, of the Allied sovereigns, Tsar Alexander and King Frederick-William of Prussia (the Austrian Emperor had de-clined the invitation). As a friend of the Regent and Lord Liverpool's sister-in-law, Bess was invited to the numerous entertainments hosted in the visitors' honour by both royalty and government: she could be relied upon to charm their guests with her beauty and the intelligence of her conversation. Though she met and talked with everyone from the Tsar to the Duke of Wellington, she had lost her appetite for such festivities. The reception at Carlton House she thought over-crowded and hot; a breakfast at Chiswick House 'was very brilliant, but to me melancholy. Alas, how different, yet how like the same.' A dinner given by her sister and Lord Liverpool was marred by the Regent, who 'seem'd to have drunk rather more than he ought'. But she enjoyed 'a magnificent Supper & Waltzing party' thrown by Hart at Devonshire House. 'The garden was brilliantly illuminated . . . The P. Regent was extremely amiable & kind to me & spoke with a feeling about D. House which makes me quite love him.' Though Bess was often crit-ical of the Prince, she could never forget his affection for Georgiana and the Duke, or his kindness to herself. Nor could she resist, as few can, the potent aura of royalty.

On 21 June Bess observed that 'The singularity of circumstances are so great that the appearance of a Cardinal in London & at Carlton House has made little sensation, but Lord Bessborough said that he was well receiv'd & was a remarkably dignified looking Man with a fine countenance – and that his name is Consalvi.' Cardinal Consalvi was the first Catholic of his eminence to set foot in England since

Elizabethan times; Bess had no premonition that he was to play a significant role in her life.

The peace ended two decades of Britain's isolation from Europe, and it was perhaps inevitable that Bess should have joined the stampede of the *beau monde* across the Channel. Her journals and her correspondence prior to her trip – initially to Spa in Belgium 'in search of relief to my mind & restoration of my health' – contain no evidence that it was intended to last more than a few months; in the event, it was four years before she returned to England.

On 6 August 1814 Bess, Caro and Fred left London. Bess, Caro, Madame Pallé and a manservant, Jaquiery, travelled together in a special carriage Bess had had built, at considerable expense, for the journey – the one possible indication that she intended her absence to last some time. Fred followed in his own carriage with his servant Thomas. Even those fortunate enough to travel in their own conveyances were obliged to rely on the supply of post-horses *en route*, and Bess and Fred were often delayed by finding none available.

Spa provoked painful memories: 'Above twenty years have elaps'd since I was here with those dear friends who made every place a place of happiness to me . . . Thus it is & ever must be with me.' But she was determined to restore her health, so she kept 'capital hours' and arrived at the well every morning at seven o'clock. After six weeks of healthy living, they made for the glamour and the gossip of Restoration Paris. The city had changed little during Napoleon's regime. Versailles, however – 'a vast and melancholy desert' when Bess went there in 1803 – was thronged with workmen employed by Louis XVIII to repair the effects of fifteen years' neglect.

Bess was at once besieged by many old friends, some of whom – like Madame Récamier – had only recently returned from exile. At dinner at Madame de Staël's, Bess and the Duke of Wellington were the only English guests. The Duke, when asked who in his opinion was the best French general, replied that Napoleon '*on the battlefield* was superior to all other generals'. To Bess he added: 'His great fault was going into Russia.' Dining with the Duke at his splendid new house in the Faubourg Saint-Honoré, Bess found herself placed next to her host, with Marshal Soult – the Duke's principal opponent in the Peninsular War – seated opposite. In an aside to Bess, the Duke remarked: 'Opposite to us is one whom I never could tame. The only one of their generals with whom I never could have any friendly communication.' Bess's niece Caroline Wortley, who was also in Paris, told her father Lord Erne that Bess was 'very popular with the Foreigners of all nations'. It is a measure of her status in society that even without the Duke of Devonshire at her back Bess was granted a private audience of Louis XVIII. She believed him to be well-intentioned, but the French people were already tiring of their weak, fat and gout-ridden king.

In November the Bessboroughs, their son Willy and his new wife arrived in Paris. The plan, presumably hatched in England, was that they should accompany Bess and Fred to the south of France while Caro returned to London and to George. By Christmas they were all at Marseilles. Bess was worried about money, and Marseilles was cheap, beautiful and by the sea. In February 1815 she wrote to Hart in sombre mood asking him to continue her allowance for a year after her death (if it occurred abroad) in order to clear her debts. 'Above all I do implore your continued affection & kindness to my darling Caroline . . . & never quite forget me who loved & adored both your Parents with an entire & faithfull affection.' She concluded with a request that she should be 'laid next my dear Husband'.

A week after writing this letter, Bess received the news that Augustus was to marry Albinia Hobart, granddaughter of the third Earl of Buckinghamshire. Though he had previously hinted at something of the kind he had not named the lady, having 'made himself ridiculous' in the past with his numerous *affaires du cœur*. He had apparently consulted his aunt Louisa, which upset Bess deeply. Why consult her and not his mother, who had shared everything with him? And if Louisa had influenced his choice, she really would be in 'despair'. Augustus hastened to explain that while he had discussed Albinia with Louisa, she had not influenced his decision. Bess's next letter shows that her fit of jealousy had passed: 'I am anxious to tell you that your letter speaks too much the happiness of your heart for me not to feel rejoiced at the choice you have made.' The couple were married in March and left for Copenhagen, where Augustus had been appointed minister. Before leaving England he rented Piccadilly Terrace for a year to Lord Byron and his new wife Annabella Milbanke, for a long period the object of Augustus's affections. With her customary biting wit, Haryo neatly summed up this particular match to Little G.: 'How Wonderful of that sensible, cautious prig of a Girl to venture upon such a Heap of Poems, Crimes and Rivals.' Wonderful, possibly; foolish, certainly, as events were to prove.

Despite her money worries and her initial chagrin over Augustus's marriage, Bess had begun to enjoy herself. She and Fred had moved into a handsome villa; the view was glorious and there were 'clusters of blossoms on the almond trees and violets in profusion in the gardens'. Her health had improved, the war was over, the Bourbons had been restored and Napoleon was safely incarcerated on Elba, a combination of circumstances which brought her 'much ease & relief'.

On 4 March 1815 their peace was shattered. 'Here's pretty news indeed,' Fred wrote to Augustus. 'I was woke this morning out of a sweet sleep with "You had better get up, Sir, there are crowds of soldiers and people in the streets. Bonaparte is landed at Cannes."' Napoleon had kept his promise to return to France when the violets were in bloom. Looking 'very sun-burnt and excessively fat', the Emperor set out for Paris accompanied by some one thousand men. 'I shall reach Paris without firing a shot,' he prophesied. He was right. On 19 March, in the pouring rain, the King and his government left Paris by the north gate; twenty-four hours later Napoleon entered by the south.

Accurate accounts of Napoleon's progress north filtered slowly through the Alpes Maritimes, rumours travelled faster, and Bess recorded both assiduously. She and the Bessboroughs had been advised to leave Marseilles as it was no longer safe. But where were they to go? Napoleon's escape had thrown the Continent into turmoil. To go north through central France was too risky. Nor was the coastal route to Italy secure, since it passed through towns known to be Bonapartist, and with Murat making threatening moves against the Austrians, Italy itself might be hazardous. Nevertheless, on 1 April they left Marseilles for Nice. From Nice they went by sea to Genoa, risking attack by corsairs 'which to us who are going in feluccas', Bess remarked, 'is not pleasant'. They reached Genoa safely, to find the city thronged with British tourists fleeing Murat's advance on Rome. Among the refugees was Pope Pius VII; Bess was presented to him. 'His manner was mild & pleasing, his voice gentle . . . About England he said "The English are a brave nation".' (Had Cardinal Consalvi not been representing the Papal States at the Congress of Vienna, he would almost certainly have been present at this interview.)

At Milan Bess and Fred separated from the Bessboroughs, who were to attempt the northern route home through Switzerland. Bess, however, was determined to make her way to Rome, now safe since Murat's defeat by the Austrians in early May. They parted with the Bessboroughs with 'great regret'. Bess and Harriet had remained close over the years, each supporting the other through crises in their lives. Harriet had continued to write to Granville, but her letters had lost their sparkle, and often went unanswered. In a note written in 1812 found among her papers, she laments the fact that for seventeen years she had loved 'almost to Idolatry . . . the man who has probably lov'd me least of all those who have profess'd to do so – tho' once I thought otherwise'.

Bess's urge to travel was obsessive – as her father's had been. 'Every change of place brings relief to my mind,' she wrote. There was always another church, another palace or ancient monument to visit, another painting to see. Almost every town she passed through had its associations, either personal or historical. Eager to see the new causeway across the Simplon Pass – one of Napoleon's greatest engineering achievements – she and Fred travelled north from Milan. As they approached the pass they found themselves surrounded by Austrian cavalry *en route* to join the Allied armies against Napoleon. Intrigued by this encounter with an army on the move, she described everything in vivid detail, adding little sketches to her journal. As she drew soldiers roasting an oxen for their evening meal, three hundred miles away at Brussels news of Napoleon's defeat of the Prussians at Ligny was spreading among the guests at the Duchess of Richmond's ball. On 17 June, as Wellington was deploying his forces along a ridge to the south of the village of Waterloo, Bess was watching the Austrian troops marching 'silent & quiet' through the pouring rain towards the Simplon Pass. 'I did pity them from my heart,' she wrote. But her pity was wasted: by the evening of the 18th, Napoleon had been defeated at the battle of Waterloo.

Bess and Fred received news of the Allied victory twelve days later at Venice, as they savoured a 'granalita' in the cool mirrored interior of the Café Florian in St Mark's Square. 'This extraordinary end of this once extraordinary Man has so astonish'd us we can talk or think of nothing else.' On 22 June Napoleon abdicated; on 8 July Louis XVIII took up residence once again at the Tuileries.

Bess hated travelling in haste, preferring to linger in places of interest. After three months in Florence, on 25 October she and Fred set off for Rome. From Nepi, the last major town before Rome, the road enters the desolate Campagna, impoverished land deserted save for an occasional mounted herdsman, his gun slung at his side. About five miles from the Imperial City, on a clear day the traveller catches his first glimpse of the seven hills of Rome, and the vast dome of St Peter's surmounted by its glittering cross.

13

Rome
1815–1819

'I am here [in Rome] in a terrestrial paradise, nor can
there be a more delicious abode to an inquisitive and
speculative mind.'

The Earl-Bishop to his agent, John Strange, *c.*1778

———————◆———————

ON A VISIT there in 1740, Horace Walpole confidently predicted
that in 'an hundred years Rome will not be worth seeing'. For
centuries the city's Classical heritage had been sacked, plundered and
neglected, its monuments buried beneath debris and newer buildings.
The Pantheon was used as a fish market, cattle grazed in the Forum,
the Palatine Hill was a wilderness of weeds, and since the fourteenth
century the Colosseum had been quarried for stone. In the early years
of his reign Pope Pius VII had begun an extensive programme of
excavation and restoration, but work had ceased with his overthrow
and exile by Napoleon. It was resumed by the French during their
occupation of the city between 1809 and 1814, a contribution under-
estimated both at the time and since; Bess, however, arriving there in
October 1815, was immediately struck by the changes. As she entered
the city by the Porta del Popolo, she noted that the French had
improved the gateway by 'throwing down old houses and convents'.
Before she had even unpacked, she had made a quick tour of the
Classical sites and visited St Peter's. So well did she remember the city
from her last visit in 1793 that she was able to list the work carried out,

monument by monument, in a long letter to Lord Morpeth. 'It is some thing inconceivable what has been discovered since we were here . . .'

Bess's interest in Rome had begun in 1781 when she made 'a particular study' of the first three volumes of Gibbon's *Decline and Fall*, followed two years later by her first visit during her Grand Tour. Unlike the majority of tourists, whose initial enthusiasm for Rome's Classical past was seldom sustained, her sense of wonder had intensified each time she returned; nevertheless, her journals and correspondence for 1815 give no clue that she intended to make the city her home. Yet there was little to keep her in England. Fred was with her, and Caro, Clifford and Augustus were all married. The Devonshire House Circle no longer existed, its most brilliant members extinguished by untimely deaths. Of her women friends, only Harriet Bessborough and Lady Melbourne remained. In Rome she could begin with a clean slate and create her own society. With the cost of living a fraction of that in England, she could afford to live in the style to which she had long been accustomed. Travel was cheap and the Italian peninsula lay at her door.

Above all, Rome for Bess came to mean Cardinal Ercole Consalvi. He was an exceptional man by any standards, in character, appearance and achievements. Bess described him to Clifford as 'tall, thin, of the most dignified yet simple manners, a dark and animated eye, a thick dark brow, a smile of inexpressible sweetness and benevolence . . .' Dressed except on state occasions in a black silk ecclesiastical robe picked out in scarlet, and with a scarlet skull-cap, the Cardinal was an arresting and familiar figure around Rome. Born a year before Bess, his life had been a series of dramatic changes of fortune, some of which might have been avoided had he not remained fiercely loyal to the papacy and to his own principles.

Following his education at the diocesan college established at Frascati by the Cardinal Duke of York (brother of Charles Edward Stuart, the 'Young Pretender'), which imbued him with a great love for the English, Consalvi had joined the *familia* or civil household of Pius VI. As a prominent member of the curia (the papal court and government of the Roman Catholic Church) he had been caught up in the momentous events following Napoleon's invasion of the Papal States in 1796. To protect Rome, the Pope consented to sign the Treaty of Tolentino, which required the surrender of certain territories and the removal to France of a hundred major works of art. When in 1798 Rome was occupied by French troops led by Bess's old friend

General Berthier, the Pope was sent into exile and Consalvi imprisoned in Castel Sant' Angelo. Threatened with a public flogging and deported to Naples, he eventually found his way to Venice in time to act as secretary to the conclave which had been summoned to elect a replacement for Pius VI, who had died in exile.

The new pope, Pius VII, was a saintly Benedictine monk, described by Chateaubriand as 'pale, sad and religious'. He at once appointed Consalvi his Secretary of State and made him a cardinal (only now did Consalvi take minor orders; he never became a fully ordained priest). Effectively the Pope's prime minister, in June 1801 Consalvi became involved in the final stages of negotiations for a Concordat with Napoleon to re-establish the Catholic Church in France. He travelled to Paris, where despite Napoleon's bullying tactics and attempts to double-cross him, the Concordat was concluded on 15 July. But Napoleon's megalomania increased, and the Pope refused to join the Continental Blockade by closing ports in the Papal States to British, Russian and Swedish vessels. Blamed by Napoleon for the Pope's obduracy, in 1806 Consalvi resigned his office.

Relations between the Emperor and the Pope could only end in disaster, however: in 1808 French troops again occupied Rome, snatched the Pope from the Quirinal Palace and deported him. Consalvi remained some months in limbo before being forcibly ejected from Rome and sent to Paris. There he lived as a virtual recluse, resolutely declining to collaborate. This passive resistance ended when in 1810 the Pope refused to annul Napoleon's marriage to Josephine and Consalvi refused, together with twelve of the other cardinals exiled to Paris, to attend his marriage to Marie-Louise of Austria. Enraged, Napoleon threatened to have him shot, but in fact the recalcitrant cardinals had their property confiscated and were exiled to the provinces, until January 1813 when Napoleon and the Pope came to an agreement at Fontainebleau. When the Allies crossed the Rhine in January 1814 the Pope was freed, and immediately restored Consalvi as Secretary of State. In this capacity he attended the Congress of Vienna, where the skill with which he negotiated the restoration of the Papal States profoundly impressed fellow ministers such as Castlereagh, Metternich and Talleyrand. His trip to London during the visit of the Allied Sovereigns (where he had been spotted by Lord Bessborough) had won him the support and friendship of the Prince Regent. Described by Napoleon as 'a lion in sheep's clothing' and by Chateaubriand as 'one of the greatest statesman of the century', such was the man with whom Bess formed a remarkable friendship during her last years.

Her initial introduction to Consalvi was through the Countess of Albany, yet another of the celebrated European women with whom she maintained a long association. Married to the 'Young Pretender' (known as the Count of Albany because the Vatican refused to recognise him as Charles III), she had for some years lived in Florence 'in a state of dubious intimacy' (Lady Holland's description) with the Italian poet Alfieri, and latterly with the French painter Fabre. Worldly, cultured and charming, she possessed, according to the Irish novelist Lady Morgan, 'one talent that is worth twenty others. She knows *how to laugh*, and *at whom*, right well!' Consalvi had almost certainly met the Countess through her brother-in-law, his friend and mentor the Cardinal Duke of York.

Bess's first encounter with Consalvi occurred in November 1815, two days after her arrival in Rome. She clearly knew something of his history, as she at once questioned him about Napoleon. Far from showing resentment towards the man who had threatened his execution, Consalvi replied that the Emperor was 'made up of such contradictory qualities that he look'd on him as the most extraordinary person who ever lived'. Ten days later Consalvi called on her. They talked again of Napoleon, and of the work accomplished by the French archaeologists during the occupation, Consalvi lamenting 'that they had not done more'. The restoration of Rome's antiquities was one of his greatest ambitions – not least because tourism was the city's chief source of income – and one which Bess passionately shared.

For Consalvi, involved as he was with the monumental task of repairing the damage done to the papacy since the French Revolution, Bess became a haven from cares of state. Her intelligence, her knowledge of European affairs and her absolute discretion equipped her to be the ideal confidante. As a foreigner, she was untainted by the cabals and gossip at the papal court, and could bring a fresh and objective view to the problems that beset him. Within four months of their first meeting, as she told Augustus, 'Consalvi and I are such friends that when we are at the same place the crowd gives way for him to come up to me'.

Though now in her fifty-eighth year, Bess was still a beautiful woman. The two drawings Lawrence made of her in 1819 indicate the fine bone structure, the profile still sharp and clear. Although she no longer habitually wore mourning, as a rule she dressed soberly. 'Black has given way to a suit of Light Grey,' Lizzy told Hart when she and Clifford visited Bess in the autumn. 'Such a Long Waist, & a *flat* Grey silk Cap as if it had been sat on, much flatter than any thing I ever saw in England.'

Her energy, too, was undiminished. Her journals reveal the zeal with which she explored Rome, often making her first foray before breakfast – always her best time of the day. Undeterred by fatigue, the cold dry *tramontana* which swept down from the mountains, or the chill which permeated the shadowy ruins even on the hottest day, she pursued her investigations with an ardour verging on the obsessive. One visit to a building or ancient monument was never enough; in six months she visited the Pantheon no fewer than twenty times. 'Pass'd near five hours in the Vatican & still did not see the Loggia!' she records with frustration.

Fred was equally obsessed: 'F.F. is in a state of ecstasy,' Bess told Lord Morpeth, 'it is the only place that has answered his expectations, which are large.' But only a month after their arrival, poor Fred succumbed to malaria. At that time the disease was believed to be caused not by mosquitoes but by bad air (*mal'aria*) which drifted into the city from the 'pestilential marshes' (infested, of course, with mosquitoes) and collected in the low-lying, sparsely populated areas where local people planted their vines. The cure was to 'take bark', but Fred was unable to keep it down in sufficient quantities. Consalvi, with a solicitude typical of him, sent Bess his own physician. The malaria was brought under control and mother and son resumed their exhaustive survey, Bess with a copy of Eustace's *A Classical Tour through Italy* under her arm, Fred at her side, and her little dog Ting (Lilli's successor) trotting at their heels.

During the first three years of her residence in Rome Bess occupied an apartment in Casa Margherita in the Strada San Sebastianello, a shady street leading off Piazza di Spagna, the area most frequented by foreign visitors (her father had once lived in the same street, possibly in the same apartment). Her niece Caroline Wortley, visiting Rome in 1817, was 'all astonishment at the size of the rooms . . . which I had imagined were so much larger'. Bess, however, seemed perfectly content: the area was well supplied with banks and shops; she could buy the English newspapers and was within easy reach of the Corso, the most fashionable street in the city despite its reputation for smelling strongly of cabbages.

Undeterred by the size of her rooms, Bess soon began to hold *con-*

versazioni. Such entertainments, according to one weary traveller, could be 'the dullest things in the World. You go in, you make your Bow to the Lady of the House, you Stare at the Company playing at Games for Sixpences . . . and then you huddle with the groups of English into a Corner, talk loud, often at the Expence of the Company, grow tired & go home.' Bess's *conversazioni*, however, rapidly acquired the reputation of being among the best in Rome. Free of the constraints of London society, she blithely mixed foreign ambassadors with English residents, artists, scientists and writers with members of the papal court like Consalvi and his secretary, a cultured cleric named Molajoni. These gatherings were often enlivened by excellent music. 'I went to the Duchess of Devonshire's *conversazioni*', reported the American scholar George Ticknor, 'as to a great exchange, to see who was in Rome, and to meet what is called the world.' Such an eclectic mix today might be crippled from lack of a common language, but among educated people of the early nineteenth century national distinctions were blurred by the universal use of French. One notable absentee from Bess's gatherings was Princess Pauline Borghese, Napoleon's sister. The Pope had granted asylum to several members of the Emperor's family, a gesture of which Bess approved – except in the case of the Princess, whom she accused of coquetry and arrogance.

Bess's refusal to invite certain people to her house naturally caused ill-feeling. Mrs Bunsen, an Englishwoman married to Charles Bunsen (later Baron Bunsen) of the Prussian embassy, was piqued at receiving no summons despite having left her card, but told her mother it was a '*relief*' not to be invited, 'for I have a sort of *cold creeping* when I think of venturing into those rooms' – an indication that Bess's unconventional past was still capable of affronting the bigoted and the intolerant.

One of the most distinguished and delightful of Bess's visitors was the sculptor Antonio Canova, renowned throughout Europe for the beauty of his work. He had reported to her father, his old friend and patron, his meeting with Bess in Paris in 1803, when he was modelling a bust of Napoleon. 'Canova speaks to me in raptures of you', the Earl-Bishop had proudly informed her, and the sculptor's studio in the Palazzo Barberini had been one of her first objectives when she arrived in Rome. Thereafter she became a constant visitor, growing to revere the artist and love the man. In his courteous and flowery letters – addressed to the 'Most Illustrious Lady Duchess' – he demonstrated his affection and regard for her.

The Danish sculptor Bertel Thorwaldsen also became a good friend. 'He is very clever,' Bess told Augustus in April 1816, 'but terribly lazy.' Six months later she had changed her mind. 'Thorwaldsen is grown excellent, some of his works are really admirable, and he is so modest and so excellent a man that he is liked and esteemed by all.'

Canova had called on Bess the day after his return from Paris, where he had gone at Consalvi's request to arrange for the shipment back to Rome of the works of art looted by Napoleon. Their restoration was entirely due to Consalvi's persistence at the Congress of Vienna and to the support he received there from Castlereagh and the Duke of Wellington, who were united in their determination to see these fruits of conquest returned to their rightful owners: Britain had also paid the cost of packing and transport. Out of gratitude 'to the Nation who had render'd such services to Italy', Canova had made a special trip to London to thank the Prince Regent in person.

The return of these masterpieces after an absence of some twenty years delighted Bess. During her journey south from Venice the previous year she had recorded her outrage at the plundering of so many works of art by the French, principally the removal of Ariosto's tomb from Ferrara. Ariosto was her favourite poet – it was a preference she shared with Consalvi – and she visited his house. The leaf she took from the grotto where he used to write is still pinned to a page in her journal. When the first shipment reached Rome in January 1816, she was at the Vatican Museum in time to see some of the cases unpacked, including those containing the *Laocoön* and *Apollo Belvedere* which she had last seen in the Louvre.

At a private audience with Pius VII – arranged for Bess by Consalvi shortly after her arrival in Rome – the old man had recounted his chagrin on seeing the statues during his visit to Paris in 1804 to officiate at Napoleon's coronation, and expressed his joy at their return to Rome. 'He was all in white', she noted, 'except his crimson velvet Hat which he took off as he came in . . . He made me sit down by him on the couch & talk'd cheerfully and agreeably . . .'

On 17 April 1816, Bess wrote in her journal:

We have been at Rome five months & a half & except during the time of Frederick's illness I have not pass'd any such space of time for many years with so much relief to my spirits & benefit to my health . . . Of society too I can truly say that I have a love and admiration of Cardinal Consalvi's character which has increas'd each day & hour that I have seen him. His views are enlarg'd, his mind full of vigour is elevated, noble & pure, a heart full of goodness & humanity, an inviolable love of truth, faithfull to his promises, a noble Patron of the Arts, a kind Master, generous to all, of a noble ambition of glory & an ardent Patriotism, he has by his Talents, his noble frankness in his publick as well as private conduct placed Rome in a higher rank in Europe than she has experienc'd for many centuries. By every Sovereign whether Catholick or Protestant he is treated with mark'd distinction & in his manners he unites all the dignity of his high rank with the polish'd ease of a Man of the World.

For nearly thirty years Bess had loved and revered the Duke of Devonshire and extolled his nobility, generosity and kindness – the same qualities she now praised in Consalvi. The Duke's lethargy and reluctance to engage with life were however in marked contrast to the Cardinal's phenomenal energy and the sheer scale of his achievements. While the Duke's apathy had been a hindrance to Bess, Consalvi's industry was an inspiration. She longed to do something, to contribute in some way, however small, to Rome's renaissance. Consalvi not only understood this, but was prepared to flout the convention that women existed but to breed and to look decorative: he obtained permission for her to begin an excavation in the Forum Romanum, the very heart of Classical Rome.

By December 1816, when Bess began work on her excavation, the Forum's principal monuments, such as the Arch of Titus, had been freed of earth and debris and all the post-Classical buildings had been demolished, including those by the Column of Phocas. It was this column that Bess was to be responsible for excavating. Unlike other English enthusiasts, who used galley slaves to carry out their excavations, Bess had elected to hire workmen, 'with which I see that he [Consalvi] is much pleas'd'. To her delight, a small chalice was turned up on the very first day.

There has been some confusion over what the excavation actually achieved. Bess did not – as has been previously claimed – 'discover' the column: it was standing proudly upright amid the rubble, as it had since its erection in AD 608. As to the inscription establishing the identity of the pillar, the French claimed to have unearthed it in March 1813 – yet in her journal for 1783 Bess had noted 'One other column also nearer the Capitol very fine: on the pedestal an inscription to Phocas'. According to Lady Morgan, whose attention to detail is impressive, the inscription reads: 'To the most clement and felicitous Prince Phocas, Emperor, the adored and crowned conqueror, always august, &c.' Lady Morgan was clearly acquainted with that Emperor's reputation as a tyrant whose catalogue of crimes included the slaughter of his predecessor and the immolation of prisoners for his amusement, for she adds: 'So much for triumphal arches and laudatory columns.'

An accurate account of the work carried out was given by the director of the excavation, Bess's friend Johan Akerblad, the Swedish orientalist and diplomat. Akerblad states that Bess's workmen unearthed 'the pyramid of eleven marble steps on which the column rested at 35 palms (7.7m) depth, on the ancient travertine paving of the Forum'. Two beautiful porphyry columns were also discovered, which were removed to the Capitol Museum. Bess herself did not exaggerate her achievement: a letter to Augustus (since lost) incorporated drawings of the excavation in which she clearly showed the work carried out by the French, and then by herself. She was, none the less, understandably proud of what she had done. 'The excavation', she told Augustus, 'acquires great interest & some celebrity from Consalvi & the Pope having both been to visit it.' Since the Pope could do nothing informally, but was driven about the city in a coach and four surrounded by half a dozen mounted guards, this papal visitation was a tribute to the importance of Bess's excavation. She also financed the dragging of a stretch of the River Tiber for antiquities, but this proved a disappointment. 'The Tyber', she told Hart in late 1819, 'has brought up great bits of marble . . . but as yet no bust or statue.'

Such activities naturally aroused comment. Lavinia Spencer, on a visit to Rome in 1819, told her daughter Sarah that the 'witch of Endor has been doing mischief of another kind to that she has been doing all her life, by pretending to dig for the good of the public in the Forum. She, of course, has found nothing, but has bought up a quantity of dirt and old horrors, and will not be at the expense of carrying it away and filling it in, so that she has defaced every place where she has poked.' That Valadier, the papal architect, included a drawing of the column – showing the marble steps excavated by Bess – in his *Raccolta delle più insigni fabbriche di Roma antica* ('Collection of the most outstanding buildings of ancient Rome'), is a measure of the injustice of Lavinia's remark. A more charitable account of Bess's enterprise reached Haryo from Granville's nephew Lord Gower on his return from Rome. 'He says', Haryo reported to Little G., 'that the Duchess, Cardinal Consalvi, and Souza are digging *à qui mieux mieux* [in emulation of one another], and that they rout up great curiosities, that the

Duchess is adored, as she protects all the artists, employs them and pays them magnificently, and that all the way on the road the innkeepers ask, "*Connaissez-vous cette noble dame?*"'

Bess was indeed employing artists, though there is no record of what she paid them. In 1816 she conceived the idea of publishing de luxe editions of Virgil's *Aeneid*, and of Horace's *Fifth Satire the First Book*. The *Satire*, which describes Horace's journey from Rome to Brindisi, was to be illustrated with eighteen plates; the two-volume *Aeneid* with more than fifty. The illustrations for both these editions, to be made from drawings executed by a number of the artists and engravers of all nationalities then living in Rome (they included Canova, Vincenzo Camuccini, Charles Eastlake, W. F. Gmelin and F. L. Catel), would depict places and landscapes mentioned in the texts. Consalvi was to procure a good edition of Annibale Caro's sixteenth-century translation of the *Aeneid* and his secretary, Abbé Molajoni, was to translate the *Satire*.

For Bess this was a venture close to her heart. Her admiration for the two poets, both of whom had spent long periods in Rome, pervades her journals, and in her travels through Italy she had visited many of the places with which they were associated. In 1793 she and Georgiana had gone to see the tomb alleged to be Virgil's near Pozzuoli, and Georgiana had commemorated the visit with a poem. Yet this project too had its detractors. To her mother, Mrs Bunsen quoted her husband as saying that Horace's *Satire* was 'one of the most indecent works that exist in any language, & it is almost incomprehensible how a woman could translate it, as she must not only be in a common way profligate, but have studied deeply the records of profligacy to be able to make a sense of expressions'. Poor Bess: it seems a little unfair that she should be accused of profligacy for lines such as

> First at Aricia we alight,
> And there refresh, and pass the Night.
> Our Entertainment? rather coarse
> Than sumptuous, but I've met with worse.

Before commissioning the printing, Bess carried out some detailed research: with Fred, she visited the principal libraries in northern Italy to examine their early editions of these and other Classical works. Her journal notes reveal not only the number and diversity of the books she perused but the respect with which she was treated by the library directors. Having refined her ideas, she commissioned De Romanis of Rome to begin work on both the Horace and the Virgil (Filippo De Romanis, the head of the firm, belonged, like Bess, to the 'Arcadians', Rome's foremost literary academy). Unfortunately, the 1816 edition of the Horace contained various errors, both in Molajoni's translation and in the printing. Consalvi himself undertook to correct the translation and Bess commissioned a second edition from the Bodoni Press at Parma, visiting the widow of Gianbattista Bodoni, the greatest Italian typographer of the eighteenth century, in person. The new edition, published in 1818, contained only eight plates (six line engravings by Riepenhausen and two aquatints by Catel and L. Caracciolo), and instead of showing the locations, depicted incidents which had taken place during Horace's journey.

Bess's involvement with these publications was temporarily suspended by a long-awaited visit from Caro, Clifford and his family in September 1816. Fred and Bess travelled north to meet them at Milan, where Fred was to leave her and go on to Copenhagen to visit Augustus. It was a sad parting: for two years mother and son had been inseparable. Fred had shared all her enthusiasms, including her friendship with Consalvi, and had fallen in love with Rome. Too idle to write many letters, he has left little of himself to posterity, but Haryo has made good the deficiency by painting, in one sentence, an endearing picture of Bess's singular offspring: 'F. Foster, the greatest love that ever was, very drole and surly and stuffing more boiled pork and boiled mutton than any person ever did before.' Fred did, however, bestir himself to write to Haryo when her first baby was late arriving: '*Tu est toujours à pigger et tu ne pigge jamais!*'

It was two years since Bess had seen Clifford. He and Lizzy were blissfully happy; they now had two sons, and Lizzy was again pregnant. But for Caro, condemned to a barren future by George's impotence, the eighteen months since she had seen her mother had been tense and unhappy. Having resisted other approaches, particularly from George Eden (who became Lord Auckland in 1814), she finally succumbed to that slippery but charismatic bachelor Henry Brougham, England's future Lord Chancellor. 'He flatters her Understanding and excites her compassion,' Haryo told Little G., '. . . and I know he has that peculiar sort of Ugliness (like a Truffle with white Teeth) which charms.' By the end of 1815 Caro was desperate, embittered towards the Melbournes and threatening to leave George. Clifford, Haryo,

Little G. and Hart all urged her to pull back from the brink. Extra-marital affairs were beginning to be less lightly regarded than they had been in the passionate and unruly days of the later eighteenth century, when virtue was an ideal often profoundly desired but seldom attained.

In February 1816 Clifford had told Bess that Caro was 'still with' Brougham; what that meant in practical terms is unclear, but society would never have countenanced them living under the same roof. When Caro and the Cliffords left on their journey to Rome, Brougham followed, catching up with them at Geneva. Lady Melbourne wrote suspiciously to her daughter-in-law in Geneva. Caro replied that she had 'for many years thought myself slighted and not loved . . . I have struggled seven years, and my courage at last failed me.' If she could be convinced that George really loved her, she would return to him; she was too kind to cite George's impotence as the principal cause. In August she told Little G. that she and Brougham had parted for good at Milan, yet in November he was in Rome urging her to return with him to England. Fearing that their arrival together in London would confirm the rumours of their liaison, Bess pleaded with Caro to delay her return for three months, 'but his power over her is great,' she told Little G. 'What is done by me in our one hour, is overruled by him the next five minutes.' But Bess's counsel prevailed: in December Brougham left Rome alone, and in January 1817 Bess carried her grieving daughter and the Cliffords off to Naples for the rest of the winter.

At Naples they behaved like true tourists, visiting Pompeii and Herculaneum and climbing Vesuvius. In early March Lizzy gave birth to a little girl. Caro, no longer able to resist Brougham's pleading letters, left for England. Bess, dining with the King of Naples, found herself embroiled in a discussion about Consalvi with the Minister of Finance, who maintained the Cardinal had too much power over the Pope. Any criticism of Consalvi to Bess was a mistake, and she delivered a lecture on the Cardinal's incomparable virtues; when she had finished there was a brief silence. '*Vous aimez donc beaucoup le Cardinal, Mad. la Dss?*' the Minister enquired politely (as faithfully recorded by Bess in her journal).

In May Bess abandoned the Cliffords and their new baby to the beauties of a Neapolitan spring and took the road for Rome. Experienced traveller that she was, Bess makes light in her journal of the numerous perils which were apt to beset the wayfarer. Inns were primitive and the roads, especially outside the Papal States, appalling. Constantly jolted to a jelly, bathed in perspiration and choked by dust, travellers prayed to escape the most recent scourge – attack by the *banditti* who infested the countryside. The blackened remains of those who had been caught, and strung up by the *carabiniere* as a deterrent, must have been revolting, but travellers were less squeamish in those days: Caroline Wortley records her son's delight at seeing a still 'fresh head' stuck on a pole by the roadside. Augustus had been horrified by his mother's 'too noble Contempt for Robbers', and she now travelled with an armed escort, but on this occasion her journey was uneventful. Once over the border into the Papal States she found that Consalvi had instructed the post masters 'to attend in every possible way to my convenience', a thoughtfulness expressive of the Cardinal's unceasing benevolence towards her.

Bess's principal reason for returning to Rome was to supervise the artists who were to make drawings for the *Aeneid*. Accompanied by her friend Akerblad and two of the artists, she made several day excursions to the sites she had selected from the text; so much had changed since Virgil's day that matching them to his descriptions was often difficult. Once a site had been chosen she left 'a countryman with each of the Artists to carry their books and umbrella' and spent the day exploring, returning at intervals to suggest minor alterations to the drawings. Despite such attention to detail she was dissatisfied with the first drawing of Ostia, and returned with the artist two years later to find a better viewpoint. 'If one undertakes a thing,' she told Hart, 'it should be well done.' Her patronage of artists, some of whom were little known at the time, has echoes of her father, who wrote in high spirits from Rome in 1778 describing the painters who worked in his room all day and boasting proudly that he was 'the midwife of talents'. But though he undoubtedly gave employment to numerous artists, the Earl-Bishop had a reputation for high-handed behaviour and a reluctance to pay for his commissions.

Curiously, Bess's journals contain no mention of the illustrations for Horace's *Satire*. The Classical archaeologist and traveller Sir William Gell supplies a glimpse of them; writing to Miss Berry from Naples he described Bess at the Hotel Gran' Bretagna giving 'tea, ice, and cakes on Thursdays, besides allowing an admiring public to tumble over, tear, spoil, elbow, and deface all her very nice portfolios of prints and drawings, to say nothing of some very pretty drawings of all sorts with which her Grace proposes to illustrate a new edition of Horace's "Tour to Brundusium" . . .' Gell had offered her a view of the Cathedral of Canosa for the *Satire*, which Bess in her desire for authenticity had refused, 'for she thinks Horace not likely to have seen it'; he did, however, supply at least one drawing for the *Aeneid.*

Almost every evening while she was in Rome Consalvi would call on Bess, often very late and frequently exhausted. 'Consalvi sat with me a long time this evening, was amiable and confidential to the greatest degree' is a typical entry in her journal. She was careful not to abuse his trust by recording their conversations, but when the Pope's life was endangered by a bad fall in June 1817, she did reveal Consalvi's view of his master: '"He has a very quick understanding, but is full of self-doubt. But he is so good, so virtuous, so gentle that I do not always have the courage to contradict him. I give way sometimes – when I do not lose by it . . . These are my faults. It is what I do not do, not what I do."' In the event of the Pope's death, Consalvi would automatically cease to be Secretary of State but this, he assured Bess, would cause him no regret: '"I would not lead the life I have led for another pope for whom I did not have the same affection or commitment – not for anything in the world."' Instead, he would retire happily to Frascati and become a parish priest.

Consalvi expressed his affection for Bess in countless ways, but one in particular symbolizes the depth and sincerity of his attachment. Following the death of his adored brother Andrea, Consalvi had created a garden in his memory which no one but himself was allowed to enter; in 1816 he gave Bess a key. Yet despite such proofs, Bess never ceased to marvel that she possessed the friendship of such a remarkable man. Throughout the years she knew him, virtually every journal entry concerning him includes some reference to his 'pure and elevated mind', his kindness to her, or to his 'selfless devotion to the affairs of Rome'.

The Cardinal was a well-known figure in Rome, and it was only to be expected that his intimacy with Bess should arouse comment. Gell had told Lady Charlotte Bury, at one time lady-in-waiting to the Princess of Wales, that Bess was 'desperately in love with the Cardinal . . . that no girl of fifteen ever betrayed a more romantic passion for her lover than did this distinguished, but then antiquated lady for the Cardinal. It is to be doubted whether he returned the tender passion; but his idea of the Duchess's consequence at the English court induced him to "*se laisser aimer*".' An entry in Bess's journal for June 1817 indirectly refutes this ludicrous and spiteful allegation: 'It seems to do him [Consalvi] good to come and talk to me openly, and on my part I feel about him *as for a beloved Brother* [author's italics].'

Before rejoining the Cliffords at Naples, Bess had two unexpected encounters. 'At the Colosseo I met Lord Byron who just alighted from his carriage and darted by.' Well might he dart, since he still owed her rent for Piccadilly Terrace. After a single tormented year of marriage – passed entirely in Bess's house – Byron and Annabella had parted; enveloped in a fog of scandal, Byron had fled to Europe. A few weeks later, at Albano, Bess met Baron de Rocca, Madame de Staël's husband. Germaine had suffered a stroke in February and according to Haryo, who had seen her in Paris in May, was 'in the most terrible state; paralytic, dropsical and dying...' She had died in July. Rocca, himself in the last stages of consumption, was devastated. Bess tried to talk to him about Germaine, but 'big tears fell from his eyes into the street as we were leaning over the balcony. I felt so affected I could not go on.'

In September the Cliffords left for England. 'We parted this morning... many tears were shed, many projects were formed for meeting again.' Bess had come to love Lizzy and her grandchildren, particularly the eldest boy Willy, who called her 'Duch' and reminded her 'not only of Clifford but of him who is ever present to me, tho' the first long bitterness of grief is soften'd into deep felt regrets.'

Bess was not alone for long: in October Augustus, Albinia and their two children, aged eighteen months and four months, arrived from Copenhagen. Bess had never met this daughter-in-law. 'Alb. seems very amiable' was all she could muster after this first meeting; Albinia's hysterics at the sight of Vesuvius 'in great glory' were scarcely calculated to win her approval. That winter, Bess was inundated with relations: her brother Lord Bristol came with his family, her niece Caroline Wortley with hers, Lady Hervey with her granddaughter. Bess was in her element in the role of *cicerone*, conducting them about Rome, and Consalvi was kindness itself, ensuring they were supplied with escorts and accommodation when they travelled to Naples. By April 1818, everyone had departed.

It was now four years since Bess had left England, three since she had taken up residence in Rome. To Augustus she confided: 'Here I have almost an ideal world, a great deal of occupation with much quiet, great interest, a feel of doing good in a manner pleasant to myself, & with great regard for many – & real friendship for *one* [Consalvi].' But for some time she had felt that she ought to return to England, if only briefly. Caro's situation weighed on her mind, as did

Augustus's wish to be transferred to a more active European post. She also wanted to follow up Canova's request to the Prince Regent for plaster casts of the Elgin marbles, to be presented to the Papal States. But she was reluctant to leave 'dear majestic Rome': 'I would not go to England', she told Augustus, 'with the chance of not being able to return for anything. I should have the *imprison'd* feel again which you may remember I hated so.'

Just before her departure, Caro wrote with the news that 'all London' was agog over rumours that Bess had 'turn'd Catholick' and confessed that Hart was her son, not Georgiana's. The latter was a revival of stories current at the time of Hart's birth which, Bess told him, she believed was intended to make trouble between them. Hart assured her this was impossible, since he could never forget 'the obligations I owe to you, and the affection of my parents for you'. Bess determined to do nothing to refute the conjecture, a decision applauded by Consalvi. Mary Berry, who kept her finger firmly on the pulse of society, dismissed it as 'a strange mad story', but the French writer Lamartine, whom Bess met later in Paris, included a highly coloured and inaccurate version in his *Souvenirs et Portraits* of 1872, even maintaining that Hart had vowed never to marry because he was illegitimate.

On the eve of Bess's departure, Consalvi 'came and staid late . . . He has given me a beautifull Cameo, *une marque d'amitié*, he said.' This no doubt took its place among the other precious objects which went everywhere with her: a locket and a bracelet, each containing Georgiana's hair; another locket showing Georgiana and the Duke; an enamel miniature of the Duke in uniform which she carried in her pocket; and a diamond watch, the Duke's last gift to her.

Bess left Rome on 15 June 1818, pausing briefly at Parma to collect copies of the second edition of the Horace from Madame Bodoni. In every city along her route there were old friends to greet her. At Florence she was received with open arms by Madame d'Albany. At Paris she was thanked in person by the King for the Horace she had given him. To her delight, Hart was the first to greet her in Paris, and again in England where, having travelled on ahead, he was 'dancing along the Quay' at Dover. But her arrival was marred by the death of her sister-in-law Lady Hervey: 'I have lost . . . a kind, steady and excellent friend.' Bess's meeting with the Prince Regent was however satisfactory: he praised Consalvi, agreed to send casts of the Elgin marbles to Rome, and promised to do what he could both for Clifford (who longed for a command) and for Augustus. Bess also broached a subject which had long concerned her: that Britain should send a representative to the Papal Court. 'We are the only Protestant power who does not,' she reminded him. The Prince replied that 'could there always be a Pope like Pius 7th, & a Minister like Consalvi there could be no hesitation at sending a Minister . . .' She raised the same point with her brother-in-law, Lord Liverpool, and later when she saw Castlereagh in Paris on her way back to Rome.

One of London's few enduring attractions for Bess was the theatre. Caroline Wortley reported seeing her every day in her box at Drury Lane, 'and as she always contrives to have a few men about her . . . she has a pleasant little *société*'. In honour of her return to England, Edmund Kean staged a special performance of *Othello*.

After three months, Bess said her goodbyes. She was to travel to Paris with the Cliffords before continuing on to Rome with Hart for what would be his first visit to Italy. As they waited for a fair wind at Dover, 'Caro and I walk'd and sat long on the beach. The past, present and dimly seen future all pass'd before us. To do as far as one can what is right and to leave the rest to providence – this was our determination.' This was the nearest Bess ever came to an acknowledgement of her daughter's unhappy situation. Haryo, who saw Caro a month later, told Little G.: 'She looks very ill and is very low. B[rougham] was with her looking like something just dug up.'

Though Bess may have parted from her family with regret, England was no longer her home. The terrible void left by Georgiana and the Duke oppressed her; Lady Melbourne had died earlier in the year, Sheridan in 1816, and with them vanished the last echoes of the glories of Devonshire House. There were now more old friends in Paris than in London. But it was in Rome that she preferred to live, not so much for its society but because of the city itself, its history, its climate and its grandeur. Above all, it was the city of Consalvi. 'Rome and Consalvi call on me,' she wrote to Augustus, '& I am on the road to the Eternal City.'

Bess spent ten weeks in Paris. Though it was more than a year since the death of Madame de Staël, her ghost met Bess at every turn. Of those who welcomed her to Paris, two, Talleyrand and Benjamin Constant, had been Germaine's lovers; Constant was now the lover of Germaine's closest friend, Juliette Récamier; and Mathieu de Montmorency had been intimate with both Juliette and Germaine. Bess also spent time with Germaine's son Auguste and her daughter

Albertine, now Duchesse de Broglie. (A papal dispensation had been required before Albertine, a Protestant, could marry her Catholic duke, and Bess, with Consalvi's help, had been instrumental in obtaining it.) Apart from these friends, Bess dined with the Queen of Sweden (French wife of the former Napoleonic general Bernadotte), was received by the King's younger brother, Monsieur (later Charles X), and discussed politics with one and all. To the Duke of Wellington she talked of Rome and of his support at the Congress of Vienna for the return of the looted works of art. 'I sacrific'd all my popularity', he told her, 'to return the statues to Rome.'

Within a week of the Cliffords leaving Paris for England, Bess too had gone. 'Are you not a little touched', Juliette Récamier asked her on the eve of her departure, 'by the way in which you are loved here? In my *petit cercle* you are adored.' Even Talleyrand, who had pleased her with his praise of Consalvi – his old sparring partner at Vienna – pressed her to remain until the spring. 'But for Rome, and Consalvi still more than Rome, I should be tempted,' she confessed in her journal. Hart was to travel separately, with a friend and a private doctor. Possibly to Bess's embarrassment, the friend proved to be Henry Brougham's brother James. The two parties met first at Lyons and then again at Marseilles, where Hart declared that 'a passion for antiquities' had come upon him when he glimpsed the wonders of Nîmes and Arles.

Susceptible as ever to every new sensation, at Aix Bess rose one morning before dawn to write to Augustus: 'I have been to the window to see the advance of morning & the interests of earth appear pitifull when fixing one's eyes on this firmament. I could fancy I saw all in motion, the rapid advance of light, the Stars quickly fading from their brightness, & soon the bright, bright & glorious sun will rule over all, & I hope will shine on Copenhagen.' On the road between Aix and Cannes they passed through the little town of Luc, where five years earlier Consalvi, on his way home after his years of detention in France, had encountered the party taking Napoleon into exile on Elba. They did not speak, but Napoleon remarked to his escort: 'There, that man, who would never become a priest, is a better priest than them all.' In her journal Bess recounts this well-known anecdote, adding that Consalvi, 'to avoid an appearance of triumph over him, would not apear at the window of the Inn as he pass'd'.

Previously Bess had made the journey from Nice to Genoa by *felucca*; this time she was determined to take the coastal route, and as sections of it were too perilous for a carriage, they were to travel by mule. Augustus had been horrified when Bess told him: 'You really ought to be scolded for your *folies de jeunesse* – who ever after five & twenty set out [in February] to make a journey to Italy by the Corniche?' To Little G., Hart described their procession of seventeen mules winding along the rocky track, on their left the snow-capped Col de Tende, on their right the sea. 'The Duchess did wonders, she rode most of the way and the road is extremely difficult and bad . . . The inns are horrible, the Duchess slept at one last night . . . which was too filthy.' At Genoa Bess received a letter from Consalvi (one of many he wrote during her absence) containing the distressing news that her friend Akerblad had died suddenly. It ends: 'I am beginning to count the days until you return . . . Yours with my heart and soul.' Leaving Hart to proceed at his leisure, Bess hurried on to Rome. From Pisa, Hart wrote to Clifford: 'The Roman [as he now called Bess] has risen very much in my estimation, she is a delightful traveller, she was *rayonnante* [radiant] and goodhumoured all the way we went together. The only times that produce blinking fits are on the eve of a journey after being long in a place.'

This letter marks a fundamental shift in Hart's attitude to Bess. Though he had never forgotten her kindness to him as a child, those early memories had long been suppressed by the animosity of Lady Spencer, Miss Trimmer and Haryo. He had been too young to understand Bess's love for his parents, but her grief following their deaths had brought about a dawning comprehension. He was now nearly thirty, charming, wealthy, the idol of society. Far from home and freed from outside influences, he was at last able to judge his stepmother on her own merits. This was a new Bess: a woman who had commanded the affection of a towering personality like Madame de Staël, who was 'adored' by Madame Récamier (a great favourite of his) and by men of the calibre of Benjamin Constant; a woman who was treated with respect by everyone from European monarchs to humble innkeepers; who could remain serenely good-natured whether dining with Talleyrand or riding on a mule. His view of her was further enhanced when he saw her in her element – in Rome.

14

Last years
1819–1824

'I press you to my heart and kiss you tenderly . . . Believe
that I will always pray for your happiness and I pray that
you love me as much as I love you. Farewell, excellent
Duchess and matchless friend.'

Consalvi to Bess, 26 June 1821

———————

AFTER AN ABSENCE of nearly nine months, Bess resumed her life in
Rome as if she had been away no more than a week. Within hours
of her arrival she had seen Consalvi, examined drawings for the *Aeneid*
executed in her absence, inspected the new fountain in front of the
Quirinal Palace (an embellishment instigated by Consalvi), checked
the progress of work both at the Colosseum and at her excavation,
and paid her customary visit to St Peter's. 'You are alive to everything
that is good or noble or interesting,' Augustus once told her. 'Nothing
escapes you, however minute, that has the slightest claim upon your
attention.' It was this energy, this passionate involvement in everything that made Bess such an invigorating and enchanting companion
in her last years. Not for her a slow withdrawal from life; instead, she
met life head on, and met it with gusto.

Hart's response was unequivocal: 'This day week I arrived at Rome,'
he wrote to Little G. 'It is an epoch in one's life, it is an interest, a sensation and an enjoyment as great and as pure as the mind of educated
man can partake of.' He rented the Palazzetto Albani on the Quirinal

Hill, some distance from Bess's apartment off the Piazza di Spagna, and began to explore the city, gazing on objects 'which seem sublimer every day'. When his excellent *cicerone* was purloined to the service of the Austrian emperor, on a state visit to Rome, Bess took his place. 'The Duchess shows things wonderfully well,' he told Little G. And it was Bess who made the momentous introduction to Canova, whose work so captivated Hart that over the next four years he acquired no fewer than six pieces of his sculpture. Such was his affection and admiration for Canova that, commissioning a marble statue before departing from Rome, he left the choice of subject to him.

Eager though she was to show off her wealthy and charming stepson, Bess was careful not to encroach on his independence – perhaps a little too careful. 'Her grace', Hart told Little G. somewhat wistfully, 'is entirely taken up with *la bella arti* and *il bello Cardinale Segretario di Stato.*' But her friendship for Consalvi he well understood. 'He is a very remarkable and distinguished person,' he told Little G. The Cardinal treated the young duke with his habitual courtesy and kindness, and offered him his houses at Tivoli and Albano: Hart was well aware it was 'all for love of the Duchess'.

On his birthday on 21 May Bess gave Hart a half-column of *verde antico* which had been found in her excavation. Accompanying it was a short verse asking him to accept her gift 'without scruple', since it was due to his generosity that she had been able to continue 'the works' which gave such value to her life in Rome. It was, Hart told Little G., 'a magnificent present'. His newly-developed collecting mania did however cause 'one grand quarrel' with Bess which, as he told Clifford, 'brought on a blinking fit for a week. It was about some columns which the Cardinal could not or would not get leave for me to export; I told her she was unnatural to side with the Cardinal against me, which she rather did.' Hart was well aware, however, that Consalvi's introduction of new laws blocking the export of antiquities had saved Rome from being denuded of its Classical past. (Bess's half-column was not considered important enough to be subject to the laws.)

When Hart left Rome in June, Bess wrote to him sadly: 'I really can't bear to look at Palazzetto Albani, there is no saying how I miss you, & how much I want you – never shall I forget your kind, your most dear & amiable manner to me & generous conduct.' Hart told Clifford that despite Bess's emotion at parting, she was so engrossed and occupied that 'it does not alter her enjoyment of life whether one is there or not, as it would with some people'.

Bess's principal occupation at this time was the visit of Sir Thomas Lawrence, at the request of the Prince Regent, to paint the Pope and Consalvi for the series of portraits of Allied sovereigns and statesmen destined for the Waterloo Chamber at Windsor. Consalvi provided Lawrence with a carriage and an apartment in the Quirinal Palace, while Bess acted as his guide, deriving special pleasure from seeing Rome through the eyes of someone of his 'discrimination & knowledge of the Arts . . .' Before he arrived in Rome, Lawrence had been carefully primed by Bess: 'You will be struck by [Consalvi's] dignified animation and benevolent expression . . . you will agree with me that a three-quarters or nearly a full face is what will do justice to the beauty of his countenance . . .' Lawrence evidently did agree, as he told his friend Joseph Farington: 'The Cardinal is one of the finest subjects for a picture I have ever had. A countenance of powerful intellect, and great symmetry . . .' Bess declared the finished portrait to be a perfect likeness, and Lawrence gave her a drawing of it which became one of her most treasured possessions.

Before he left Rome Lawrence also made two drawings of Bess, one showing her in a jaunty hat, the other in profile. She clearly preferred the latter, since she used it as a frontispiece to the *Aeneid*, confessing to Lawrence: 'I am myself rendered quite vain by it and it is your particular talent to extend the term of looks that may have been reckon'd good.' She sent engravings of the profile to Augustus. 'I think them beautiful,' he replied, '& so like you & it has an Imperial look about it which pleases me.'

In June Bess moved to the lofty splendours of an apartment in the Palazzo Spada (now demolished) in the Piazza Colonna. From her balcony she looked 'full on the column' and could watch all the events which took place on the Corso. The rooms, though not much larger than those of Casa Margherita, were higher-ceilinged and more numerous, and she now had space for her rapidly increasing collection of books, paintings, marbles and curiosities. One visitor described the apartment as resembling a museum. Lady Morgan, lamenting the lack of patronage of the artists then working in Rome, declared that it was only the 'saloons of the Duchess of Devonshire' that 'were . . . crowded with recent works'. To Augustus, Bess wrote: 'All my visitors are delighted with my change of house & say that I am more suitably lodg'd; even poor Lawrence said "I find again the Dss of Devonshire", so I suppose I was thought to be ill off before.' Ten months later Bess told Lawrence that Consalvi had 'made a lamb of Piombino' (her landlord), persuading him to rent her two more rooms and contrive her a new kitchen.

Hart had joked to Clifford that Bess was much happier after the Austrian Emperor departed, when she was once again Queen of Rome, but there was some truth in the jest. Charles Greville's retrospective view of her – that 'In old age, Popes and Cardinals, Savants and Artists, attended her *levées*, rendered her an unceasing homage, and were obedient to all her wishes or commands' – was no exaggeration. Whether she could have achieved such eminence without the friendship and protection of Consalvi is perhaps open to doubt, but there were few foreigners in Rome who could hope to aspire to her crown. In the years following Waterloo, the British who visited Italy were of a very different type from the Grand Tourists of the previous century. In general they lacked the manners, taste, Classical education and seriousness of purpose of their predecessors. Clutching their guide books they rushed from one antiquity to another; they looked, but they did not *see*, still less did they *feel* – a 'parcel of staring boobies', Byron called them. In Stendhal's view, they were only tolerated by the Romans because they spent money lavishly. Why, he wondered, did they have to behave in Italy in a way they would never dare behave in London? Stendhal considered that Bess and Hart were 'the only English, to my knowledge, from whom the Romans make exception in the profound hatred they bear towards their countrymen'.

Bess's success was sometimes the target of adverse comment. Lavinia Spencer on her visit to Rome in 1819 claimed that Bess made herself 'the laughing-stock of all Rome with her pretensions to Maecenas-ship'. But Lady Morgan's opinion more than offsets Lavinia's malice: 'While Ciceroni dispute and Virtuosi stare, and Roman Princes and Cardinals boast of the past glories of the "*eterna città*", the Duchess of Devonshire is more effectually doing the honours of Rome, ancient and modern, by illustrating Horace, reprinting Virgil, making excavations, giving countenance and patronage to living talent and bringing forward modest professors into the distinguished circles of her own society.' Mrs Bunsen could still be relied upon for spiteful gossip, however; though she and her husband might consider themselves far too respectable to attend the assemblies of 'that intolerable old Witch of a Duch of Devonshire', she was not above hinting to her mother of something improper in Bess's friendship with Consalvi, or perpetuating the rumour that Bess was going to 'turn a Catholic'.

This rumour was founded, perhaps not implausibly, on Bess's

association with Consalvi and his clerical colleagues and her frequent attendance at Catholic services. But her god was a universal god, her attitude to religion as tolerant and as ecumenical as her father's. She believed that 'in every rite the religion of the heart is felt, & I think one can enter a Catholick church & as fervently offer up prayers & thanksgiving in it as in one's [own] country'. (In Leghorn, out of curiosity, she had even visited a synagogue, and described the proceedings in some detail in her journal.) With her love of the theatre, it was natural that she should respond to the drama of the great Catholic rituals. 'I never was so struck with the beauty and magnificence of the ceremony at St Peter's as today [Easter Sunday 1816] . . . The beauty of the Church, the Pomp of High Mass, the number of Cardinals with their splendid dresses & above all the sanctity of the Pope's countenance & manner made it the most impressive solemnity I ever saw.'

On a visit to Rome in late 1820, Mary Berry wrote to Hart that 'the Dhs goes on *à merveille*, I really give her credit for the existence she has contrived for herself here – she is a sort of English Minister who costs nothing to Government, & is very useful to her Country for this.' Since Bess never lost an opportunity to promote, explain or extol Consalvi's policies to all and sundry, including such powerful connections as Lord Liverpool, Lord Castlereagh and the Prince Regent, she was also discreetly useful to the Papal government. Miss Berry adds, however: 'It would be well if she meddled less with politics, in which (they say) she does harm . . .' This may be a reference to the last visit made by the Princess of Wales to Rome, in February 1820. George III had died on 29 January, so that she was technically now Queen – but no *official* notification had yet reached Rome: should the Papal government accord her the honours due to a visiting monarch? It has been suggested that Bess influenced Consalvi's decision not to provide the royal visitor with the guard of honour she demanded; she certainly discussed the problem with him, but there is otherwise no evidence to support the allegation. Nor was she unsympathetic to Caroline's predicament; as she told Hart, she was quite prepared to call on her rather than 'degrade Royalty at a time when it requires being upheld as much as possible'. Indeed, there is a hint in one of Consalvi's letters that she had tried to persuade him to give in to Caroline's demands – 'Your kind heart betrays you in this affair,' he told her – and she did call; her name is one of the last to appear in the visitors' book on 8 April, the day Caroline left Rome.

Bess was always careful not to abuse her influence. To Hart, who had asked her to do what she could for an Irish bishop, her reply was that she had told the bishop 'it would be improper for me to interfere in any ecclesiastical affairs both as a Woman & a stranger', and that she had made it a rule to restrict the use of her influence with Consalvi 'merely to acts of kindness' to individuals.

Bess's own 'acts of kindness', especially to foreign visitors, were legion. As well as showing them around Rome itself, she organized excursions to Hadrian's Villa at Tivoli or south along the Appian Way to the lakes of Albano and Nemi. Even Charlotte Bury had to admit that Bess was 'an invaluable friend here to the English'. But the arrival in Rome of Lord Spencer and her old enemy Lavinia gave her pause: how was she to react? Her decision to swallow her pride and be kind to their son and daughter was praised by Clifford as 'taking the only revenge Worth taking of a Noble Mind'. (If she felt a surge of malicious pleasure at the news that it had taken the Spencers thirteen hours to cross the Simplon Pass, who could blame her?) Bess also took pity on Hart's private physician, Dr Eyre, who had been too ill to return with him to England. Eventually she moved the poor man, now raving and threatening suicide, to her apartment to be nursed by her staff, an act of charity for which Hart was profoundly grateful.

Bess was now in regular correspondence with her stepson, her letters spontaneous, affectionate, often amusing, and full of news of Rome. In September 1819 she sent him an ecstatic report on the sculpture he had commissioned from Canova. 'It lives, it breathes, it is all life, & youth, & beauty; yet it looks not, it wakes not. It is not Apollo, but it is a form so beautiful, of such nature, taste & loveliness, that I really think it is the most perfect of all his works . . . He had worked at it as he says "*con amore*" & done it in the space of a fortnight . . .' The sleeping figure of Endymion, a dog at his feet, now lies in marbled beauty in the Sculpture Gallery at Chatsworth. Canova was also modelling Bess's sister Louisa for Lord Liverpool. To Lawrence Bess confided that she hoped Canova would not do 'too holy a figure for Lord Liverpool who is a great admirer of female beauty and would like a Nymph or a Venus better than a Magdalen'. Canova, however, resolutely continued to model a Magdalen.

In 1819, the first volume of Bess's edition of Virgil's *Aeneid* was printed by De Romanis of Rome, but throughout 1820 she was still commissioning artists to do drawings for the second volume. One view shows the Forum; discreetly tucked away in the right-hand corner is a woman wearing a long veil, with a book in her hand and a small dog at her heels – unquestionably Bess herself. She also contributed two of the drawings. She gave the first copies of the Virgil to Consalvi and to the Pope. Others were distributed to 'the Royal libraries of Europe' and to friends and family, including one to the Duke of Wellington. Scholarly observers like George Ticknor thought her edition 'a monument of her taste and generosity'. It was also praised by art critics of the day, not only because Bess had employed contemporary landscape painters but because the illustrations broke with the baroque tradition of depicting the actions of Aeneas and instead portrayed the locations in which they took place.

Work on Bess's excavation was still in progress. Just before her return to Rome the workmen had discovered another inscription on the base of the column, and in August she reported to Augustus that a road had been found near her column 'which seems to have cross'd the Foro, or to denote that the Foro only began where the Pillar stands'.

All these undertakings were expensive, and Bess was constantly worried about money. Clifford, who looked after her finances in London, told her in March 1819 that Byron had finally paid the last of the rent for Piccadilly Terrace, 'so that I hope there will be sufficient to Answer your Drafts . . .' This outstanding debt to Bess had been a contributory factor in a quarrel Byron had had with Caro's lover Henry Brougham: apparently Brougham had gossiped about it, and Byron declared his intention of challenging him to a duel when he returned to England. Bess came into more direct contact with the poet in July 1821 when he wrote asking her to use her influence to secure the reversal of the sentence of exile imposed on the father and brother of his auburn-haired mistress Teresa Guiccioli. The letter, oozing flattery, admits that while Byron's acquaintance with her Grace's character was slight, he had only to 'turn to the letters of Gibbon (now on my table) for a full testimony to it's [*sic*] high & amiable qualities'. The letter missed Bess, who had left again for England, but she wrote in August promising to do what she could and assuring Byron that 'there is a character of justice, goodness, and benevolence in the present Government of Rome' – by which of course she meant Consalvi.

Bess's return to England had been precipitated by news that her sister Louisa was seriously ill. She also longed to see her children, Clifford's intended visit to Rome in 1819 having been postponed. Although still in the navy, he was now also MP for Dungarvan, one of the Cavendish seats, and Hart, anxious that one of his members should not miss a whole session, had cautioned him against the trip: 'that little Roman will do all she can to keep you when you are with her & she is like sticking plaister'. A sad little entry in Bess's journal reveals her awareness that she now took second place in her children's affections; if she wished to see them, it was she who must make the effort. But her priorities had also changed, as Consalvi's friendship became increasingly precious to her. 'If there is a pure and angelic mind on earth now, it is his.' He called her his 'protecting goddess', and in handwriting she found difficult to read sent her frequent notes addressed to his 'Dear Friend' and ending 'All yours with all my heart and soul': none of her letters to him has survived. Shortly before her departure from Rome in June 1821 she heard that Louisa had died, but she was determined to make the trip. Before setting out she received a note from Consalvi. 'His friendship supports my courage – but it is a bitter moment that of leaving him & Rome – Rome is him.'

After only ten days in Paris Bess travelled on to Spa, where she was reunited with Hart, Caro, Clifford and Augustus. From Spa they all moved to Brussels, where their arrival coincided with a visit by George IV, who was to tour the field of Waterloo with the Duke of Wellington. Over the next five days Bess was called upon by the Duke, Lord Castlereagh (the Foreign Secretary, now Marquess of Londonderry) and Frederick, Prince of Orange. In her journal she expresses neither surprise nor conceit that her company should be sought by men of such eminence; with the exception of the Prince of Orange, they were old friends. With the King she spent more than two hours. They discussed his recent visit to Ireland, and his estranged wife's death some seven weeks previously. 'He talked of the event with great propriety, but I thought him too credulous of the accusations against her . . . Of Consalvi he said "I love that man as my Brother. You cannot in speaking of him to me say too much of my love, esteem & respect for him."' At her first meeting with the Duke she questioned him closely about the battle, her questions revealing an already detailed knowledge of the day's events. Undeterred by this third degree, he called again the following day. 'His countenance is quite brilliant as he speaks & his manner simplicity itself.'

While she was in Brussels, Bess visited the studio of Jacques-Louis David. She thought him 'a horrid man to look at from an excrescence in his mouth', and condemned 'his character in the Revolution' as 'atrocious'. As she was leaving, she records, David said: "'May I ask to whom I have the honour of speaking?" "I am the Duchess of Devonshire," I said. "My God, that name is known, and honourably known, throughout all Europe." The horrid mouth which pronounced this did not, I am afraid, prevent my being pleased at it.'

Bess and her children arrived in England in early October. She went at once to stay with Lord Liverpool, still shocked by Louisa's death. From there she, Caro and Augustus travelled to Chatsworth. This might have been a distressing pilgrimage for Bess, but she found the house 'so altered, and indeed improved, that I have borne returning here far better than I expected'. Four days later the Morpeths arrived. Bess had doggedly continued to write to Little G., especially during Caro's unhappy affair with Brougham, but it is impossible to avoid the impression that Little G. replied not out of affection but from a sense of duty. Hart had tried but failed to bring them together during Bess's last visit to England, but this time he was determined to succeed: 'I think it would really be unkind and wrong of you to let her leave England another time without seeing you.' A similar plea to Haryo had fallen on stony ground, however.

That Little G., like Hart, had managed to separate the Bess they knew now from the Bess of the past is evident from a remark made by Hart to his sister shortly after the visit: 'I am so glad you met her Grace, and I think we shall be glad of it and look back to that time all our lives.' A year later he wrote to Bess from Chatsworth: the Morpeths were with him 'and we think of you a great deal; it was just this time last year that you was here and we wish with all our hearts that the same party be now assembled'. Though Hart was the kindest of men, he would never have said this unless it were true.

Bess passed November in London with her children. Fred, still showing no inclination to marry, had suffered a long illness which left him permanently lame. Freed from Brougham by his marriage in 1819, Caro had quietly resumed her life with George, but she was not happy. The marriages of both Clifford and Augustus were contented and prolific. To his delight, Clifford was to take command of the *Euryalus*, due to sail to the eastern Mediterranean, where the Greeks were fighting the Turks for their independence. Though they could not know it, this was to be the last time the family were together, the last time Bess saw Fred and Augustus.

Accompanied by Caro, Bess left London at the end of November. At Dover they heard that at Florence Harriet Bessborough was dangerously ill, the result of weeks spent nursing a dying grandson. 'I cannot bear to think of it,' Bess wrote on 29 November. 'She is so connected with the recollections of all that was dear to me that I feel a great anxiety, as if she were indeed my sister.' The following day she wrote: 'We have lost her and our loss is irreparable.' Though through force of circumstances she and Harriet had seen little of each other in recent years, they had corresponded regularly. Apart from Georgiana – and perhaps, briefly, Germaine de Staël – Harriet was the only other woman Bess ever loved.

On 6 December 1822 Bess and Caro arrived in Paris, where they stayed with Bess's brother Lord Bristol and his family. He had been living abroad since 1817, partly to recoup his finances but also to rebuild the collection of works of art which the Earl-Bishop had spent thirty years assembling for his house at Ickworth, only to have it seized by the French. At the Earl-Bishop's death in 1803 only the shell of Ickworth's vast rotunda had been built, and the flanking wings were a mere three feet above ground level. Though he was briefly tempted to demolish the whole unwieldy structure, the new earl pledged himself to proceed with the house according to his father's ambitious plans; the house was not completed in its entirety until 1841. Today, the rotunda and curving colonnades rise with comic grandeur from the flat green Suffolk landscape; they would look more at home on the banks of the Tiber.

In April, Bess parted from Caro and left for Rome. At Évian she succumbed to an outburst of sorrow. 'What a fearful chasm is made in all I then possessed of friends and relations!' But once back in her beloved Rome her old zest for life returned. Consalvi was thinner, but 'well & most kind and delightfull', and the city more beautiful than ever. During her absence much had happened. 'Something is going on in all parts of Rome,' she told Lord Morpeth, 'a great deal of planting, house building, or repairing, & a general activity prevails . . .' The summer of 1822 was unusually hot, and she seldom left the house until evening. 'Every body dines at six,' she wrote to Little G., 'the blinds begin to be opened as the evening breeze refreshes one, & carriages begin to roll. I generally go to some artist, or musician till Sun set & then walk either in a villa or on the Pincian hill . . . In coming home I stop to eat ices, either alone or with my companions to promenade, then come home about nine.' On moonlit nights she would take a party to the Colosseum to watch dancers performing a quadrille. 'Here, long after the midnight hour,' wrote Lady Morgan, one of

Bess's guests, 'we have seen the twinkling of beauty's fairy-foot tread-
ing its maze where martyrs bled, and heroes fell.' Bess described it to
Hart: 'The finest tho' darkest night possible shewed St Peter's to
immense advantage & made me think so of you & your admiration of
it. Not a breath of air & the dome like a Topaz!'

In July Bess left for the sea breezes of Castellammare on the Bay
of Naples where she had taken a house for Lizzy and the children;
Clifford was to join them there for a month's leave in November.
'Roman is arrived from Paris in new Costumes,' Lizzy told Hart. 'Pink
& yellow & all sorts of colours. The Heat however keeps her within
bounds, & we haven't yet even been to Pompeii . . . She brought me
such pretty things from Rome . . .' During the day they kept out of the
sun, but the evenings were spent with the children by the seaside.

Bess had always possessed the knack of being in the right place at
the right time, and in October Vesuvius erupted – the first major eruption for thirty years. It is typical of her that viewing the spectacle from
afar was not enough; she must take her carriage to a point where she
could see 'an immense stream of Lava moving on & setting fire to
Trees & Vineyards, the wretched inhabitants flying & carrying their
furniture, children, aged & sick along with them'. That night forked
lightning 'in a hundred shapes & directions like fire rockets fill'd the
whole firmament whilst the Moon pale and blighted scarce gives light'.

In September Bess had been shocked to hear of the suicide of her
old friend Castlereagh: she thought he must have been 'either mad or
guilty of a criminal act'. Hard on the heels of this sudden death came
news of another: 'My dearest D.,' she wrote to Hart, 'how you will
grieve to hear of the loss which we have all sustain'd on the death of
Canova! . . . It seem'd as if fate should have respected such a genius
. . . What a loss to Rome, to Italy, to Europe.'

Before leaving Naples, Bess visited her little dog's grave. Ting had
died in the summer of 1820, and she had buried him close to the steps
leading to Virgil's tomb. Even this mild indulgence was pronounced
'impudence' by Mrs Bunsen, who told her mother that some wit had
composed an epitaph to mark the grave which read: 'Here lies a young
dog and an old witch, A faithful creature and a d—d b—.'

Bess returned to Rome in early December to find her old friend
Adrien de Montmorency (now Duc de La Val), cousin of Mathieu,
eagerly awaiting her arrival. She had known both Montmorencys since
meeting them in Paris in 1802; Adrien was the newly appointed French
ambassador, and his presence was to prove a great consolation in the

months to come, not least because he shared Bess's love and admiration for Consalvi. To her surprise, Hart also arrived in December. As he told Clifford, he 'found Roman blink blink because she had no notice of my coming . . . She is all kindness and we live a great deal together.'

On 1 January 1823 Bess's summary of the past year was unusually positive. She expressed gratitude for 'seeing dear Clifford', for improved health, for Hart's kindness, for the continued prosperity and beautification of Rome, but above all for Consalvi: 'Long & happy may his life & administration be!!' Within a month, however, the Cardinal was showing signs of illness. Bess's entry of 5 February sets the tone for what is to come: 'I have been most sick at heart from anxiety.' There is hardly an entry during the ensuing months which does not alternate between hope and despair over Consalvi's health. Her anxiety for him and his gratitude to her for her concern and kindness are unbearably touching. 'He is to me the kindest, most feeling friend . . . For above 7 years he has been a constant source of every distinction, comfort & advantage to me here, & more than all he has shewn me a constant affectionate, kind confiding friendship; he has been the object of my residence at Rome . . . His illness therefore weighs on my heart.'

Consalvi's first symptoms were spasms in the chest and restricted breathing, then his legs became so swollen and painful that he was unable to walk without assistance. 'I have no peace of mind whilst he suffers so.' With his customary tenacity, he continued to work long hours, still finding time to write to Bess twice a day. In her distress, the Duc de La Val was her greatest comfort. 'I shall love him ever for the feeling which he has shewn!' Lacking any faith in Consalvi's doctors, Bess recommended another physician, whose change of medication had immediate results. By Easter, Consalvi was 'astonishingly recover'd', and her life briefly returned to normal. Hart had left in mid February, but with a little coterie of friends who included La Val and Artaud de Montor (Secretary to the French Legation, 'a true Frenchman' who wore a huge white ring and earrings) she made trips to Albano and Porto d'Anzio; attended the numerous Easter ceremonies; went to the theatre and to the races; and on Fridays held her regular *soirées*. 'My Friday event', she told Hart, 'went off well, good musick, whist, & *écarté* till four in the morning.' In April, Consalvi's regular Thursday evening visits were re-established. Bess had also begun to raise money for a monument to Canova, a figure of the artist to be modelled by her friend, the neo-classical sculptor Bertel Thorwaldsen. (Through no fault of Bess's, this ambitious project was later abandoned.)

In July the Pope fell and broke his hip. Consalvi, still recovering from his illness, exhausted himself by devoted attendance on the now dying man, his friend and master for twenty-three years. Two weeks after the Pope's fall, St Paul's-Outside-the-Walls, one of Rome's most ancient and best-loved churches, was burned to the ground. Appalled, Bess returned again and again to the smoking ruin. 'Piety, love of the Arts, respect for high antiquity, every thing conspires here to encrease one's regret & sorrow.' The Pope's death on 20 August was signalled by the tolling of the great bell on the Capitol, followed by all the bells of Rome. Consalvi's resignation as Secretary of State was automatic. Grief and fatigue, the loss of St Paul's and the preparations for the necessary conclave to elect a new pope sapped what little strength remained to him, yet at his last meeting with Bess before going into conclave she thought him never 'more animated in look & manner'. Her principal fear, as she told Hart, was that he was on the point of being shut up 'with a *swarm* of wasps, all men [who,] with the exception of some very few, would put things back to where they were one hundred years ago'.

Bess's fears were realized: Pope Leo XII and his new Secretary of State could hardly have differed more from their predecessors; the pendulum had swung from an enlightened, liberal papacy to one that was reactionary and bigoted. To Sir Thomas Lawrence, Bess confessed that she could barely contain her indignation at the 'ingratitude & artfull conduct of government'. Hart, however, assured Little G. that 'in six weeks she will have the new government at her feet'. But Bess was too loyal for that. Consalvi, bruised in mind and sick in body, retired to Porto d'Anzio.

For some time Bess had been plotting with Lawrence for a portrait by him of George IV to be presented to Consalvi. Bess knew Consalvi would be deeply touched by the gift, but also saw it as a way of proving to his ungrateful fellow cardinals how much he was valued by the world beyond Rome's frontiers. The King not only agreed, but gave Bess permission to tell Consalvi the portrait was on its way. (In the event, Consalvi died before it arrived, but the King instructed Lawrence to give it to Bess, on the condition that after her death it should go to Hart. It is now at Chatsworth.)

In October Bess left to join Lizzy at Naples, where together they waited for Clifford to arrive on leave. To their astonishment, who should disembark with him from his ship but Hart, whom he had picked up at Genoa. It was two years since Hart and the Cliffords had met, and it was a joyful reunion. 'This is delightfull,' Bess wrote. Ten days later Clifford returned to sea in the *Euryalus*: 'She sail'd nobly out, one straight course, ever like her dear Commander.' Bess hurried back to Rome to be near Consalvi, who was still at Porto d'Anzio. He did his best to spare her feelings, but his letters left her in no doubt that he knew his illness to be mortal.

Consalvi returned to Rome on 11 January 1823, and seemed to rally. 'His conduct since the sovereign power fell from his hands has been perfect,' Frances Bunsen told her mother, 'there has not been an instance of meanness, not a symptom of querulousness or discontent, he has been throughout dignified, courageous, & consistent . . .' He was twice sent for by the Pope, and on the 14th was named Prefect of the Propaganda Fidei, an important post. But it was all too late. His illness returned with renewed violence. Bess visited him once, often twice a day, optimistic and desperate by turns. He was now in terrible pain, but 'always patient & courageous'. On the 22nd she sat with him. 'I could not help crying, he press'd my hand, let me place his pillows, but cast such piteous looks it went near to break my heart . . . He thank'd me so for all the feeling I shew'd him. How could it be other wise!' Her entry for the 24th reads simply: 'O Heavens – all, all is over.' To Hart she was more expressive: 'Oh dearest D. how [to] tell you how unhappy I am . . . This morning that pure & noble spirit, that kind & benevolent heart ceas'd to exist.'

Consalvi's body lay in state for a week in the Palazzo Farnese. 'And when the last sad ceremonies took place,' Bess wrote to Lawrence, 'all Rome pour'd out to pay homage & respect to his memory.' On the day of the funeral, Bess took refuge from the crowds in the grounds of the Villa Borghese. Madame Récamier and her niece Amélie, who had been in Rome since December, came upon her by chance, walking alone in the deserted gardens. Amélie left a description of the haunting encounter: 'The solitude was complete, and Madame Récamier had alighted from her carriage to enjoy it freely, when she noticed in the distance, in an alley, the . . . elegant figure of the duchess, who by the contrast of her black clothes with the pallor of her complexion, looked like a ghost. Her image has remained with me as a striking example of smothered despair.' On impulse, Bess asked Juliette to take her to the Palazzo Farnese to see Consalvi once more. Lamartine takes up the story: 'The duchess gazed once more in the stillness and holiness of death at that face which she had seen every day . . . animated with all the beauty and grace which characterised his expression.' Overwhelmed with grief, she fell insensible into the arms of Madame Récamier, who took her back to Palazzo Spada. (In his will Consalvi left Bess a beautiful *pietradura* snuff box.)

'To me Rome seems a desert,' Bess told Lawrence on 3 February, '& were not Duc de La Val here, who has been like a brother to me, I don't know that even the cold could detain me here.' Bess was now sixty-four, a good age for that time. She had outlived Georgiana by eighteen years and was, on the face of it, still full of vigour. But life in Rome without Consalvi was inconceivable.

Determined that the city should not be allowed to forget its former Secretary of State, Bess threw herself into the task of raising money for a memorial. With the help of Artaud de Montor and the Hanoverian minister Reden, she commissioned a pair of commemorative medals to be struck in his honour, proceeds from the sale of which would pay for a marble bust by Thorwaldsen, modelled from the death mask he had made. (She ordered a copy of the bust for herself – possibly the one now at Chatsworth.) 'The occupation pleases & soothes me,' she wrote in her journal. The bust, which was placed above Consalvi's tomb in the Pantheon, was considered a remarkable likeness. 'The eyes, particularly,' wrote one contemporary, 'are full of the nobility and kindness which he always had.' On 12 February Hart arrived from Milan and went immediately to see her. 'She was less afflicted than I expected,' he told Little G., 'she has been out since the Cardinal's death & has made no fuss.' But Bess was dissembling; to Lawrence she wrote, 'I cannot tell you of my grief.'

Since his return from Milan Hart had become ensared in a flirtation with Princess Pauline Borghese, who teased and charmed him by turns. The very last entry in Bess's journal reads: 'D. has made me promise to dine at Prs Borghese on Sunday.' This was the first time Bess had accepted an invitation from the princess, and it was while waiting in the biting March wind for her carriage after dinner that she caught a chill.

The course of her illness was charted by Hart in his diary. His account is a testament to his affection and to his tender care of her through her last days. The first intimation that she was dangerously ill came on 23 March, when she developed a high fever and pains in her chest. A dozen leeches were applied, which relieved her. 'I should be grieved to lose her,' he wrote on the 24th, adding with candour that 'selfish thoughts come on my mind of all the trouble and difficulty I should have being her only connection here.' Copious amounts of blood were taken from her. As Bess seemed to prefer solitude, Hart kept most visitors at bay but was obliged to admit La Val and Juliette Récamier: 'They are truly attached to the Dss.' The only other person he allowed in was young George Howard, Little G.'s eldest son. He had been in Rome for some time, and Bess had become very fond of him.

For two days Bess rallied, but when the decline began on the 26th, it was swift. Hart, though now living at Palazzo Spada, dined out, 'for her servants are so unhappy I do not make them work . . . She expectorates about every two hours which harasses her very much.' On the 27th he thought it wise to write to Lord Bristol and to Lord Morpeth. On the 28th he and George agreed that Bess should be warned of her danger. 'She bore it with astonishing fortitude', begged him to take care of Clifford and of her servants, and directed him to a red box which contained her will and instructions for her funeral. La Val, Artaud de Montor and Juliette came to see her. She was also visited by a clergyman, Dr Nott. Clearly well acquainted with her past, and perhaps alerted to the rumour that she had contemplated 'turning Catholic', he grilled her mercilessly as to her beliefs and urged her to make a full confession. He then waited for her to ask to take the Sacrament. 'I thank you – but not now,' he thought he understood her to say. Having reduced Bess to a shred, he was driven away by the physicians. 'My poor Dss, what a day this has been!' Hart exclaimed in his diary.

The following day she seemed a little better, but was anxious that Hart should obtain from Consalvi's executor the *pietradura* snuff box the Cardinal had bequeathed her, as she wanted Hart to have it. 'I was more touched than I can say by her recollection of me at such a moment.' The box is at Chatsworth.

On 30 March Hart wrote: 'On this day 18 years ago my poor mother died – and between 3 and 4 this morning I lost her whom my mother loved with enthusiastic affection. I had a premonition that the poor Dss should die on this day.' At midnight Bess's condition had begun to deteriorate, and he had sent for Juliette, La Val and Artaud de Montor. 'Her breathing by degrees became more and more oppressed, she sank as if into a sleep and one cry terminated her suffering, her hand in mine, she recognized me and kissed my forehead . . . Oh God bless her.' Later that day he wrote to Fred Foster: 'Nothing was ever

so tranquil, so kind to all, so calm as the Duchess in her illness . . .'
Bess had died with grace, considerate and composed to the end.

Hart was now faced with what he had dreaded: the onerous task of
putting Bess's affairs in order, and arranging for her body to be
returned to England for burial alongside the Duke's in the vault at
Derby, as she had requested. He had also to inform her children, who
were scattered about Europe: Clifford was somewhere in the eastern
Mediterranean, Caro in London, Augustus in Copenhagen. Fred's
whereabouts were a mystery: when last heard of he had been at Turin
en route for Rome.

Although all Hart's letters were sent by courier, Clifford's still had
not reached him nearly a month later. Fred's letter finally found him
in Paris. His barely legible reply betrays his remorse for failing to be
with Bess when she died. Those from Caro and Clifford express their
great love for their mother, and their profound gratitude to Hart for
his kindness to her in her last days. 'If any thing could soften my grief
at having been away from her at such a moment,' wrote Caro, 'it would
be your having been there. If I could have chosen who should be with
her, I should have said you – she loved you so truly – as if you had
been her son.' Even Haryo admitted to Little G. that she and Granville
had been shocked by the news. 'She had so much enjoyment of life . . .
It also brings back past times to one's mind, and many nervous and
indefinable feelings. This is a bitter cup, dearest sister.'

Lizzy's letters to Clifford are touching in their concern for him. She
was afraid he would be told the news by a passing ship. 'I did love her
so much,' she wrote. She advised him to have his 'epaulettes covered
with black crape & your sword to make it as deep as possible & the
gold round your hat', and told him she intended putting their horses
into mourning.

No letter from Bess's sister Mary survives, but Lord Bristol wrote
to Hart: 'To me the loss is indeed irreparable – & the Chasm which it
has left in my Heart shall be kept sacred to her Memory to the latest
moment of my life.' As head of the family, Lord Bristol received the
physicians' autopsy report. Though Bess had died of pneumonia, her
lungs and one of the large arteries were in such a diseased state that
death had been inevitable.

Others outside the family spoke of her death with deep regret.
'There never was anything like the grief felt in Rome,' Hart told Caro.
'I believe it is sincere, and it is from all classes.' Bess would have been
astonished by such proofs of affection on the part of her adopted city.

'Those who saw her die', wrote Artaud, 'might say of her . . . "She was as gentle in death as she was to all the world".' Thomas Lawrence told a friend: 'I *have* lost a very true and sincerely valued Friend in this amiable Woman, and the many, the daily obligations that I ow'd to her during my stay at Rome, rise perpetually before me.' He was anxious that Rome should 'not be without some just Memorial of its Bene-factress', and asked to be one of the first to contribute to its cost. A medal was duly struck in her honour, showing that imperious profile Lawrence had drawn.

Nor did Bess's death go unremarked in the wider world. On 5 May the French *Journal des Débats* – one of France's most prestigious news-papers – devoted virtually its entire front page to an assessment of her character and reputation. Almost certainly written by Artaud de Montor, it pays tribute to her patronage of the arts, her 'inexhaustible benevolence', the success of her excavation, the splendour of the de luxe editions, her intelligence and taste, her gift for friendship and, above all, her unfailing *douceur*.

As one of Bess's two executors, with Lord Bessborough, Hart was able to open her will in Rome and pass on its general contents to her children. Fred and Augustus were left any property she had inherited from her own family, while all that she had received from 'her beloved husband', the Duke, was to go to Caro and Clifford. Any money in the bankers' hands, beyond the sum of five thousand pounds bequeathed to Caro, was to go to Fred 'who left himself poor to increase my income before I became Duchess of Devonshire'. (This clause must have come as quite a shock to the Cavendish family who had surely always assumed that all the expense of her upkeep was an item to be added to Bess's other sins.) The list of her minor bequests shows her concern to distribute her most precious possessions to those who would appreciate them most. The enamel portrait of the Duke was left to Little G. and the miniature of him to Haryo; the cottage at Richmond she left to Clifford; her papers to Caro; her clothes to her faithful maid, Madame Pallé; and to her brother Lord Bristol, Lawrence's drawing of Consalvi, to be carefully preserved as that of 'one whose friendship has stored my mind and whose constant kind-ness makes Rome delightful to me'.

To preserve Bess's body for the long journey home it was first embalmed, then soldered into a lead coffin which was enclosed in an outer one. 'There is a glass through which one sees the poor face.' Hart had been concerned by the redness of her 'poor face', but this had faded, and 'nothing could be better than the whole appearance'. The double coffin was loaded on to Bess's landau, altered to keep its heavy burden in place. A second carriage was to transport her servants and personal possessions (her books, 1500 of them, were to follow later). Bess's steward, Jaquiery, was in charge.

On 10 April the two carriages, with Bess's two coachmen, Loton and Philippe, riding postilion, left Rome for the long journey to Calais, Hart accompanying them beyond the city walls. Before taking leave of the little cavalcade, he 'looked into the carriage, saw all was right and stuck some white blossom I had just gathered into the band of the outer covering'.

The reports Hart received from Jaquiery reveal all too clearly the trials of such a journey. Two days of incessant rain had made the roads impassable at Bologna; a broken spring delayed them at Turin; the passage over Mont Cenis took seventeen hours – as no one had thought to warn them of a heavy fall of snow in the mountains. So that the coffin should not be searched for stolen goods at the numerous custom houses – as had happened to Harriet Bessborough's coffin – embassies between Rome and London were alerted, to ensure its protection. La Val and Artaud de Montor took responsibility for the frontiers of France, Lord Liverpool for the customs at Dover. At Calais the coffin was met by Hart's steward, with a hearse for its conveyance to London. After lying in state at Devonshire House, Bess's mortal remains left on their journey to Derby.

On 29 May Hart wrote to Little G.: 'The Lambs & F. Foster came here on Monday, she [Caro] never meant to be at the funeral, & I see she regrets it now, but it was as well not. It was very melancholy from poor Frederick being in such a state. I felt a sort of relief and satisfaction all the time from seeing the poor Duchess's remains placed where she wished after so long & difficult a journey!'

Thus was Bess laid to rest beside the Duke and Georgiana in the Cavendish vault at Derby. They remain as inseparable in death as they were in life.

Epilogue

The suddenness of Bess's death came as a severe blow to her children. That none of them had been with her added to their grief. 'Oh why was I not there,' Caro wrote to Hart, 'that is the pang that never never will go, I ought to have been with her.' Though they might not see her for long periods, Bess's interest in everything connected with them – communicated by her vivid monthly letters – ran like a thread through their lives. And there was always the joyful prospect of their next trip to Rome; Fred had been on his way when Hart's courier found him at Paris. 'Poor Frederick continues very low,' Caro told Clifford in June. 'He is unable to make up his mind to any plan. I wish him to take rooms at Albany as somewhere, and to allow himself a carriage and some little comforts, but I think he will probably go and see Augustus.' This glimpse of Fred is one of the few to survive, although there is evidence that he continued to be a welcome guest of various members of the family.

Caro, childless and trapped in a sterile marriage, was equally adrift. She had just let the London house for a year in anticipation of her visit to Rome in the summer. 'I have no wish to go now,' she told Clifford. 'Who should I go to? What should I go for?' Writing to Haryo sometime in 1824, Hart paints a grim picture of Caro's situation: 'I went to Melbourne [the family's house in Derbyshire] for 2 nights, poor Caro does her best to be cheerful but it is the most dismal place in the world . . . and the Lambs [George and Frederick] damn and whistle in the room with their hats on, very cross too . . . it is really terrible for her and when I come to settle here [Chatsworth] in November I shall try to rescue her from that gloomy den. In the meantime there is no good, no charity you can do to equal the kindness of writing her a few lines would have, she lives upon your letters.' Caro, loved for her sweet nature, kindness and discretion, was everyone's favourite sister, half-sister, sister-in-law and aunt. It was she who was keeping vigil at the bedside of Caro William when she died in 1828; when George died at the age of fifty, it was her brother-in-law William who 'staid with me night and day.' And it was Caro who frequently acted as nurse and companion to William in his last years.

Caro did have one task to perform for her mother: to sort through her papers when they were returned from Rome. 'I am very much occupied in arranging & looking over her papers,' she told Clifford. 'There is an immense quantity, but much that is to be burnt. Letters from interesting people, all yours are in separate bundles . . . Most of Mad. d'Albany's & Consalvi's I shall burn . . .' Caro did her job well: none of Madame d'Albany's letters escaped this conflagration, and of the fifty-two remaining from Consalvi, only a handful contain anything of interest.

As for Augustus, Bess's death deprived him of his greatest resource. Her love and ceaseless encouragement had sustained him ever since his reunion with her at the age of sixteen and during the lonely years spent in foreign postings. Although he had achieved some success in his profession, was a good husband and a loving father to his three sons, he struggled all his life with a crippling lack of self-confidence. 'For all the Prestige of Public Station,' he wrote in 1847, '& even the applause I obtained from such Men as Lord Wellesley, [George] Canning, etc. etc. were not strong enough to counteract the effect made by Impressions in early Life . . . and I certainly would chuse rather to have never been, than to exist as I have sometimes done – afraid to meet my friends for fear of blushing in their Presence.' A year after he made this entry in his journal, he committed suicide.

Cushioned by a sweet and loving wife and a large family, it was perhaps Clifford whose life was least affected by his mother's death. Like Bess before him, he reaped immeasurable benefit from the Cavendish connection. He and Hart were not just half-brothers, but close friends. Clifford and his family were frequent visitors to Chatsworth, Chiswick and Devonshire House. In 1826, when Hart was asked to represent George IV at the coronation of the Grand Duke Nicholas (a friend of his since 1817) as Tsar of All the Russias, it was Clifford who captained the yacht which carried him to St Petersburg. But Hart, despite his wealth, his many friends and diverse interests, was frequently alone.

With the Cliffords he could enjoy the ease and informality of a family life that was denied him. An undated letter to Lizzy shows what a delightful uncle he must have been to Clifford's large brood: 'I never saw such adorable people as your children, they have all their merits, and I like best the one I have last had on my knee. I am particularly intimate with Helen Augusta, how beautiful Charles is, engaging and loveable Bella, sensible William & God how like poor Roman Spencer is, he has got exactly her face & I think he will be very handsome.'

In 1832, soon after he had been instrumental in appointing Clifford (now Sir Augustus) a Gentleman Usher of the Black Rod, Hart wrote to his half-brother: 'My dearest Rod, I am quite touched by your letter, and the mention of Roman whom I loved.'

Bibliography

I would like to select a few sources for special mention. The Prologue to the biography was inspired by David Cecil's wonderful Prologue to *The Young Melbourne*, and by Desmond Shawe-Taylor's illuminating and beautifully illustrated *The Georgians: Eighteenth-Century Portraiture & Society*. No one writing about this period can survive without Lawrence Stone's *The Family, Sex and Marriage in England 1500–1800* and Roy Porter's *The Greatest Benefit to Mankind: A Medical History of Humanity from Antiquity to the Present*. I am also indebted to John Martin Robinson for his excellent biography *Cardinal Consalvi*, not least because the majority of his sources were in Italy, written, naturally, in Italian. Another invaluable source was *A Dictionary of British and Irish Travellers in Italy, 1701–1800; Compiled from the Brinsley Ford Archive*, edited by John Ingamells. I am also grateful to Francisca Kuyvenhoven for her article 'Lady Devonshire, an English Maecenas in post-Napoleonic Rome', and to Ronald Ridley for his *The Eagle and the Spade*, which examines the French contribution to the restoration of ancient Rome. Two unpublished manuscripts have been very useful: the late Mary McNeill's 'Virtues of Delight' filled in several gaps in Elizabeth Foster's life during her years in Ireland, and Larry Ward's 'Postscript' supplied information on the illegitimate daughter and mistress of the third Duke of Richmond.

MANUSCRIPT SOURCES

British Library
Althorp MSS. Correspondence of the Spencer family
Melbourne MSS, Add MSS 45548, 45911. Papers and Correspondence of
    Elizabeth, Lady Melbourne
Gibbon MSS, Add MSS 34886. Lady Elizabeth's letters to Edward Gibbon

Castle Howard, Yorkshire
Carlisle MSS. Papers and Correspondence of the sixth Earl of Carlisle (Lord Morpeth) and Georgiana, Lady Carlisle (Lady Morpeth)

Chatsworth House, Derbyshire
Chatsworth MSS. Correspondence of the fifth Duke of Devonshire, Georgiana, Duchess of Devonshire, the sixth Duke of Devonshire

Dormer Archives
Journals, scrapbooks and sketchbooks of Lady Elizabeth Foster; memoirs and sketchbooks of Caroline St Jules; correspondence of Lady Elizabeth Foster with her son Augustus Clifford, and with James Hare; the sixth Duke of Devonshire's letters to Augustus Clifford; letters of Cardinal Consalvi; letters of Edward Gibbon to Lady Elizabeth Foster

Hertfordshire Record Office
Panshanger MSS. Papers and correspondence of the Lamb family

National Library of Wales
Letters of Mrs Frances Bunsen to her mother, Mrs Waddington

Public Records Office, Northern Ireland
McNeill MSS D3732. Papers and research notes of Mrs Mary A. McNeill for a biography of Frederick, 4th Earl of Bristol, unpublished at her death; papers, notebooks and research notes and the corrected draft of 'Virtues of Delight', consisting of studies of Frederick, 4th Earl of Bristol, Lady Elizabeth Foster and Augustus Foster, unpublished at her death. The MS incorporates papers given to Mrs McNeill by Vere Foster's (Augustus Foster's youngest son) great-great-niece, Mrs A. C. May

Royal Academy of Arts
Lawrence MSS. Correspondence of Sir Thomas Lawrence with Lady Elizabeth Foster (later Duchess of Devonshire)

Sheffield Archives
Wharncliffe Collection. Correspondence of the Earl and Countess of Bristol; correspondence of Lady (Mary) Erne

Suffolk Record Office
Bristol MSS. Papers and correspondence of Frederick Hervey

East Sussex Record Office
Holroyd MSS. Correspondence of the Earl of Sheffield with the Revd. Thomas Foster, John Foster, and Lady Elizabeth Foster

West Sussex Record Office
Bessborough MSS. Papers and correspondence of the Bessborough family
Richmond MSS. Correspondence of the third Duke of Richmond

PRINTED SOURCES

Airlie, Mabell, Countess of, *In Whig Society, 1775–1818* (Hodder and Stoughton Ltd, 1921)

Adair, R., *Sketch of the Character of the Late Duke of Devonshire* (William Bulmer & Co., 1811)

Adeane, Jane (ed.), *The Girlhood of Maria Josepha Holroyd, Lady Stanley of Alderley* (Longmans, Green and Co., 1896)

Artaud de Montor, Alexis-François, *Histoire de Pape Leon XII*, vol. I (Librairie de Adrien le Clere et Cie, Paris, 1843)

Askwith, Betty, *Piety & Wit: Biography of Harriet Countess Granville 1785–1862* (Collins, 1982)

Aspinall, Sir Arthur (ed.), *The Correspondence of George, Prince of Wales 1770–1812* (Cassell, 1963–71)

Ayling, Stanley, *George the Third* (William Collins Sons & Co. Ltd, 1972)

Bakewell, Michael & Melissa, *Augusta Leigh: Byron's half-sister: a biography* (Chatto & Windus, 2000)

Bayne-Powell, R., *Travellers in Eighteenth-Century England* (John Murray, 1951)
——, *Eighteenth-Century London Life* (John Murray, 1937)

Bazin, Germain, *The Louvre* (Thames and Hudson, 1957)

Bessborough, Earl of, and Aspinall, A. (eds), *Lady Bessborough and Her Family Circle* (John Murray, 1940)

Bessborough, Earl of (ed.), *Georgiana: Extracts from the Correspondence of Georgiana, Duchess of Devonshire* (John Murray, 1955)

Black, Jeremy, *The British Abroad: the Grand Tour in the Eighteenth Century* (Alan Sutton Publishing Ltd, Stroud, 1992)
——, *The British and the Grand Tour* (Croom Helm, 1985)

Blyth, Henry, *Caro, the Fatal Passion* (History Book Club, 1972)

Booker, John, *Travellers' Money* (Alan Sutton Publishing Ltd, Stroud, 1994)

Bowron, Edgar Peters, and Rishel, Joseph J. (eds), *Art in Rome in the Eighteenth Century* (Merrell Publishers Limited in association with Philadelphia Museum of Art, 2000)

Brewer, John, *The Pleasures of the Imagination: English Culture in the Eighteenth Century* (Farrar Strauss Giroux, New York, 1997)

Briggs, Asa, *The Age of Improvement 1783–1867* (Longmans, Green & Co., 1959)

Browning, Oscar, *Despatches from Paris 1784–1790* (n.p., London, 1909)

Bruyn Andrew, C. (ed.), *The Torrington Diaries*, 4 vols 1934–8 (Eyre & Spottiswoode, 1935)

Buck, Anne, *Dress in Eighteenth-Century England* (Batsford, 1979)

Bull, Duncan (ed.), *On Classic Ground: British Artists and the Landscape of Italy, 1740–1830* (Yale University press, New Haven, 1981)

Burton, Elizabeth, *The Georgians at Home 1714–1830* (Longmans, 1967)

Byron, George Gordon, Lord, *Letters and Journals*, ed. Leslie Marchand (John Murray, 1973–82)

Calder-Marshall, Arthur, *The Two Duchesses* (Hutchinson, 1978)

Cecil, David, *Young Melbourne* (Constable, 1939)

Chapman, Pauline, *The French Revolution as seen by Madame Tussaud, Witness Extraordinary* (Quiller Press Ltd, 1989)

The Memoirs of François René, Vicomte de Chateaubriand, sometime Ambassador to England (being a translation by Alexander Teixeira de Mattos of *Les Mémoires d'Outre-Tombe*) (6 vols, Freemantle & Co., 1902)

Childe-Pemberton, W. S., *The Earl Bishop* (2 vols, E. P. Dutton and Company, New York, 1924)

Clifford, Sir Augustus W., *A Sketch of the Life of the 6th Duke of Devonshire* (privately printed, 1864)

Chisholm, Kate, *Fanny Burney: Her Life 1752–1840* (Chatto & Windus, 1998)

Coke, Lady Mary, *Letters and Journals*, 4 vols, 1889–96 (David Douglas, Edinburgh, 1889)

Colley, Linda, *Britons: Forging the Nation 1707–1837* (Yale University Press, New Haven, 1992)

Carne-Ross, D. S., and Haynes, K. (eds), *Horace in English*, Penguin Books, 1996)

Craddock, Patricia B., *Edward Gibbon, Luminous Historian 1772–1794* (The Johns Hopkins University Press, Baltimore and London, 1989)

The Creevey Papers, ed. Sir Herbert Maxwell (John Murray, 1905)

Cunnington, C. Willett and Phillis, *Handbook of English Costume in the Eighteenth Century* (Faber & Faber, 1957)

Dallas, Gregor, *1815: The Roads to Waterloo* (Richard Cohen Books, 1996)

De-la-Noy, Michael, *The House of Hervey: A History of Tainted Talent* (Constable, 2001)

Devonshire, 6th Duke of, *Handbook of Chatsworth and Hardwick* (privately printed, n.d. [?1845])

Devonshire, Deborah, Duchess of, *The House: A Portrait of Chatsworth* (Macmillan London Limited, 1982)

Devonshire, Georgiana, Duchess of, *The Sylph* (printed for S. Price, J. Williams, etc., Dublin, 1779)

Doyle, William, *The Oxford History of the French Revolution* (Clarendon Press, 1989)

Eeles, Henry S. and Earl Spencer, *Brooks's 1764–1964* (Country Life, 1964)

Falkiner, C. L., *Studies in Irish History and Biography, Mainly of the Eighteenth Century* (Longman's & Co., 1902)

Farr, Evelyn, *Marie-Antoinette and Count Axel Fersen: The Untold Love Story* (Peter Owen Publishers, 1995)

Foreman, Amanda, *Georgiana, Duchess of Devonshire* (HarperCollins, 1998)

Foster, Elizabeth, *Children of the Mist* (Hutchinson, 1960)

Foster, Vere (ed.), *The Two Duchesses* (Blackie & Son Ltd., Glasgow and Dublin, 1898)

Fothergill, Brian, *The Mitred Earl: An eighteenth-century Eccentric* (Faber and Faber, 1974)

Frampton, Mary, *Journal, 1779–1846*, ed. Harriot G. Mundy (Sampson Low & Co., 1885)

Fraser, Flora, *The Unruly Queen: The Life of Queen Caroline* (Macmillan, 1996)

Garlick, Kenneth, Macintyre, Angus and Cave, Kathryn (eds), *The Diary of Joseph Farington* (16 vols, Yale University Press, New Haven and London, 1978–84)

Garlick, Kenneth, *Sir Thomas Lawrence* (Routledge and Kegan Paul, 1954)

Gash, Norman, *Lord Liverpool: The Life and Times of Robert Banks Jenkinson 1770–1828* (Weidenfeld and Nicolson, 1984)

George, Mary Dorothy, *London Life in the XVIIIth Century* (Kegan Paul & Co., A. A. Knopf, New York, 1925)

Girouard, Mark, *A Country House Companion* (Century Hutchinson Ltd, 1987)

——, *Life in the English Country House: A Social and Architectural History* (Yale University Press, New Haven, 1978)

Goethe's Travels in Italy . . . (George Bell & Sons, 1892)

Grosvenor, Caroline (ed.), *The First Lady Wharncliffe and her Family*, vol. I, (William Heinemann Ltd, 1927)

Granville, Castalia, Countess of (ed.), *Lord Granville Leveson Gower: Private Correspondence 1781–1821* (2 vols, John Murray, 1917)

Halsband, Robert, *Lord Hervey: Eighteenth-Century Courtier* (Clarendon Press, Oxford, 1973)

——, *The Life of Lady Mary Wortley Montague* (Clarendon Press, Oxford, 1956)

Hampson, Norman, *The French Revolution: A Concise History* (Thames & Hudson, 1975)

Hale, J. R. (ed.), *The Italian Journal of Samuel Rogers* (Faber and Faber, 1956)

Hawes, Frances, *Henry Brougham* (Jonathan Cape, 1957)

Hemlow, Joyce, and Douglas, Althea (eds), *The Journals and Letters of Fanny Burney (Madame d'Arblay)* (Oxford University Press, 1972–84)

Herold, J. Christopher, *Mistress to an Age: A Life of Madame de Staël* (Hamish Hamilton, 1959)

Hibbert, Christopher, *The Grand Tour* (Thames Methuen, 1987)

——, *Rome: the Biography of a City* (Viking, 1985)

——, *The Days of the French Revolution* (Penguin Books, 1980)

——, *George IV* (Penguin Books, Harmondsworth, 1976)

Hilles, F. W. (ed.), *Letters of Sir Joshua Reynolds* (Cambridge, 1929)

Hobhouse, C., *Fox* (John Murray, 1934)

Hobsbawm, E. J., *The Age of Revolution 1789–1848* (Weidenfeld & Nicolson, 1975)

Holland, Henry Richard Vassall, Baron, *Memoirs of the Whig Party During My Time*, vol. I (Brown, Green and Longmans, 1852–4)

Holmes, M. R. J., *Augustus Hervey: A Naval Casanova* (Durham, 1996)

Hope, Annette, *Londoners' Larder* (Mainstream Publishing Company (Edinburgh) Ltd, 1990)

Hudson, Roger (ed.), *The Grand Tour 1592–1796* (The Folio Society, 1993)

Ilchester, Countess of, and Lord Stavordale, *The Life and Letters of Lady Sarah Lennox 1745–1826*, vol. I. (John Murray, 1901)

Ilchester, Earl of, *The Home of the Hollands 1605–1820* (John Murray, London, 1937)

——, *The Journal of Elizabeth, Lady Holland 1791–1811* (2 vols, Longmans, Green, & Co., 1908)

Ingamells, John, *A Dictionary of British and Irish Travellers in Italy, 1701–1800: Compiled from the Brinsley Ford Archive* (Yale University Press, New Haven and London, 1997)

Jarrett, Derek, *Britain 1688–1815* (Longmans Green & Co. Ltd, 1965)

Jesse, J. H., *George Selwyn and His Contemporaries* (n.p., London, 1843–4)

Jupp, C., and Gittings, Clare (eds), *Death in England: an Illustrated History* (Manchester University Press, 1999)

Kelly, Linda, *Richard Brinsley Sheridan: A Life* (Sinclair-Stevenson, 1997)

Knight, Cornelia, *Autobiography*, vol. I (3rd edn, W. H. Allen & Co., 1861)

Kunstler, Charles, *Fersen et Son Secret* (Librairies Hachette, Paris, 1947)

Lamartine, A. de, *Souvenirs et Portraits*, vol. II (Hachette & Cie, Paris, 1871–2)

Llanover, Lady (ed.), *The Autobiography and Correspondence of Mary Granville, Mrs Delaney*, vol. II (Richard Bentley, 1861)

Lecky, William, *A History of Ireland in the Eighteenth Century*, vol. II (1902)

Lees-Milne, James, *The Bachelor Duke* (John Murray, 1991)

Leveson Gower, Sir George, and Palmer, Iris (eds), *Harry-O: The Letters of Lady Harriet Cavendish 1796–1809* (John Murray, 1940)

Leveson Gower, F., *Letters of Harriet, Countess Granville 1810–45* (Longmans, Green, and Co., 1894)

Leveson Gower, Iris, *The Face Without a Frown: Georgiana, Duchess of Devonshire* (Frederic Muller Ltd, 1944)

Lewis, Lady Theresa (ed.), *Extracts of the Journals and Correspondence of Miss Berry*, vol. III. (Longmans, Green, and Co., 1865)

Litten, Julian, *The English Way of Death* (1991)

Longford, Elizabeth, *Byron* (Hutchinson, in association with Weidenfeld & Nicolson, 1976)

Lyttelton, Lady Sarah Spencer, *Correspondence 1787–1870*, ed. Mrs Hugh Wyndham (John Murray, 1912)

Marshall, Dorothy, *Eighteenth-Century England* (Longman, Harlow, 1962)

Masters, Brian, *Georgiana, Duchess of Devonshire* (Hamish Hamilton, 1981)

Mayne, Ethel, *A Regency Chapter: Lady Bessborough and Her Friendships* (Macmillan & Co., 1939)

Mead, W. E., *The Grand Tour in the Eighteenth Century* (Houghton Mifflin Company, Boston & New York, 1914)

Mitchell, L. G., *Charles James Fox* (Penguin Books, 1992)

——, *Lord Melbourne* (Oxford University Press, Oxford, 1997)

Morgan, Lady (Sydney), *Italy*, vol. II (Henry Colburn and Co., 1821)

Moore, Lucy, *The Amphibious Thing* (Viking, 2000)

Moritz, C. P., *Journeys of a German in England: A Walking Tour of England in 1782* (Eland Books, 1982)

Murray, Venetia, *High Society: A Social History of the Regency Period 1788–1830* (Viking, 1998)

Norton, J. E. (ed.), *The Letters of Edward Gibbon*, vol. III (Cassell & Company Ltd, 1956)

Nugent, Thomas, *The Grand Tour*, vols. III & IV (printed for S. Birt . . . D. Browne . . . A. Millar . . . and G. Hawkins . . ., 1749)

Olson, Alison G., *The Radical Duke. Career and Correspondence of Charles Lennox, third Duke of Richmond* (Oxford University Press, Oxford, 1961)

Oman, Carola, *Nelson* (Hodder and Stoughton, 1947)

O'Toole, Fintan, *A Traitor's Kiss* (Granta, 1997)

Pange, Victor de (ed.), *Le Plus Beau de Toutes les Fêtes: Mme de Staël et Elisabeth Hervey, duchesse de Devonshire d'après leur correspondance inédite, 1804–1817* (Éditions Klincksieck, Paris, 1980)

Paston-Williams, Sara, *The Art of Dining* (The National Trust, 1993)

Piper, David, *The English Face*, ed. Malcolm Rogers (National Portrait Gallery Publications, 1992)

Plumb, J. H., *England in the Eighteenth Century (1714–1815)* (Penguin Books Ltd, Harmondsworth, 1950)

Ponsonby, D. A., *Call a Dog Hervey* (Hutchinson, 1949)

Porter, Roy, *The Greatest Benefit to Mankind: A Medical History of Humanity from Antiquity to the Present* (HarperCollins, 1997)

——, *English Society in the Eighteenth Century* (Penguin Books Ltd, Harmondsworth, 1982)

Porter, Roy and Hall, Lesley, *The Facts of Life* (Yale University Press, New Haven and London, 1995)

Porter, Roy and Rousseau, G. S., *Gout: The Patrician Malady* (Yale Univesity Press, New Haven and London, 1998)

Powell, David, *Charles James Fox: Man of the People* (Hutchinson, 1989)

Price, Cecil (ed.), *The Letters of Richard Brinsley Sheridan*, vol. I (Oxford University Press, Oxford, 1966)

Priestley, J. B., *The Prince of Pleasure and his Regency, 1811–1820* (William Heinemann Ltd, 1969)

Reeve, Henry (ed.), *The Greville Memoirs* (Longman, Green & Co., 1875)

Ribeiro, A., *The Visual History of Costume: The Eighteenth Century* (Batsford, 1990)

Ridley, Ronald T., *The Eagle and the Spade* (Cambridge University Press, Cambridge, 1992)

Riley, John, *Rowlandson Drawings from the Paul Mellon Collection* (Yale Center for British Art, New Haven, 1977)

Robinson, John Martin, *Cardinal Consalvi 1757–1824* (Bodley Head, 1987)

Rousseau, Jean-Jacques, *Émile*, transl. B. Foxley (Everyman, J. M. Dent, 1993)

——, *La Nouvelle Héloïse*, transl. Judith H. McDowell (Pennsylvania State University Press, University Park & London, 1968)

Sackville-West, Vita, *Knole and the Sackvilles* (Heinemann, 1934)

Schama, Simon, *Citizens: A Chronicle of the French Revolution* (Penguin Books, 1989)

Sedgwick, Romney (ed.), *Lord Hervey's Memoirs* (William Kimber, 1952)

Shawe-Taylor, Desmond, *The Georgians: Eighteenth-Century Portraiture and Society* (Barrie & Jenkins Ltd, 1990)

Sheridan, Richard Brinsley, *The School for Scandal* (J. M. Dent & Sons Ltd, 1963)

Sichel, Walter, *Sheridan* (Constable, 1909)

Smith, E. A., *George IV* (Yale University Press, New Haven and London, 1999)

Smollett, Tobias, *Travels through France and Italy, 1766*, ed. Frank Felsenstein (Oxford University Press, Oxford, 1979)

Söderhjelm, Alma, *Fersen et Marie Antoinette: correspondence et journal intime inédits du Comte Axel de Fersen* (Éditions Kra, Paris, 1930)

Spencer, Charles, *The Spencer Family* (Viking, 1999)

Squire, Geoffrey, *Dress, Art and Society, 1560–1970* (Studio Vista, 1974)

Starke, Mariana, *Travels in Europe, for the use of Travellers on the Continent, etc.* (A. and W. Galignani and Co., Paris, 1839)

——, *Letters from Italy*, vol. II (printed for G. and S. Robinson, 1815)

Stendhal (Henri Beyle), *Voyages en Italie* (Éditions Gallimard, Paris, 1973)

Sterne, Laurence, *A Sentimental Journey through France and Italy* (Oxford University Press, Oxford, 1968)

Steuart, A. Francis (ed.), *The Diary of a Lady-in-Waiting by Lady Charlotte Bury* (John Lane, London and New York, 1908)

Stokes, Hugh, *The Devonshire House Circle* (Herbert Jenkins Ltd, 1917)

Stone, Lawrence, *The Family, Sex and Marriage in England 1500–1800* (Weidenfeld & Nicolson, 1977)

Stuart, Dorothy Margaret, *Dearest Bess* (Methuen & Co. Ltd, 1955)

——, *Molly Lepell, Lady Hervey* (George G. Harrap & Co. Ltd, 1936)

Surtees, Virginia (ed.), *A Second Self: The Letters of Harriet Granville* (Michael Russell, Salisbury, 1990)

Sykes, Christopher Simon, *Private Palaces: Life in the Great London Houses* (Chatto & Windus, 1989)

Thompson, Francis, *A History of Chatsworth* (Country Life, 1949)

Thompson, J. M., *Napoleon Bonaparte* (Basil Blackwell Ltd, Oxford, 1952)

Thorold, Peter, *The London Rich: the Creation of a Great City, from 1666 to the Present* (Viking, 1999)

Ticknor, George, *Life, Letters and Journals*, vol. I (Boston, 1876)

Tillyard, Stella, *Aristocrats: Caroline, Emily, Louisa and Sarah Lennox 1740–1832* (Chatto & Windus Ltd, 1994)

Trease, Geoffrey, *The Grand Tour* (Heinemann, 1967)

Trevelyan, G.M., *Illustrated English Social History*, vol. III (Penguin Books Ltd, Harmondsworth, 1944)

Trouncer, Margaret, *Madame Récamier* (Macdonald & Co., 1949)

Vickery, Amanda, *The Gentleman's Daughter: Women's Lives in Georgian England* (Yale University Press, New Haven & London, 1998)

Villiers, Marjorie, *The Grand Whiggery* (John Murray, 1939)

Walpole, Horace, *Letters*, ed. Mrs Paget Toynbee, 19 vols (Clarendon Press, Oxford, 1903–25)

———, *Memoirs of the Reign of King George the Third*, ed. G. F. R. Barker, 4 vols (Lawrence & Bullen, 1894)

Watkins, Susan, *Jane Austen in Style* (Thames & Hudson, 1996)

White, T. H., *The Age of Scandal* (Jonathan Cape, 1950)

Williams, D. E. (ed.), *The Life and Correspondence of Sir Thomas Lawrence* (Henry Colburn and Richard Bentley, 1831)

Wilson, Harriette, *Mistress of Many*, ed. Max Marquis (Paul Elek Limited, 1960)

Wilton, Andrew and Bignamini, Ilaria (eds), *Grand Tour: The Lure of Italy in the Eighteenth Century* (catalogue of the 1996–1997 exhibition in London and Rome: Tate Gallery Publishing Ltd, 1996)

Winegarten, Renee, *Mme de Staël* (Berg Publishers, Leamington Spa, 1985)

Wraxall, Nathaniel, *Historical and Posthumous Memoirs of My Own Time*, 5 vols (n.p., 1904)

Articles

Ford, Brinsley, 'The Earl-Bishop: An Eccentric and Capricious Patron of the Arts', *Apollo*, n.s. Vol. 99, 1974

Hall, Ivan, 'A neoclassical episode at Chatsworth', *Burlington Magazine*, June 1980

Kenworthy-Browne, John, 'A Ducal Patron of Sculptors', *Apollo*, Oct 1972

———, 'A Patroness of the Arts: The Duchess of Devonshire in Rome', *Country Life*, 25 April 1971

Kuyvenhoven, F. R. E., 'Lady Devonshire, an English Maecenas in post-Napoleonic Rome', *Mededelingen van het Instituut te Rome*, Nova series 11, vol. XLVI, 1985

Rankin, P., 'Downhill, County Derry', *Country Life*, vol. CL, nos 3865–6, 8 and 15 July 1971

Salmon, Frank, '"Storming the Campo Vaccino": British Architects and the Antique Buildings of Rome after Waterloo', *Architectural History*, vol. 38, 1995

Journal des Débats, 5 May 1824 (Paris)

Booklets

Hewlings, Richard, *Chiswick House and Gardens* (English Heritage, 1989)

Pitt, I. T., *The Davers of Rushbrook and the Hervey Connection* (1997)

Index